Football

Women's Basketball

HAIL TO PITT

Hail To *Pitt*

A Sports History Of The University Of Pittsburgh

Edited By Jim O'Brien

Illustrated By Marty Wolfson

Sponsored By The Panther Foundation

●

Assistants to the Editor:
Kathleen O'Brien • Mary M. O'Brien

Contributing Writers:
Eddie Beachler • Frank Carver
Myron Cope • Jack Henry
Pat Livingston • Roy McHugh
Maria Sciullo • Bob Smizik
Paul Sullivan • Norm Vargo

Photographic Services:
Marlene Karas

Reprinted Columns By:
Rudy Cernkovic • Arthur Daley
Jerry Izenberg • Harry Keck
Dana Mozley • Grantland Rice
Chester L. Smith • Stanley Woodward

CATHEDRAL OF LEARNING • UNIVERSITY OF PITTSBURGH

 WOLFSON PUBLISHING CO., INC.
Pittsburgh, PA

DEDICATIONS

During my student days at the University, a trip to Fitzgerald Field House was always a delightful experience because of the presence of such special Pitt people as Doc Carlson, Frank Carver, Beano Cook, Carl Peterson, Leo "Horse" Czarnecki, Boo Connors, Roger McGill and Bobby Lewis. This book is also dedicated to the memory of my brother, Dan, who showed me the way to Pitt in the first place.

—Jim O'Brien

This book is dedicated to all those individuals who have been associated with sports at the University of Pittsburgh, as athletes, administrators, support groups, students and fans. Hail to them, too!

—The Panther Foundation

Books are living legacies of time. They are recorded documents of efforts and accomplishments of people and the events they created. Books help create the special character of yesterday, today and tomorrow. Books survive the passage of season and time. They provide us with information to learn and through learning we grow. This book is dedicated to everyone who made it happen. I am proud to be part of this documentation of time.

—Marty Wolfson

ACKNOWLEDGMENTS

"HAIL TO PITT: A Sports History of the University of Pittsburgh" was made possible by the private sponsorship of The Panther Foundation, with special support provided by Equibank, the Golden Panthers, and the University of Pittsburgh.

We are indebted to the following firms, corporations, businesses and organizations for the boost they provided: Alcoa, Allegheny International, Baierl Chevrolet, Carnegie Library, Cold-Comp, Copco Papers, Inc., Cost Brothers Inc., Dravo Corporation, Fisher Scientific Co., Frank B. Fuhrer & Associates, Froggy's, Geyer Printing, Inc., H.J. Heinz Co., Koppers, LMV Leasing, Inc., Massaro Corporation, Mellon-Stuart, Meyer-Darragh-Buckler-Bebenek & Eck, Modern Reproductions, Oliver Realty Inc., Oxford Realty, PPG-EAA, Pittsburgh Athletic Assn., Pittsburgh Brewing Co., Pittsburgh Chamber of Commerce, Pittsburgh Convention and Visitors Bureau, Pittsburgh National Bank, Reed Smith Shaw & McClay, The University Club.

Special thanks to the following individuals for their interest and support in promoting this project: Bill Baierl, Bill Bierer, John Besanceney, Ernest Buckman, Charles "Corky" Cost, Frank B. Fuhrer, Jr., Robert J. Gallagher, Stan Goldman, Justin T. Horan, Ed Lewis, Joseph A. Massaro, Jr., Steve "Froggy" Morris, Christopher Passodelis, Ron Puntil, Larry Werner.

Our special thanks and gratitude to the following individuals who helped in some way, by contributing information, memorabilia, backing or service in some respect to make this book possible: Beth Adams, Barrie B. Adrian, Dr. Nate Apple, Joyce Aschenbrenner, Ted Atkins, Lenore Bayus, Dr. Herman J. Bearzy, Donald Bebenek, Bob Bernardini, Dean Billick, Mary Bonack, Taylor Brittain, Betty Brown, Mayor Caliguiri, Harry M. Carroll, Frank Carver, Doug Chambers, G. Reynolds Clark, Cold-Comp Staff, Ed Conley, Randy Cosgrove, Dave Crantz, Leo "Horse" Czarnecki, Frank E. Davis, Jr., Vincent C. DeLuzio, Robert J. Dodds, Jr., Herbert P. Douglas, Jr., Tom Farrell, David F. Figgins, Barbara T. Germaux, Flora Giancola, Merle E. Gilliand, Frank Gustine, Jr., Bud Harris, Charles Hartwig, Joyce Hayden, Bob Heddleston, Stan Hoehl, Mary E. Holbert, Bill Hoop, Edward C. Ifft, Jr., Albert Kamper, George Kanidis, Sam Kerr, Carlton G. Ketchum, Mr. and Mrs. John Kifer, James A. Knight, Jr., Bernard J. Kobosky, Bernie Koperec, Alex Kramer, Joe Kristufek, Dr. Bobby LaRue, Elmer C. Leitholf, Russ Lindberg, Elmer A. Lissfelt, Fred B. Loeffler, A. J. Luppino, Ed Lutz, John C. Mascaro, Dan McCann, John S. McKean, Don Mellon, Cas Myslinski, Emil Narick, Gloria Nelson, Sarah H. O'Brien, Dorothy Otis, Charles W. Parry, John D. Paulus, Cathy Pawlowski, John Pelusi, Steve Petro, Joel Platt, Robert J. A. Pratt, Bob Prince, David A. Progar, Jimmy Joe Robinson, Bob Rosborough, William T. Rush, Walter Sarraf, Mrs. Helen Roe Sawyer, Evelyn Schildhouse, Robert E. Schooley, Adele Schwadron, Richard Skaare, Kimball Smith, Rose Mary M. Stidmon, Hazel Swetonic, Robert E. Todd, Jr., Vee Toner, William F. Trimble, John Troan, University Archives, Rich Vangennewit, Linda Venzon, James M. Walton, Mike Weisberg, Dave Welty, Dolores S. Wilden, Reggie Wilson, Irene Wolfson, Bill Work, Bob Wydo, Fred Young, Dr. Paul E. Zehfuss.

—Jim O'Brien and Marty Wolfson

"It's nice to have the memories. It was a lot of work and a lot of fun, and I'm proud of it. But you still need 50 cents to buy a cup of coffee."

— Dr. Bobby LaRue, '36

Published by Wolfson Publishing Co., Inc.
Pittsburgh, PA

First Printing

Designed by Marty Wolfson

Manufactured in the United States of America

Printed by Geyer Printing Company, Inc.
Pittsburgh, PA
Typography by Cold-Comp

Photo reproductions by Modern Reproductions, Inc.

Library of Congress Catalog Card Number #82-50778

ISBN Number #0-916114-08-2

Contents

CHEERLEADERS and Panther mascot have always helped provide the proper atmosphere for Pitt sports events.

Points of Pride:

- **PITT** has won nine national championships in football, and two in basketball.
- **PITT** has won Eastern team championships in football, basketball, track & field, wrestling, swimming, boxing and women's sports.
- **GLENN "POP" WARNER** — whose football teams went undefeated four years in a row, winning three national championships in that span.
- **DOC CARLSON** — Coached basketball team for 31 years, winning two national titles and gaining entry into the Basketball Hall of Fame.
- **CHARLEY HYATT** — the first of five All-America basketball players produced by Pitt, and a member of the charter class of the Basketball Hall of Fame.
- **SAM PARKS, JR.** — Pitt's first golf team captain won U.S. Open Golf Championship at Oakmont in 1935.
- **JOHN WOODRUFF** — Pitt's only Olympic gold medalist, for winning 800 meter run at Games in Berlin in 1936.

- **HERB DOUGLAS** — won bronze medal as third-place finisher in long jump at Olympic Games in London in 1948.
- **PEERY FAMILY** — Rex and his sons, Hugh and Ed, all won three consecutive national wrestling championships and were named to Wrestling's Hall of Fame.
- **JOE SCHMIDT** — Captained 1952 Pitt football team and went on to become school's only member in the Pro Football Hall of Fame for his outstanding play with the Detroit Lions.
- **JOHN MICHELOSEN** — Coached Pitt football team to back-to-back bowl games, the Sugar Bowl in 1955 season, the Gator Bowl in 1956.
- **BILLY KNIGHT** — Led Pitt basketball team to NCAA tournament in 1973 and became school's first All-Pro in basketball with the Indiana Pacers.
- **JOHNNY MAJORS** — Coached Pitt to its ninth national championship in 1976.
- **TONY DORSETT** — Led Pitt to national championship in 1976 and became school's only Heisman Trophy winner.
- **JACKIE SHERRILL** — Completed four-year career with back-to-back 11-1 seasons to move ahead of Jock Sutherland with Pitt's all-time winning percentage as football coach.

SUGAR BOWL BLISS

HOW SWEET IT IS! — Pitt's Dan Marino (13) celebrates with John Brown (89) after Panthers beat Georgia, 24-20, on a 33-yard touchdown pass from Marino to Brown with 35 seconds left in 1982 Sugar Bowl. —UPI Photo

4

Message From The Chancellor

CHANGING OF THE GUARD — New athletic director Dr. Ed Bozik, left, is congratulated by Chancellor Wesley W. Posvar, right, and Dr. Jack Freeman, the vice-chancellor for administration, upon accepting important Pitt post in late June.

CHANCELLOR WESLEY W. POSVAR

High achievement in the classroom and success on the playing fields, far from being contradictory, are mutually beneficial, and there is good reason to expect an institution with stellar academic programs to support similarly successful athletic programs. The University of Pittsburgh maintains a policy of excellence throughout, with strong academic standards for athletes, winning records, and emphasis on leadership.

Pitt athletics provide a large measure of the fun of attending a University. Sport, in one sense, is entertainment, and in another elevates community spirit and morale. Just as books and ideas and intellectual exchange stimulate us, sport offers to the spectator the change of pace, the opportunity for involvement and dedication to a cause. A good athletic program also projects an image of institutional well-being and helps attract to the classroom intellectually alert young people from near and far.

For the participant, an athletic experience imparts a discipline seldom found elsewhere in the learning process. We are proud that the leadership and scholastic record of Pitt athletes is a long and illustrious one of many alumni who have left the playing fields to distinguish themselves in professional careers.

The history of sports at the University of Pittsburgh has ebbed and surged with the fortunes of the times; but, in the main, the athletic tradition has been and is a noble one. There have been lean years and spectacular ones, extraordinary triumphs and national championships.

In these pages are transmitted some of the thrilling accounts of young men and women who pushed themselves to demonstrate their skills in winning. Throughout, there are the great spirit of challenge and the essential fun that is sport.

I am charging Dr. Ed Bozik, our new athletic director, not only with maintaining the continuity of our successes in the major sports — football and basketball — but also with developing non-revenue sports to levels of distinction. In addition, greater efforts lie ahead in developing even more alumni and public support, improving facilities, and serving the interests of our student-athletes in their development for their future careers. We want to have winning programs in everything we do.

Wesley W. Posvar

Wesley W. Posvar
Chancellor

Pitt Is It!

5

MESSAGES FOR STUDENT-ATHLETES

"Athletics are an integral part of the educational curriculum"

From Dr. Sutherland:

I have seldom been called sentimental — in fact, we hard-headed Scotch are more often accused of being just the opposite — but I want to say that I am profoundly touched by the significance of this occasion. I have a deep affection for the University of Pittsburgh. It is my University. I am proud that for more than twenty years — as an alumnus, and as a member of the faculty — I have had a small part in the development of this University. As a Pitt man, I have always felt a responsibility to further in every way possible the best interests of the University.

Naturally, I feel that athletics are an integral part of the educational curriculum, but I have never for a moment permitted the glamour and the thrill of the athletic spectacle to overshadow in importance the fundamental educational values for which the University stands.

The success of University of Pittsburgh athletic teams is a reflection of the indefinable spirit that imbues all students of the University, not only on the athletic field but in the classroom and laboratory. Pitt students, as I have known them, are serious and earnest. They pursue their objectives aggressively, yet always with a sense of responsibility and a consideration for the traditions of fairness and sportsmanship.

The record of our athletic teams naturally has been gratifying to me, but, as an alumnus, I am even more proud of the University's achievement in the field of scholarship, and in its part in training young men and women for lives of useful service to the Commonwealth of Pennsylvania, and to the many other communities in which they live throughout the United States and the world.

SEDATE SUTHERLAND . . .
Pitt's Hall of Fame football coach was a silent Scot, an introspective sort.

Words Of Wisdom From Two Of Pitt's Finest

"Our goal is always TO WIN 'EM ALL"

From Dr. Carlson:

I should like to preface this discussion of the 1936-37 basketball team with a few general remarks. Like all the other squads I have coached at Pitt, the present one is composed of fine, well-mannered boys whose primary interest is to gain an education. Basketball comes second, as it should.

Every player this season is from the Pittsburgh district. With the exception of two or three boys who room near the campus and do their own cooking, they live in their own homes. They are streetcar riders — "one check commuters" — who eat hurried breakfasts and run for the trolley. Their noon meals are of the conglomerate type, non-scientific in quality and probably insufficient in quantity.

Basketball practice necessarily starts late in the afternoon and lasts beyond the dinner hour, so one can imagine the boys arriving home at the end of a long walk or a drafty street car ride and finding a cold meal on the table.

The point I want to make is that our basketball players make real sacrifices to play the game. They work hard because hard work is essential to the success of any undertaking. But hard work means fatigue.

This year, as every year, our players have had to dig deep into their physical and nervous reserves. Last season, these reserves were depleted by the time of the Olympic finals, but even so we finished with a winning percentage of .800.

This year we have 13 eligible players — no cuts are ever made in the varsity squad — and these boys, three seniors, five juniors, and five sophomores, are the sole survivors of previous academic and basketball wars.

They are the crusaders, the boys with the will that the mail must go through. Our goal is always to WIN 'EM ALL, and although we have only succeeded in that ambition once, in 1927-28, nevertheless our will to win always gives us a better-than-average record, year after year.

CHEERLEADER CARLSON ... Pitt's Hall of Fame basketball coach stirs up students at campus pep rally.

INTRODUCTION

Scrapbooks. Everybody seems to have one. Those who did not, or those whose scrapbooks disappeared on them through the years, wish they had them. They were stored away, in attics, cellars, out-of-the-way places. Musty memories. Some sons and daughters, as well as grandchildren, did not know they existed. Now they do.

They had been kept, for the most part, by proud parents, adoring aunts, secret admirers, given as graduation gifts. "I wish I had kept one," some said, sadly. Going through them was like being on an archaeological dig. There were so many discoveries, finding out so much you never knew about Pitt, your old school, and its rich and proud athletic tradition. Once you got used to the mildew...

Memories. Kenny Rogers singing "Through the Years" on the car radio as you raced off to visit another old-timer, someone who could tell tales about the good ol' days at Pitt. Barry Manilow singing "Somewhere Down the Road."

Shaking hands with sports heroes from Pitt's past. Feeling bad that too many of those hands were shaking before they held yours. Glad eyes. Sad eyes. "I'd love to do what you're doing," said Bob Rosborough, who once played football for the Panthers and now works in the alumni office, looking after the affairs of the Pitt Varsity Letter Club. "I'd love to know more about the sports history of this school. I envy you."

Yellowed newspaper clippings, flaking, fragile to the touch. Photographs, fading, cracking, chipping. Faces from another time, faces and uniforms that look funny now. Yet so beautiful to behold. Just different, from another day. Some of the faces were familiar, to begin with; others you came to recognize from sorting through them so often. Pitt people, all of them.

Meeting so many men — and women — who had meant so much to you, growing up in Pittsburgh, just three miles from the University campus, then going to school there in the early '60s, and growing up on its campus. Graduating, by God. Hazelwood was home, but Pitt was a nice place to visit and to spend so many days and nights. It was so close, yet another world completely.

You were always proud of your Pitt ring, yes, even during those three straight 1-9 seasons in football in the '60s, but this experience made it an even more prized possession, more than a memento of school days.

Talking to Gibby Welch, Herb McCracken. Frank Carver. Bill Kern. Herb Douglas. Corny Salvaterra. Mike Ditka. Don Hennon. Bobby LaRue. Emil Narick. John Woodruff. Joe Schmidt. Paul Zehfuss. Paul Fisher. Joe Kristufek. Bimbo Cecconi. Dodo Canterna. Ira Hill. Dick Conti. Corky Cost. Everett Utterback. Woody Harris. Reggie Wilson. Mickey Zernich. Christopher Passodelis. Don Smith. Ave Daniell. Miller Harbaugh. Johnny Majors. Carlton Ketchum. Jackie Sherrill. Arnie Sowell. It was a thrill each time around.

Learning so much from the likes of John Brosky. Marshall Goldberg. Bobby Timmons. Bobby Lewis. Leo Bemis. Carl Rees. Warren Neiger. Carl Peterson. Boo Connors. Beano Cook. Dave Havern. Kenny Lucas. Bill Kaliden. Fred Mazurek. Ernie Bonelli. Nate Apple. Hank Zeller. Timmy Lawry. Paul Martha. Rick Leeson. Phil Dahar. Ed Assid. Ralph Jelic. Dick Bowen. Darrell Lewis.

Goldberg became a millionaire after his All-American career at Pitt, and he has put it all into perspective so well:

"Pitt, its administration, faculty and student body," he wrote to us, "has always been to me a warm, aggressive Team, striving and reaching to be better. They make me do the same."

It's that sort of sentiment that was expressed by so many Pitt grads, most grateful for the opportunity and experience provided during their school days.

It was great talking to Vee Toner, who was Venus Shakarian in her school days at Pitt, who was bouncing back from serious surgery. Our research showed she hasn't been fibbing all these years when she insisted she had been awarded honest-to-goodness varsity letters in the '20s. She was a bundle of energy back then, too.

This book, hopefully, will bring back some pleasant memories for all these people. For some, it will be sad, too, for many of the people portrayed herein have passed on. Their memories remain, however, and this book will help perpetuate their accomplishments.

Elmer Lissfelt, a fine basketball player and swimmer as well as an outstanding student in the '20s, wrote: "Looking at these bits, I could almost weep for a great group of men with whom I had the privilege of associating in my years at Pitt. I should have kept their letters, to give you a chance to know them."

In a sense, this is a scrapbook. It was put together with the wonderful help of a man with a steady and deft hand, my friend and colleague, Marty Wolfson. It was a pleasure to work with him again, to admire his artistic talents and thoroughness. He went to Carnegie Tech to learn more about art, but through his task in putting all the pieces together here — and reading and re-reading the contributions by an outstanding staff — he has learned to love and respect Pitt as well. Now, he's a Pitt man, too.

We hope it will have the same impact on others.

Hail to Pitt.

Jim O'Brien

Pitt PORTRAITS

Text By Jim O'Brien
Illustrated by Marty Wolfson

Blessed boomerangs . . . they keep coming back at you like blessed boomerangs. Doc Carlson not only spoke about the blessed boomerangs, but he diagrammed them for you as well, wanting to make sure you understood where he was coming from. Here are 15 profiles or reflections on outstanding athletic performers from Pitt's past and present, including Doc Carlson, who showed you how to sail those blessed boomerangs. They touched you when they did it, and theirs was a personal touch. They epitomize Pitt at its best, both on and off the field of sports combat. There are others, of course, just as special and some of them are written about elsewhere in this book by other writers who knew them better. Pitt can be proud of all of them, as they have voiced their pride in Pitt. Hail to them. Hail to Pitt.

- DOC CARLSON
- MIKE DITKA
- HERB DOUGLAS
- TONY DORSETT
- DON HENNON
- BILLY KNIGHT
- DANNY MARINO
- DOC MEDICH
- JOHN MICHELOSEN
- CARL OLSON
- REX PEERY
- JERRY RICHEY
- JOE SCHMIDT
- GIBBY WELCH
- JOHN WOODRUFF

DOC CARLSON

A Man to Remember

Marty Wolfson

"He had a gift for laughter and a sense that the world wasn't so bad."

Henry Clifford Carlson, who died November 1, 1964, at his summer home near Ligonier, Pa., had been associated with the University for half a century.

The famed and beloved Pitt basketball coach had national championship teams to his credit in 1928 and 1930. During his tenure of office from 1922 to 1953, his teams had 369 wins versus 247 losses.

Dr. Carlson had just retired in September of 1964 as director of the student health services at the age of 70. He was a member of the Helms Foundation Basketball Hall of Fame, the Pittsburgh Dapper Dan Hall of Fame, and the Curbstone Coaches' Hall of Fame. He was honored posthumously as one of the lettermen of distinction at the Pitt-Notre Dame Homecoming game on November 7, 1964.

Where do you find the words to say what you feel about one who was so much a part of the University that now it seems incomplete without him? Jim O'Brien was faced with that dilemma as he sat down at his typewriter to write a tribute for the PITT NEWS. But somehow the words just came. They are reprinted here.

It was Thursday and Doc Carlson was fussing about his sometime office in Fitzgerald Field House.

Doc wasn't really supposed to be there. They had retired him late this summer, and told him to take it easy. It was like telling Mahatma Ghandi to go to war. The desk and chair, scale and stethoscope would always be there. The fatigue curve chart remained on the wall. No one had the heart to take them away for they knew Doc would always return for another day.

He called to me in the hall: "Come here, James, I want to show you something." Soon I was in his office, and it didn't take Doc long to go off on a tangent. This time it concerned the footwork necessary to achieve balance when you're running with a football. There he was, a white-haired man of 70, a little less nimble than Astaire, but shifty enough to elude an open drawer at the bottom of his desk.

He explained the mechanics of a wide base, the muscles involved, mentioned something about the center of gravity. I guess I was doing some footwork of my own at the time — backward; I was too busy this day. Anyhow I seldom understood these lessons in kinesiology.

It was Friday and I wasn't too busy. I was playing football on the lawn by the Student Union. Strictly for kicks. Then my man threw a pass my way and I lunged and caught it and fell to the grass. An unexpected "Hurrah!" went up from the sideline and when I looked up it was Doc Carlson, walking along Fifth Avenue in the afternoon. "It's a good thing you caught that ball, Sourpuss," he cried. "You'd a caught it good from me." He smiled. And suddenly that catch was a Rose Bowl catch.

It was Saturday and Doc had gone to his other home, in Ligonier, his idea of paradise, out where he planted things, like flowers and fruit trees. Imagine planting a tree when you're 70. Imagine uprooting a tree when you're 70, making sure there's plenty of sod clinging to the roots, and dropping it into your car trunk to deliver to a friend who'd like it. Even if your friend had a helluva time getting it out of the trunk because it was too heavy for one man to carry. But then Doc took it easy sometimes, too, like when he'd send a pack of petunia seeds to a friend's little girl.

This man was a stubborn man although he didn't tolerate stubbornness. You remember him telling you last winter about his wife ordering him to get a new topcoat. "Bah," he said. "You don't buy a topcoat at my age."

So he went out and bought two topcoats, a suit, a pair of shoes and a new hat. "That'll teach her," he said, smiling. He always referred to his second wife — the first one died — as "my girlfriend."

It was Sunday and you woke up late, feeling poorly from staying out too late. The phone rang. It was Beano Cook. All your mother heard you say was "Doc Carlson" and "one-thirty," but it was enough. She knew. And then you felt worse.

You sat there for awhile, on the kitchen steps. Images of Doc Carlson came and were gone as in a Fellini film and the images did not stop coming, and they were rich images. Doc Carlson was something special.

That afternoon you were in Fitzgerald Field House, next to Doc's office. You went through the green door which separated the two offices. No one was there and you looked about. The burgundy cover on his examining table was dusty and you could streak it with your fingers. The pillow at the head of the table was the kind firemen find when they are rooting through a flophouse.

Maybe they were right when they said Carlson could no longer doctor for the University. Perhaps his practice was outmoded. But he found fault with his successor because "things are too regimented now." He recalled how anybody could come into his office for help, the profs, the dishwashers in the cafeteria, the mechanic in the garage.

But Doc Carlson forgot that the University where he lived for fifty years had grown up, had gotten more sophisticated. He didn't consider how there were now a thousand or more students living on campus these past few years who hadn't been there before. There wasn't time anymore to pull the thorn from the landscaper's finger. A kind word or an aspirin was not enough.

And he didn't know what breed of student he was dealing with now. His favorites had been the poor kids who needed a few bucks to replace their worn slacks. He'd only shake his head and mumble if he knew there were some today who wanted them that way. He didn't know the students' hometowns anymore. It's a good thing he didn't. He used to say, "Hiya, Braddock!" and "Hiya, Hazelwood!" when he didn't know your name. It would sound awful today if Doc had to call "Hiya, Jamaica Heights!" or "Hiya, Great Neck!"

But Doc Carlson was a healer. He could seize your heart without a scalpel and sutures. And he could ease the pain. His smile was more quieting than a sedative.

Perhaps he wasn't a great surgeon. You remember how he once burned a wart off your knuckle, and you watched the sparks fly and how it scorched and turned to charcoal and how it hurt like hell, and how you didn't say a word because Doc was smiling and you couldn't complain.

When you were down in the dumps, you wondered whether you should speak to your priest or Doc Carlson. He'd smile and say, "Let me buy you an ice cream cone," and you felt much better.

You remember him calling you into his office, and telling you to reach into his drawer where there were all sorts of candies and chocolate bars. There are probably file cards now in his old desk.

Doc used to write you little notes now and then. They were always encouraging. He wanted you to be more compassionate in your writing. There were too many good guys in this world, he argued, to bother criticizing the bad ones. Yet he said if there were heroes in games, then surely there were goats.

There's a book in your library that Doc sent you. It's called **The Tumult and the Shouting.** It's a collection of stories by Grantland Rice, the dean of American sportswriters in Doc's day. It doesn't belong on that shelf with Tolstoi, James and Twain, but Doc thought it did, so it stays. It's a cherished possession.

Inside the cover there is a message and a diagram — of course — from Doc Carlson. There's an arrow pointing upward toward "Grantland Rice (compassion)" and an arrow pointing downward toward "Westbrook Pegler (sarcasm)" and the footnote from Doc read: "the choice is yours."

He wanted you to see the good in everyone. Robert Louis Stevenson once wrote: "There is no duty we underrate so much as the duty of being happy." That's why Doc Carlson is underrated. Try to overlook his achievements in sports, his plaques, and trophies. Look instead at the man.

People who generate inner sunshine make life pleasanter for those around them. Their impulses lead to right action; their thoughts are usually true. They have their roots in some deep, shining faith.

Very naturally we resent those tiresome Pollyannas who foist their cheerfulness upon us regardless of our fate and feelings. But Doc Carlson found pleasure in a sunset or the face of a friend at the door and he felt that his daily duty was doling out happiness.

Doc Carlson gave out gaiety and he felt it coming back at him. It was like a boomerang — a blessed boomerang. He got a high rate of return. He often spoke of the "dividends one receives."

I didn't like the way he went away, but I'll bet there was a gentle smile dancing at the corner of his mouth. He didn't even tip us off with a cough or a cry. He didn't want any fuss. He probably entered laughing.

MIKE DITKA

Chicago Bears' New Boss Has Always Been A Leader

"Mike is one of the finest No. 1 picks I ever made. What desire and determination he has."
—George Halas

Mention Mike Ditka to anybody who played with or against him and there is an instant response. Some smile. Some frown. Some shake their heads, and are happy to still have them on their shoulders. Everyone has a story.

Mike Dynamite, maybe that's what he should have been called. Then again, Mike Ditka may be a perfect name. It's hard-hitting. Ditka. There's a crunch to it.

One-time and for-all-time Pitt sports publicist Beano Cook encouraged Bob Anderson to tell me his story about Mike Ditka.

Anderson was an All-America halfback at Army in his senior season at West Point, playing in the same backfield as Pete Dawkins, another All-America. Dawkins became a career officer; Anderson a saloon keeper on New York's fashionable East Side.

Anderson was sitting at a sidewalk table at Mr. Laff's, naturally laughing as he talked about his first meeting with Mike Ditka. "We were playing Pitt about midway through our schedule, and we were undefeated, and I was feeling pretty good about myself," Anderson said.

"I was getting a little cocky, and I hadn't paid much attention to the scouting report that week. Before our game at Pitt, I checked a program to see who was in their lineup.

"I saw they were starting Mike Ditka at the one end. A sophomore. That's good, I thought. I didn't even know until later that it was also his first start. But I figured I'd have an easy day sweeping that end.

"The first time we did it, I was an advance blocker ahead of Dawkins, who carried the ball. I went at Ditka. Well, he hit me in the chin with a forearm shot that sent my helmet back over my head. I was reeling after that. My mouth was bleeding. I wanted no more of Mike Ditka that day."

That was vintage Mike Ditka. No one ever got him out of Pitt's starting lineup after that. Pitt tied Army, 14-14, that day, just for the record. It was a morale victory.

Ernie Hefferle, the 66-year-old pro personnel evaluator for Bum Phillips and the New Orleans Saints, smiles when he talks about Mike Ditka.

"He was the damndest player I ever came across; you get one like him in a lifetime, if you're lucky," said Hefferle, who coached the ends as an assistant to Johnny Michelosen in Ditka's All-America days at Pitt.

"He used to forearm our own guys in practice. He used to complain that our practices weren't tough enough. He wanted more hitting. All he wanted to do was hit, hit, hit."

Said Bob Timmons, who coached Ditka in two sports: "He'll hit the first guy he sees."

Ditka was like that whether he was playing football, baseball or basketball — all of which he competed in on a varsity basis at Pitt — or in wrestling, where he was the heavyweight champion on the intramural circuit. Rex Peery, who coached the varsity wrestling team, once said Ditka could have been an NCAA mat champion.

He was such a tenacious competitor. He once punched two Pitt guards in the same game during huddles because he didn't think they were putting out.

In Ditka's senior season at Pitt, he went after teammate Chuck Reinhold at halftime. Reinhold, a well-mannered, scholarly type, was a safetyman from Mt. Lebanon. He did something wrong near the end of the first half of the game with Michigan State, permitting Herb Adderly to escape his grasp and go for a touchdown.

Not long afterward, as the Pitt squad clattered into the dressing room, Reinhold hollered, "Let's get 'em the second half!"

Ditka cried out, "If you hadn't given up that touchdown we wouldn't be in the fix we're in!" With that, he went for Reinhold. It took about six teammates to restrain Ditka.

Ditka demands a lot from his teammates. Said Mike Pyle, who co-captained the Chicago Bears with Ditka: "He lets you know right away. If you do something wrong, he'll tell you. If you do something right, he'll tell you. And he expects to be told himself."

Ditka was a devastating defensive end at Pitt, but the Panthers seldom passed the ball under Michelosen, so his offensive talents were kept under wraps for the most part.

He was named first team All-America as a senior in 1960, and was joined by Joe Bellino of Navy, Ernie Davis of Syracuse, Bob Ferguson of Ohio State, E. J. Holub of Texas Tech, Dan Larose of Missouri and Bob Lilly of Texas Christian, to cite a few of the college elite that year.

He was also named the winner of the Charles C. Hartwig Award as the senior who did the most to promote the cause of athletics at Pitt.

Upon closing his Pitt career, Ditka declared that he had a special desire to beat Notre Dame and Penn State because he almost went to those schools.

"I was lucky to play on three winning teams against Notre Dame," he pointed out, "but my only regret in my career is my showing against Penn State. They beat us two out of three and not once in three years did I catch a pass against them."

He was always the leader of his team. He captained Pitt in his senior year, he captained the East against the West in three post-season games, he captained the 1961 College All-Star team against the National Football League champions. And, as an all-pro tight end with the Chicago Bears, he captained their offensive unit.

Soon after he became the Bears' coach, Ditka came back to Pittsburgh to play in Foge Fazio's Leukemia Open golf tournament, and was one of the main attractions — along with former coach Johnny Majors — in a fund-raiser that netted more than $50,000 for the Leukemia Society. Ditka looked great as he strolled the Pittsburgh Field Club.

Ditka was delighted to help a good friend out, and to re-establish ties with Pitt people. He had been named the Bears' coach on Jan. 19 — the same day Fazio got the Pitt job.

"Looking back to my college career," Ditka declared, "Pitt means to me my whole life — what I am now. As a kid growing up, I wanted to go to Notre Dame. But they didn't get interested in me till late in the summer after my senior year at Aliquippa.

"When they finally invited me to visit their campus, I had to turn down an invitation to meet my boyhood idol, Stan Musial. It came down to choosing between Pitt and Penn State, or, really, the recruiting coaches, Jack Wiley and Joe Paterno. I loved them both.

"At the last minute, I decided I wanted to be a dentist, so I went to Pitt. I owe Pitt so much. They played the finest schedule, and they gave me a publicity guy on my side in Beano Cook, and he helped me to become an All-American.

"Johnny Michelosen may never go down as one of the great coaches of all time, but he had a lot of character. He taught you how to play basic fundamental football. We tried to double-team everybody on the field, but, of course, you couldn't do that.

"I never thought I was a good athlete. I thought I was determined. That's what I'm looking for with the Bears — people with the right attitude."

Ernie Stautner, the former Steeler who is enshrined in the Pro Football Hall of Fame, and was on the same coaching staff as Ditka for five seasons with the Dallas Cowboys, offers: "I'm so pleased for Mike. He'll be great for the Bears. To me, Mike Ditka epitomizes what the Bears used to be. Now if they can get back to that."

He broke in with the Bears in a big way. The burly, 230-pound bone crusher from Aliquippa caught 56 passes for 1,076 yards and 12 touchdowns to win NFL Rookie of the Year honors.

"Mike's the best tight end I've ever seen," said Billy Wade, who was one of the Bears' quarterbacks. "The way I always picture Mike is with one hand on the ball, and the other hand free, looking for someone to hit."

Rudy Bukich, the Bears' other fine quarterback, described Ditka similarly: "He's a leader. He's 100 percent for the team. He drags you along with him."

Both descriptions were fitting for Ditka's performance upon returning to Pittsburgh as a pro the first time. That was in 1963, when Pitt was putting together a great 9-1 season of its own, and the Bears came to Forbes Field to play the Steelers.

I watched that game from the roof above the rightfield stands, and saw one particular play which I will never forget, and it's the way I'll always picture Mike Ditka.

"It was the most amazing play, perhaps, that I have ever seen in football," wrote Pat Livingston, the sports editor of The Press, in a reflective piece about Ditka when he was hired in January of 1982 to become the new head coach of the Bears.

MIKE DITKA   —Photo By John Alexandrowicz

"For hopeless human effort, it was exceeded only by the Marines at Tarawa or Iwo Jima."

Here's what happened:

With the Steelers ahead, 17-14, and the clock spinning down, Billy Wade threw one of those dinky passes to Ditka. At the 30, Mike brushed off the Steeler who was covering him. At midfield, he struggled to break free of a couple of safety men, but was swarmed over by a pack of linemen.

Somehow he outfought them. At the 40, hugging the sideline, Ditka broke another tackle. At the 25, he was reeling, staggering on limp, drunken legs. Yet he managed to get the ball close enough for the tying field goal before collapsing from his effort.

"And that play," wrote Livingston, "had something to do with George Halas's decision to hire Ditka."

After that game, Halas stood in the Bears' dressing room and pointed to Ditka.

"Ditka's going to be one of the greats of this league if he isn't there already," said Halas of his star end. "What desire and determination that young man has!

"Did you see him fight his way out of the grasp of all those Steelers after catching a pass when it was third down and 35 for us deep in our own territory? What he did separates the good from the great.

"Mike is one of the finest No. 1 draft picks I ever made."

Ditka was a four-time All-Pro tight end with the Bears. He later played for the Philadelphia Eagles and concluded his career with four seasons with the Dallas Cowboys, twice going to the Super Bowl with that ballclub. He stayed on as a coach, and for five years he was in charge of both special teams and receivers.

Whether Ditka will be a success in Chicago is anybody's guess, but several who know him are willing to offer their thoughts on the subject.

Ditka was known for his fiery temper in his playing days.

"I know a lot of guys with the same temperament who were successful — John Madden is one who comes to mind," said Denver Broncos' head coach Dan Reeves, who coached with the volatile Ditka in Dallas for several seasons. "As long as you control it, it's good. Maturity has helped. Mike made great strides in that area."

Broncos' assistant Stan Jones, who played with Ditka for five years at Chicago, observed, "Ditka changed a lot of his ways working under Tom Landry. He will be fiery, but under control."

Said Doug Atkins, another former Bears' teammate: "I think he's lost some of the temper he had while he was playing ball. We all get mellow as we get older, and lose a little fire when we don't have to play."

The Bears' job came open after the 1981 season and Ditka claimed it. "He's certainly ready for the challenge," said Tom Landry, his boss at Dallas. "And no one likes challenges more than Mike."

"Ditka is going to be one of the greats of this league."
—George Halas

Chicago Bears owner George Halas (r) introduces his new head coach, Mike Ditka.

TONY DORSETT

Tony Dorsett wins Heisman Trophy.

Marty Wolfson

Tony Dorsett always stood out in a crowd, even during those first few days at Pitt's football practices.

Johnny Majors, the new coach at Pitt, had gone out in 1973 and brought back players by the carload. He brought back in the neighborhood of 80 new players. That's about the size of some college teams—with four years of recruiting—and Majors brought them all in at once.

He believed there was quality in quantity.

One young man named John Hanhauser hardly knew anyone after the first week of practice when Majors held his first scrimmage.

"I was playing linebacker then," Hanhauser recalled, "and it was a screen pass. I went out to get this guy. It was easy. I'm not the fastest guy in the world, but I had this guy easy. I thought. When I got out there, he wasn't there. He was gone!

"I remember I went back to the bench and I said, "Who in the hell was that? Who's 33?"

Someone named Tony Dorsett, he was told.

"I'd never heard of Tony Dorsett myself," admitted Hanhauser. "I didn't know a thing about him."

He learned quickly, and so did the rest of his teammates. So did Pitt's opponents. Some of the coaches on the other side will tell you the rest:

• "I have not seen a running back like Tony Dorsett since O. J. Simpson," said Homer Smith, Army.

• "I don't know if I've ever seen a better running back," said Joe Paterno, Penn State.

• "It was (Dorsett's 303-yard day as a junior) as fine a performance as I've seen in 28 years of coaching," declared Dan Devine, Notre Dame.

Pitt's backfield coach at the time was Harry Jones. He had been a two-time All-America running back at Arkansas and a wingback for five years with the Philadelphia Eagles.

"I used to think Gale Sayers was the greatest runner I'd ever seen," said Jones, "until I saw Tony. He works harder than anyone I've coached. And he hasn't lost his modesty with all that exposure over the years."

Chancellor Dr. Wesley Posvar congratulates Tony Dorsett.

**OCTOBER 23, 1976
PITTSBURGH -VS- NAVY
THE DAY TONY DORSETT BROKE
THE NCAA RUSHING RECORD**

Alumni Loved Tony Dorsett, And He Loved Them Right Back

"It's a lot more fun when you win."
—Dr. Marvin Zelkowitz

Reprinted from SCORE!   *Nov. 6, 1975*

Mrs. Myrtle Dorsett, the mother of Pitt's All-America running back Tony Dorsett, sat directly behind me in a 40-yard line seat on a Saturday afternoon at West Point's Michie Stadium.

She never stopped smiling, though she wore rain gear, and watched much of the Pitt-Army football game that gray afternoon from beneath an umbrella. It was easy, though, to appreciate her good humor.

Her son, Tony, always a source of pride to her anyway, was having one of the best days of his already spectacular three-year career, cutting here and there, and darting by the dark-shirted Cadets on one long run after another. Her son-in-law, Richard Kimbrough, who also played football at Hopewell High and before that at Aliquippa High just after, he said, Mike Ditka had left there to enroll at Pitt, was keeping track of Tony's yardage. He was kept busier than the Cadets' defensive unit.

"What do you think of him?" Kimbrough would ask after Tony would break off a 20- or 30-yard gain.

At halftime, Kimbrough said his brother-in-law had already gained 218 yards. A fan nearby corrected him, saying he had just heard on the radio it was 191 yards.

As it turned out, Kimbrough had credited his brother-in-law with only a yard too many. Altogether, young Dorsett, just a junior but already the holder of every important rushing and scoring record at Pitt, gained 268 yards and scored four touchdowns as the Panthers pelted the Cadets much more than the rain, winning by 52-20. Dorsett would have only one better ground-gaining effort, an unreal 303 yards against Notre Dame later the same season.

From the very first play of the game when Pitt was on its own 20-yard line following a touchback on the kickoff, and sophomore quarterback Robert Haygood threw a dangerous sideline pass to freshman receiver Gordon Jones, the Panthers provided one thrill after another for their fans, mostly family and alumni sitting in a capacity Homecoming Day crowd on the scenic West Point campus.

I remember telling my friends that Pitt never would have attempted a pass on the first down of a game when Johnny Michelosen was the coach. Surely one of the "C-Boys" — Fred Cox, Jim Cunningham or Bob Clemens — would have been sent off right guard to get things underway when I first came to Pitt at the outset of the '60s. I then cursed myself for sounding so much like an old grad.

I was surrounded by friends who had gone to Pitt with me, and now reside in New York. We commented about Pitt's majorettes, something new to the Pitt football scene, and wondered why the cheerleaders didn't lead cheers anymore, but were more of a gym team.

Dr. Marvin Zelkowitz, who was two years behind me at Pitt and sports editor of The Pitt News his senior year, sat directly in front of me at Michie Stadium. He had wanted to be a sportswriter, but had to settle for being a pediatric neurologist. He was carrying on this afternoon like the teenager he had been at Allderdice High in Squirrel Hill.

"This is fun," he shrieked at one point, continually jumping up and down as Dorsett and Elliott Walker waltzed through the Army line. "It's a lot more fun when you win."

Alumni feel that way everywhere, of course. And the alumni are so important to a football program like Pitt's. Before the game, at a brunch at Bear Mountain Inn, athletic director Casimir Myslinski, himself an All-America center in his student days at West Point, told the alumni: "Without your support, we couldn't have gotten a great football coach like Johnny Majors to come to Pitt."

It was Myslinski, of course, who was the mover and shaker behind the organization of the Golden Panthers, the fund-raising booster group that has become the lifeblood of University athletics.

It would be difficult to contemplate anyone enjoying the romp over Army anymore than Mrs. Dorsett and Dr. Zelkowitz, but I bumped into other old school chums who were equally ecstatic.

Dr. Ron Ellsweig, a dentist in New Jersey, who came to Pitt in 1960 from East Stroudsburg, Pa., played a trumpet in the school's marching band as a freshman, but quit when "my lip went bad." There's a persistent image of him, as a freshman, standing above the crowd at a campus pep rally behind Forbes Field, outlined by a bonfire.

He, too, was at West Point, and he is an amazing example of the extremes to which some alumni go to pursue their interest in the Panthers.

Ron and his wife, Susan, traveled to Georgia this season for the opening game with the Bulldogs at Athens, and to Philadelphia for the Temple game. He planned to go to Pittsburgh for the Notre Dame game on Nov. 15.

Whenever Ron is unable to attend a Pitt football game — get this — he telephones the WTAE-Radio studio each Saturday. Someone there has gotten to recognize his voice and leaves the telephone line open in the studio so that Ron can listen to the entire Pitt football game as broadcast by Bill Hillgrove and John Sauer.

Ron spent $20 to buy an amplifier that he hooks up to the telephone and then he and Susan sit back in their living room in New Jersey and listen to the game. Last season it cost him $120 in phone charges to catch all the action.

At Army, he was talking to some equally fervid fans, making plans to attend the Pitt basketball game at Temple this winter. That's the closest the Pitt team will get to New York. I bumped into Ron the previous spring at the National Invitation Tournament at Madison Square Garden, and two years before that at the Fordham gym when Pitt was playing there.

Ron sends $100 each year to the Pitt athletic fund, "and I wound up getting tickets on the goal line for the Notre Dame game," he complains. And he's helped them recruit.

"I got them one guy, but he flunked out," said Ron, with a laugh. "He was so stupid, even Majors admitted he was stupid."

Sanford Levine, '64, also lives and dies with Pitt's sports teams, and he turns up in all the same places as Dr. Ellsweig. Pitt sports is all he talks about, it seems.

His heart is in the right place, right behind the Pitt monogram he wore on his gold blazer at the Pitt-Army game. He wore a gold shirt as well, with a dark blue club tie that had the Pitt emblem all over it. It was held in place by his fraternity pin. He wore stockings, which he proudly displayed for all to see, that had P-I-T-T on the sides in a vertical stripe.

A member of the student choral group in his days at Pitt, as well as a member of the tennis team, he even sang the alma mater for us at our luncheon table. "I love this whole scene," he said.

HEISMAN TROPHY WINNER TONY DORSETT

19

Marty Wolfson

HERB DOUGLAS

Hazelwooder Long Jumps From Obscurity To Olympic Stardom

The two-story brick house at 160 Hazelwood Avenue has always been something of a local landmark. Youngsters going to Gladstone Junior High across the street for released-time classes in wood shop and metal shop would pass it coming from St. Stephen's Grade School, and somebody would invariably point it out as the home of Herb Douglas Jr.

Herb Douglas Jr. was a point of pride in Hazelwood. He had won a bronze medal in the long jump at the 1948 Olympic Games in London.

So was his father. He went blind after suffering a stroke at age 41, but lived to be 92, and was among the first to have a seeing-eye dog in this country. "He and my mom were the real champions," says their son.

Jim O'Brien, who was one of those youngsters who used to stare at the Douglas house when he passed, was present in the fall of 1980 when Douglas was honored as a Letterman of Distinction at the Varsity Letter Club's Annual Homecoming Dinner at the Student Union Ballroom.

A year later, he discovered Douglas on an airplane departing the Greater Pittsburgh Airport for Philadelphia, where Douglas now resides in suburban Wyncote. He had been in Pittsburgh for the Christmas holidays to hand deliver a present to his mother. His mother has lived in that house since she was 16.

I f I had to do it again, I'd do it the same way," Herb Douglas declared. "I really enjoyed going to Pitt, regardless of the obstacles we had to overcome as blacks back then. We led the frontier for the Tony Dorsetts and Hugh Greens. They may not realize it, but it's true."

A warming glint shined through the eyeglasses of Douglas, now 60 and a vice-president at Schieffelin & Co. of New York City, importers of wines and spirits. He spoke proudly of his accomplishments at Pitt, as well as those when he was a dashing young man at Gladstone Junior High, just across the street from his home, or at Allderdice High School in Squirrel Hill.

"I got to Pitt on a football scholarship in 1945," said Douglas. "Clark Shaughnessy gave me a football scholarship. I was the only black along with Jimmy Joe Robinson. We were the first blacks to play football at Pitt.

"I had first gone to Xavier of Louisiana in 1940 and 1941, and I had a great track coach there in Ralph Metcalf. He was the only one who ever beat Jesse Owens and he did it consistently, but he never got the acclaim.

"That's like, when they talk about the 1936 Olympic Games in Berlin it's all Jesse Owens. They don't think of Johnny Woodruff, who came out of Connellsville and Pitt to win a gold medal in the 800 meters, or of Mack Robinson, Jackie's brother, who inspired young Jackie Robinson. Robinson was second to Jesse in the 200 meters in the Olympics.

"My dad was blind, and I dropped out of Xavier during the War to help him. But I couldn't work with him anymore — he could be tough on you — and so I went to Pitt. I didn't have to go far. See, my dad was in business for 30 years. He was really the champion of our family. We never knew what the depression was at our house. He was in the garage business, parking and maintaining cars for people who lived in apartments in Shadyside. His place was on Ellsworth Avenue.

"Pitt was practicing at Ellsworth Center, and I walked down there one day. Jimmy Joe was practicing. That's how it all happened.

"I became a halfback, but I was a man in motion, like a wide receiver. Shaughnessy was one of the early exponents of the T-formation. I wasn't much of a football player, but I did have one big moment.

"We hadn't scored in three or four years against Notre Dame, and the first time we had the ball I scored a 57-yard touchdown. I was the second black ever to score against Notre Dame. Buddy Young of Illinois was the first.

"The next year I concentrated strictly on track. My potential in track was greater then because there were very few minorities in pro football. If I were coming through today, I'm sure I'd be a wide receiver.

"Carl Olson came back to Pitt from the Navy in 1946, and he was responsible for my not playing football any more. He didn't believe in it. He wanted total dedication to track. He was a stickler for conditioning. I'm not so sure he was a great coach as far as teaching techniques were concerned, but you were always in condition to compete at your best.

"If you didn't win, or came up short when you were expected to break a record, Olson would say, 'What happened?' I wanted him to tell me what happened, or what went wrong."

Douglas won the AAU broad jump in 1945. The next year, he won the 100 yard dash and broad jump in the IC4A outdoor meet, and was second in the broad jump at the NCAA meet that season. In 1947, he dominated the broad jump in all meets.

"I went to the Olympics in 1948," said Douglas, "and won a bronze medal. I was second in the Olympic trials. I was the last Pitt man to win a medal in the Olympics. There's only been two of us, Johnny Woodruff and me.

"Being on that stand, listening to the Star Spangled Banner being played . . . that was the greatest moment of my life," recalled Douglas.

"I had a friend who went to ruin when he didn't make the Olympic team. I've thought about that. I worked 12 years toward that one goal. I wonder what would have happened to me if I didn't make it.

"When I was in junior high, my mother took me to see Jesse Owens. He'd just come back from Berlin where he had won four gold medals. He was appearing at Watts Grade School in The Hill district. He was campaigning for Alf Landon, the Socialist candidate for President.

"As Jesse was leaving the building, I stopped him, and he put his arm around me. I said, 'Mr. Owens, I go to Gladstone Junior High. I run the hundred in 10.4, I broad jump 21-8, and I high jump six feet.' He said, 'You did better than I did when I was your age. Keep up the good work and get an education.'

"I learned later that he was a real kidder, but back then I believed him. I knew that I'd make the Olympic team for sure. That was my ultimate aim. There was no way in the world you could tell me I wouldn't make the Olympics."

His effort of 25'3½" at the Olympic tryouts stood as the Pitt record for 23 years.

Douglas earned letters in basketball, gymnastics and track at Gladstone Junior High. He was the City champion in the 75-yard dash in 1936 and the 100-yard dash in 1937, and in tumbling in gymnastics competition both years.

At Allderdice, Douglas earned letters in four sports, playing football in addition to his other endeavors.

He was the City champion in the 100 and 220 yard sprints and the broad jump in 1939 and 1940, setting City records in all three events as a senior. He was the state champion in the broad jump in 1939 and 1940, and in the 100 and 220 yard dash in 1940.

In addition, he won the tumbling event in the 1938 City gymnastics competition. "That might have been my best event of all," said Douglas.

He was All-City in 1938 and 1939 in basketball as Allderdice won back-to-back championships. "I was the only 'brother' on the basketball team, but I led the team in scoring," he said.

After Allderdice, it was Pitt and a daily street car commute from his home in Hazelwood to the Oakland campus. "The athletes today wouldn't consider something like that," he said.

"Things were tougher for blacks back then. What I gained from it is that I have been able to go out in the competitive world, and feel equal to anyone. I learned I could compete equally."

Douglas, at right, during 1948 Olympic medal presentation ceremonies. The long jump winner was the U.S.A's Bill Steele.

Douglas was a long jump bronze medalist as a third-place finisher at the 1948 Olympic Games in London.

"We are all proud to have been athletes and to be part of Pitt's athletic history . . ."

Herb Douglas was the most stirring speaker when he was one of four Pitt graduates and varsity letter holders who were honored as Awardees of Distinction at the Varsity Letter Club's Annual Homecoming Dinner at the Student Union Ballroom back on Oct. 1, 1980.

In addition to Douglas, others honored were John R. Kountz, a member of the varsity track team (1952-54) who is vice-president, secretary and general counsel of H. K. Porter Co., Inc., Bob Timmons, who played varsity football at Pitt in 1933 and later served on a long term as varsity basketball coach and as an assistant football coach, and Dick Cassiano, a member of the "Dream Backfield" in 1938, who was honored posthumously.

The text of Douglas' address follows:

Being honored for accomplishments that took place thirty years ago is a strange and, in many ways, a sobering experience. The roar of the crowd is now only a distant, echoing memory.

The strength, spring and speed of youth has long since faded. But the memories do indeed linger on. When I think back to those years, I remember the competition, the camaraderie and the companionship of teammates.

But most of all, I remember the many people who made it possible for me to stand here today and receive this great honor.

During one's lifetime, there are very few occasions when an opportunity is presented to publicly say thank you. So forgive me if I take this moment to do just that.

To all my teachers: Thank you for your time, your dedication and your patience.

To my coaches: God bless all of you for caring enough to teach me, read me the riot act and push me to the limits of my abilities. In many ways, this honor is more yours than mine.

But most of all, I reserve a special debt of thanks, appreciation and love for two very special people who made it possible for me to earn this honor — my parents!

There's a union that lasted over fifty years and brought forth two children. They raised and trained their children not only with words, but more by their love and dedication to each other and to us.

They taught by example: When I was five years old and entering kindergarten, my mother gave birth to my sister. On that very same day, she learned that her husband, my father, had suffered a massive stroke and was permanently blinded.

Her unfailing support, devotion and courage set an example for her children that will never be forgotten. With her help, my sightless dad went on to build a business, support his family and be a devoted father.

My father died two years ago at the age of ninety-two. He never saw me win a race, score a touchdown or win an Olympic medal. He didn't have to . . . my mother told him about it. She was his eyes for more than fifty years . . . the best eyes a man ever had.

Mother was twenty-seven when he went blind, and to him — in his mind's eye — she always remained young and beautiful. And I think you will agree that he was right!

I'd like you to meet the real champ of the Douglas family . . . mother, would you please stand up?

I know that Dick Cassiano, John Kountz and Bob Timmons, all of whom are being honored here tonight, also received guidance, devotion and courage from their parents.

I regret that Dick's honor comes to him posthumously, as he died two days after having been nominated. I recall very vividly a chat I had with Dick several years after he had graduated. He said how appreciative he was that Pitt had given him an athletic scholarship, because he came from a family of meager means. He remembered how his father fed his family for years on the mushrooms he gathered and cooked.

John Kountz . . . John emerged to scholastic excellence by graduating summa cum laude. John's father moved his family to Mt. Lebanon so that John could receive a good education, even though his family was not financially prepared for such a high income community.

Bob Timmons . . . Bob was called the silent threat . . . but he had a traumatic setback when both his parents died of influenza during his sophomore year at Pitt.

His father was a policeman who believed in discipline. This facilitated his ability to coach basketball and develop men both on and off the courts. Examples such as All-American Don Hennon, who is now a surgeon and Julius Pegues, the first black to play basketball here at Pitt, and who is now an aeronautical engineer.

Being a Pitt athlete has in so many ways opened the door to success for all of us. Of the nominees mentioned here tonight, there is not one who could not have been so honored as a Letterman Of Distinction.

As I reflect back, there are also many athletes who were not nominated . . . and some of you are in this audience . . . who I think equally deserve this honor.

I know that we are all proud to have been athletes and to be part of Pitt's athletic history. Pitt was one of the first universities to say to a student: "It doesn't matter what color you are, or if your parents are rich or poor. What does matter is that you develop to your full potential."

I am also proud to be part of the Pitt community of lettermen who have contributed so much to the success of sport in our country.

Sport is now big business . . . a multi-million dollar business. But I sometimes wonder if all the athletes who say they are "number one" or "they are the greatest" stop to remember all the people who made their success possible.

One of the beautiful things about sports is that no one person makes it solely on their own . . . and no one nationality is supreme. Sports is truly a melting pot where all men and women of ability can compete on equal terms.

The lessons learned in competition transcend the playing field to the business and professional fields. Trying your best, working with others and being a winner has made our country great!

Thirty-five years ago, a coach by the name of Clark Shaughnessy gave Jimmy Joe Robinson and myself a chance to try out for football. Jimmy made the first team, while I was a miserable flop . . . my only claim to fame was that I ran like a ghost for 57 yards for the first touchdown we had scored against Notre Dame in four years. Thus, I was the second black at the time to score against Notre Dame.

Today, Jimmy is a fine minister on the North Side of Pittsburgh, while I continue to help the devil by supplying the wines and spirits to his church goers.

I think the golden age of Pitt sports was in the thirties. Pitt had the number one basketball team, football team and an Olympic champion. Two of the recipients tonight are of that era. More importantly, the majority of all the Pitt lettermen have graduated, gone on to raise families, build careers and contribute to their communities and to the nation as a whole.

What do we all have in common? I think Dick Cassiano best described this, shortly before his death, in a letter to Bob Rosborough as follows.

"Dear Bob: Concerning your recent letter, I am not quite certain of your meaning . . . letter winners who have achieved success in life.

"If you mean material success, such as money, position and property; then I have failed. But if you mean non material and/or spiritual success; such as a loving wife, family and good friends . . . then indeed I am a rich man who has achieved success."

And a friend who wrote to Dick . . .

"Dear Dick: I was saddened to learn that you have not been well, but I understood that your courage is an inspiration to all who know you. You have a great many friends going back over the years who are thinking of you and praying for you during this difficult time, and I just wanted to be sure that you count me among those rooting for you. With warmest regards, Jerry Ford."

During the course of my athletic and business career, I have been fortunate to receive many honors. But none will I cherish more than being elected by my peers . . . my fellow athletes . . . to be a Letterman of Distinction!

I know that I speak for John Kountz, Dick Cassiano and Bob Timmons. I thank you for the honor you have bestowed upon us.

DON HENNON

"He's a living monument to great teaching."
—Doc Carlson

Reprinted from The Pittsburgh Press   March 8, 1981

There were six of them and they represented Pittsburgh at its best in basketball.

In their time, they could dribble, shoot and rebound with anybody. They included Chuck Cooper, Dick Groat, Ed Fleming, Don Hennon, Connie Hawkins and Brian Generalovich. What a team they'd be!

They were sitting together at a showcase table for the Curbstone Coaches' Eastern 8 Basketball Championship luncheon at the Allegheny Club in March of 1981, and a sellout crowd paid tribute to them as well as the league's award winners.

"It was nice for old-time's sake," said Dr. Hennon, now a 43-year-old general surgeon here. "I like to see those guys, and find out how they're doing these days."

Dr. Hennon is the smallest of the six, but that is nothing new. As a junior at Pitt during the 1957-58 season, Hennon, at 5-8½, 185, was the smallest member of a six-man All-America team that had to be the greatest of all time.

It included Wilt Chamberlain of Kansas, the tallest at 7-1, Bob Boozer of Kansas State, Elgin Baylor of Seattle, Oscar Robertson of Cincinnati, Guy Rodgers of Temple, and Hennon. Pitt's sports publicist at the time, Beano Cook, pushed unsuccessfully to get a picture of Hennon posed with Dr. Jonas Salk, who developed a polio vaccine during his stay at Pitt, and label them "Pitt's two greatest shotmakers."

In his senior year, Hennon and the Panthers slipped somewhat from their previous season's performance. While he was not a consensus All-American in his final year, he was named to the UPI first team that included Robertson, Boozer, Bailey Howell of Mississippi State and Jerry West, a junior at West Virginia University.

Hennon's No. 10 was retired, and he still holds many of Pitt's all-time scoring records, averaging 24.2 points over three varsity seasons. Only Larry Harris, who played for four seasons, scored more career points (1,914) than Hennon (1,841).

Hennon had been schooled in basketball since he was 10 when his father, L. Butler Hennon, hung up a basketball hoop in the cellar of their home. He played for his father at Wampum High School, near New Castle, and they were a winning combination, taking the state Class B title in Don's senior year. Don's dad was a brilliant basketball coach, and used all sorts of practice innovations — dribbling blindfolded and around chairs — to improve fundamental skills.

As Pitt's Hall of Fame basketball coach, Dr. H. C. Carlson, said of Don Hennon: "He's a living monument to great teaching. He is also living proof that a great basketball player cannot be measured by size alone. The heart still has a lot to do with winning games."

DR. JONAS E. SALK — Pitt's great shot-maker.

Bob Timmons was the basketball coach at Pitt when Hennon was playing, but Doc Carlson, then the head of the student medical service, helped sell Hennon on staying here to play college ball.

Dr. Hennon, who was among the record crowds at this weekend's Eastern 8 Tournament at the Civic Arena, said he came across a letter Dr. Carlson had written him when he was going through some of his memorabilia.

"Doc was a very realistic person," said Hennon, "and he said in his letter when I was being recruited, 'Look, you'll go to North Carolina State and Duke and Maryland and they've all got beautiful campuses. They're out of this world. But, remember, you can't eat grass. Come to Pitt and play where you're going to work someday.'"

It was sound advice.

"I wanted to be a physician when I came to Pitt," he recalled. "I wanted to be a doctor; I didn't know then that I'd be a surgeon. I never worried about not being 6-6. Doc Carlson used to tell me about Bobby Brown, a third baseman for the New York Yankees, who went to medical school and became a doctor when he retired from baseball. He thought you should have a future beyond basketball."

Dr. Hennon thinks that too many of today's youngsters see sports as an end in themselves. "They see the big money the pros are making, and you can't blame them for wanting that," he said.

But the odds are so heavily weighed against realizing such goals. Of every senior starter on a high school basketball team in this country, one out of 40,000 makes it in the National Basketball Association. In truth, it's easier to become a doctor, a lawyer, a scientist, a teacher, a contributing citizen.

After playing in a series of exhibitions for the Cleveland Pipers of the American Basketball League, along with the likes of Dick Barnett and Ben Warley, Hennon devoted full-time to his medical studies at Pitt. He's not sorry.

He's a general surgeon at Allegheny General Hospital, Passavant Hospital and Surburban General Hospital. And he still plays basketball with his boys in their backyard in the northern suburb of Franklin Park. Don Jr. is a 6-foot freshman on the jayvee team at Westminster, Rob is a 5-11 junior at North Allegheny High School, and Scott is a seventh grade member of the Ingomar Middle School team. Don also has a daughter, Kim, who's a junior at Penn State University.

Dick Groat says Hennon had one of the best outside shots he ever saw in basketball, and apparently he hasn't lost his touch. "He can still shoot," reported Don's wife, Madeline, a former nurse from Weirton, W.Va., "but he can't run anymore because he has arthritic knees."

Which means he doesn't shoot that running push shot going into the corner anymore.

"I've always loved basketball," he said, "but I tell my boys that basketball isn't necessarily going to be your life."

Don Hennon's tutor in high school was his father, L. B. Hennon.

DON HENNON — Pitt's other great shot-maker.

25

BILLY KNIGHT

From Braddock To The NBA With A Winning Smile

Billy Knight is one of the nicest guys in the NBA. He ranks right up there with Julius Erving, one of his heroes when he was still a student at the University of Pittsburgh, and Dr. J was among the many pro players pictured on the posters of Billy's dormitory wall. Playing pro ball was just a dream for Billy back then.

Knight has not been spoiled by the big dough and the pampered (what-can-we-do-for-you-next?) world of professional sports. He is the same clean-cut, bright-eyed, bright-smiling young man who came out of Braddock High to push Pitt into the national limelight in basketball for a brief, but exhilarating period in the '70s.

He set all sorts of scoring records and, as a senior, led the Panthers to the NCAA Eastern Regionals, before they fell to high-flying David Thompson and the North Carolina State team that went on to win the national title in 1974.

He was recruited mainly by Tim Grgurich and coached mainly by Buzz Ridl during his reign at Pitt, and he has enjoyed more success in the play-for-pay ranks than anyone else in the school's history.

He had his ups and downs during his first six years in pro basketball, the first two with the American Basketball Association, and, following a merger, the next four in the National Basketball Association. He was twice an All-Star selection in the ABA, and was second in scoring (28.1 ppg) only to Dr. J in his second ABA season. He was an All-Star Game selection his first time out in the NBA, too, but has been in and out of the starting lineup ever since. It's never been quite the same.

He started out with the Indiana Pacers, then played for the Buffalo Braves and Boston Celtics before coming back to the Pacers. He's never complained publicly about anything since he's been in the pro ranks, which right away cuts him apart from the pack.

When he broke into pro ball, his first coach, the Pacers' Bobby Leonard, allowed, "Knight is one of the all-time great kids. He doesn't smoke, he doesn't swear, he doesn't drink, he's very easy to coach, he's very easy to get along with. I'm telling you, he's something else."

When Billy was on a scoring tear one time, teammate George McGinnis groaned, "If this keeps up, he'll have us all drinking Hi-C."

During the 1981-82 season, it was written somewhere that Knight was in Coach Jack McKinney's doghouse. It didn't ring true, and Knight scoffed at the suggestion. "Me and him have never had words or gotten into it," he explained, "or had any kind of confrontation.

Marty Wolfson

"Knight is one of the all-time great kids."
—Bobby Leonard

LOCAL LOOK — Coach Buzz Ridl, at right, recruited mostly local talent, which included these members of the 1972-73 team (left to right) Ken Wagoner (Beaver Falls), Mickey Martin (Baldwin), Billy Knight (Braddock), Jim Bolla (Canevin) and Bill Sulkowski (Canon-McMillan).

AS A PACER — Another former Panther, Mel Bennett, is behind Billy in pro action at right. On the attack against Army, Billy as Panther below.

"When the season started, I was prepared to do what I was asked to do. The coach decided to go with a different kind of team, and it called for me to come off the bench as a forward. Hey, it's his team. That's what he wants to do.

"I'm not the type of person who'd try to undermine the team, or knock the guys who are playing. We have good guys, good personnel. I try to keep a positive attitude and approach."

He has always maintained a proper perspective about pro basketball, and his role in it. He may have lost something along the way, but it wasn't his smile. He looks back fondly on his days at Pitt.

"That was a great experience," he said. "First of all, Coach Ridl had a lot to do with forming and developing my attitude, seemingly laid-back. The way you handle things ... by not outwardly always showing your emotions. It doesn't mean you're never down or disappointed. It's the way I try to be.

"Coach Grgurich was a very emotional type of person. Sometimes I'm like that, too. I think about those people. Coach Ridl and Coach Grgurich and Coach (Fran) Webster have all come to see me in Indianapolis, and have stayed at my place. Coach Ridl came to see me in Cleveland, too. He brought along Ron Galbreath, the basketball coach at Westminster, where Coach Ridl is now the athletic director. Coach Grgurich is in constant contact. He calls me regularly, and I telephone him if I have a problem.

"Not only were they my coaches, but also my good friends. They had a positive influence on me. We accomplished a great deal there. It was something that wasn't supposed to happen."

Knight got his start under Moe Becker at Braddock. Becker, one of the original "Iron Dukes" at Duquesne, and Billy still get together for dinner whenever Knight is in Phoenix where Moe is living in retirement. "He still uses the salt and pepper shakers to show me his new plays," says Knight.

When Knight was a senior at Braddock High, he had scholarship offers from Georgetown, St. Bonaventure, N.C. State, Arizona and Pitt. "Basically, I wanted to stay home," he said. "I hadn't been away from home. We had a large family, with 11 kids, and I wanted to be near them.

"Most of the guys on the team came from the Pittsburgh area. Yet we won 22 in a row my senior season, and we were featured in **Sports Illustrated.** They made a big deal about all the guys being local products. We thought that was quite an accomplishment.

"If I had to do it all over again, I'd go to Pitt. It was a great experience and I learned quite a bit. I made so many friends there, with the coaches and the players, and we keep in touch. There's still a lot of closeness.

"I can call on the alumni, too. Bill Baierl was a good friend. I bought my mother's car from him. Sam Sciullo, the attorney, is another. I knew them before I had anything, and I can always call them for advice on business matters. They have nothing to gain from me."

It's not surprising that anybody who rubbed shoulders with Billy Knight when he was the No. 1 basketball player at Pitt remains a friend. Billy Knight will never forget where he came from.

Marty Wolfson

DANNY MARINO

A Home-Town Boy Who's Glad He Stayed In Oakland

"Somewhere down the road it might help him. It'll help him be a man."
— Dan Marino, Sr.

Dec. 27, 1981

Danny Marino's mother says she can't stand to hear somebody say something bad about her boy, who just happens to be an All-American quarterback at the University of Pittsburgh.

"There's not a better college quarterback in the country," said Jackie Sherrill, who coached Dan for three seasons, but not everyone shared his enthusiasm.

Daniel Constantine Marino Jr., a 20-year-old junior at Pitt, already holds all the school passing records, could win the Heisman Trophy as the nation's outstanding college football player in the '82 season, and is a popular young man on campus. He has danced to the tunes of glory more than most his age.

He is the best home-grown quarterback in this town since Johnny Unitas came out of St. Justin's on Mount Washington and worked his way to the Hall of Fame in Canton, Ohio. Even so, Danny has his detractors and when they shoot arrows at him they pierce Veronica Marino's heart. She bleeds easily.

Whether she is sitting in the stands at Pitt Stadium, with the bony-hard knees of a Penn State fan pressed into the small of her back, and needling catcalls from the same source ringing in her ears, or listening to the critics who call Cope, Savran and Nover to voice their opinions on the radio sports talk shows in town, Mrs. Marino has no defenses to ward off the pain she experiences when anyone puts down Pitt or Sherrill or Sal Sunseri or her son. Especially her son. But sports fans are sports fans . . .

"Inside, I'm just grinding, because of some of the things they say," she says, shaking her head. "Danny is still a little kid to me."

Her husband, Dan, Sr., sits across the room, and shakes his head, too, only with a smile. "I enjoy those shows," he says. "I get a kick out of them, I don't take it that seriously. And I don't look at Danny as a little kid anymore. He can handle it. He's a big boy now. It'll help him be a man."

He looks at the loss to Penn State on the final Saturday of the regular schedule in the same way. "Somewhere down the road, it might help him," he says. "It's certainly not going to ruin his life. Forty years from now, will his life be a complete failure?"

His father recalls how a reporter from the Philadelphia Inquirer came up to him when he was watching practice before the Penn State game, and asked him if Danny was behaving any differently because of the pressure of the upcoming contest. "The game is just fun," he said. "I think pressure is being a father with five or six kids, and having the boss tell you you've been laid off. That's pressure."

Bourbon Street, New Orleans, the Sugar Bowl, and the New Year's Day meeting with mighty Herschel Walker and the University of Georgia Bulldogs seemed so far away as Dan and Veronica Marino talk about the oldest of their three children.

It is three days after Pitt's shocking 48-14 setback by Penn State, Pitt's first loss in 17 games, and a loss which cost the Panthers their No. 1 rating, and the national championship. In the wake of that defeat, Pitt people are wearing black armbands, emotionally anyhow. It doesn't hurt anybody as much as it hurts the Marinos, yet they keep things in perspective better than most.

This is a gray, rainy Tuesday, but it is brightened by meeting the Marinos in their modest home on Parkview Avenue, which borders Schenley Park at the southernmost tip of Oakland.

Once you get through the steel gate and the sign — BEWARE OF THE DOG — and through the front door, you get comfortable in a hurry in their home. You feel like you're with family. "Don't worry, the dog won't bite you," says Dan Marino, Sr., and you believe him. "How about a coffee, a beer or some pop?"

The dog is called Watson. It looks like a German Shepherd. "In part, but he's also collie and who knows what else," says Veronica Marino. "He's just a mongrel."

Within an hour, the three children come home from school. Cindi, an 18-year-old freshman at Pitt, is the first to arrive, having walked the mile from the campus. She's a live wire.

Then Danny comes through the door, and drapes a brown leather coat over a chair in the living room. He is 6-foot-4, 215 pounds, but still a "little kid" in his mother's mind. He says he comes home about three nights a week during the season, to drop off his laundry and get a good home-cooked meal.

"Just like Sal Sunseri does," Danny says with a smile. Sunseri is from Greenfield, and was a teammate at Central Catholic High as well as a fellow All-American at Pitt. His mother has gotten a lot of publicity for her great cooking.

Finally, Debbie, a 14-year-old freshman at Sacred Heart High in East Liberty, arrives. Debbie is demure, a bit bashful, and quite a contrast to Cindi.

"I always told Cindi she was like a little butterfly," says her father. "Debbie is shy, but she's coming out of it. She says everybody says she's shy, so that's why she's the way she is. They're all good kids."

There are hugs and kisses, pats on the back, honest how-was-your-day inquiries, reassuring smiles for all. "What's up, Deb?" Danny says to his kid sister. She smiles and shrugs her shoulders in reply. "How was your day, Deb?" asks Mrs. Marino. She and Cindi compliment Debbie on her new haircut.

Danny and Cindi have their Mother's ice-blue eyes, and Debbie has her dad's dark brown eyes. The Marinos all have the same smile. It's always starting in the corners of their mouths, and ready to spread from ear to ear.

"After a loss like the one to Penn State," declares young Dan, "it's nice to have a family so close. It was reassuring to come home and talk to my dad and my family, and know they still love me."

His dad interrupts at this point. "Hey, he knows I'm not all wrapped up in what he's doing athletically, or that his athletic success is so important. I treat him the same way I do my daughters. No matter what he does on that football field, I'm not gonna love him any more or less.

"What I want from Danny is that when he comes out of Pitt after four years there . . . what matters to me . . . is that I want to see him the same person with the same feelings and the same compassion as when he went in there. My responsibility is to make sure that happens, and to have some input into building his character."

When young Dan reaches out to touch someone, he doesn't have to get a dial tone first. He can drive home from his dorm room at Lothrop Hall, just off Fifth Avenue, in about five minutes, when it's his turn to borrow the family's 1974 Chevrolet Impala. "If that breaks down," Danny laughs, "I'll be walking."

Penn State football coach Joe Paterno praised Danny Marino after the big game as the best quarterback he'd ever gone up against in collegiate competition. He said Danny's two touchdown passes on Pitt's first two possessions were the best he'd ever seen.

Even so, when things went badly for Dan and the Panthers, and Penn State started its own roll, some familiar critics surfaced. There's one in Section 2 who waves a blue-and-gold pom-pon, and has steel wool for hair, and something less for a brain, who's always barking, "Break Marino's legs!" Other fans were fuming after the game, and Marino was on their minds and lips.

"How'd you get Danny Marino to throw that game?" one young woman was overheard asking a Penn State grad. Or, from another, "Did Danny Marino just fall apart or what? What happened?"

They should ask Veronica Marino. "Something just happened to them, they're just kids," she says.

Backing up their quarterback are the Marinos: Cindi, Dan Sr., Veronica and Debbie, from the left. Watson the dog plays center.

There were about eight minutes to go in the game, says Danny, when it started to sink in that he was in a lost cause. An undefeated season, the No. 1 ranking, the national championship, were all going up in smoke. "I knew it was gone," he says. "I was in my back pedal."

His sister, Cindi, was sitting in the student section. "I started crying with about eight minutes to go in the game," she interjects. "I just sat there and I couldn't stop crying. Then, I looked around, and saw that so many people had left. They were good weather fans. Then I got mad. I stood up and started cheering."

She turns to Danny and says, "That interception you threw at the end — the one Mark Robinson ran back 91 yards for a touchdown — I was worried that you were going to try to tackle him. I thought you'd get hurt. That made me cry, too."

The two of them laugh about that.

She wishes she could live on campus, the way Danny does. "I'd have to hit the lottery first," says her dad.

"Sometimes I think I'm missing out on getting to know other kids better," she says. "But, I wouldn't have gone anywhere else to school. It's the only school I applied to. I would never want to leave my family. We're close. And I wanted to watch my brother play football. Not just when he was on national TV."

Cindi is considering a career as an actress — she had a role in the recent Studio Theatre production of Leonard

Football has been at Danny's doorstep since he was in fifth grade. "There's not a better quarterback in the country," said his former coach, Jackie Sherrill.

Bernstein's "Wonderful Town" on the campus, but she's also thinking about being a psychologist or a sportswriter — all lofty ambitions.

"People at school make a big deal about Danny being my brother," Cindi continues in an animated manner, much to the amusement of the rest of the Marinos. "So do teachers. 'What's it feel like?' they ask me. What do they mean? It's no big deal, he's my brother. I'm going to take this course, Acting I, and the teacher asked me if I had trouble identifying with myself because of my brother. He said, 'In the class, we'll try to find you.' I didn't know I was lost."

The Marinos can take credit for their children's confident posture. There are as many pictures of the girls gracing the wall unit in the corner of the living room as there are photos and plaques hailing Danny's athletic prowess.

The Marinos are the kind of family you'd like to have as next-door neighbors. The girls would be great baby sitters, and if a problem arose they could call their mother and she'd be home. So would their dad. "Why would I want to drink in one of the bars upstreet when I can stay here with my family?" he asks.

Mrs. Marino would share her recipe for chicken. She implored a visitor at the dinner table, "Please, you can use your fingers to eat the chicken." And her husband added, "Yeah, you don't have to impress anybody here."

He would help you if you were building something in the back yard or remodeling the kitchen, and she'd send over a cake if you weren't feeling well. "Some people put down Oakland, but I wouldn't want to live anywhere else. We don't go door to door every day, but they're always there. If you needed them, they'd be here in a hurry," she said.

Her parents were Polish and she grew up on Polish Hill. "My girlfriend and I used to get passes to the Pitt football games in the mid 50's and we went there to see the boys," she recalls.

Dan Sr. drives a delivery truck for the Post-Gazette, working the late-night shift. He once was the newspaper boy on the street where he now lives. He managed a Little League team that played at Billy Mazeroski Field, out behind where Forbes Field once stood.

He frequented Forbes Field as a youngster, and knows all the Oakland sports characters. He played football at Schenley High and sandlot ball with the Greenfield Preps. "I knew how Danny felt after the Penn State game," he says. "Hey, when I was at Schenley, we lost one game to Connellsville by 61-0, and the next week to Westinghouse by 61-6. So I've been there. And it didn't ruin my life."

The house on Parkview Avenue has been home to the Marinos for 17 years. Dan Sr. has lived in the same neighborhood all his 45 years. His mother, 68-year-old Julia Marino, lives one block away, on Frazier Street, in the only other home Dan Sr. has known.

Willie Stargell once lived next door to Danny Marino's grandmother, during Willie's early years with the Pirates, when they were playing at nearby Forbes Field. "I used to go over there and he'd catch ball with me in the street," recalls Danny.

Dan Sr. went to St. Regis Grade School, which is right across the street from his present home, and Schenley High School. Bruno Sammartino, who became the world's wrestling champion, was a classmate. They were patrol boys together. He remembers Bruno lifting a sewer lid over his head when they were at their weekly woodshop class at the nearby Holmes Grade School.

All the children went to St. Regis until it closed because of declining enrollment two years ago. "There just aren't enough little kids in the neighborhood anymore," explains Cindi.

Danny directed the St. Regis football team for several seasons in the City Catholic Grade School Football League. The team was 6-1 his last year there. "We beat St. Philomena, 14-6, to tie them for the first place in the section," he recalls. "I dropped back to pass and ran 80 yards for the game-winning touchdown. That's when I was fast."

This memory was spurred by a stroll from his home to nearby Frazier Field, where he played football and Pony League baseball. It's an abbreviated ballfield on the edge of a hill overlooking the J&L blast furnaces below, as well as Bates Street, the Parkway East and Second Avenue.

There's quite a view from up there. Directly ahead, the rusty mill stretches along the Monongahela River, and, to the left or east, coal barges are visible in the bend of the river. The sound of railroad cars being connected below punctuates the air. The blast furnaces are dormant these days, but there's still some smoke coming out of stacks nearer the shoreline.

Looking west, you can see the U.S. Steel Building, topping the Downtown skyline. Looking back toward the Marino home, you can see a montage of homes painted in pastel shades, or covered with aluminum and false-brick siding, all in rows. And on the not-so-distant horizon, through the crooked TV antennas and the gray mist, rises the 42-story Cathedral of Learning.

"I made a good decision," Danny declares at the sight of his current school. "It's great to be able to play in front of my friends and my family. It's been good from the standpoint of playing. I've played a lot and I couldn't have played any more anyplace else. I've been home and I've gotten great publicity. I'm a home-town boy.

"My sister is a smart girl, and she could have gone anywhere in the country with her grades, but she picked Pitt, too."

Danny's second choice was UCLA. He also visited Clemson, Michigan State and Arizona State. He had planned to visit Notre Dame, but decided not to, and caught a lot of flak for that. He laughs about those letters now.

Football has been at Danny's doorstep since he was in fifth grade, and he walks tall when he tours his neighborhood.

As he stands on the sidewalk in front of St. Regis, he points to a broken window on the second floor. "I must've broken 20 of those when I was a kid," he says.

There is an official looking sign posted in the window at the entrance to the school. It reads: "NOTICE — No Playing During Services, Mass, Weddings Or Funerals. ATTENTION — No Batting In School Yard. No Hard-Puck Hockey. Catching With Soft Ball Permitted."

Danny smiles at the sign. "I always played right here," he says. "We played touch-tab football and street hockey here, and games like release-the-peddler. This was the home base."

A young black walks by, and hollers to Danny. He is Kenny Holiday, who played Little League ball with Danny. A blue-and-white Cadillac Eldorado passes, and the driver honks the horn at Danny. That's Dominic Lauterio, who's going to school to be a welder.

"They don't treat me any different when I go down to watch the Oakland Softball League games at Frazier Field," says Danny.

The Marinos produce a scrapbook that has a clipping on the first page where Danny is pictured receiving a trophy for winning the 9-year-old division of the Punt, Pass and Kick competition. In the same picture is Sal Sunseri, the 11-year-old winner. They go back a long way.

"I could get out of bed five minutes before school started and beat the morning bell," Danny boasts. He obviously liked the idea, since he went to high school and college close to home, too, all within walking distance.

At Central Catholic, Danny was an outstanding athlete, an ace pitcher in both football and baseball, and he was one of the most sought-after scholastic sports stars in the country his senior season.

"Quite naturally, as a mother, I thought it would be nice for him to stay here," says Mrs. Marino. "I never really let him know I felt that way. I told him, 'Whatever you choose to do, I want you to be happy.' But I'm so glad he's here.

"When I first saw him play for Pitt, I had to pinch myself. I knew it was happening, but it seemed like a dream. It's exciting to know this is all happening to my son. I think what he has is something God gave to him. I just pray to God that he stays the same nice kid he is all his life."

—Photos by Marlene Karas

DOC MEDICH

"No one is going to die if I give up a hit."

Pitt has always taken great pride in how many of its former athletes went on to become physicians.

George "Doc" Medich did that and more. He not only became a doctor, but he became a big league baseball pitcher during the same period.

Medich somehow managed to mix a minor league and then a major league sports career with his off-season studies at the University of Pittsburgh medical school, and he's been enjoying the best of both worlds.

The 1982 season was his tenth in the major leagues. He is presently pitching for the Texas Rangers, after earlier stints with the Oakland A's, the Pittsburgh Pirates, the New York Mets, and the New York Yankees.

He spent the winter as a resident in orthopedic surgery at St. Francis Hospital in Lawrenceville, his second straight off-season tour there.

The winter before, Medich looked in as much as possible on a patient who particularly enjoyed his visits. That was Elmer Merkovsky, who had been a big, tough tackle in the days of Jock Sutherland and the "Dream Backfield" at Pitt in the late '30s, and later played three seasons (1944-46) with the Pittsburgh Steelers.

Merkovsky was having a difficult time of it. He had already had one leg amputated because of blood clotting and gangrene, and was going to have the other amputated as soon as he was strong enough to undergo a second operation.

Medich cheered up the former professional athlete, and they got along swell. Merkovsky, an optimistic soul, cheered up everyone who entered his room.

Seeing Medich again brought some memories to mind: when he was going great with the Yankees and I was covering the team's activities for the New York Post. Because we had both gone to Pitt, Medich was more than just another Yankee to me . . .

Dick Howser, a coach with the Yankees, joked that George "Doc" Medich was playing baseball only so he could make enough money to have a down payment on his malpractice insurance when he became a doctor.

But Doc has always been as dedicated to his ballplaying as he has been to his medical studies.

For five days and as many ball games in July of 1974, there just wasn't a better baseball pitcher to be found than Medich, the pride of the Yankees, Aliquippa and the University of Pittsburgh School of Medicine.

That month, Medich pitched five consecutive complete game victories for the Yankees — he had a no-hitter going into the ninth inning of the fourth game but had to settle for a two-hit victory — and he was named the American League's Player of the Month.

He would have preferred to have been named to the American League's All-Star team for the showcase contest back home in Pittsburgh on July 23, but his storybook career didn't contain that chapter.

During the previous winter, he lived 15 minutes from Three Rivers Stadium in an Oakland apartment while pursuing a medical degree from Pitt. "It would have been something," he said, "to go home as an All-Star."

From the start at Shea Stadium or at Yankee Stadium, Medich has always been able to pitch well under pressure. Two years earlier, the Yankees borrowed him from their Double A farm team in New Haven to pitch against the Mets at Shea in the Mayor's Trophy Game, a mid-season exhibition for New York fans.

Medich responded with a four-hit, 2-1 victory before a crowd of 53,949.

In 1973, in his first full season in the majors, he twice pitched before 60,000 fans at Yankee Stadium. He pitched on Bat Day and then on Ball Day.

"I think the kids came out to get a free ball and bat," he offered, "rather than to see me. But I loved it anyway."

Medich was amazing. Until he showed up at Shea that day to pitch against the Mets his name had never come up for conversation when major league pitching prospects were discussed.

He was big enough, at 6-3, 230 pounds, but he was better known at Pitt as a tight end on the football team. He was the second best tight end that ever attended Pitt from Aliquippa. Mike Ditka, of course, was the best. Much was made about Medich by Dave Hart, but much was made of all the football recruits in those days, and all that came of them were three straight 1-9 seasons.

Medich pitched for the Pitt baseball team, too, but Dave Welty was the best pitcher on the team back then. "When I was growing up, I wanted to be a baseball player more than anything," he recalled. "But I thought my future was as a hitter, not a pitcher, because I couldn't throw hard enough.

"At Pitt, I played first, third, outfield and did some pitching. As a senior, I was 4-3 with a 1.50 ERA and hit .400. Yet, as a senior, I only pitched."

Medich became a bona fide pitcher in the Greater Pittsburgh Federation League, where his team won the sandlot title with a 27-1 record. "It was there that my stuff got better and I was able to get good velocity on the ball," he remembers. "So the scouts started coming around again like they did in college before being scared off by my interest in medical school."

He says Harding Peterson, the Pirates' scout then, shied away from him when he spoke of going to medical school.

"I took a day off from working a summer job at the hospital in Aliquippa," said Medich, "and went to Forbes Field for a tryout. I thought I had a good tryout with the Pirates, and that's the team I really wanted to pitch for. Peterson told me I'd never play because I wasn't dedicated to baseball."

Medich has proven he could succeed in both fields. His desire to become a doctor came after his dream of being a big league baseball player. "I always admired medical people, especially with their personal attitudes," Medich said. "I found I was able to relate to them."

The Zernich brothers, a trio of doctors, interested Medich in medicine. "We came from the same place," he said, "our families went to the same church, and they attended Pitt and played sports. So it was natural that I became friends with them."

Although he went to Pitt as a pre-med student, sports was still his prime concern. "I thought I was a pretty good quarterback in school, but at Pitt they made me an end without even giving me a chance to throw the ball."

Pride of the Yankees   As a Texas Ranger

As a Pitt pass receiver

After Pitt, he signed with the New York Yankees for a $5,000 bonus. Shortly thereafter, he married Donna Creekmore and reported to Oneonta (N.Y.) to begin his minor league career in 1970. Medich had made it clear to Randy Gumpert, a scout for the Yankees, that he had been accepted by Pitt's medical school and he intended to pursue that career for life.

"Gumpert told me he knew the name of a Yankee player who had done just that," said Medich. "He suggested I call the Yankees and get his address and inquire how that fella did it."

Gumpert only knew the name of the player. It was Bobby Brown. Dr. Brown had become a well-known cardiologist in Fort Worth, Texas after his playing days ended in 1954. In a later development, Dr. Brown became president of the Texas Rangers.

"Dr. Brown motivated me in both directions, baseball and medicine," Medich said. "He convinced me it could be done. I explained my situation completely to the Yankees."

Medich played baseball and read books in between, such as the Journal of Medicine, the Journal of Bone Joint Surgery, the Journal of Sports Medicine, and his regular textbooks on everything from anatomy to pediatrics. When each season was over, he would go back to school at Pitt.

"I put the game in perspective," he said. "It might be some of the things I've seen around the hospital. I realize baseball is important, but there are more serious things. So in a tight situation, there's less pressure on me than maybe someone else.

"I've seen sad things in the hospital. People die. I don't want to sound high-handed, but your perspective does change. When I'm in a tight situation in a game, sometimes I have to remind myself that if I give up a hit no one is going to die. When someone dies on the operating table, the game is really over.

"I like to pitch. Baseball's always been fun for me ever since I can remember. When I was a kid, I'd just throw it up myself, hit it, chase it and hit it again. I'd break a window occasionally and get a spanking, but I'd go right out and play some more.

"When I get tired of baseball, I'll quit and be a doctor. But right now it's still a lot of fun."

JOHN MICHELOSEN

Seen Through The Eyes Of His Players

Marty Wolfson

Reprinted from Alumni Times　　　*September, 1962*

Age has a way of improving things — like wine, cheese, tobacco, legends, and Jock Sutherland.

The cynical Scot, a demagogue cast in the Legree mold, blew such fear into the timid souls of his contemporaries, that ever since they have gone forth as disciples, extolling the adulterated virtues of the greatest coach in Pitt history.

This has put a paradoxical personality named John Michelosen in a myriad of lights, few of which shine through a rose-colored prism. Michelosen is supposedly the ghost of the Scot, Sutherland reincarnated. Humbug.

Michelosen himself has contributed as much as anyone to this illusion. His forced staccato step about the practice grounds, his timely aloofness, his reluctance to drop the single-wing some years ago.

He was Sutherland's quarterback, and senile folk would have you believe that Jock is still in the heavens pulling the strings of a puppet-like coach, sort of a Paul Brown-Otto Graham relationship. Every time a Pitt fullback plows headdown into the buttocks of his own center, the comparison is renewed.

His pupils, the football playing students of the University, see right through the masquerade. To them the image is mere putty and greasepaint, resulting in an Emmet Kelly-like figure — sad and lovable.

"He tries to be like Sutherland," one said, "only he can't be. He tries to stay away from his players, and then soon as one of them's in trouble, he's patting them on the back, consoling them. He doesn't have the guts to be like Sutherland."

Paraphrased, the player may have meant that Michelosen has too much heart. When a kid gets in trouble, has problems or is stumped by his schoolwork, he goes to Michelosen. He's a father-confessor. Such intimacy doesn't coordinate well with the stern taskmaster image that he otherwise strives to enact.

Most of the time Michelosen is just a gentle-hearted man, quiet and patient and, fortunately, very peaceful. His rare rages have been directed at himself or fate. "So far as I know," says a senior letter-winner, "he has never chewed a player out while anyone else was present. And if he had I would know. Those things get around."

In the eyes of the copy-seeking press Michelson is as tight-lipped as King Tut. He never fingers a player. He resorts to cliches, or invokes team play. "He cares for them, that's the difference," one of his aides claims. "He assumes all blame, never picks a goat for a whipping-boy."

This facet differs sharply from Sutherland who once benched a promising quarterback for two years for calling a poor, misfiring play as a sophomore.

Michelosen was a player himself and, like anyone else, had his bad moments as well as a lot of good ones. He can understand a player's problems and sympathize with them. Up to a point. After all, he is a coach now, and his job is to win ball games. He expects his players to do their jobs, too.

"But I guess he's too easygoing," says one of Sutherland's cronies. "I like John, but when he loses a game, it doesn't seem to be important enough. With Jock, when you lost, you knew it was important. 'We're going to win Saturday,' he'd say — and you could tell he meant it. We were going to win. We'd better."

A present day star had another opinion. "There's a difference," he says. "I like Mike. I don't know him very well. He's not particularly close to the players. But you know that Michelosen is serious about winning games. He lets you know that's what you're out there for. You really have to respect him."

Apparently everyone in football respects Michelosen. He is not the most successful coach around, nor, as he will tell you himself, the smartest. But he is sincere and, above all, he is honest. The pensive eyes, the silent lips and that tough firefighter's jaw, the long face, and the semi-scowl which it frequently wears, does, indeed, appear formidable. To strangers, Michelosen sometimes seems unapproachable or, at best, reserved.

Actually, however, he is a warm, friendly man, with great character, strong opinions and intense loyalties. With those he knows well, the eyes twinkle and the scowl is replaced by a strange little lopsided grin and the voice is full of zest. He isn't the best conversationalist, but he does reveal an earnestness to talk with people, and share their thoughts. And this in turn, inspires loyalty among those who have worked with him. Everywhere he has been, they would be happy to have him back — if he would only quit sending his fullback off tackle so much.

Professional coaches swear by his conditioning tactics. Many say that they know a Pitt graduate will be tough, hard, and won't pant in the dying moments of a game if they draft him. They also claim that an ex-Panther is sure to be soundly schooled in the fundamentals of the game.

In his seven years as head coach here his record is 36-30-5 against a schedule that reads like a mine-field in the Argonne Forest. It's still disappointing, smudged especially by last year's disastrous 3-7 campaign which had only one clear-cut victory in it. The early years were the glorious ones for Michelosen. He piloted the 1955 and 1956 clubs into the Sugar Bowl and Gator Bowl respectively. Georgia Tech won both affairs.

In Michelosen's only major league job, Art Rooney was forced to get rid of him when the Pittsburgh Steelers found the single-wing which Sutherland had left to his pupil wouldn't sell tickets, and the disciple was too stubborn to change.

Till the day they write his epitaph, John Michelosen will revere the old bachelor who taught him his football. He has a right to cherish his memory. Perhaps the conflict arises today because Michelosen is a family man, he is not lonely, and the old dictum that times have changed is perhaps most significant of all.

A radio announcer who has watched both the Jock and Michelosen in action, says that perhaps the reason Mike doesn't play the austere, iron-handed role to the hilt is because kids today wouldn't stand for that sort of stuff.

He noted that fathers in Jock's day were far more demanding, too, and took the switch to their sons more often. Curfews, teetotaling and non-smoking edicts were also upheld by stern fathers. Today most fathers would rather spare the rod, than have their sons wrest it from them, and turn upon their fathers with the switch.

The old-timer doubts that players would endure the same treatment under which boys of the Sutherland era sweated. The carefree students of today would be tempted to tell a coach off for ill treatment, and would even risk a scholarship to have their own way. Sutherland would have convulsions if he saw what goes on nowadays, not just at Pitt, but all over the country. Whether it's better or not is more conjecture.

Bear Bryant, the arch-ruler of Alabama, still gets away with it, however, and he had the No. 1 team in the country last year. Bryant has been known to raid a delinquent player's locker and toss his clothes out in the street. Michelosen would never do such a thing. He is too much of a gentleman. He would be more apt to take the boy aside, and set him straight.

WORDS OF WISDOM ... Michelosen chats with Pop Warner, one of the sport's legendary coaches.

JOHN MICHELOSEN ... the single-wing quarterback.

That is why most of Michelosen's men swear by him as a man. Some of them, however, second guess his strategy. A fullback on his team some years ago said, "When we were huddling before a play, we were astounded to hear the defensive team actually calling the same play. That's how well they had us pegged. They knew what was coming, and it was no wonder we went nowhere."

Whether this was the result of an unimaginative offense or a self-cleansing fullback is mere presumption, but Michelosen's players have stuck by him in recent years. When a rabid lynching party threatened to hoist his effigy at half mast on the flag pole in front of the Student Union a few seasons back, his boys went into action.

They policed the campus till late at night, searching for the culprits who made the boast. The team had just lost to an underdog opponent and, as always, Michelosen was bearing the brunt of the blame. His likeness flying in the trees would demonstrate the wrath of the student body. But, alas, football players have curfews, and playboys do not. About 2 A.M. a papier mache figure rose in the air on the Student Union lawn.

Michelosen has been hung in effigy two or three times at Pitt, but this doesn't rankle his composure. "I've been stabbed in the back too many times before," he says, "to let anything they do nowadays bother me. I don't care what anybody says about me as long as they don't harm the boys. They are just young kids, and something pinned on them can hurt their chances in the future. It bothers them more because they haven't experienced it before."

Sounds like a martyr. And his players stick by him because of his loyalty for them. They want to win for him, they want to get the general public off his back. They want to silence the critics. According to Michelosen, who claims he is not a pessimist, just a realist, this might be the year. No, he didn't come right out and say so. That would be heresy. But he's not throwing up white flags of surrender, either.

He noted, however, that this year's team has more experience than last season's outfit. Spirit has been generated at the spring drills that never existed before. In search of a stimulant to advance this new found enthusiasm, the coaches have been tabbed a third unit, keyed primarily for defense, the "Head Hunters." The "Chinese Bandits" did wonders for spirit down at LSU when Paul Dietzel was winning there, and the Pitt staff hope lightning strikes twice.

Enemy scouts say Pitt is loaded this year. This will put Michelosen on the spot more than ever. And Athletic Director Frank Carver has asserted that no one in the department, himself included, is a standard fixture. A football coach's life can take as many turns as a fumbled football.

No matter what happens this fall, one may expect Michelosen to get tagged with whatever losses the team may suffer, and Traficant, Martha, Leeson and Co. to get credited with the wins. That's the way it goes in the life of a coach at Pitt. Michelosen knows he has to produce this fall. He knows the fans are crying for a winner.

Last season at the Baylor game his youngest son, Jock, learned of the fandom's cruelty. "You stink, Michelosen!" one cried from his bleacher seat in the Stadium.

Taken aback, young Jock glared forcibly at the mocking gentleman, and cried, "and so do you, sir!"

That's the way his father would have wanted him to answer. Like a gentleman.

CARL OLSON

"Those kids might not know it, but he loves them. He has a heart of gold inside."
—Jim Banner

Reprinted from Pittsburgh Weekly Sports
Nov. 15, 1968

The rain fell in a light drizzle on this wet afternoon, and the trees about Flagstaff Hill in Schenley Park bent when the wind rushed in. A cross-country run between Point Park College and Westminster was about to begin.

It seemed like a hellish time to go jogging through the park, especially in one's underwear. The boys were game, however, and they went about their warm-up exercises with much vigor and enthusiasm. Suddenly it made good sense to warm up.

They jumped around, shaking their arms, kicking their legs about. Clasping their gloved hands together. Eager to be off so they would perspire and be warm. Carl Olson, the crochety old man who coaches the Point Park team, stood under a tree nearby, and surveyed the hillside.

His facial muscles were twitching, and his teeth were rattling, yet the mere suggestion that it wasn't a very good day for running through the woods raised his eyebrows, and illuminated his piercing blue eyes.

"Any weather is good weather for a cross-country meet," declared Olson. And, yet as he said this, his old gray head seemed sunken in his shoulders. He was wearing a rain coat, a windbreaker, a wool coat, a sweater and a shirt. His green baseball cap with the white "P" was pulled down near his ears. And he smiled, as he must so often, to soften the harshness of his stormy declaration.

Carl Olson, now in his mid-70's, never merely speaks to anyone. A bit of a despot, he is argumentative in manner. "He is most dogmatic," says Jim Banner, the track and cross-country coach at Pitt, who once ran for Olson, and now watches him each afternoon as their respective teams go through their paces in the park. "He is a mean guy on the surface, but he really does have a heart of gold inside."

Olson coached at Pitt for 27 years before he was retired. Then came a call from Carnegie Tech. Would he be interested in coaching their cross-country team? Sure, he said. "I don't go looking for these jobs," said Olson, when asked why he won't quit. "They come looking for me."

So he went to Tech, now Carnegie-Mellon, and he coaxed enough kids to come out for the team to win three of ten meets his first season. After that his teams posted a 61-8-1 record over the next seven years, including a streak of 31 straight victories.

Then Mel Cratsley, who had left Tech to become athletic director and basketball coach at Point Park, asked Olson to follow him to the downtown college to coach cross-country. Olson agreed, and this first year he turned in a record of nine victories and one defeat. He toasted his team at an informal banquet after the final meet with Malone College in a backroom at Frankie Gustine's Restaurant in Oakland.

Olson is still smarting from the one setback, to Indiana University of Pennsylvania, because some of his best boys were sick the day of the meet.

Olson in 1937

The win over Westminster was the next-to-the last victory of the season. After he fired the starting gun that wet afternoon, he dashed for his automobile. He wanted to drive out to the three-mile mark to see how the race was progressing.

As the boys blazed the cross-country trail, Olson wheeled around the sharp serpentine roads that run through the park. He stopped by the side of the road, and hurried to the edge of a hill. He surveyed the trail below which came out of the gold-brown foliage, carried across a moss-covered bridge, and came up to the level on which he was standing.

As he waited for the first runner to appear, he talked about his career, and gave a hint as to why his competitive zeal is still so keen. "I'm just the son of a Swedish immigrant trying to make the grade," he said. "I've traveled across five continents . . . I have a special commendation from the U.S. government for my coaching work in South America . . . do you know I get just as much of a kick today with these kids as I ever did with the Olympians (four) I worked with at Pitt?"

"I like to work with youngsters," he went on. "I like kids — if they're trying. It's great to see progress, to watch a kid you're coaching come along. That's the joy of it."

He squinted his eyes as he searched the woods for a figure. "They should be here," he said in an undertone.

"Here they come now!"

The first runner to appear, as expected, was Dan Moriarity. He came up the slight hill, and moved easily past his proud coach. "Atta Boy, Danny," cried Olson. "You got 'em by 50 yards!" Moriarity acknowledged the news with a confident nod.

Olson scurried once again to his automobile. As he was driving along, gripping the wheel with a nervous intensity, he talked about his sport once more.

"If a kid has two arms, two legs and a good heart," he said, "he can run cross-country. He doesn't have to weigh 300 pounds, or be seven feet tall. That's the beauty of it, it takes in everybody." That is, except 300-pounders and seven-footers.

Olson slowed his car down, as a police patrol car halted on the road to allow the runners to cross the street. Olson spied a rival runner, his hair locks long and shaggy, flying as he bounded across the pavement. "Isn't that awful?" snapped Olson. "I'd fire him so fast he wouldn't know what happened."

At Pitt, Olson once suspended a runner who was the Eastern 100-yard sprint champion for breaking training rules.

Olson was now driving down the road next to the No. 1 tee at the Schenley Park golf course. The boys were running along the fairways. "Let's go, Chuck ol' boy," bellowed Olson as Chuck Devine, his second-best runner, raced along.

Devine accelerated his pace. "See how much he gained on that guy just by hollering at him," exclaimed Olson, smiling once more, like a wise old cat with a fish on his tin plate. At the finish, Franny Webster, the coach at Westminster, was cheering on Moriarity of Point Park as he came down the hill.

The Pioneers had plenty of other green-jerseyed runners at the head of the pack, and it was an easy win. "We ate 'em up," Olson told Moriarity.

Later, Moriarity munched on an apple Olson had given him and his teammates, and talked about his coach. "He expects a lot from you," said Moriarity. "I believe he eats nails for breakfast."

Moriarity doesn't mince words, when he discusses Olson. "Sometimes he makes you so mad . . . ," he said. "He's so damn demanding."

Olson, at right, alongside trainer Herman Bearzy, and assistant Jim Potts flank 1938 cross-country team.

One of 16 children in an Oakland family, Moriarity is a sophomore out of Central Catholic High where he ran the same Schenley Park course. He enjoys running the familiar trails. "I just like being out there," he said. "I like to get away from school, my home, the coach, everybody."

He thinks there should be more fun in his sport. Otherwise it's a real chore, lifting those legs up and down, up and down, mile after mile, hill after dale. "I try to catch the leaves," he said. "One guy on our team caught twelve. I only have four. That's the trouble, you should have more fun out there."

There are no crowds to coax the kids on to greater glory. They only gather there in the spring and summer when the coeds are sprawled about the grass, sunning themselves in their skimpy swimsuits.

Olson's no-nonsense, spartan training is a contrast to Moriarity's ideas of training. "I never try to run a popularity contest," says Olson. "If you do, the kids end up running you. I train these kids the same hard way I used to work the kids at Pitt. Kids want guidance. In the long run, they appreciate it.

"Show me a kid I've coached who's not a good citizen," he demanded. And he talked about John Brosky, now a judge here, who ran for him, and was honored that same weekend at Pitt's Homecoming ceremonies as a Letterman of Distinction.

"I know how the kids feel," he snapped. "Sometimes they get mad at me and they go out to show me up. Sometimes it takes years to get a kid psychologically right to run his race."

He will never change, says Banner, whose own cross-country team is undefeated going into Saturday's Penn State meet. "He's from the old school," said Banner, smiling about the old man, remembering some of the tricks he pulled to push Banner to his best efforts. "He's like Jock Sutherland, I guess. He was way ahead of his time in training techniques, things that carry fancier names now. These kids might not know it, but he loves them."

Crack relay teams were Olson's passion. This exchange from Bill Lape to Olympian Arnie Sowell would have pleased him.

Olson Lists His Top Thrills

By Harry Keck
Pittsburgh Sun-Telegraph

June 1, 1958

When a man has been on a job for over 25 years and, indeed, has devoted his entire working life to a profession, he must have some fond memories.

Such a man is Carl Olson, Pitt's track and field and cross-country coach and head of the required physical education and intramural programs of the University.

Carl, on the occasion of his 65th birthday, named his top thrills.

No. 1, he said, was when his team won four relay championships in the Penn Relays Carnival of 1939 — the sprint medley, 440, 880 and mile.

No. 2 was when Pitt's Johnny Woodruff won the Olympic half-mile championship in Berlin in 1936.

No. 3 was the winning of the IC4A cross-country championship in 1955 with a Pitt team that included Arnie Sowell, his great half-miler.

No. 4 was the brilliant running of Sowell.

Woodruff was his No. 1 protege with Sowell close up. Frank Ohl, who ran on those four winning teams in the Penn Carnival, is rated next. Others are Hap Stickel, the hurdler; Bill Carter, a sprinter; Dick Mason, a sprinter who won IC4A titles in the 100 and 200-meter and 220-yard dashes; Charley Gongloff, the javelin thrower; Mel Barnwell, the sprinter; Clarence Doak, the hurdler; Herb Douglas, the sprinter and long jumper who competed in the 1948 Olympics; Pete Bennett, the high jumper, and Wally Monahan, the hurdler. He also had a fine sprinter in Jimmy Donahue.

"I've probably forgotten a few," Carl said. "If so, I hope they'll forgive the oversight."

Olson's teams won the sprint medley and half-mile and mile relay championships at Penn in 1938 with Ohl, Al Ferrara, Mason and Woodruff running in the sprint and half-mile and Al McKee replacing Mason in the mile.

His Pitt teams won both the sprint and half-mile relays three times to retire the trophies.

Virtually all of his stars were products of Olson's skill as a coach and conditioner. The athletes, with few exceptions, came to him green and had to be developed.

His work carried Olson far afield. He attended Olympic Games in Los Angeles in 1932; Berlin, '36; London, '48; Helsinki, '52 and Melbourne, '56. He has taken all-star teams on tours of Europe.

REX PEERY

Mum's The Word
In Peery Family

Reprinted from The Pitt News, 1962

This Saturday wrestling coach Rex Peery will seek his 100th victory when Pitt takes on Lehigh, the second-best wrestling team in the country, at the Field House.

The human heifer smiles with intoxicating good nature when he dwells on the idea. "It sure will be nice to win," he said. "Mum sure will be tickled pink."

"Mum" is Peery's wife, the tiny woman who has been deciphering telephone calls for 13 years when Rex is on the road with his Pitt matmen. "He always shouts himself hoarse," Mum said. "I can hardly hear him."

But the raspy whisperings that Mum strains to hear have been on the happy side in most cases, for Peery seldom calls home about a loss. He doesn't avoid phone booths in disgust; he just doesn't lose too often.

Peery's lifetime chart at Pitt is 99-31-4. His first team in 1950 lost all ten matches, his second split even, losing seven. He hasn't had a losing season in the 11 years since, and he's had a 26-meet winning streak in between.

It was in the early '30's when Rex first entered Oklahoma A&M where he learned the skills of wrestling. A remarkably large number of gray-haired men wore silk toppers, white-piped vests, and worried expressions in that era.

Not Peery. He was wearing red tights, a confident smile, and he was embarking on a four-year career in which he would not lose a regular match. He won three NCAA titles and 102 matches against two losses.

He learned well, too, for his own coach was as competent as they ever come in the sport. Edward Clark Gallagher's teams won 70 consecutive meets from 1921 to 1932. They also won 11 of the 13 national championships contested from 1928 to 1940. Peery inherited the winning habit. He was going to need it when he later came to Pitt.

Peery spruced up on his tactics, coaching high schools in Oklahoma for awhile, when Cliff Kean, then wrestling coach at Michigan, recommended him to Athletic Director Tom Hamilton, who wanted to reactivate the sport at the University of Pittsburgh.

The sport was born at Pitt in 1914. The Panthers lost their first outing, 4-3, to Lafayette, and that was the closest they ever came to winning for quite some time. They lost to the likes of MIT and Johns Hopkins.

Even the presence of a heavyweight with a heavier Scottish brogue named Jock Sutherland could not keep the inexperienced squad from losing 12 matches with nary a win. The sport was dropped from the program in 1917.

The wrestling sport would not stayed pinned. Pitt tried again in 1935, but 17 straight losses dampened its pioneering spirits once again. Then Peery came along. He was not an overnight miracle worker, either. His first team recorded an 0-10 mark.

Ed, Hugh and Rex Peery. This hold is called a "high wing."

His curtain lecture was worth all the sermons in the world for teaching the virtues of patience and long-suffering endured during his first year.

Peery teaches wrestling the way they teach chemistry or economics — no nonsense. His wrestlers give him their undivided attention, no gawking, no wisecracking. He teaches them more than techniques. He conditions men mentally. He toughens them.

For him they have learned the joy of terse, even bitter competition in practice as well as in meets. He has hungry wrestlers under restraint. At lunch they must pass up the chicken, potatoes and pie that get a strong play from the rest of the students.

"They eat lettuce and steak," Peery says. "They do what other people call making sacrifices. That is, they get big helpings of rest and sleep, and they don't stuff themselves with food.'

Peery has a private battle with the paunch, and he joins in with his team in the daily violent exercise sessions in the Miami temperature of the wrestling room. He is the biggest man in the swarm of little people, and his voice echoes about the room like rumbling peals of thunder.

The wrestlers lift their necks quickly from the mats and swing them hard sideways, looking like freshly-hooked trout. The few that aren't in top-notch shape breathe like rhinoceroses.

Peery's success is due to sweat. And his wrestlers are constantly reminded of the message which Rex first greeted his initial Pitt team with: "I want no one who is satisfied with mediocrity."

When his boys go out on the mat against Lehigh this Saturday they should think of another of his favorite expressions: "The true indication of a champ is when he is in a rough spot, he reaches down for another handful of guts and then comes through victorious."

Pitt wrestlers work out at the Field House as Coach Rex Peery (top right) supervises.

JERRY RICHEY

He's A Member Of The 4-Minute Mile Club

Reprinted from Pittsburgh Weekly Sports

June 14, 1968

Most milers bluff it, and speak lovingly of their long-distance running. Sure, there's pain, they say, but there's also a joy, a sense of accomplishment.

The newest mile prodigy, 19-year-old Jerry Richey of Pitt, is much more honest in his observations. Last Saturday at Franklin Field in Philadelphia in the IC4A meet, he finished third in one of the greatest mass-finish miles ever run anywhere, the fastest ever run in the East, with the first five finishers under four minutes.

Reflecting on the race a few days later, he was something short of poetical, certainly not philosophical, when he allowed that as he was trailing the pack after running about 300 yards, he thought to himself, "What am I doing out here? I hate this stuff!"

He thought he'd quit while he was behind. "I just wanted to step off the track, lie down on the grass, and watch the race," he admitted afterward.

It appeared for a while that Richey would become a spectator. "I thought he would drift back too far," said Pitt coach Jim Banner, who admitted he became anxious on the sidelines in the early going.

The writer happened to be in the Philadelphia area last weekend, and watched the IC4A meet on a local educational television station. Richey completely disappeared from the picture after the first 440 lap.

"I ran a pretty stupid race," Richey remarked the other day. "My tactics were bad. I let a big gap open up. The whole race I was just thinking four minutes. If I had been thinking about the competition instead of time, I might have had a shot at second or even first.

"I didn't feel I was competing," Richey went on. "I know that doesn't sound like a very good attitude, and maybe it isn't. But I heard the splits (lap times) and I knew there was a chance for a four-minute mile. When I heard the three-quarter time (3:02), I knew I could do it, if I didn't tie up. So I kicked."

He was running alongside George Wisniewski of NYU, and he went by him, Harvard's Jim Baker and Fordham's Jack Fath and caught Villanova's Frank Murphy at the finish line with a :56.6 last lap.

On the TV tube, you could see this guy with glasses, wearing a jersey with P-I-T-T in letters across his chest, lunging into the picture. "I think Richey snuck by Murphy at the finish!" the announcer shrieked.

His face grimaced in anguish, his arms flailing, Richey says he was "hurtin'" at the end. "At the end," said his coach, "I think he was moving faster than anybody in the race."

Richey regaled in his achievement. He said Fordham's Fath was angry. "Imagine running a 3:59 mile," cried Fath, "and finishing fifth."

WORLD RECORD HOLDERS
Pitt's distance medley team, coached by Jim Banner (r.), consisted of (l. to r.) Jerry Richey, Mike Schurko, Smittie Brown and Ken Silay. They set indoor record on Feb. 27, 1971.

42

He was a state champion runner at North Allegheny High.

Coach Banner embraced Richey, and offered, "You could have won the whole thing."

"Jerry just shook his head," Banner recalled, "and gave me a funny look like 'you're never satisfied, are you!' " But Banner was beaming, and Richey started smiling again.

Richey ran the four-minute mile he thought he was going to be denied that day. Coach Banner had told him for the last month that he was going to run him in the three-mile at the IC4A's.

"I think he started getting mad at me," Banner said.

"I sure was," admitted Richey without any reluctance. "I thought he was really going to mess me up. I thought I was ready."

"I wanted to keep the pressure off him," Banner explained. "But I kept pointing him for the mile and just before the meet I said, "You're a miler. What do you think you can do?' He said, 'I'll run a four for you, Coach.' "

Banner said he thought Richey had a chance to win.

"I told him to stay in the middle and not drift back," Banner said, "but he slid back. He does that, he still doesn't believe he has all that ability. I think he'll start believing it now. He's a member of the four-minute mile club."

Despite the number of sub four-minute clockings now in the book, it remains a magic figure. Spectactors still stand and root for it. There have been 300 four-minute miles since Roger Bannister ran the first one, 14 years ago, but the magic and the drama live on.

It is the glamour event. Villanova's Dave Patrick, the winner of the IC4A in 3:56.8 was on the cover of Sports Illustrated a few days before the meet. "I saw that," said Richey, "and thought about it."

So did Pitt football coach Dave Hart, always concerned about Pitt's national image. "I said I wish that were Jerry Richey with Pitt across his chest," snapped Hart.

Contrary to local TV and newspaper reports, Richey is not the first, nor the second Western Pennsylvanian to run a sub-four-minute mile. Sam Bair of Scottdale, who runs at Kent State, and Cary Weisinger of Mt. Lebanon, running for the Quantico Marines in 1963, have done it.

But Richey is the youngest of the trio to accomplish the feat. He's a sophomore at Pitt because he's in the accelerated trimester program. Only one year ago, Richey was running for North Allegheny High School, in Pittsburgh's north suburbs, and was winning the state mile and half-mile championships.

He had a 4:10.6 mile and people who watch clocks knew he was a hot prospect.

It's been a long time since Pitt has had his like. Before this year the Pitt record in the mile was 4:12.8, set by John Woodruff in 1939. Woodruff was an Olympic gold medal winner at Berlin in 1936 before the demoniac eyes of Adolph Hitler.

JERRY RICHEY — Pitt's 4 minute miler.

JOE SCHMIDT

From Brentwood To Canton— Joe Schmidt Stayed Home And Became Hall of Famer

"I have a soft spot in my heart for Pitt."

Joe Schmidt is the only University of Pittsburgh graduate to gain induction into the Pro Football Hall of Fame in Canton, Ohio.

He achieved the honor in 1973, eight years after he completed his playing career with the Detroit Lions. He was one of the greatest linebackers in the National Football League for 13 seasons, competing in the Pro Bowl 10 of those campaigns. In the interim, he had coached the Lions for seven seasons, six as the head man, and become a successful businessman as well.

In his rookie season of 1953, the Lions repeated as NFL champions. Even though he had not played on the Lions' 1952 team, Schmidt was invited to attend a dinner honoring that group at a dinner hosted by teammates Cloyce Box and Bobby Layne on the eve of Super Bowl XVI in January of 1982.

The affair was held at the Hyatt Regency in Dearborn, Mich., and members of the 1952 team were given champion rings for the first time. Schmidt spoke of his days at Pitt at a prior luncheon in the same hotel. Joe Schmidt, at age 50, is still a formidable figure, as thick-necked and barrel-chested and firm, yet soft-spoken, as ever.

"I love Pittsburgh," said Schmidt. "It's my hometown, even though I've lived most of my life in Michigan. It's still my home."

I went to Pitt at age 17," recalled Joe Schmidt, "and you don't realize the opportunity you have. My main goal was to be an All-American and to play professional football. I didn't apply myself in school as I should have, but most athletes can say that.

"Pitt provided me with the opportunity to do what I've wanted to do, and further myself through my athletic abilities. Everything I have stemmed from that opportunity. So I have a soft spot in my heart for the university.

"Looking back now, it served my purpose. My deal was probably different from a lot of kids. I felt I should stay home."

His dad died when Joe was just 13. That was in February of 1945. Seven months earlier, an older brother, Bill was killed in World War II action in France, shot dead by German soldiers as he rode in the turret of an American tank that had been called up to provide artillery support for an infantry unit that had been pinned down by gunfire from Germans holed up in a French farmhouse.

Another brother, Robert, died 15 years earlier, at age 11, when he fell from a tree in the Schmidt's Mt. Oliver neighborhood, and was impaled on a tree stump.

Joe's only other brother, John had played center and linebacker for the fine football teams at Carnegie Tech from 1937 through 1939, and was now out on his own. He later became an executive at Duquesne Light Company.

So it was just Joe and his mother, Stella, "a very strong-willed and religious person," as her youngest son recalls her, at home when Joe was starring for the high school football team in nearby Brentwood.

"It was just the two of us together, and it was difficult for awhile," said Joe Schmidt. "She was a domestic, and provided day help for other families."

Schmidt's story, in many respects, is similar to that of another Pro Football Hall of Famer, Johnny Unitas, who came out of the nearby community of Brookline a few years later.

Joe was offered scholarships to Penn State, Maryland, Virginia, VMI and Cincinnati — he remembers Paul Dietzel came to visit him when he served as an assistant to Sid Gillman at Cincinnati — and was called upon by the service academies.

"I had made my mind up already, though," he said. "I was going to stay home. My dad was dead and my mother was by herself."

Joe had a soft spot in his heart for Pitt back then, too, though he might have gone to Carnegie Tech if they had continued their top-flight football program.

"My parents had taken me to Pitt and Carnegie Tech games when I was a kid," said Schmidt. "I went to the Pitt-Tech game in 1938."

That was the season in which Pitt compiled an 8-2 record, defeating the likes of Wisconsin, SMU, Fordham, Nebraska and Penn State, yet they were toppled by Tech, 20-10.

"I remember being at Pitt Stadium back then, and I remember the uniforms and the marching band," said Schmidt. "My brother would bring the guys home. Those teams were using the single-wing attack at that time.

"Tech had two terrific backs in Georgia Muha and Merlyn Condit, and I admired those guys. My brother would take me into the dressing room, and I guess it just excited me. Everybody wants to be a running back, but I didn't have the speed."

Schmidt played fullback at Brentwood High School, and was a quarterback as a freshman in 1949 at Pitt. He was a T fullback as a sophomore, and became a linebacker as a junior. "I didn't care," he said. "I just wanted to play football."

Schmidt not only found his proper position as a junior, but also a place to room on campus. That was in University Hall. Before that, he commuted each day to and from home. "After practices, I'd get on the 77/54 street car. It went through the South Side and up through Mt. Oliver."

Schmidt recalls that his teammates were always scattered about, some commuting home as he did, some living in rooming houses about the campus, some staying in shelter provided under Pitt Stadium, and in a small brick building — which came to be known as the "Animal House" when wrestlers were put up there years later — located between the Stadium and a cemetery.

"We had to make our own fun," he recalled. "So we'd go to dances and stuff on and off the campus."

He remembers the guys used to frequent an Italian restaurant — John's — at the corner of Fifth Avenue and Bouquet Street. "You could get a plate of spaghetti for 50 cents," he said with a smile.

"Tom Hamilton was the athletic director back then, and the football coach for awhile, and he wanted to have a building on campus where we could all stay. He had that in the back of his mind. Tom Hamilton did a helluva job. He was always a first-class guy. He eventually got that thing at Ellsworth Center, and we finally had a training table.

"If he had stayed at Pitt, the program would have improved. When he left, I was disappointed. Tom's the kind of guy if you gave him the ball he'd run with it. He always had big thoughts; he never thought small. He had dreams."

So did Joe Schmidt, and some of his teammates, but they were mostly frustrated. There were four different head coaches during Schmidt's four-year stay at Pitt.

Schmidt signed on under Mike Milligan in 1949, and played varsity ball for Len Casanova in 1950, Hamilton in 1951, and Lowell P. "Red" Dawson in 1952. The Panthers compiled a 1-8 record in 1950, a 3-7 record in 1951 and a 6-3 record in 1952.

"We changed coaches so much," said Schmidt, "that the team never realized its potential, like a lot of teams. We had some good football players, some all-star players."

He flipped through a copy of the 1952 Pitt football press guide, in which he and Coach Dawson shared the cover with a blue Panther, and called out some of the standout

NOTRE DAME VICTORY CELEBRATION

Pitt captain Joe Schmidt is flanked by Ray Ferguson (left) and Billy Reynolds at a Cathedral of Learning Commons Room rally two days after Panthers upset Fighting Irish at Notre Dame, 22-19, for first win over ND in 15 years. Reynolds outrushed the entire Notre Dame backfield.

members of that team: Dick Deitrick, Joe Zombek, Lou Pallatella, Eldred Kraemer, Henry Ford, Rudy Mattioli, Billy Reynolds, Bobby Epps, Paul Chess, Richie McCabe and Paul Blanda.

"I was disappointed with what happened in our senior season," said Schmidt. "I thought we could really have a good football team. With a couple of offensive players, we'd have been a real good football team. We really wanted to go to a bowl game, but it didn't work out."

Schmidt spoke of the season-opening victory over Iowa, 26-14, at Pitt Stadium, and that sparked memories for us as well. That was the first Pitt football game we ever attended, on a pass for getting a certain number of new subscribers as a carrier boy for the Post-Gazette.

Pitt went to Oklahoma the following week and went up against Bud Wilkinson's powerful Sooners, led by Billy Vessels, who would win the Heisman Trophy. Oklahoma walloped the Panthers, 49-20. "They really stampeded our butts," said Schmidt, shaking his head at the memory.

The task was no easier the next week when Pitt played at Notre Dame. Schmidt was the captain of the Pitt team that year, and before the kick-off he went to Coach Dawson and asked if he and his assistants would kindly leave the locker room for a minute or two.

Schmidt then described in graphic terms what he would personally do to each and every one if they dared to let Notre Dame beat them.

"I more or less presented the situation to them," said Schmidt in 1982, nearly 30 years later. "Notre Dame had guys who were from Western Pennsylvania and hadn't been any better as high school players than our guys. 'They think they're so great,' I told them, 'because they have the image of Notre Dame going for them.' I talked a little bit more, and I think they realized that I had a good point. They said, 'Dammit, let's go out and win the game.' And we did."

Pitt defeated Notre Dame, 22-19, that day. "It was a helluva game," recalled Schmidt, "and I don't think Notre Dame expected it. I got knocked out in the tail-end of the third quarter, and it almost ruined our relations with Notre Dame. They sent in a reserve named Joe Bush, and when their quarterback threw the ball to my left, and I looked that way, this Joe Bush hit me with a forearm across my face. And I went down.

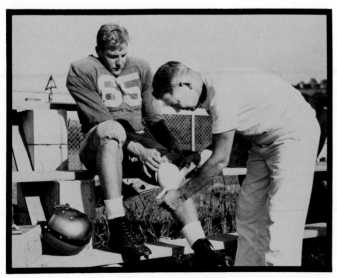

Oft-injured Joe Schmidt is treated by trainer Howard Waite at Allegheny College pre-fall training camp site.

"I must have been out for 10 minutes. I had a severe concussion, and I had some bleeding. They gave me a spinal tap, and everything else.

"They were lined up late in the game for a field goal, and Jim Schrader of Scott Township, who later played with the Washington Redskins, attempted a short field goal that would have tied the game. The holder wasn't ready, and he fumbled the ball. The kick was no good.

"I saw Jim later on, and he said that his coach, Frank Leahy, caught him at midfield after that and told him, 'James, may your soul burn eternally in hell.' Leahy took the loss seriously, I believe."

Schmidt missed the Army and West Virginia game the following two weeks. The Panthers won at West Point, 22-14, but were beaten by the Mountaineers, 16-0, in a stunner at Pitt Stadium. Pitt bounced back to defeat Indiana, Ohio State and North Carolina State. "It all came down to the Penn State game," said Schmidt.

Penn State shut out Pitt, 16-0, and that was the end of the bowl hopes. "I thought we might go to the Orange Bowl before that," said Schmidt.

He was named a first-team All-American by International News Service, and hoped to parlay that into a pro career.

"I dreamed of playing for the Steelers," he said. "I'd go to their practices sometimes with Richie McCabe, who was from the North Side — he'd gone to North Catholic — and was a ball boy with them. They had a linebacker named Jerry Shipkey, and McCabe told me, 'You're better than he is right now.'

"McCabe introduced me to Art Rooney one day, and the old man looked at me and smiled. He said, 'You're the kid who gets hurt all the time.' That hurt."

As a sophomore at Pitt, Schmidt separated a shoulder and had a couple of broken hands. As a junior, he hurt his knee in training camp and missed the first game. As a senior, he had that bad concussion and a bad knee. Somewhere in between, he had broken ribs.

"Richie told me I'd be drafted by the Steelers, about the third or fourth round," recalled Schmidt. "I sat home and listened to Joe Tucker on the radio, and he gave a rundown on the draft. I wasn't taken until the seventh round, and then by Detroit. They'd won the championship that season, and I thought I didn't have a snowman's chance in hell of making that team."

He talked to his brother, John, about it. "I don't think I'll report," he said.

"Give it a shot," said John. "What can you lose?"

Reluctantly, Schmidt drove to camp with Gene Gedman, a halfback from Duquesne who had played at Indiana University. "I never saw a guy so unsure of himself," Gedman said later.

Nick Kerbawy, the Lion's general manager, glad-handed Gedman, a top pick, for five minutes and then, with a glance at Schmidt, asked if he had brought a fraternity brother along.

Schmidt stayed, and soon became a leader on the Lions. Soft-spoken off the field, he'd shout and scream on it, or in the locker room. Some of his teammates remembered Schmidt's halftime speech during the 1957 Western Conference championship playoff when the San Francisco 49ers were leading the Lions by three touchdowns. One of Schmidt's less-violent epithets was "lousy, yellow quitters." The Lions won, 31-27.

He has succeeded in private business, as the owner of Joe Schmidt Sales, which provides original parts to Ford, General Motors and Chrysler. He is a partner in a Ford dealership in Orlando, Fla., and has real estate holdings in Fort Lauderdale.

"Football opened a lot of doors for me," said Schmidt "and I'm grateful."

JOE SCHMIDT
At Canton, Ohio Shrine Ceremonies

"Joe is the best linebacker in the league."
—Paul Hornung

Joe Schmidt grew up in Mt. Oliver, not far from Mt. Washington, and played sandlot football with older fellows when he was a youngster. Then he played at Brentwood High School, and went from there to the University of Pittsburgh.

He was a fine football player at Pitt, but his career there was hindered by injuries. He was not drafted by the Detroit Lions until the seventh round in 1953, and the Lions were a lot more interested in another Western Pennsylvania product, Gene Gedman, who came out of Duquesne, Pa., to star at Indiana University, and was the Lions' second pick.

Schmidt turned out to be one of the greatest middle linebackers in the history of the game. He was voted to the NFL all-star team eight times, and was named to the Pro Bowl nine straight years from 1955 through 1963, and he was named the MVP of the Lions by his teammates in four of those years.

"Joe is the best linebacker in the league," said Green Bay's Paul Hornung.

"He's always in the way," said John Henry Johnson, one of the NFL's all-time great backs who resides in Shadyside these days.

Schmidt was a 1973 inductee into Pro Football's Hall of Fame.

"He should've been a Steeler" —Art Rooney

Mention Joe Schmidt to Steelers' owner Art Rooney and he responds by shaking his white-haired head. "Oh, he should've been a Steeler," says the 81-year-old patriarch of the Pittsburgh pro football club.

"Sure, he got hurt a lot when he played at Pitt, but I thought he was a good one, and I told Walt Kiesling to get him. But I only mentioned it once; that was the right way. 'Kies' was such a stubborn Dutchman, and he didn't like anyone telling him what to do.

"Ed Kiely, our publicity man, cost us Joe Schmidt. He kept telling Kiesling to select Schmidt. I warned Kiely to cut it out, that he was killing our chances."

Art Rooney, Jr., the second-oldest son who looks after the Steelers' scouting department these days, and earlier an aspiring actor, picked up his cue there.

"This happened before I was working here, but I've heard the story," said the younger Rooney. "We had a guy named Ray Byrne working for us part-time then, as a personnel man. He knew all the college players; he was phenomenal."

"He was a funeral director, that's what he did for a living," his father interjected with a smile, and a stab of his cigar.

Without missing a beat, Art Rooney, Jr. continued his story. "Everyone was sitting around at the league draft, each team at its own table. It was getting down to the seventh round, or where the Steelers started thinking seriously about taking someone like Schmidt.

"The Detroit Lions took a guy and handed in a slip of paper with his name on it. Ray Bryne spotted his name on the slip, and told the guy from the Lions, 'Hey, your man is ineligible for the draft.' The Lions' man said, 'Thanks for telling me.' And he turned in a second slip with Joe Schmidt's name on it. That's how the Lions got Joe Schmidt."

With their seventh choice, the Steelers selected Claude Hipps, a running back from Georgia.

"He said he liked to go hunting and fishing, and I said there was no place to do either in Pittsburgh," remembered Art Rooney, Sr. "So he signed with Canada."

GIBBY WELCH

Days when Welch swept the ends for Pitt, and dashed between fallen bodies seemed so long ago, yet the vibrance of his story-telling made them seem like yesterday.

Still, he hardly seemed capable of stepping on the back of a fallen teammate, and using it to pivot and veer elsewhere as he did one summer day at Camp Hamilton in Windber, Pa., where the Panthers conducted their pre-season training. That's when Sutherland realized he had something special on his hands.

Only Tony Dorsett gained more total yardage in his Pitt career than Welch, who ran and passed, and caught passes and returned kicks for the Panthers in the '20s.

"I played 60 minutes, and I did everything," recalled Welch with a warm smile. "I only missed one game, and that was the opener in my junior year after I injured a kidney at camp. I was a busy boy when I played at Pitt."

Welch played in the first game ever played at Pitt Stadium, as a sophomore in 1925, and led the school team to its first bowl game ever — the Rose Bowl on January 2, 1928 — and was a legitimate athletic hero in his day. He set a school record in the javelin event as a member of the Pitt track and field team. There wasn't anything he couldn't do.

He mentioned all his ailments and the list of body repairs was as long as his achievements as an All-America running back at Pitt, but he seemed to gain strength from recalling his halcyon days.

He spoke of Sutherland and "Doc" Carlson and "Horse" Chase and Charley "Chipper" Hyatt and other Pitt greats of yore, yet he seemed equally aware of what Dorsett and Danny Marino and Doc Medich were doing, and was even more impressed by the modern day performers. On a nearby table were the most recent issues of Sports Illustrated, and that day's Pittsburgh Press turned to the sports section, and he said, "I like to keep track of things."

When Welch watches today's ballplayers on the small TV that sits atop a chest of drawers in his room, he is awed by what he sees.

"In the first place, there are so many great athletes today," he said. "The level from my day is so high on the average. To me, as an old-timer, there are just innumerable great athletes in this world today.

"The thing that astounds me is the size of these people. The height and the weight! And the ability to retain quickness and speed. With so much height and so much weight.

"It's almost unbelievable. In my sophomore year, the captain of our team was a guy called 'Horse' Chase. Ralph 'Horse' Chase. Now he stood 6-4, and weighed 225, and we thought he was a giant. He was the only guy that big.

"Today, they have halfbacks that are as big as that running around. I look at these guys today, and say, 'Hey, maybe they'd let me carry the water. That's the way I look at it. I don't know what the limit is. Every year or two there's a new innovation.'"

Welch was 5-11, 175 pounds when he played at Pitt, and he was the best in the nation in his time. But he has kept his impact in proportion.

"I was a busy boy when I played at Pitt."

Gibby Welch was sitting in a well-worn armchair, snug by his bed, in the corner of a room where he lives in the home of Louis and Helen Salerno on Pauline Avenue in Beechview.

"You've gotten bigger," he told a visitor he had not seen in 16 or 17 years, or since Welch worked in the alumni office at the University of Pittsburgh in the mid '60s. In truth, Welch was smaller, slightly stooped at age 77.

His right hand shook somewhat when Welch extended it in greeting, but his grip was firm, and definitely that of a former athlete.

He seemed happy to be talking about his glory days at Pitt — Jock Sutherland said Gibby Welch was the best player he ever coached there — and there was a gleam behind Gibby's eyeglasses as he reminisced.

The midday sun reflected from the snowy hillside into the window and lit up his pale and wizened face.

His memory was good, though he often apologized for the gaps in his stories, and he laughed easy and coughed hard. "My mind isn't so good since my sick spell in 1981," he apologized when he failed to pluck an elusive name out of the air.

Once, Alex Kramer, an administrative assistant to Jackie Sherrill, approached Welch about coming to the campus and speaking to the football team.

"I refused," recalled Welch. "I told him, 'Those guys will think I'm crazy, an old sonuvagun like me.' I said, 'I can't do a thing like that. I don't believe in that bullcrap. What the hell, those guys don't want to hear a lot of crap.' I remember they used to bring in all those old ducks in front of us and, cripes, we'd chuckle to ourselves."

He is pleased that Pitt's football teams are again among the nation's finest, and that the Steelers and Pirates all put out so many championship teams in the last decade.

"I'm very proud," said Welch. "I'm a hundred percent Pittsburgh. It doesn't make any difference whether it's Central Catholic or the Steelers."

Welch was asked to discuss his days at Pitt, and talk about what football at Pitt was like in the '20s, and he was quick to attack the challenge.

"We were very strong," he began. "The University of Pittsburgh has been strong in football ever since 1908-09-10. And by the time I got there in 1924, it was a warm situation. We had the interest of the community, we had a live wire student body, and we had an interested alumni.

"I remember when I first showed up on the campus that George Carson came to see me, and took me to the top of the hill, up there where the Veterans' Hospital is today, and showed me the campus. Then he took me on a tour of it. I was just a stinkin' freshman, and I never forgot his kindness. But George was always like that. Eventually, he became, in a sense, the Varsity Lettermen's Club, looking after all the former athletes and the records of that organization. He was quite a guy.

"I remember in my senior year — the team that I captained — we had a squad of 38 men. When we won the privilege of going to the Rose Bowl to play against Stanford, we took 23 men. How's that for starting from the bottom? Twenty-three men! To play a game of football! That was bad. I always felt bad about that. But there wasn't the big money back in those days. It was just a short-changed deal in my book.

"Pitt's football team back then didn't have the Golden Panthers. What Pitt football was back then was one, two or three wealthy men — the big guns — supporting the program. The big fellow was a coal operator — A.R. Hamilton, Al Hamilton. He was the big money fellow back then.

"We dedicated the Stadium in 1925, in the fifth game against Carnegie Tech, for the city college championship. It was pouring down rain, and the drainage system wasn't working properly. The water was standing on the field about three or four inches deep. We were slopping around in it. It was a real slophouse. The half ended with no score.

"We sat on a cold cement floor. We didn't have the kind of dressing rooms these boys have today. We didn't even have benches. It was cold and dank. Nothing but tin lockers, and cement floor and cement walls. No nothing. Nothing else. But here's the thing . . . we didn't know any better. So what the hell was the difference? We were walking around on cement and that was all right with us.

"I remember I was leaning against a wall when this A.R. Hamilton came in. His face was so red, and he was livid. He later died on a B&O train in my senior year coming back from Washington, D.C. He died of a heart attack. By God, I thought he was gonna have one there. He called Sutherland, he called 'em all in, even the trainer. He says, 'I want everybody in this room to know that we're in a dedication

TWO GREAT ONES GET TOGETHER. Gibby Welch, All-American halfback at Pitt back in 1927, and for a long time holder of the Pitt record in both javelin and discus, meets a world famous Panther, Arnie Sowell.

Welch was reputed to have been a nifty passer, but Pitt didn't pass much in those days. "We had two ends who complained to Sutherland that I was throwing the ball too hard," said Welch. "You wouldn't catch anybody today complaining about a ball being thrown too hard. They'll handle them even if they're like a bullet.

"We didn't know much about passing in those days. Sutherland didn't know much at all about passing. He'd get behind me at practice, and he'd say, with that Scotch brogue of his, 'Lob it, Geeb. Lob it, Geeb.' Well, I lost my sense of timing from lobbing it."

Welch started laughter here, and ended up coughing. For a good spell.

"Hell, I'd been used to throwing it like a bullet at Bellefonte Academy, and having guys catching it. Like 'Honey' Guarino and this little Irishman — doggone I can't remember his name — but he came back here as a fireman for the City Fire Department. Damn, he died just a few years ago. Bucky O'Neill! That's it!

"After my time, Sutherland took a team out to Ohio State one time and he never threw a forward pass the entire game. Jock Sutherland never did adjust himself to the forward pass. He never believed in giving anybody a chance to get hold of the football. He was a possession-football man.

"He was a perfectionist. He never over-loaded us with plays. But we ran them over and over again, until we could run them in our sleep, or if we were unconscious. He was absolutely, to the nth degree, a perfectionist.

"I'll never forget him. We had to play defense, too, and I'll tell you what Sutherland's pass defense was. He'd stand on the side, and say, 'Identify your man and get him immediately and go helter-skelter.' "

There were other terrific athletes at Pitt when Welch was there. The 1927 basketball team was also undefeated, and won the national championship with an All-American named Charley "Chipper" Hyatt leading the way.

"Charley Hyatt was a fraternity brother of mine," said Welch. "We lived in the same house, and we had 14 guys from the football team there, too. That was the Phi Gamma Delta house, at 4725 Wallingford. Charley was a tremendous player. He'd be good today. They're moving up and down the floor like they're running a 100-yard dash. He was that kind of guy. He was fantastic.

"I remember we had a Canadian boy come down here named Vic Pickard, and we were on the same track team. Vic tried for a world's indoor record in pole vaulting in the Millrose Games, aiming at 12 feet. And now they're going pretty near 19 feet. But Vic was one of the best pole vaulters in the nation.

"We had a track man — and I was responsible for bringing him in; he came down from Bellefonte with me, and he was from West Virginia, like me — and he was a hammer thrower. His name was Don Gwinn. He weighed only 165 pounds. In the 1928 Olympic Games in Holland, he took fifth place in the world.

"He revolutionized the hammer throw. He was the first man to ever take three turns before he delivered the hammer. He had to have the centrifugal force development, at his size, to get the hammer out there.

"We had lots of good ones. Ralph Chase and Bill Kern and Mike Getto were great linemen when I was there, and Joe Donchess started with us as a sophomore at end, and was an All-American two years later. He became a doctor. He's dead now, too."

It was mentioned that Sutherland usually snubbed

game, and if we don't win this ballgame there'll be a housecleaning from top to bottom.' I was cringing; he was raising so much hell. That will give you an idea of what it was like in those days. We won it, 12-0."

When Welch was a sophomore, the offensive stars were fullback Andy Gustafson, who scored the first touchdown at Pitt Stadium, and quarterback Jack "Spike" Harding. Those two later combined to establish a football program at the University of Miami as coach and athletic director, respectively. Jess Brown was the right halfback and punter for Pitt, playing opposite Welch.

"We used the single-wing attack, and the ball was usually snapped directly back to me or to the fullback. The quarterback was a blocker, more than anything. I called the signals in my junior and senior seasons. We had an unbalanced line, with two tackles on the right or left, on the strong side, depending on which way we were running. You'd have the guard and end on the weak side.

"Everything was direct center in those days. I think my center, Andy Cutler was his name, was the best direct-pass center who ever played the game. He never made a bad pass in the three years I played. He was just magnificent. He knew how to lead me and he was just perfect.

"Andy Cutler . . . he died within the last year. As a matter of fact, there are only five starters left from my ballclub. There are two tackles, Bill Kern and Chet Wasmuth, a guard, John Roberts, and a quarterback, Paul Fisher. Only Paul Fisher and I are left from my senior backfield, the one that played in the Rose Bowl."

sophomores, and that Donchess and Welch were exceptions to the rule.

"It was really a great compliment to me that Sutherland started me in my sophomore year. He didn't think a guy could do the job until he was a junior or senior. He didn't believe sophomores could play football. In fact, Sutherland didn't believe I could play football.

"Doc Carlson told a story about that one night when we were all up at Camp Hill the night before a Big 33 football game; we were at the home of Dr. Skippy Hughes, the dentist who had played basketball at Pitt and later coached at St. Francis of Loretto.

"He said Sutherland didn't think I could play until he saw me as a sophomore at Camp Hamilton. I stepped on the middle of a guy's back when I was going through the line, and used it as a pivot foot to turn on. The guy's name was John 'Juggy' Breen.

"He was a guy from Hazelwood. They picked him off the B&O Railroad. Back in those days, they recruited off the railroad or any place a guy looked husky. They sent him to Bellefonte Academy first, just like me. He and I roomed together at Bellefonte for awhile. Anyway, I told the linemen to watch out for me. I said, 'I'm comin' and if you're in the way I'll step right on you. I don't give a damn, I'm comin' through.' Poor ol' Juggy was laying out there on his belly, and I stepped right on his back.

"Carlson coached me as a freshman. He coached the varsity basketball team then, and the freshman football team. He and Sutherland were completely different. Carlson was quite a guy. He had a sense of humor. He'd give us a breather and say, 'Up on your toes while you're resting,' and 'fight for the inches, the yards will take care of themselves.' That was Carlson; he'd pull that sort of stuff. Sutherland never had any of that.

"Carlson was very kind to me. That same night up there at Camp Hill, he said, 'Over there sits the man that saved Jock Sutherland's job.' They said, 'Who are you pointing at?' And he said, 'I'm pointing at Gibby Welch.'

"He said, 'If Gibby hadn't had the success that he had Sutherland would have lost his job.' He said there was a contingent of people who wanted to get rid of Sutherland because 'Pop' Warner left, and they were Warner people, and they wanted Sutherland out of there. He said I saved Sutherland's life, and that's all there was to it. I never knew anything about that before. I was busy trying to win ballgames. I didn't know anything about all that stuff.

"Pitt unfortunately, you know, has had too much rancor and unpleasantness in their athletic department over the years. Too much bickering, too much jealousy, or anger. There was a big fight between Jimmy Hagan, the athletic director, and Jock Sutherland, and Chancellor Bowman and Sutherland, and all that stuff. I never got in that."

Welch personally had a great experience at Pitt, and only wishes he had taken greater advantage of it. "I've had things going my way because of my experience at Pitt," he said. "But I spoiled my own life with alcohol. I was a tremendous alcoholic for 30 years. I ruined three marriages, and who knows what else because of it.

"I quit drinking in 1958, and I stopped smoking in 1964. I finally got a win. I battled. If you had seen me drinking — week-long binges and stuff — you'd know how bad I was. My experience at Pitt provided me with sufficient character to fight through it. I may be living on borrowed time now, but I never felt better. I'm thankful to Pitt and to God, above all, for giving me a second chance.

"I was damn near dead a year ago. I was living in an apartment by myself out in Oakland. One day I was talking to the Salernos — they've been friends of mine for about 20 years — and they knew something was wrong with me, by the tone of my voice. I damn near starved myself, and I couldn't take care of myself. They drove to my apartment and told me to pack my things, that I was coming to stay with them. They said, 'C'mon, you've got to come with us.' They saved my life. He's 85 and she's in her 60s, but they have taken me into their home, and I have it good here. They're wonderful people, and the food's terrific."

"Gibby Welch Was My Greatest Player"

By Jock Sutherland
Reprinted from The Pittsburgh Press

Oct. 12, 1932

Some great linemen and outstanding backs have come and gone during the 10 years I have been coaching football at Pittsburgh.

The names of "Horse" Chase, Ralph Daugherty, Mike Getto, Ray Montgomery, Joe Donchess, Tom Parkinson, Jess Quatse, Toby Uansa, Bill Kern, Zonar Wissenger, Alec Fox, Jim MacMurdo and Luby DiMeolo were placed on All-America rolls in their day at Pitt.

But I think the greatest player I ever coached was Gibby Welch.

He had all the qualities a great halfback needs. He was a brilliant runner and a splendid passer. He dazzled with his speed and dash. He weighed around 180 and physically was like a Greek god.

Welch called signals, and his own ability to run with the ball under pressure saved many plays. On defense he showed marvelous discernment of the plays our opponents were about to use. And he was a deadly tackler.

Twice during his last year at Pitt — that was 1927, the year he was captain — he ran back kickoffs for touchdowns.

His last game in 1927 — it was against Penn State — is memorable to me. We had not been beaten and felt that a victory over Penn State would win for us the invitation to play against Stanford in the Rose Bowl game. Penn State had defeated Penn and Syracuse and tied New York U.

Usually it is my custom to shake hands with the captain before the kickoff and wish him the best of luck. It always seemed to me that handshake relieved the player of some of that tense apprehension that comes while waiting.

It was unnecessary to relieve Welch of any apprehension. After the toss, he came galloping across the gridiron and his eyes were shining.

"This is my last one, coach," he shouted, "and I'm going to make it my best."

He went whooping into the game with the zest of a boy.

Welch's inspiration that day led us to a smashing victory over the team we had expected to give us a hard contest. We won, 30-0, and we were honored by an invitation to the Rose Bowl.

JOHN WOODRUFF

John Woodruff Ran To Glory In 1936 Olympics At Berlin And Was Cheered In Connellsville

"It was a real good feeling. I did something as an athlete and for my country."

John Woodruff stared at Adolph Hitler, not sure what he should do next.

Woodruff, a freshman middle-distance runner from the University of Pittsburgh, had just won the 800 meter event in a most unconventional manner in the 1936 Olympic Games, and he was standing on the top perch of the winners' platform.

Hitler, the chancellor and fuhrer of Nazi Germany, stood in his private box at Berlin Stadium, to acknowledge the presentation of medals, as he did throughout the Games.

Joseph Goebbels, the minister of propaganda, approached the platform. Woodruff lowered his head, and Goebbels slipped the Olympic gold medal about the tall young man's head.

"I was kinda confused," recalled Woodruff while sitting in a room at the Grand Hyatt in New York City, in the winter of 1982, 46 years later, and reminiscing about his athletic accomplishments at Pitt. "They didn't school us as to how we were supposed to respond.

"They started to play the Star-Spangled Banner, and I didn't know whether to give Hitler the Nazi salute or the American salute. I went through three or four gyrations before I put my hand above my right eye, and saluted him in an American manner.."

Woodruff was sure of one thing. "It was a real good feeling," he reflected on his experience as a 21-year-old Olympic gold medalist. "It was a very inspirational feeling. I did something as an athlete and for my country."

What Woodruff did was something special. To this day, he is the only student in the history of the University of Pittsburgh, or athlete from Western Pennsylvania, to win an Olympic championship. "Long John" is justly proud.

The 1936 Olympic Games in Berlin were dominated by Adolph Hitler and J. C. Owens, who became popularly known as Jesse Owens, a spindly sprinter from Ohio State University who won four gold medals.

Owens finished first in the 100 and 200 meter sprints, anchored the 400-meter U.S.A. team to victory, and won the broad jump, now known as the long jump.

Owens was black, and his success in the XIth Games was supposed to have been a jolt to Hitler's theory of Aryan supremacy. In one report of those games, it was written that "the Nazi government disgracefully attempted to turn the Olympic movement into a propaganda vehicle for the glorification of their creed."

Woodruff, who is also black, says he was unaware of the political implications back then, and believes the American athletes were just as naive, including Jesse Owens.

John Woodruff and Frank Ohl, members of the Pitt Track Team, 1937-40.

"You could see all those flags with the swastikas about the stadium, but they didn't mean the same thing to us then that they do now," said Woodruff. "You could see the German soldiers marching around. It was impressive.

"The treatment was superb. Everything was fine. They couldn't have treated us any better. Old-timers on our Olympic team said the facilities were the finest they had ever experienced. Everything was just right.

"A young German athlete came to our village. He spoke some English. We asked him about Hitler, and he made a statement that Hitler was doing a fine job, that he had improved the economy, and had people working again.

"We knew nothing then about his Aryan supremacy theories, that pure-blooded whites were to rule the earth. If he was advancing all this political stuff, we weren't conscious of it.

"Hitler came to the Games every day, and sat in his box with his lieutenants. We didn't pay much attention to him. I know Jesse Owens always told the story about Hitler refusing to shake his hand. He said he snubbed him. I don't know about that. Hitler and Jesse exchanged waves, I know that. I saw that.

"One day Hitler invited some American athletes to his box. Jesse wasn't one of them because he was busy competing in events. So I don't know when the opportunity came up for Hitler to snub him."

There were more than 110,000 spectators who witnessed Woodruff's winning effort in the 800-meter run that overcast and otherwise gray day of Aug. 4, 1936.

Owens won his second gold medal that same day with an Olympic record broad jump of 26 feet, 5 inches, but Woodruff's victory was more unexpected and certainly more unorthodox.

The race was run in bad weather conditions, the pace was slow, and Woodruff's winning time of 1:52.9 didn't threaten any existing marks. It was still remarkable.

"Winning the race itself, and how I won it," said Woodruff, "is still vivid in my mind, and always will be. In the preliminaries when I ran, I jumped right out in front and stayed there. I did the same thing in the semi-final heat. Why I ran the way I did in the finals still escapes me.

"I laid back in the beginning. Phil Edwards, a Canadian who went to NYU, set the pace. He set a slow pace. I fell in behind, and ran second or third. I ran that way for 400 meters. Then I realized that all the field was around me, and I was boxed in. I had to get out of there."

What Woodruff did next was recounted thusly by Olympic historian R. D. Mandell:

"Seemingly disgusted, the American giant slowed his pace until he was, briefly, walking."

Recalls Woodruff:

"I actually stopped. I got spiked, but I didn't realize it until I saw the blood on my leg after the race. I moved out into the third lane, and was last in the pack. I felt I had to do something drastic. I couldn't break between the two leaders because I would've been disqualified on a foul.

"From the third lane, I got around everybody, and took the lead. They said I ran a lot more than 800 meters."

Woodruff was able to make up the lost ground because he had a running stride that hadn't been seen before in track and field competition. The average athlete took in about eight feet at a stride, while Woodruff was believed to be putting his spikes up and down nine feet apart.

The 6-3, 168-pound freshman had what was described as "the longest stride of any human being in the world" and, in another report, as "heron-legged."

Pitt Takes Half-Mile, Mile Relay
Fighting Fox Wins Wood Memo

Jesse Abramson, the track and field writer for the New York Herald-Tribune, wrote that Woodruff was "the Negro wonder whose stride has to be seen to be believed." Another Abramson story described Woodruff as "an ebony vision in gold pants and blue shirt."

This tells you of the awe in which Woodruff was held, and maybe even more about the journalism of that era. Damon Runyon referred to Woodruff as "the Black Shadow of Pittsburgh."

Whatever, Woodruff won his Olympic gold medal by beating out Mario Lanzi of Italy, who finished second, and Edwards of Canada, who was third. It was the first victory by an American in the 800 meters in Olympic competition in 24 years.

The U.S.A's Olympic team was celebrated when it came back home in a parade in New York City. Then Woodruff came home to Connellsville and an even more important parade. "The people really turned out," recalled Woodruff.

According to an Associated Press report of that day of Sept. 5, 1936 there were 10,000 townspeople on hand to welcome Woodruff home. It was a Labor Day event that also marked the golden jubilee of the class of 1886 at Connellsville High School.

"They presented me with a fine watch, a Lord Elgin, with an engraving on the back acknowledging my Olympic achievement," said Woodruff. "That fall, on the first day of practice at Pitt, we were told to put our clothes in baskets in open lockers when we changed into our sweat suits. We would be assigned lockers with keys the next day. I put my watch in the pocket of my pants. When I came back, it was gone. It was gone for good. I had it for only two months. I was told not to make a big fuss about it."

That watch meant a great deal to him. It was presented to him by his high school coach, Joseph A. Larew. His college coach, Carl Olson, was there that day, too, as were the mayor and most political officials of the Fayette County city.

Connellsville is a coal-mining community located about 50 miles southeast of Pittsburgh. It's where Woodruff was born and bred, and where he first learned, almost by accident, that he had an exceptional ability to run.

His grandparents were slaves in the Virginia tobacco fields. His parents were born free in Virginia and moved to Connellsville.

It's a town that also turned out two other exceptional athletes in the mid-40s, namely Johnny Lujack, a Heisman Trophy winner at Notre Dame, and Jimmy Joe Robinson, a running back who became the first black ever to play football for the University of Pittsburgh.

Lujack went on to play pro football for the Chicago Bears. Robinson went to a seminary, and is now a minister at the Bidwell Presbyterian Church on Pittsburgh's North Side.

"I remember Robinson as a youngster," said Woodruff. "His home was right beside the Union Baptist Church. His father, Franklin, was a chauffeur. Jimmy Joe was raised so properly. He impressed me as a Little Lord Fauntleroy, but I never thought he'd be an athlete.

"Johnny Lujack's brother, Stan, would have been a great athlete if he had gone to college. He came earlier, about the class of '32 or '33. There were other good athletes, but they just finished high school and got married, and didn't have the opportunity to continue playing ball.

"They worked in the coal mines, or the glass factory, or the box factory, or at the B&O Railroad. I quit school when I was 16, and that's what I was gonna do. I tried to get a job. I wanted to go into a factory and make some money. They wouldn't hire me. Looking back, that's the one time I'm glad I was rejected because I was black."

Woodruff had been working right along, and as far back as he can remember, on his parents' small farm on the outskirts of Connellsville. "We raised some hogs and some chickens," he recalled. "And I had to cut wood and bring in the coal."

There wasn't much money to go around, especially during the Depression. The Woodruffs had 12 children, though several died in infancy, not uncommon in those days.

Silas Woodruff was a hard-working man. "He was a laborer," said his youngest son, John. "He dug coal, he worked in the steel mill, and in the coke ovens in Clairton. He worked in a stone quarry. He was a powerful man, about 5-11, with great girth. I heard stories about him lifting stone slabs and rocks that normally required two or three men.

"I was built more like my mother, Sarah. She was tall, about 5-9, and slim. She took in washing to make extra money. I had one sister who was younger than me. Two of my older brothers, Clarence and Roger, died. And so did

for 3 Titles in Penn Carnival;
ial at Jamaica by Three Lengths

30,000 Watch Woodruff Anchor Panther Teams To Rainy-Day Triumphs

Negro's Giant Strides Dethrone Indiana by Three Yards in Shorter Race as Meet Mark Is Tied; Manhattan Four Retains 2-Mile Crown, Borck Coming From Behind; Hoosiers Score in 4-Mile

By Jesse Abramson

PHILADELPHIA, April 30.—On the flying feet of John Youie Woodruff, six-foot four-inch Negro wonder, whose stride has to be seen to be believed, the University of Pittsburgh rode to two more relay championships on the closing day of Pennsylvania's forty-fourth annual Relay Carnival as three meet records were shattered and another tied today.

Through the wind and rain that swept Franklin Field off and on during the eight-hour day of blazing competition, Ol' John stood out above the road of the crowd of 30,000 spectators. Back in hot form this week end after a nine-month respite from super-achievements, Woodruff opened the show this forenoon by anchoring Pitt's half-mile relay that tied the carnival record of 1 minute 26.6 seconds, then he closed the relay fireworks in the squally twilight by anchoring Pitt's mile foursome that defeated New York University by seven yards in 3 minutes 17.8 seconds.

Indiana Beaten 3 Yards

An ebony vision in gold pants and blue shirt, Woodruff had run his anchor half on the record-smashing sprint medley yesterday in 1:49.9. Today he approached 21 seconds for his furlong stint on the half-mile relay, carrying his team from second to a three-yard triumph that dethroned Indiana. And in the classic mile test, Woodruff, for once, was given a lead and he was off and away to a 47.4 second quarter that gave Pitt its first mile title since 1918 and its third crown of the meet.

The same Panther foursome of Frank Ohl, Albert Ferrara, Edgar Mason and Woodruff that won the sprint medley ran in exactly the same order to snatch the half-mile relay in 1 minute 26.6 seconds, tying Texas's two-year-old record. Woodruff was touched off a yard back of

8 Marks Fall As 14,000 See Drake Relays

San Romani Runs Third to Fenske in '1,000'; Rice and Wisconsin Win 4 Events Each in Meet

DES MOINES, Iowa, April 30 (*AP*). —Fourteen thousand spectators, sitting in the warmth of a bright sun, saw eight meet records go tumbling into oblivion in the finals of the twenty-ninth Drake Relay Carnival today.

The athletes, in bursts of dazzling speed, opened the meet with a record-breaking performance and continued it until the gun barked for event.

from Rice In-several of my sisters when they were young. There's just four of us left now; three sisters and myself."

Just as Jimmy Joe Robinson and Johnny Lujack would be lucky to later escape Connellsville, John Woodruff was fortunate to find a way out of the coal mines and factories.

"When I couldn't get a job," said Woodruff, "I went back to school, and I went out for the football team. The coach had the football players running wind sprints. They had a quarterback named Ralph Marilla and he was fast. Marilla was also a sprinter on the track team. The line coach of the football team, Mr. Larew, was also the track coach. He saw that when we ran that I could keep up with Marilla.

"My mother made me quit the football team because I was getting home too late after practice to do my chores. She told me to quit and that was it. When the indoor track season started, though, Coach Larew invited me out for the team and I did. I remember we ran from the high school to the cemetery — Hill Grove Cemetery — and back. It was a mile up and back. We didn't have a regular track at our school; just a dirt path around the football field."

In the interim, his mother died. John was just 19 at the time. Woodruff was on the track team for only two years, his junior and senior seasons. As a senior, he set a national interscholatic record for the mile with a 4:23.4 clocking.

"My technique wasn't that classical," he conceded. "I was just powerful. I didn't have good control of my limbs." But they were some limbs.

Woodruff was sought by several colleges, but was leaning toward Ohio State because Jesse Owens was there. "I had met him at some meets," explained Woodruff, "and he stimulated my interest in Ohio State.

"But there were people in Connellsville who convinced me to go to Pitt. They were mainly business people, and they had a Pitt alumni club. There was a dentist, Dr. 'Muzz' Campbell, and he was a dyed-in-the-wool Pitt man. He kept after me pretty good.

"They got me a scholarship to Pitt. If it weren't for the scholarship, I couldn't have made it. I'm the only one from my family who went to college. Things were bad. I came to Pitt with 25 cents to my name. I had to go see the coach, Carl Olson, and he let me have $5 so I could feed myself for the rest of the week. And it did, which tells you about the times."

Actually, things were looking up in 1936 when Woodruff first came on the campus at Pitt. The Depression was almost ended. Pitt, Carnegie Tech and Duquesne all had great football teams. Pitt had quite a basketball team, too, so, with Woodruff on hand, it was truly a golden era for sports at the Oakland school.

"I had mixed feelings about the school," said Woodruff. "Back in those days, things weren't for the blacks. But it was a good experience for me, coming out of a small town, and never having been to the big city too much."

He roomed at the Centre Avenue YMCA, at Centre and Francis Street, in The Hill district, just across the street from the offices of the Pittsburgh Courier, a nationally-distributed and respected Negro newspaper.

"That first year was rough for me, trying to get adjusted," he recalled. "Irvin Brown was my roommate. He was from Norristown, Pa. 'Irzie' was a good sprinter and hurdler. I was a freshman, and he was a sophomore. He didn't go to class on cold days, and he flunked English, and was put on probation. Then he was sent home altogether.

"I didn't want that to happen to me. I came from a poor family, and if God hadn't given me the ability to run I couldn't have gone to college. If I didn't make good, I'd

WOODRUFF ON WAY TO WIN — "Long John" enroute to gold medal victory in 800 meter run before 110,000 at Berlin Stadium in 1936 Olympics. This German photo was found in a bomb-destroyed photo shop in Nuremberg, Germany in 1944 by Baldwin's Elmer C. Leitholf, who was there with the American Armed Forces.

already made up my mind I wasn't going back to Connellsville. I was a good average student in high school. I had to work hard at Pitt; I had to dig. And we all had to work, too, at Pitt. I cleaned up the Stadium after football games, and the stadium pavilion after basketball games.

"I had no idea I'd make the Olympic team in 1936. I figured I'd go back to Connellsville for the summer, that's what I thought. Then I won the 800 in the Allegheny Mountain Association meet, and moved on to the semi-final Olympic trials at Harvard Stadium. I won there, too. Then I came back to Randalls Island in New York and won the finals. I was going to Berlin, and I couldn't believe it."

Woodruff should have realized right then and there that he was an exceptional performer. He beat world record holder Ben Eastman of Stanford to win at Randalls Island.

"At Pitt, I reached the ultimate right from the beginning, but I enjoyed the rest of my student days, too. It was stimulating," Woodruff went on. "I got more experience, and I accomplished a lot of the goals that were set for me."

He won the 440 and 880 three years in succession in the IC4A track and field championships. "That had never been done before in 58 years," he said. During the same three-year span, from 1937 through 1939, he also won the NCAA half-mile all three years. "That was quite an achievement," he said. "You can't do much better than that."

He also set records and anchored record-setting Pitt relay teams at the Penn Relays in Philadelphia, and at various meets in Madison Square Garden. He won the 800 meters in the 1937 Pan American Games.

He recalled his relationship with Carl Olson, the Pitt track coach. It was a satisfying, yet stormy relationship. "Coach Olson was a very ambitious coach," he said. "He tried to get the ultimate out of you. But he had a tendency to make you run too much.

"I often ran in four events: the 220, 440, 880 and the mile," said Woodruff. "I didn't mind it so much in dual meets. But in the IC4A and NCAA, I felt you were fortunate if you could win one event. I remember in 1938 at the University of Minnesota, he wanted me to run the quarter- and half-mile events, and I had to run heats as well as to qualify for the finals. He got mad at me when I protested. He was like a little dictator, a Napoleon. I just thought it was too much to ask in national competition."

Woodruff ran and won, though, and Pitt won its share of IC4A titles, and gained a national reputation as one of the top teams in the nation in those days.

In 1937, for instance, Woodruff established a world mark of 1:47.8 for the half-mile as Pitt won the IC4A title. That same campaign, he won the same event in the NCAA meet held in Berkeley, Calif., with a 1:50.3 clocking.

On Friday, April 30, 1938, at the 44th Penn Relays Carnival in Philadelphia, Woodruff made up a deficit to anchor Pitt's sprint medley unit (Frank Ohl, Al Ferrara and Dick Mason) to a world record 3:34.5 time, as he ran the 880 in 1:49.9. The following day, he anchored the half-mile relay team (the same foursome) to victory, and then the mile unit (Allen "Red" McKee replaced Mason on the third slot) to victory. On May 27 of the same summer, Woodruff won the 440 and 880 in the IC4A track and field meet, equalling the college mark of 47 seconds for the 440.

In his senior season of 1939, he repeated his IC4A and NCAA titles, and anchored three winning relay teams at the Penn Relays. The Pitt teams on which he ran, and he captained the 1939 outfit, were undefeated in dual meets.

"I graduated in four years in 1939," Woodruff was eager to point out. "Then I went to NYU for a master's degree in sociology."

While attending NYU, Woodruff worked as an elevator operator at a local department store — from 6:30 A.M. to 4:30 P.M., six days a week. He rose at 5 A.M. to start each day. They were long days, and they required a man with his determination and long stride.

Later, he served in World War II as a second lieutenant in the South Pacific, and compiled a remarkable record.

"Pitt gave me an opportunity to get a good college education," he said. "Without it, I couldn't have achieved what I did: winning the Olympics and getting a degree. It made it possible for me to make a good livelihood. Some others did better economically, but I did all right. I always had a job.

"I raised two children. My son, John Woodruff, Jr., is an attorney, who got his degree from Howard University. My daughter, Mrs. Randilyn Gilliam, is a school teacher, and she's married to an attorney.

"I'm retired now. All my life, I worked with disadvantaged kids. I retired from the Job Corps at Camp Kilmer in Edison, N.J." He serves as a deacon at his neighborhood Baptist church. He still keeps a busy schedule as an AAU official at track and field meets on the high school and college level. "It gives me something to do," he said.

Only the previous week, he had worked a meet at Jadwin Stadium at Princeton, and at the Brendan Byrne Arena in the New Jersey Meadowlands, and was looking forward to officiating at the Millrose Games at Madison Square Garden, once a showcase for his speed and skills.

"I love to be involved with kids in athletics," he said. "That's why I like officiating."

That's also why, in 1976, he turned over his Olympic gold medal, and some of the mementoes of his glorious track career, including a photo showing him with Jesse Owens at the 1936 Olympics in Berlin, to Connellsville High School. "We have a nice, glass-encased trophy display with all of Woodruff's stuff in there, and the kids appreciate it," reports Michael Bell, the athletic director.

"It's a living memorial," said Woodruff. "I gave it to them to try and inspire some kids."

In that respect, he believes baseball's Jackie Robinson provided the greatest inspiration to young blacks. "I knew his older brother, Mack, who finished second to Jesse Owens in the 200 meter dash at the 1936 Olympics," said Woodruff, "and I later met Jackie. He told me of some of his experiences when he was coming up with the Brooklyn Dodgers. He was treated worse than a dog. But he had to take it. Branch Rickey selected him because he was the right man, as much as for his great ability. He had the right temperament to break the barrier, the color line. Today's young blacks owe it all to Jackie."

They owe something to John Youie Woodruff as well. The recognition has come late.

In 1966, Woodruff was named a Varsity Letterman of Distinction at Pitt, inducted along with Allan Booth, Charles Hartwig and Regis Toomey. To Woodruff's way of thinking, he wondered what took so long.

"I was hurt before that," said Woodruff. "I was the only Olympic champion in the history of the school, yet I was not in Pitt's Hall of Fame in the school yearbook. People like Marshall Goldberg, Curly Stebbins and Johnny Chickerneo — all classmates of mine — were in, but I wasn't. Those guys brought national recognition to Pitt. I brought the school international recognition."

Woodruff had some second thoughts on the subject. "I do not have any more bitterness concerning my college days at Pitt," he added. "I have put all those unpleasant experiences behind me. I now want to help and encourage some young promising black athletes to enter Pitt.''

In 1978, Woodruff was elected into the National Track and Field Hall of Fame. As he spoke that afternoon in New York, he pointed proudly to the large gold ring he wore that acknowledged his admission into that hallowed group.

Woodruff was wearing that same prized ring when Pitt paid tribute to him in May of 1982 at the Pitt Invitational Track & Field Meet which attracted 25 college teams to Pitt Stadium.

He presented a plaque to the winner of the "John Woodruff 880-yard run," an idea fostered by his friend, another former Pitt Olympic medal winner, Herb Douglas. "John deserves something like this," declared Douglas.

"I haven't been forgotten," said Woodruff. "When the Olympics were held in Munich in 1972, German officials made arrangements for the 1936 Olympic champions to be there, and they paid my way.

"We were given a tour of Berlin. We saw the Berlin Wall, and we heard the Berlin Symphony Orchestra — I appreciated that — and we went to the stadium where I'd run in 1936. I'm looking out at the empty stadium, and I had a quick flash. Suddenly, I could see all those flags, and the soldiers marching, and I could imagine all those people. For a second, there were over a hundred thousand people in the place again, and I was running. It was like it was yesterday."

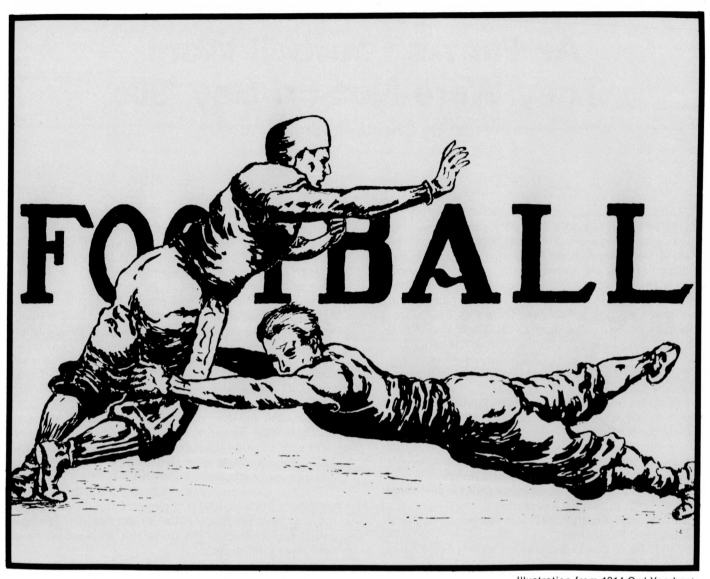

Illustration from 1914 Owl Yearbook.

"Upon the fields of friendly strife,
are sown the seeds that, upon other fields
on other days, will bear the fruits of victory."
—General Douglas A. MacArthur

"We met an old grad who didn't care whether you
roasted or boosted his college football team . . .
or whether you even mentioned it. It was the first
funeral we had attended in years."
—Grantland Rice Sportlight,
Oct. 17, 1924

As Far As Football Went, They Were Not-So-Gay '90s

By Chester L. Smith

Football at Pitt began in the Fall of 1889 when the first football team was organized and a game played — the result being a defeat at the hands of Shady Side Academy. That pioneer team, organized by Bert H. Smyers and John D. Scott, started the University on an athletic caravan which made its name known wherever sports are discussed.

Actually, Pitt was not Pitt until 1908. From its founding until that time, the school was known as the Western University of Pennsylvania, or WUP. There was a time, believe it or not, when the Pitt players were referred to as Wups.

The change in the name of the school also brought on a new nickname.

At a student meeting the nickname "Panthers" was proposed by an undergraduate, George M.P. Baird, who pointed out that it was alliterative — Pitt Panthers rolled off the tongue easily — and that in early times the panther was the fiercest animal to roam the Pennsylvania forests.

So the Pitt Panthers began their hunt for prey.

The early formative years scarcely count in the overall picture except to provide a background.

The 1889 squad, pathfinder that it was, should be known to every loyal Pitt follower.

In addition to Scott, captain and center, and Smyers, quarterback, it included Anson B. McGrew and Frank Rhea at guards, Harry S. Calvert and John McGrew at tackles, E. C. Shaler and George H. Calvert at ends, Joseph B. Griggs and William C. Gill at halfbacks, and John M. Hansen at fullback. The names of the substitutes, if there were any, are not on record.

The first full schedule was played during the following season, 1890, when the personnel of the team was much the same — the original ends were replaced by J. A. Hartrich and Albert A. Marshall, and Hansen's place was taken by George Neale, All of this group remained in '91 save Scott, and to the squad were added Joseph C. Trees, Dudley D. DuBarry, J. Harvey Evans, J. A. Morrow and Walter Witherspoon.

From 1890, the team played for three seasons without a coach, winning seven and losing nine games, and meeting such opponents as Washington & Jefferson, Geneva, the Allegheny A.A., West Penn Medics, East End Gymnastics and Indiana Teachers.

The first game with W&J was played in 1890; the first with Penn State in 1893. No games were played against those opponents between '95 and 1900, that period being a dull one in athletics at the University, although teams of sorts were maintained.

MORE LIKE RUGBY — This looks more like a "scrum" than a scrimmage, but it's Pitt's first football team in action.

Anson F. Harrold, a Princeton graduate, was the first formal coach, coming on the scene in 1893.

Then came J. P. Linn of W&J in 1895, G. W. Hoskins of Penn State in 1896, Thomas Gawthrop Trenchard of Princeton in 1897, and Dr. Frederick A. Robinson of Penn State in 1898 and 1899.

The revival in athletic enthusiasm at the school commenced in 1898 when schedules were improved, and Pitt posted its first winning season, a 5-2-1 record, with victories over the Duquesne AC, Pittsburgh Academy, Westminster, Natrona AC and Cal Teachers. The setbacks were by West Virginia and Grove City, and the tie a 6-6 standoff with the New Castle Terrors.

The Panthers closed out that first decade of their football program with another winning record under Coach Robinson, a 3-1-1 mark.

Pitt tied Westminster, 11-11, in the opener, then defeated Grove City, Swissvale AC and Bethany before bowing in the final game to the J.F. Lalus A.C.

One can easily determine that those were pioneer days, that things were still quite primitive, and that the clubs were just this side of sandlot sports in their make-up.

But it was the start of something big, the basis for today's big-time program, acknowledged as one of the finest in the nation.

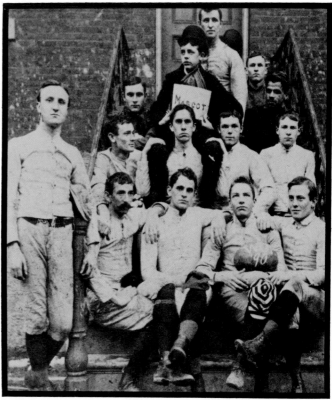

OUR GANG — This was WUP's first organized football team, the 1890 bunch that won one of three games, beating Geneva.

—Photos from University Archives

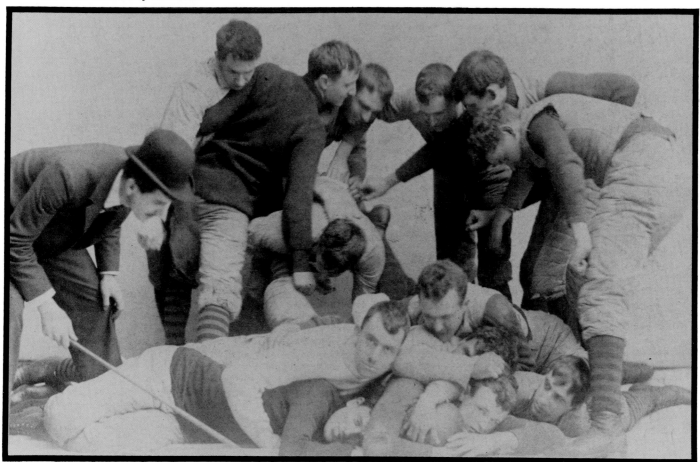

CHARLIE CHAPLIN, THE REFEREE — Well, the chap wielding the pointer on the left sure looks like the great comic of silent film days. Back in the beginning, the refs wore bowlers and kept order as best they could.

A Saint And A Colonel Began Century With Winning Records

By Chester L. Smith

Pitt kept coming up with a new coach each football season at the start of the 20th century, and there was no consistency to the program or the results.

Dr. M. Roy Jackson of Pennsylvania was the coach in 1900 when the Panthers posted a 5-4 record, Wilbur D. Hockensmith, a Pitt man, was in charge in 1901 when the team had its best-ever record of 7-2-1, and then Frederick Joseph Crolius of Dartmouth was the main man when the Panthers slipped to 5-6-1 in 1902.

Along came Arthur St. L. Mosse of Kansas in 1903 and he stayed for three seasons, and compiled an impressive 20-10-1 record. He did it the hard way.

His first team didn't win a game, going 0-8-1, and losing to the likes of the Manchester AC, Bellevue Outing Club, East End AA and getting crushed by Penn State, 59-0.

Then a few enthusiastic alumni emerged and came to the aid of the coach. They set up a training table and helped recruit a sufficient number of prospects. It paid off.

"Their plans bore fruit," went a report in the Owl yearbook, "and the progressive betterment in athletics of the last few years, and the present efficient plan is the direct result of this effort of theirs."

The following season, Pitt went undefeated for the first time in its history. The Panthers won all 10 of their games, and finished the season with a 22-5 victory over Penn State. It was Pitt's first win over Penn State in seven games, and the Panthers had been shut out in five of the earlier meetings.

Those five points by Penn State, however, were the only ones scored against Pitt that entire season. The Panthers outscored their opponents 406 to 5. Penn State scored that touchdown — then worth five points — late in the fourth quarter of that final game.

Some of the members of that team were Dr. Leslie Waddill, a tackle who turned to dentistry and practiced in Pittsburgh's Jenkins Arcade; Dr. Joseph Edgar, who practiced medicine in Oakmont; Dr. Albert T. Schmidt, who practiced medicine in Wilkinsburg; Dr. O. H. Mehl of Edgewood, who was on the medical staff of the Edgar Thomson Steel Works in Braddock for many years.

There were also W. W. Zieg, an insurance adjuster; Arthur McKean, a New Kensington attorney, and Frank C. Rugh, who quarterbacked the 1904 team and became an attorney.

Then, too, there were Walter East, a lawyer in Akron, Dr. Charles Henry Boisseau, a dentist who practiced in Smithton, Pa., and there was Colonel Joseph F. Thompson, who may have been the most famous member of that '04 team.

Joe Thompson came from Beaver Falls, where he had gone to Geneva College before transferring to Pitt. He captained the first of the school's undefeated, untied teams and in his three years on the team the Panthers achieved an excellent 26-6 mark.

In 1905, the final one for Coach Mosse, the Panthers posted a 10-2 record. In 1906, under Coach E. R. Wingard of Susquehanna, the Panthers were 6-4. Coach John A. Moorhead of Yale directed the team to a 9-1 record in 1907.

Following graduation from Pitt's law school in 1908, Thompson took the reins of the football team. Under Thompson, the Panthers went 8-3 in 1908 and 6-2-1 in 1909.

Perhaps the first player to win attention far beyond the bounds of Western Pennsylvania was Jack Turner, a great center of the 1907-09 period.

In 1908, a junior right end named Homer C. Roe, 5-8, 162 pounds, established a record that remains in the Pitt archives and is the longest-standing record in those books. He intercepted a pass and returned it 105 yards for a touchdown against West Virginia.

Roe was named the captain of the 1909 squad.

A most interesting development that year was the establishment of training quarters in a large roomy house at 3456 Bouquet Street. "The sixteen rooms were pleasantly furnished," according to a report, "and the members of the team who stayed there felt quite at home."

The school was first referred to as Pitt in 1908.

At that same time, The Pittsburg Leader, a newspaper that boasted it was "the paper which does things in the sporting world," originated the idea of numbering the players. Joe Thompson thought it was a great idea. The Leader even donated the numbers worn by the Panthers.

Pitt boasted that it was the first school in the country to have numbers on the players' jerseys.

"This system," said The Pittsburg Leader in a 1909 Pitt football game program, "enables the spectators to keep close tab on the work of each player and has been endorsed by such authorities as Walter Camp, George H. Brooks, Dr. Bull, Penn's great center, Amos Alonzo Stagg of Chicago, Coach Joseph H. Thompson of Pitt and Prof. Andrew Kerr, Coach of Pittsburgh High School Team."

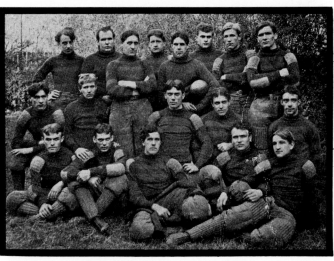

Pitt Grid Team, Vintage 1900

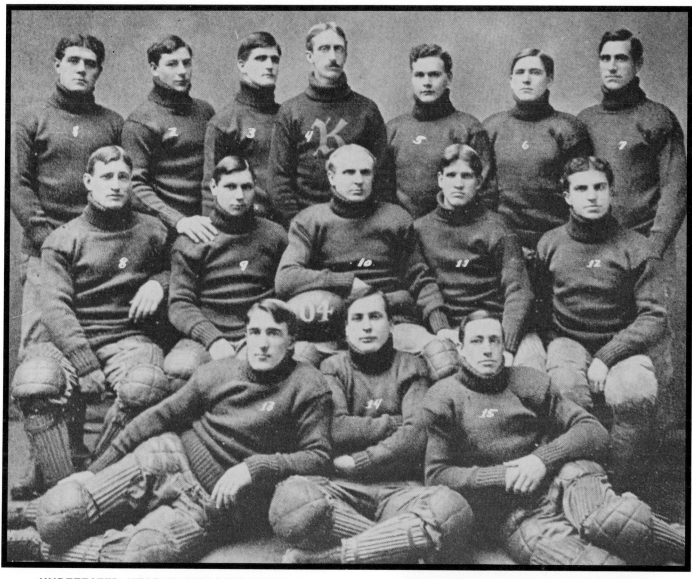

UNDEFEATED, NEARLY UNSCORED UPON

Members of the famous '04 football team of the Western University of Pennsylvania: (1) Cal Marshall (Med. '08); (2) Joe Edgar (Med. '08); (3) Arthur McKean (Col. '05); (4) Arthur St. Ledger Mosse, the coach; (5) Curt Leidenroth (Dent. '06); (6) W. W. Zeig (Mines '10); (7) Leslie Waddill (Dent. '07); (8) Walter East (record of school and class lost); (9) Albert T. Schmidt (Med. '08); (10) Joseph F. Thompson (Col. '05, Law '08); (11) Omar Mehl (Med. '08); (12) Theodore Perry (records lost); (13) Charles Henry Boisseau (Dent. '07); (14) Frank C. Rugh (Law '05); (15) Walter Ritchie (Dent. '07). Coach Mosse came from Kansas, hence the "K".

Homer C. Roe — Record Interception Return

COLLEGE SONG . . .
JOE THOMPSON
(Tune — "Ol' Black Joe")

Who plans the plays to spring upon the foe?
Who fought for Wup, five years or more ago?
Who's still for Pitt, does anybody know?
Just hear those loyal rooters shouting:
Joe! Joe! Joe!
REFRAIN
We're coming, we're coming;
We have the foe in tow,
So here's a cheer for Pittsburgh dear
And Joe! Joe! Joe!

Pitt had an athletic dormitory in 1909.

It was a roomy house at 3456 Bouquet Street.

"The 16 rooms were pleasantly furnished," it was written, "and the members of the team who stayed there felt quite at home."

1906 SQUAD, CAPTAINED BY CALVIN C. MARSHALL (with ball)

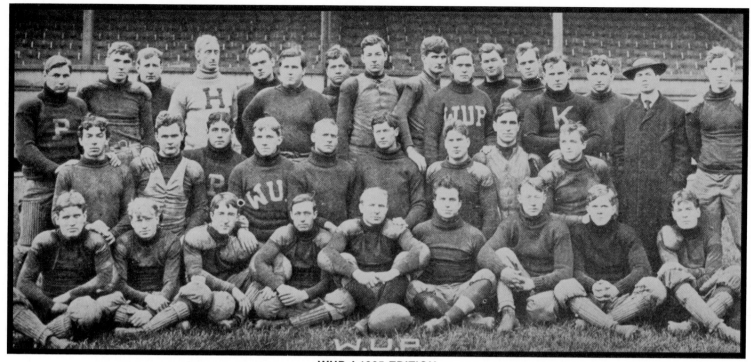

WUPs' 1905 EDITION

First row, left to right, were Omar Mehl, John S. Mackrell, Charles Boisseau, Walter Ritchie, Joe Thompson, Ted Perry, Quince Banbury, Capwell, Cathern. Second row: Fritz Klawuhn, Curt Leidenroth, Cal Marshall, Springer, Swenson, Win Banbury, Bill Turner, Leslie Waddill, Jim Frye. Rear: Al Schmidt, Sullivan, Walter East, Coach Arthur St. Ledger Mosse, Gil Miller, C. R. McKinney, Martin, Joe Edgar, Arthur McKean, Waldy Zieg, Tex Yielding, Grizzle Rice, Paul Vitte, Benjamin Jenkins, the student manager, and Frank Griggs. Some players wore jerseys from other schools, which accounts for the "P" (Princeton), "H" (Harvard) and "K" (Kansas).

AT HOME AT FORBES FIELD

The 1908 team posted an 8-3 record, playing all its games at Forbes Field with the exception of a 13-0 victory at St. Louis. With "Jam" Moorhead and "Kacie" Swenson in charge of the coaching, and "Little" Banbury as captain, the Panthers had quite a team.

Pop Warner's Teams Won Three National Titles In Four Years

By Jim O'Brien

Starting with an undefeated football team in 1910, the decade from 1910 to 1919 was one of the most productive in Pitt football history.

The ten year total of 64-14-3 is surpassed only by the record of 76-15-4 posted by the Panther football teams in the 1930s, and it's one that Pitt teams can shoot at in the 1980s.

There were three coaches during that span, starting off with Col. Joe Thompson (1908-12), Joe Duff (1913-14) and one of the greatest of them all, Glenn Scobey "Pop" Warner (1915-23). Home games were at Forbes Field.

That 1910 team won wide fame, going through the season unbeaten and unscored upon. It's the only Pitt team that can make such a claim.

In that stretch, they outscored Westminster, 18-0; Waynesburg, 42-0; West Virginia, 38-0; W&J, 14-0; Carnegie Tech, 35-0; Penn State, 11-0.

There was an interesting review of that 1910 team that appeared in the 1912 Owl yearbook:

"That football in the University of Pittsburgh in 1910 was an unqualified success is everywhere recognized. But how could it have been otherwise when the team had Joe Thompson as coach, Tex Richards as captain, ten of last year's lettermen, and an abundance of new material?

"With these men, Joe set to work to build up a team worthy of the hearty support of the student body. That he succeeded cannot be denied. However, it was not to the ability of any one individual that this success was due, but rather to the team as a whole. There was not a quitter on the squad, every man throughout the entire season displaying a vim and daring seldom witnessed in any sport.

"This was a team of brain as well as brawn. In consequence, it was able to win nine straight victories, scoring in all 282 points, and yet keeping its own goal line un-crossed. At that Pitt did not have to exert herself to any great degree. Had it been necessary, many more points could have been scored."

The stars comprising that team were topped by the mighty Robert W. "Tex" Richards, one of the greatest of all fullbacks and one of the outstanding stars of all Pitt's football history.

His name is still in the Pitt record book to this day. As a sophomore in 1908, he returned a kick-off 105 yards for a touchdown against Bucknell, a feat tied in 1927 by Gibby Welch against West Virginia.

Richards is the earliest player still listed on Pitt's all-time football team. "He was strong enough," wrote Chet Smith, "to carry through the power plays which were dominant in that era."

The graduation of many of the 1910 group resulted in a letdown during 1911 and 1912, and then came general reorganization which put the University in the front rank of the football world and kept it there.

Col. Thompson, a soldier and politican who also looked after the track team, left his post in 1912 and Duff came on.

Thompson's teams were 4-3-1 and 3-6 in his last two seasons, and Duff's posted records of 6-2-1 and 8-1.

The captain of the 1913 team was a senior named Hube Wagner, who was a brilliant end and running back. "There's a man," offers Frank Carver, who came to know him in later years, "who was even a greater human being than his legend."

Wagner was elected to the National Hall of Fame, along with Herb McCracken, a back and lineman from 1918-20, with the class of 1973 enshrinees.

He came to Pitt from Monaca High School in 1910 and immediately became a member of the great Panther team that went undefeated and unscored upon. While primarily

The 1915 Pitt team that went undefeated beginning a win streak that was to extend for four years setting a record that was broken by Oklahoma in 1956.

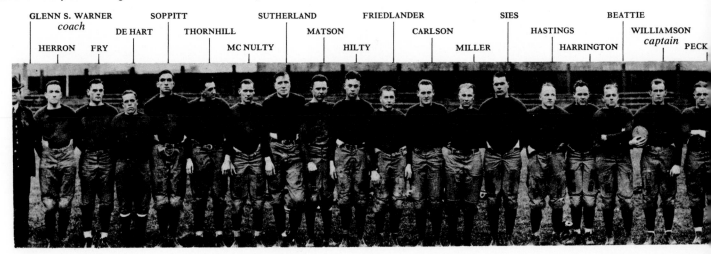

GLENN S. WARNER coach — SOPPITT — DE HART — SUTHERLAND — THORNHILL — FRIEDLANDER — MATSON — CARLSON — SIES — HASTINGS — BEATTIE — WILLIAMSON captain
HERRON — FRY — MC NULTY — HILTY — MILLER — HARRINGTON — PECK

BACKYARD HEROES — George Brown and William Hittner of 1910 team.

an end, he filled in at every other position except quarterback because of his great versatility.

He went on to become an outstanding surgeon and for 12 years was a member of the University Board of Trustees. He was also elected a Letterman of Distinction in the initial class of 1961.

Relations with Notre Dame began in 1911 and so did a significant series with the Carlisle (Pa.) Indian Training School — famous as Jim Thorpe's team — because it brought to Pitt's attention the Indians' coach, "Pop" Warner.

After the 1914 season, Pitt authorities made an attractive offer to Warner and "The Fox" accepted. It brought into the Pitt picture one of the game's early geniuses.

Who invented what in football is always a controversial subject. For instance, Warner is credited with having con-

CAPTAIN "TEX" RICHARDS

KENDRICK AMMONS MC QUISTON MORROW SEIDEL COLLINGWOOD
MEADOWS GLICQUENNOI MC CLELLAND BOND HOCKENSMITH *student manager*
TAHLMAN SIEMON MC LAREN SHAPIRA GOUGLER DOUGHERTY STAHL

BOB PECK — became the first All-American from the University in 1915 and repeated in 1916.

ceived the screen pass but Hube Wagner disputed this. "Actually," he said, "we stole the screen from Ohio Northern, one of our opponents and a little-known team. Where they got it, we had no idea."

But Warner was creator of the single and double wing offenses and a screen that sent so many men down in front of the receiver that it resulted in the "ineligible player downfield" rule being written into the book.

Pop lived in Springville, N.Y. and spent only the fall months in Pittsburgh.

At Carlisle, when one of his players came down with pleurisy, he rigged a protective shield out of an old wash boiler. He carved his own golf clubs from bed posts, and he was continually tinkering with motor cars.

Then, too, he was an author who wrote a weekly column for The Pittsburgh Press under an assumed name. It gave him the opportunity to praise or dress down his players without them suspecting that it was their coach speaking.

Under Warner, the Panthers put together an all-winning streak that stretched over four years — 1915 through 1918, the last season being shortened to four games because of a flu epidemic.

Relations were established with Georgia Tech, Lehigh, Syracuse and Pennsylvania during that period.

Pitt had become a national entity in sports.

Bob Peck, the center who "roved" and was one of the forerunners of the linebacker, became the first All-American from the University in 1915, and repeated 12 months later. "Stars may come and stars may go," wrote Capt. "Red" Carlson, "but Bob will be everlastingly revered as the greatest of them all."

Tommy Davies was an All-America running back. Harvey Harman, who was later the executive secretary of the National Football Foundation and Hall of Fame, stood out at tackle. Bill McClelland was a stout-hearted back, and became even more famous later as a dentist who became the Allegheny County coroner and later commissioner.

Several others gained All-American honors in that era, and are among the most famous names in Pitt history.

H. C. Carlson, who became better known as "Doc" Carlson, the varsity basketball coach and student health service physician in later years, was an All-American end in 1917.

Jock Sutherland, who would someday succeed Warner as Pitt's head football coach, was an All-American guard in 1917.

Sutherland was a regular guard on the great Pitt teams of 1914-1917, teams that lost only one game during the entire period. He graduated in 1918 with a dental degree and went into the military service.

Claude Thornhill was an All-American guard in 1916, and Dale Sies won the same honors at the same position the following season. George McLaren was an All-American fullback in 1917 and 1918. Leonard Hilty was an All-American tackle in 1918.

McLaren is looked upon as Pitt's all-time finest fullback. He came to Pitt from Peabody High School and played four years (1915-18) when the Panthers compiled a 29-0 record.

He was captain of the 1918 team. He scored 13 touchdowns in 1917. He holds the one-season rushing mark by a Pitt fullback with 782 yards. He also holds the longest run from scrimmage for a fullback, 92 yards in 1917. He was never stopped without a gain in his entire Pitt career.

McLaren was also a member of the school's basketball team for two years, and a performer on the track team for

PERFECT RECORD — Pitt's untied, undefeated, and unscored upon football team, the 1910 edition coached by Joe Thompson, a star of the first undefeated team in 1904, and starring among others Tex Richards and Hube Wagner. Thompson later was the Colonel Joe of World War I fame and Wagner went on to become an All-American end. This team was the most talked about at Pitt until the Glory Road days when Glenn (Pop) Warner put the Panthers on the big time to stay. R. W. Richards (with ball) was Captain.

two seasons. He was elected a Varsity Letterman of Distinction in 1965.

Davies, who was from Washington, Pa., was a two-time All-American and ranks as one of Pitt's greatest backs. After prepping at Kiski, Davies entered Pitt in 1918 and was named on the last of Walter Camp's All-American teams as a freshman. He holds two Pitt punt return records, and ranks third in the all-time total yards gained department, after Tony Dorsett and Gibby Welch, with 3,931 yards in four seasons. Davies scored over 20 TDs in his career. He spent 25 years as a coach at Penn, Geneva, Allegheny, Rochester, Kiski, Scranton and Western Reserve.

Herb McCracken came along at the same time. A native of Sewickley, McCracken was considered one of Pitt's most versatile and one of the lightest football players in the school's history.

"He made up in football instinct and desire for any lack of size," said one report of the period, "and those same attributes later made him a successful coach."

He was a varsity performer under Pop Warner from 1918-20, participating at halfback, fullback, guard, end and center. He also played three years of basketball, captaining the team his senior year.

McCracken went on to achieve outstanding coaching success at Allegheny College and Lafayette. Herb left coaching in 1935 to co-found Scholastic Magazine, Inc. He has served as a trustee at both Pitt and Lafayette. He was elected a Varsity Letterman of Distinction in 1961.

Some other standouts of that period were G. M. Williamson, Jimmy DeHart, Andy Hastings, "Pat" Herron and Randall Soppitt.

DeHart became the first student to win varsity letters in four major sports before graduating in 1918. For three years, he was a backfield star on the football team, and

COL. JOE THOMPSON — Honest War Hero

69

1913 TEAM — Top row (left to right) Wayne Smith, (captain elect), Mark Hoag, Tiny Thornhill, Charles Reese, Randall Soppitt, Cowell, Earl Ammons, Collins, Jenkins (manager). Bottom row: Bob Peck, F. F. Ward, Shoff, R. Heil, J. Huber Wagner (captain), Phillip Dillon, James Herron, James Jones, Isadora Shapira, G. M. Williamson.

TERRIFIC TRIO — The most potent ball carrying set of backs in Pitt history was the 1916 trio of George McLaren, Andy Hastings and Jimmy DeHart. These three outgained all starting combinations before them.

during an equal period of time he held down the third base position with the baseball team. He ran dashes for the track team and was a member of a winning relay team. He also starred at guard on the basketball team.

"Diminutive Jimmy is one of the most conscientious as well as modest workers in the school," according to an account in the yearbook, "and the honor bestowed upon him is a popular and deserving one."

Pitt won three national championships with Warner at the helm during this period, being selected in 1915 (8-0), 1916 (8-0) and 1918 (4-0).

After seeing the 1916 unit in action, Walter Camp, the distinguished football authority, wrote: "This team play is perfect. They are a most wonderful team. Pitt is a marvelous combination."

When war was declared in 1917, there was much speculation as to the future of intercollegiate athletics, but Pitt managed to keep things on a pretty even keel.

"Credit is due to the team members for the way they cooperated with the management in keeping down expenses," went one account. "No training house was provided for the team and the boys lived in their own homes; yet they were always in good physical shape. While the attendance at games was not quite so large as other years, the support was, as a rule, all that could be desired. The crowd at the W&J game even exceeded that of 1916. The student support was splendid, with the newly uniformed Pitt band always in evidence."

Pitt closed out the period on a positive note with a 6-2-1 record in 1919, which included a quite unexpected victory over W&J.

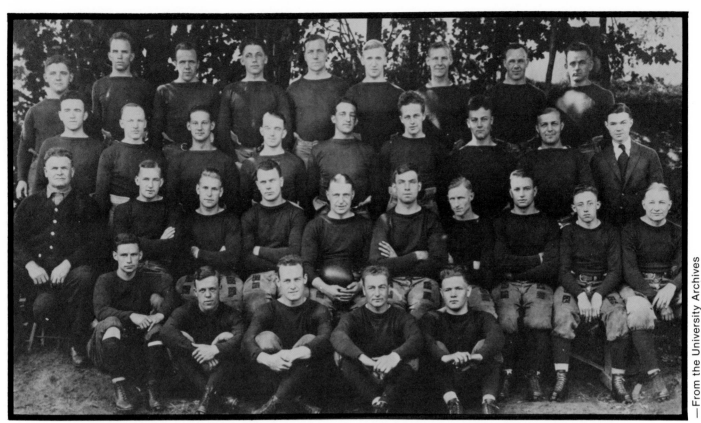

1916 GRID TEAM — Undefeated and frequently rated as Pitt's greatest. Front row (l. to r.) Eric Meadows, Jim DeHart, H. C. Carlson, Sam Friedlander, Lobaugh. Second row — Coach Pop Warner, Jim Morrow, Skip Gougler, Dale Sies, Captain Bob Peck, Randall Soppitt, Earl Ammons, Tom Kendrick, Cy Stahlman, Bill Miller. Third row — Jim Herron, Andy Hastings, George McLaren, Katy Easterday, Tiny Thornhill, Alvar Ginn, Leonard Hilty, Fred Seidel, Jack Thompson. Fourth row — Jim McIntyre, Chester Smith, William Neibels, Jake Stahl, Jock Sutherland, Bill McClelland, Frank McNulty, Bill Harrington, Cliff Brown.

JUGGERNAUT. Pitt's great 1916 team executes a perfect off-tackle play. Jim Morrow (left) has knocked down the opposing end and is lying on top of him. Pat Herron and Jim DeHart (right background) are rolling on the ground after knocking down the tackle. The interference is George McLaren (in front of ball carrier), Dale Sies, and Jock Sutherland (partly obscured by Sies). The man with the ball is Skip Gougler. H. C. "Red" Carlson is following the play.

Pop Warner Went Undefeated In Four Years At Pitt; Coached The Legendary Jim Thorpe At Carlisle

"He was a great inventor."
—Grantland Rice

By Jim O'Brien

JIM THORPE — Starred for Warner at Carlisle

Pop Warner was one of the "Grand Old Men" of the game of football, a legend in his own time we'd say now. He was christened Glenn Scobey Warner, but everyone who knew him called him "Pop" because he came across that way. There was a genuine warmth about him; he was a grandfather figure to all.

Warner was one of the founders of college football as we know it today. He was the father of the "single-wing" and "double-wingback" systems, and he wrote collegiate football history at no fewer than three Pennsylvania schools — Carlisle, Pitt and Temple. Between the last named posts, he enjoyed a great stay at Stanford.

He was an innovator, along with the likes of Amos Alonzo Stagg and Bob Zuppke. One of his good friends, sports columnist Grantland Rice wrote of him: "In 1910 I thrilled to the power Pop Warner achieved from his single-wing attack, and a year later to the deception of Pop's double-wing."

That was when Warner was coaching at Carlisle, of course, and he had a young man carrying the ball named Jim Thorpe. Thorpe was a terrific all-around athlete, and he was named to Walter Camp's All-America team in 1911 and 1912.

He was also named to our 1912 Olympic track and field team. Warner went with him as a "chaperone" to Sweden for the competition. One day the track coach, Mike Murphy, was upset because Thorpe had failed to show up for practice for the third day in a row.

"Glenn, I've seen some queer birds in my day, but your Indian beats all!" complained Murphy. "I don't see him do anything . . . except sleep!"

Warner smiled at Murphy, and said benignly, "Mike, don't worry. All those two-for-a-nickel events you've got lined up for Thorpe won't bother him. He's in shape . . . what with football, lacrosse, baseball and track back at school, how could he be out of shape? This sleeping is the best training ever — for Jim."

As Warner had figured, Thorpe took four of the five firsts in the pentathlon, and four of the ten firsts in the decathlon. As King Gustav of Sweden was giving him a gold medal, he told Thorpe, "Sir, you are the greatest athlete in the world."

Warner wouldn't argue with the King on that point, but he had some reservations about Thorpe.

"In addition to having every needed physical asset, Thorpe had a rare spirit," said Warner. "Nothing bothered Jim. When he was 'right,' the sheer joy of playing carried him through. When he wasn't, he showed it. When he was right, he was the best.

"The reason I picked Ernie Nevers over Thorpe as my all-time football player," Warner went on, "was because Ernie gave one hundred percent of himself — always. In that

POP WARNER

respect, he was a coach's ideal. Thorpe gave it only on certain occasions. It was difficult to know whether Jim was laughing with or at you."

Pitt played against Carlisle when Warner and Thorpe were teamed up at the Indian Training School. Carlisle defeated Pitt, 17-0, in 1911, and by 45-8, the Panthers' worst licking in the 1912 season. Pitt caught Carlisle without Thorpe after that, and defeated the Indians, 12-6, in 1913, and 10-3, in 1914.

Pitt pried Warner away from Carlisle to coach the Panthers for the 1915 season. "Pop's" Pitt teams went on a tear, with a record of 59 victories, 11 defeats and 4 ties over a span from 1915 through 1923. It represents one of the most remarkable coaching records in the book — a winning percentage of .843.

"I had grand helpers such as Floyd Rose and Alex Stevenson," said Warner, when asked to reflect on his Pitt experience when he was retired in later years.

"And there were many fine players, too. I remember and often think about George McLaren, Bob Peck, Red Carlson, Bill McClelland, Jock Sutherland, Jim Herron, Andy Hastings, Jimmy DeHart and a lot of other fine boys too numerous to mention."

Some of the others who gained All-America status from Warner's Pitt teams were Claude "Tiny" Thornhill, Dale Sies, Leonard Hilty, Tommy Davies, Herb Stein and Ralph "Horse" Chase.

Warner had four straight all-winning seasons at Pitt from 1915 through 1918, posting a 29-0 overall mark, and won three national championships during that stretch.

Walter Camp, who brought the word "All-America" into prominence, once came to Warner before Pitt played Syracuse and said, "I didn't get a chance to scout you this season. You have anything new . . . anything I don't know about?"

"Not a thing, lad," responded Warner, with his droll sense of humor. "We'll use about five plays . . . two reverses, an off tackle, a trap play or two and perhaps a pass. I promise not to use anything else, but I won't tell you in what order I'll use them."

WARNER'S WARRIORS — From Sutherland to Carlson

"POP" WARNER
— Pitt coach from 1915 to 1924.

Marty Wolfson

TOMMY DAVIES

Run, Tommy, Run!

"I kept praying my blockers would stay healthy."

By Chester L. Smith

Reprinted from Pittsburgh Sports Hall of Fame

There was only one thing wrong with Tommy Davies' spectacular climb to football fame and with Tommy, too, while he was jitterbugging to one record after another, first at Kiski prep school and later at Pitt: his timing was bad.

The little man from Washington, Pa., set records in an era when records were kept either sketchily or not at all. In his day — he was a member of the Panther backfield from 1918 through 1921 — football statistics were virtually unknown. What Tommy did has to be picked up piece by piece from old newspapers, scrapbooks and memory.

Had there been a "book" then, the Davies saga would be one of the greatest ever told.

Tom Davies never weighed more than 155 pounds and after a rough campaign he would drop down to just a bit more than 140. Yet he has more than one fabulous accomplishment to his credit — such as the 58-yard field goal he dropkicked at Kiski prep school in a game against the Penn State freshmen. And other items: They would include his selection by Walter Camp on the All-America in his freshman year at Pitt and twice again before he was graduated, the 4625 yards he gained during his four seasons in a Jungle Cat uniform, averaging more than 170 yards a game; and the 20-odd touchdowns he racked up in his four years on the varsity under Glenn Scobey Warner.

Warner thought so highly of his small game-breaker that he named him on his first team late in life when he was asked to pick an all-time squad from the players he had coached. The quarterback in that backfield was Jimmy Johnson of the Carlisle Indians, plus his running mate, Jim Thorpe, at one halfback and Ernie Nevers of Stanford the fullback. Davies was Pop Warner's choice to be the other halfback. Incidentally, three other Pitt men were on Warner's team: Bob Peck, center; 'Horse' Chase, tackle; and Jock Sutherland, guard.

There was the 1920 season when Davies scored 42 of the 48 points Pitt collected as the Panthers played against three powers of the East — Lafayette, Penn and W.&J. The Lafayette Leopards — coached by Sutherland — were the sectional defending champions the day Pitt defeated them, 14 to 0, on two long runs from scrimmage by Tommy.

Probably the biggest day of his life came in the Penn game, which was won, 27 to 21. As the Pitt Owl, the student yearbook, gushed later: "On November 6, Tommy Davies, Pittsburgh's wonder man, defeated the University of Pennsylvania in one of the most thrilling grid battles ever staged on Franklin Field. The Quakers played a strong game. Their aerial attack bewildered Pitt and they scored thrice. But that could not beat Tom Davies. For Pitt's first score he threw a three-yard forward pass to Tom Holleran, who crossed the goal line. On the next kickoff he ran through the Penn team 90 yards for a touchdown. In the third period Davies scored again on two 30-yard runs and to finish the day's work in the fourth period he intercepted a Penn forward pass and ran 60 yards. His feats stand out as the greatest single exhibition of the year.''

That same campaign saw Tommy rack up two touchdowns to top Lafayette, and turn in a 30-yard broken field dash against W.&J. to topple the Presidents' power pack, 7 to 0.

What was his secret? Great speed and body action were two factors but the man himself says modestly, ''I had good teams to play on — we won 21 games, lost 5 and tied four during my years at Pitt — but prayer helped, too. You see I kept praying that my blockers and the rest of the boys would stay healthy. One fellow can't do it himself. I found that out very early in my playing days and it still holds good.''

Davies' pyrotechnics against Penn were not forgotten by the Red and Blue. The fall after his graduation found Tommy a member of the staff of Head Coach John Heisman at Penn. It was the beginning of a sparkling coaching career.

A year after his term with the Quakers, Davies went to Geneva College as head coach. He remained there for one year before moving to Allegheny College for the 1924 and 1925 campaigns. Next it was on to the University of Rochester (1926 to 1935) where he transformed a perennial loser into a winner.

In 1936, Davies returned to Pittsburgh to set himself up in what proved to be a profitable insurance business and coach the Carnegie (Tech)-Mellon freshman squad. Twelve months later found him back at his old prep school, Kiski, to handle the team there during the illness of the Kiski Dean and Coach, James L. Marks.

Came 1937. Davies became the headman at Scranton University. He remained there through 1940, dropping only three games in the three-year span.

Western Reserve University of Cleveland tapped him in 1941 and he stayed with the Red Cats for five seasons, with one year's absence for defense work during World War II. Then home to Pittsburgh, an end to coaching and concentration on business — and golf, at which he was close to being a scratch player. During 26 years of coaching, Tommy had set an enviable mark of winning 141 games against 42 defeats and four ties.

Throw in a baseball career which saw him captain the Panther nine (as well as the football team) and earn a contract from John J. McGraw and the New York Giants. His stay there was brief, however, for football was his dish, and a tasty one at that.

TOUCHDOWN BOUND — The oldtimers still argue Pitt never had a better ball-carrier than Tommy Davies.

Sutherland Succeeds Warner, Wins National Championship

By Jim O'Brien

Pitt football in the '20s was a roaring success, but a switch in coaches — from Pop Warner to one of his former players, Jock Sutherland — created the same sort of concern and controversy as when Johnny Majors left the school after directing the Panthers to a national title in 1976 and was replaced by Jackie Sherrill.

Just as Sherrill was always compared to Majors, and was begrudgingly recognized as quite a coach in his own right, so was Sutherland when he stepped into the large shoes left by Warner when he departed Pittsburgh in favor of Stanford following the 1923 season.

Warner won three national championships in a four-year period in his early Pitt days, but his clubs slipped by comparison in the '20s. With Warner as coach, the Panthers posted records of 6-2 in 1920, 5-3-1 in 1921, 8-2 in 1922, and 5-4 in 1923.

The captains of those respective clubs were Herb Stein, Tommy Davies, Tom Holleran and Lloyd Jordan.

Stein should be singled out. He came to Pitt from Warren, Ohio, and for four years (1918-21) was one of Pitt's greatest offensive and defensive centers.

He was named a first-team All-American in 1921. During his four years, Pitt won 21, lost five and tied four. His brother, Russ, was an All-American tackle at Washington & Jefferson.

The career of Davies was detailed in the previous chapter; suffice to say here that he was one of the most productive runners of all time.

Holleran was rated one of the best quarterbacks in the country, as well as one of the greatest in Pitt history. According to one report, he was "a born fighter and leader, a great all-around player and a field general of rare judgement."

Holleran captained the 1922 team, and that's also when George I. Carson became the student manager, and began to make his mark as a man who could be counted upon in whatever Pitt-related activities in which he was engaged. Carson set a standard for service at the University.

The rap on Pitt's 1921 team (5-3-1) was its lack of consistency. "At times they were great with the greatest," went one story, "again they were lacking in the aggressiveness so characteristic of Warner machines."

They lost by 6-0 that season to Lafayette, coached by a former Pitt guard named Jock Sutherland.

Led by Holleran and Charlie Bowser — who would become the Pitt coach in later years — the Panther eleven came back strong at season's end and whipped W&J and Penn State in stunners.

Pitt lost only two games in 1922, but they came in back-to-back fashion in the second and third games of the schedule, by 7-0 to Sutherland's Lafayette squad, and by 9-6 to West Virginia.

Some of Pitt's top players were Jack Sack, "Pie" Williams, "Hoot" Flanagan, "Tiny" Hewitt, Marshall Johnson and John Anderson.

Bowser was named captain of the 1923 team: "Second to none as a center, unrivaled as a fighter and leader, and who has already shown himself worthy and capable of leading a Pitt football team, Bowser was an easy choice."

Warner's final year at Pitt was a difficult one. The team went 5-4 and all four losses came in succession. The season started well enough with a 21-0 victory over Bucknell with Nick Shuler and Jess Brown throwing passes with "unerring accuracy" and the two of them, along with Captain Jordan, catching them for big gainers. In the second game, Pitt defeated Lafayette, 7-0, for their first victory over Sutherland's squad in three years.

Then the Panthers hit the skids, with successive losses to West Virginia (13-7), Syracuse (3-0), Carnegie Tech (7-2) — the first Plaid victory in the history of Pitt-Tech relations — and Penn (6-0).

Pitt came out of its tailspin to whip three area schools — Grove City (13-7), W&J (13-6) and Penn State (20-3) to salvage a winning season.

Sutherland signed a three-year contract to coach at Pitt. He was a logical choice by virtue of his great record as a player at Pitt, and his exceptionally fine record as a coach at Lafayette. While head man at the Easton, Pa., school, Jock's teams lost but eight of 43 games, and split in four meetings with Pitt.

RECALLING THE GOOD OLD DAYS, Tommy Davies (left), Russ Stein (center) and Herb Stein have a reunion at a Curbstone Coaches luncheon, where the Stein brothers were inducted into the group's Hall of Fame in 1968.

HOMECOMING REUNION. Some members of the 1922 football squad got together at the 1967 Homecoming. Front row, left to right, are Karl "Jakey" Bohren, George Carson, manager; Dr. L. N. "Nick" Colonna, and Dr. Thomas H. Holleran, captain. In the second row are J. P. "Pat" Herron, assistant coach, Mike Hartnett, Yhlard "Hank" Handgartner, and Lloyd Jordan. In the top row are J. "Hube" Wagner, team physician, J. Franklin "Tiny" Miller, Jack Sack, and Dr. "Red" Seidelson.

Even so, Warner was an athletic god, with a lifetime Pitt record of 59-11-4, and Sutherland had to show in a hurry that he had what it took to be a winner.

Construction on mammoth Pitt Stadium started in 1924, at a cost of $2,125,000, and was scheduled for completion for the start of the 1925 football season. From then on, all Panther athletic teams would find permanent homes in the massive bowl rather than playing at Forbes Field, Motor Square Garden, or Trees Gymnasium. It originally seated

67,000, but was scaled down to its present 56,500 capacity.

Sutherland's first team produced a 5-3-1 record. A summary of the season in the school yearbook went like this:

"Facing the stiff task of shaping unknown material of little experience into a football team worthy of representing the University against nine of the best elevens Eastern America could boast, Coach Sutherland succeeded.

"His difficulties were neither realized nor appreciated by the public, but there is no need to make excuses, for he not

Ground Breaking
Pitt Stadium
August 7, 1924

Architects' Model

East Entrance - Pitt Stadium

only overcame them, but finally produced a lineup that compared with the finest.

"No, Pitt football hasn't died; it is only getting started."

Two of Sutherland's stars that first season were quarterback Jack "Spike" Harding and fullback Andy Gustafson, who would one day team up again to direct the University of Miami's football and athletic fortunes.

Pitt lost to Lafayette, 10-0, in the second game of the season. Sutherland had been succeeded there as head coach by another former Pitt player, Herb McCracken.

Pitt registered 28 first downs to none in knocking off Johns Hopkins, 26-0, then turned around and lost seven fumbles inside the 10-yard line (three of them inside the 5-yard line) while losing for the second time in as many years to cross-town rival Carnegie Tech, this time by 6-0.

The first Sutherland-coached team brought its season to a successful conclusion on Thanksgiving Day by defeating Penn State, 24-3. Sutherland had taken his team to Ligonier for a week-long seclusion prior to the annual holiday meeting.

"The Panthers returned to Pittsburgh the morning of the game," according to one report, "with a new spirit and determination to do or die in their last contest."

Sutherland had started a good thing at his alma mater.

Under the leadership of an All-American tackle named Ralph "Horse" Chase, the Pitt football team in 1925 compiled the school's best record since 1916 with an 8-1 mark.

Gustafson was the big offensive star, and scored the first touchdown ever scored in the new Pitt Stadium. In the later games on the schedule, a member of the school's fabulous freshman team of the previous season stepped forth and showed his stuff in earnest. That was Gilbert "Gibby" Welch. His fine running, especially his noted 80-yard run from scrimmage against Penn State, and his foward passing made him a two-way weapon.

Playing in its new stadium, Pitt re-established itself as one of the nation's finest football teams. Before a full house on the Stadium's Dedication Day, they defeated Tech, 12-0.

Pitt lost a lot of good players from its 1925 team, and hit some snags in its 1926 schedule. "It featured the grit and determination for which Panther athletic teams are famous," it was written in the Owl yearbook.

After barely beating Allegheny, tying Georgetown and losing to Lafayette, the Panthers found themselves and clipped Colgate, 19-16. Carnegie Tech was next, and the Tartans whipped Pitt, 14-0. Then the Panthers pulled themselves together and defeated Westminster, 88-0, West Virginia, 17-7, had a scoreless tie with W&J, and stopped Penn State, 24-6.

Welch was the leading ground gainer in the country that season, and he gave Pitt most of its offensive punch. "Tiny" Linn and Bill Kern were great on the line. Captain Blair McMillin was a good, dependable leader playing end opposite John Kifer.

There were 50,000 at the Stadium the day that Carnegie Tech played Pitt. The Tech team had walloped Notre Dame earlier in the season, and led by their All-American tackle Bull Yoder, and their flashy back, "Daredevil" Donohoe, who scored two touchdowns, they carried the day.

Sutherland knew he had a soft spot on the schedule with Westminster, and went to Philadelphia that day to scout W&J in action, leaving "Chalky" Williamson to guide the home team through its most decisive victory of the season. Welch scored four long touchdowns that day.

There were 55,000 at the Stadium to see "Galloping Gibby" turn the game into a track meet in the season finale, a 24-6 victory over Penn State.

Tuffy McMillan expressed his appreciation at season's end: "A spirit of loyalty, confidence in self, character were some of the things which Jock gave us," he wrote. "It is the qualities that football develops in an individual which makes the game the 'American man' sport it is. Jock and his assistants have prepared us for life."

John McGrady, the team manager, also penned an impressive reflection on the team's pre-season training headquarters:

"At the mention of Camp Hamilton to any of those who

BROKEN FIELD. Tommie Davies sprinted 19 years for TD to lead Pitt to 35-0 victory over Syracuse in 1922.

THE PANTHER — Formed by the faculty and students of The University of Pittsburgh — April 9, 1920.

have done time there brings first a glamourless memory of monotonous plugging, of sprains and bruises and fatigue; but then comes the memory of the chill of the cool evenings, the dripping dampness of white tents, the rushing murmur of Paint Creek, the discordant jangling of the first bell.

"At Camp Hamilton, acquaintances are formed and friendships sealed. There is an irrepressible spirit born of perseverance and self-sacrifice which draws and binds the men together. Inconveniences are undergone willingly, injuries borne patiently, strict training rules adhered to without protest.

"Any player will tell you that it is these few weeks at Camp Hamilton that inculcate a fighting spirit into the members of the squad, which gives zest to the whole season."

After two weeks of such hard preliminary polishing in the hills of Central Pennsylvania, at the Windber training site, Sutherland's fourth Pitt team was set for an unbeaten season. They won eight games and had a scoreless tie with Washington & Jefferson during the regular season. They outscored the opposition, 283 points to 20.

A 21-13 victory over Nebraska's big powerhouse is a memorable one for Welch. "We were two-touchdown underdogs against Nebraska, he recalled. "We had the ball on our own 19-yard line and I called a pass. I called the signals for us. Now, we almost never passed.

"Jimmy Hagan was to throw the ball and I was to catch it. In the huddle, Hagan said to me, 'Jock will raise hell.' I said, 'We'll do it anyway.'

"Hagan threw the pass. We caught Nebraska flat-footed and scored. We won the game. And Jock didn't object to the way we did it."

Welch came from Parkersburg, W. Va., and before the WVU game each year Jock would say in his Scottish accent, "Geeb, this is your week." Geeb's 105-yard kickoff return against WVU was an accident, though, he says.

Backing up as he watched the flight of the ball, Welch did not realize he was in the end zone. "If I had, it isn't likely I would have gambled," he said. Against Nebraska, Welch had a kickoff return of 97 yards.

Pitt was invited at season's end to play in the Rose Bowl in Pasadena, California. It was the first bowl invitation ever extended to Pitt. There, they dropped a hard-fought 7-6 decision to Pop Warner's Stanford Indians.

"The long train ride across the continent and the dizzying heat of California," went one explanation, "coupled with a wonderful Stanford eleven to give the champions of the East their only reversal of the season. The honor alone of being the pick of Eastern teams to represent this section of the football firmament in the Rose battle was fitting tribute to Coach Sutherland and his golden warriors."

Welch and Kern were both first-team All-American selections at the close of the season.

The 1928 team was regarded as a good one, with a record of six victories, two defeats and a scoreless tie with Nebraska. But the two defeats were to area schools, and that had to be difficult to swallow.

West Virginia, with one of the best teams in its history, came to Pitt Stadium in the third game of the season and upset the Panthers, 9-6. Two weeks later, Carnegie Tech took the measure of the Pitt men by 6-0. Those 15 points were the only ones scored against Pitt the entire season.

They shut out seven other opponents. The defensive standouts that season were Captain Alec Fox, Albert Guarino, Luby DiMeolo, Ray Montgomery and Charles Tully. Montgomery was labeled "the perfect guard" by Sutherland.

Mike Getto, a unanimous choice for All-American tackle, was the outstanding Panther of the year.

Joe Donchess, a junior end, again received All-American attention. Octavius "Toby" Uansa, and Josh Williams were two fast backs who were hard to stop. Tom Parkinson had a good year at fullback, and was a triple threat man.

CAPTAIN ALEC FOX

TOBY UANSA

LONG DASH. Karl Bohren raced 80 yards on this play in 20-3 victory over Penn State at Forbes Field on Thanksgiving Day, 1923.

The best of those ballplayers all came back for the 1929 season and what a season that was. Pitt posted a 9-1 record that season, and was named by the Parke H. Davis Ratings as the nation's No. 1 football team.

It was Sutherland's first national championship squad and the fourth in school history.

Four Pitt performers gained All-American recognition that year. Montgomery, Uansa, Parkinson and Donchess were all chosen first-team by one A-A team or another.

Pitt went undefeated during the regular schedule in 1929, running up a 53-0 victory over Waynesburg in the opener, defeating Duke, 52-7, then West Virginia, 27-7, in the next two games.

Then they knocked off Nebraska by 12-7; Allegheny, 40-0; Ohio State, 18-2; W&J, 21-0; Penn State, 20-7; and Carnegie Tech, 34-13.

For the second time in Sutherland's tenure, Pitt was invited to the Rose Bowl. The result was disastrous, as Southern Cal clobbered the Panthers, 47-14.

It was some time before Pitt and Sutherland lived down that embarrassment. It was no way to end such an outstanding decade of excellence.

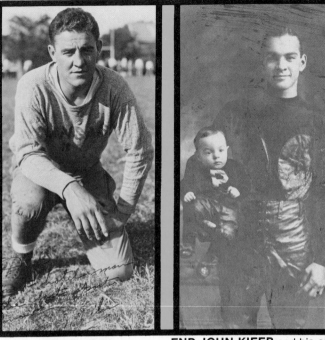

MIKE GETTO

END JOHN KIFER and his one-year-old son, Johnny, Jr., in 1925.

TRY THIS ON FOR SIZE — Paul Fisher is fitted for an old-fashioned helmet by Joe Skladany, as one-time official "Red" Friesell, left, and Tommy Davies look on admiringly at Duquesne Light sports memorabilia exhibition.

RAY MONTGOMERY

1927 PITTSBURGH FOOTBALL SQUAD

Top Row, Left To Right: Sutherland (Coach); Cutler, Center; Sargent, End; Kern, Tackle; Faw, Tackle; Getto, Tackle; Klinger, Tackle; Roberts, Guard; Marohnic, Guard; Corson, Tackle; Doverspike, Guard; Fisher, Quarterback; Shaw, Center; Sheriko, End; Wasmuth, Tackle; Second Row, Left To Right: Parkinson, Fullback; Fioch, Fullback; Bowen, Halfback; Mier, Tackle; Hogan, Halfback; Welch, Halfback and Captain; Booth, Fullback; Edwards, Quarterback; Fox, Guard; R. Goldberg, Center; Salada, Tackle; Montgomery, Guard. Lower Row, Left To Right: Donchess, End; Mahoney, Tackle; Guarino, End; Hoban, Halfback; Demoise, End; Wilps, Halfback; P. Goldberg, End; Uansa, Halfback; Trapanza, Guard; Siefert, Tackle.

That 1929 Team Had Quite A Background

They were starters on the first of the five national championship football teams turned out by Jock Sutherland and they were something special.

It was a different era and that is quickly evident by looking at the backgrounds of the members of Sutherland's 1929 squad.

Captain Albert "Luby" DiMeolo, for instance, had roots that are remarkably similar to Serafino "Foge" Fazio, the current coach. His parents were born in Naples, Italy. He was born in Youngstown, Ohio and grew up in Coraopolis.

During the summers, he worked as a lifeguard at the Coraopolis beach, yanking numerous swimming aspirants from the murky waters of the Ohio River. During the fall, he was a fine right guard for the Panthers.

Octavius George "Toby" Uansa, the starting left halfback, was born in Germany. His parents were natives of Rumania. He grew up in McKees Rocks, where he earned 16 letters in sports in high school. During the summer he was heralded as the home run king of the local sandlots while playing outfield for the Stowe Civics.

Eddie Baker, the quarterback, was a native of Nanticoke, Pa., where he was a three-sport star in high school. His parents were born in Poland. He was also a fine basketball player at Pitt. He later coached the Carnegie Tech football team.

Fullback Tom "Pug" Parkinson's parents were born in England, but he grew up in California, Pa.

Joe Donchess, the starting left end, may be the most interesting story. His parents were from Germany, but he grew up in Youngstown.

He left grammar school when he was in seventh grade to go to work to help out the family's financial situation. He remained there five years. An executive of the firm, attracted by the diligence of young Donchess, sent Joe to the Wyoming (Pa.) Seminary. His hard work obtained Donchess his college entrance requirements in four years.

As a senior on the 1929 team, Donchess gained All-American honors. He attended Pitt's School of Medicine and became a doctor in 1932. While attending grad school, he also coached the Pitt football team from 1930-32. He coached the ends at Dartmouth from 1933-37 while doing graduate work in its school of medicine. After Dartmouth, he began a career as an orthopedic surgeon. He later became a medical director at U.S. Steel.

Donchess was a big contributor to the University for over 30 years and from 1960-62 was the Chairman of the Pitt Annual Giving Fund. In recognition of his special contributions, the Pitt football training room — inside Gate 3 at Pitt Stadium — was dedicated in his memory after he died in 1978. His wife sent the school a check for $30,000 in his memory in 1982.

There were other unique young men on that '29 team that posted a 9-0 record before being stopped by Southern Cal in the Rose Bowl.

The right end was Paul "Rip" Collins, who came out of Sioux City, Iowa, on the border of the Bad Lands. The center Ralph Daugherty was a sophomore who would gain All-American recognition. He was from Freeport, but played halfback for Tarentum High, Bellefonte Academy and Kiski Prep.

The left tackle Charles Tully and the left guard, All-American Ray Montgomery, were from Wheeling, the right tackle James MacMurdo was from Ellwood City. The right halfback Josh Williams was from Mars — Mars, Pa. that is.

In a sense, they were all out of this world.

JOE DONCHESS — As Dartmouth Coach

EDDIE BAKER — Pitt Captain

Jock Sutherland

Marty Wolfson

84

Before going up on the hill to begin spring practice, I want to take a few moments of your time. You older members of the squad have heard before what I have to say, therefore my remarks will be directed to those of you who are reporting for the first time to the varsity. It won't, however, do the others any harm to have their memories refreshed.

The practice sessions which are now about to begin are limited to number and duration. This means your coaches have an allotted time to teach you the system and you have an allotted time to absorb it.

It will be necessary, therefore, for each of you, from the time you arrive on the field until you leave it, to devote your entire thought and energy to the program I have mapped out for you during this spring session. If you do this with the proper spirit and attitude, you should learn a lot of football and be well advanced when the fall practice opens.

In former years I have frequently had a boy report for practice who was under the impression that when he was called upon to practice football, his classroom activities ceased. I am sure none of the older members of the squad are laboring under this misapprehension, and I trust that none of the new candidates are.

Your school work, and I mean work, now as before and after, comes first. Unless your marks are maintained, you cannot play football, because you will become ineligible and I shall be required to take your suit away from you.

But even if this were not so, I would urge you to keep in mind that your education comes first. You are in school for the sole purpose of getting an education that will enable you to live a more useful life.

The time you spend in football will unquestionably better qualify you to find your place in the world, particularly if you play the game of life as I hope you will play the game of football, to win, putting every ounce of determination you have into it.

In three years from now, your active participation in football will be over, but that which you get from the books you are given to study will benefit you the rest of your life. It has further been my observation that a good student is an easier boy to teach football to than a poor one.

Now go up to the practice field and dig in. Football is a rugged, rough, and tough game, and that is why we like it — and play it. In playing a game of football there are certain things you must never forget. First, you should never lose your temper. Second, under no circumstances ever do anything that will bring discredit to you or your team.

Your schedule for the coming season is a tough one, but here at Pitt we are used to, and like them tough.

High Spots in Career Of Jock Sutherland

1889 — Born at Cooper Angus, Scotland, March 21, 1889.

1907 — Came to this country from Scotland at age of 18.

1910 — Prepped at Oberlin Academy, Oberlin, Ohio.

1914 — Entered University of Pittsburgh, played football under Coach Pop Warner 1914, '15, '16 and '17.

1918 — Entered United States Army, played and coached football at Camp Greenleaf.

1919 — Coach at Lafayette College for five years, 1919, '20, '21, '22 and '23.

1924 — Succeeded Pop Warner as Pitt coach and remained for 15 years through 1938.

1939 — Resigned as Pitt coach, March 4, 1939. Remained out of football during 1939.

1940 — Signed to coach Brooklyn Dodger pros. Remained two seasons, 1940 and 1941.

1942 — Enlisted as lieutenant commander in Navy. Remained in service three years.

1945 — Signed five-year contract to coach Pittsburgh Steelers on December 28, 1945. Coached for two years.

Panthers Became National Power On Single Wing During Torrid '30s

By Eddie Beachler

"Pittsburgh's pugnacious Panthers played the Trojans off their feet."

—Braven Dyer

It was a time of Hoagy Carmichael's Star Dust and the Big Bands ... and Brother, Can You Spare a Dime? It was a time of nickel hamburgers at the White Tower, dime beer at Trabert's bar, all you can eat spaghetti dinners for two-bits at Caruso's restaurant, at the foot of Cardiac Hill ... and breadlines, Shantytowns and Father Cox's Army of the jobless marching on Washington, D.C.

It was a time when grade school kids bummed a dime from Dad for a brick to finish the Cathedral of Learning ... which Pitt students called the Height of Ignorance.

It was a time before there were any thoughts of building dormitories ... when the only Pitt football players who lived decently waited on tables in fraternity houses to get a square meal, and a place to bunk.

This was the Torrid or Terrible Thirties, depending on your point of view and how much you had in your pocket ... a time when Pitt football was just about the only thing people had to cheer in the gloom of THE Depression, Same Old Steelers and Gabby Hartnett's home run that knocked the Pirates out of a pennant.

This was the time when Pitt became a dominant national power chewing up the best teams from coast to coast — Nebraska, Notre Dame, Southern Cal, Fordham, Southern Methodist, Wisconsin, Duke and Minnesota (but also lost heart-breakers to the latter two).

Yeah, with the old Single Wing. Their opponents needed the prayer.

This was the era of the Sutherland Scythe, so named by Chet Smith, Press Sports Editor. The rhythmic beauty of the off-tackle play, pulling guards, blocking quarterbacks and fullbacks paving the way for tailbacks taking four steps out, then cutting in to rip through the toughest defenses. Hartwig, Ormiston, Petro, Lezouski, Baker, Michelosen, Chickerneo, Weinstock, Weisenbaugh, Patrick, Stapulis, Heller, Sebastian, Goldberg, Cassiano.

Pitt always was in the thick of it, either winning the national championship or determining who did. One of the few college teams to win back-to-back national titles (1936-37) and the only team ever to refuse a Rose Bowl bid at a time when there no other major bowls.

Over a 9-year stretch (1930-38) Pitt lost only 10 games, playing the toughest intersectional schedules and produced the biggest crop of All-Americans. Sixteen, including three repeaters, better than one a year: the two-time All-Americans were Muggsy Skladany, Marshall Goldberg and Bill Daddio; the others were Jess Quatse, Warren Heller, Doc Hartwig, George Shotwell, Izzy Weinstock, Art Detzel, Ave Daniell, Biff Glassford, Frank Souchak, and Tony Matisi.

This was the era that established football as THE spectator sport in Pittsburgh. That drew record Pitt Stadium crowds of 75,000, more than the Rose Bowl or any other bowl up to that time. That produced intense local rivalries, putting Carnegie Tech and Duquesne in bowl games and made Pittsburgh the national capital of football.

This was the era when the first Golden Panthers recruiting organization of boosters was formed under the banner of the mythical College of the North. A fun-loving benevolent organization with stationery that bore the whimsical motto of "Not One Cent for the Chancellor — Everything for Football."

The president and poet laureate was Jim Marks, a master of doggerel and coach of Kiski Prep. Kiski, along with Bellefonte Academy, incubated All-Americans and fed them to Pitt, Stanford, Penn, Princeton, Harvard and other powers of that day. Chet Smith of The Press was a driving force behind the organization, as well as the Curbstone Coaches, a Monday morning second guessing group.

If a good prospect was too young for college, or needed extra schooling to mature and put on a few pounds, he was salted away in Saltsburg or Bellefonte.

The Golden Panther boosters in those days, *trusties,* as they were known, of the College of the North, included Bill McClintock, Harrisburg paper-box manufacturer; Bill Sullivan, McKeesport High football coach-building-real estate tycoon; Dave Thompson, Pittsburgh stockbroker-art collector; Dr. Charley Gordon, Pittsburgh dentist; Bob Herbert, Greensburg newspaper publisher; Don Saunders, Pitt alumni secretary and later editor of McCall Publications; Vince McGuinness, Philadelphia broker.

When Frank Souchak, All-American end, arrived from the coal fields with a battered overnight bag and patches on the elbows of his only jacket, a member of the College of the North marched him downtown and bought him his first suit and topcoat. This was standard procedure for many needy Panthers, just to help them survive and emerge with successful careers.

However, the basic ingredient of Pitt's success was Dr. Jock Sutherland, who taught dentistry, a master at detail and organization of a great coaching staff of former Pitt players: Bill Kern, Dr. Eddie Baker, Dr. Skip Gougler, Doc Hartwig, Dr. Ralph Daugherty, Mike Milligan, Charley Bowser, Ken Ormiston, John Michelosen, Eddie Schultz, Don Hensley and Dr. Bud Moore, the team trainer.

Dr. Jock set the pace striding up Cardiac Hill to the practice field and insisting his players do the same. He admonished those who hitched a ride, in his Scottish burr, to "get off that cur." And the penalty was extra laps.

This was the coaching staff and Golden Panther recruiters who pioneered in developing the two-team system. Two teams that were almost equal in strength. The first team played the first and third quarters, going both

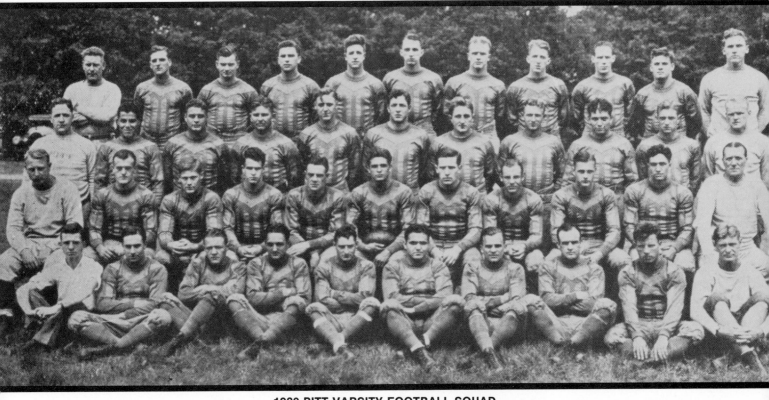

1930 PITT VARSITY FOOTBALL SQUAD

Reading from left to right: Back Row — Gougler, frosh coach; Reider, Williams, Cuba, Daugherty, R. Morris, Yentch, H. Morris, Alpert, Schindehutte, Montgomery, assistant line coach. Third Row — Hangartner, assistant line coach; Walton, Luch, Hood, Anderson, McMurdo, Hirschberg, Walinchus, Quatse, Dailey, Kern, assistant line coach. Second Row — Gustafson, backfield coach; Babic, Ciper, Miller, Collins, Captain Baker, Tully, Heller, Tommins, Cutri, Head Coach Sutherland. First Row — Kearney, manager; Brown, Sekay, Wagner, Kelly, Lewis, Schultz, Milligan, Clark, Donchess, assistant coach.

ways; the second team the second and fourth quarters, with some substitutions when the game demanded it. By the time the fourth quarter arrived the second team could beat you with this one-two punch if the first team hadn't already done it.

This was the forerunner of the specialized system we see today — offensive and defensive teams, plus the added dimension of specialty teams on kickoffs, punt returns, passing situations, punts and goal-line stands.

Sutherland introduced another new wrinkle in converting big, fast high school backs into All-American ends, guards and centers. Such as Hartwig, Ken Ormiston, Ralph Daugherty, Souchak, and Daddio.

Pitt opened the 1930 season still smarting from its second successive loss in the Rose Bowl, a 47-14 pasting of a Panther team that had rolled undefeated by what many regarded as Howard Jones' greatest USC eleven.

That was the game that gave rise to the legend of feuding in the locker room over no fewer than four Pitt All-Americans (Joe Donchess, Ray Montgomery, Toby Uansa and Pug Parkinson). Someone remarked "something smells bad in this dressing room." To which Capt. Luby DiMeolo reportedly replied "It must be the All-Americans." Uansa, a speedster, ran out of gas on the kickoff with an open field ahead of him — and the Trojan rout was on.

But this was to be just a rebuilding season. After romping through four games without giving up a point the Panthers met their Waterloo in one of Knute Rockne's last great teams, 35-12, before he was to die in a tragic plane crash. It drew a record Stadium crowd of 74,000, the first game of an Irish series that Pitt was to dominate.

Pitt had its moments, blanking no fewer than seven drives by Syracuse, which had what was regarded as one of the best lines in the East, 14-0. And Eddie Baker beat All-American Howard Harpster in a quarterback duel, booting the point in a 7-6 upset of a Carnegie Tech team that had tumbled mighty Notre Dame while Rockne was away scouting Army.

However, five successive tough games exacted their toll as personable Wesley Fesler passed Ohio State to a 16-7 win, while Bulldog Reider got some measure of revenge by scampering 57 yards around All-American Fesler's end for the Pitt score.

— From the University Archives

ROSE BOWL BOUND — Imposing lineup includes, left to right, Mike Sebastian, Bob Hogan, Izzy Weinstock, Warren Heller and Paul Reider, as they head for 1932 Rose Bowl and embarrassing 35-0 blanking by Southern Cal.

1933 ROSE BOWL TEAM — Linemen, left to right, Joe Skladany, Frank Walton, Tarcisio Onder, George Shotwell, Charley Hartwig, Paul Cuba, Ted Dailey. Backfield, Mike Sebastian, Bob Hogan, John Lynch, Warren Heller.

Fesler, later in the 1940s, was to attempt to rescue Pitt football from the doldrums, but failed.

Warren Heller's 35- and 80-yard TD runs in a 19-12 finale with Penn State left Pitt still supreme in the East, but with two scores to pay back to the Midwest.

With the entire line returning and only two regulars graduating, the Sutherland Scythe chopped down eight opponents in 1931, averaging better than 30 points, but lost to the Irish again, 25-12.

The game at South Bend was a crunching line battle, decided by the brilliant passing of Marchy Schwartz.

A fine Nebraska team will never forget a 40-0 carving in Pitt Stadium on Thanksgiving Day; and Pitt dispelled some of its reputation as a grind-it-out team, flashing some unexpected razzle-dazzle in slaying Army, 26-0.

Quarterback Bobby Hogan was hurt early in that game. Rocco Cutri replaced him, with halfback and Captain Reider calling his own plays. With Heller and Rip Collins (on an end-around) throwing to the Bulldog the future generals were given a preview of the World War II aerial bombardment. Collins, of Sioux City, Iowa, and a bona fide hog caller, was one of the first immigrants to be recruited from distant states.

How many teams have been held scoreless in two games, yet were undefeated and invited to the Rose Bowl?

Only one. The 1932 Pitt team was chosen for a rematch with Southern Cal, the first Eastern team to play in the granddaddy bowl as many as three times. All in the short space of six years. Despite two scoreless ties with powerhouse Nebraska and Ohio State.

Overlooked were Coach Andy Kerr, the canny Scot who served a stint here at Washington & Jefferson, and his undefeated-untied-unscored on — AND UNINVITED Col-

gate Red Raiders, and undefeated-untied Michigan.

Fancy that! But the reasons were considerable. Mainly a shocking 12-0 Pitt upset of high-scoring Notre Dame that had been hailed as the "Team of the Century." Pitt's first success over the Fighting Irish.

That, plus shutting out Stanford with no first downs in the first half to wreck ex-Pitt Coach Pop Warner's return to the Eastern football wars. Dumping unbeaten Penn in Philadelphia in a 19-12 thriller. Staging three long TD drives in an 18-13 come from behind nail-biter over Army.

Not to mention the fact that Pitt was a favorite of Hollywood stars, notably comedian Joe E. Brown who adopted the Panthers as "my team" on their two previous losing performances in the Roses and Joe never sued for non-support. The romance with Pittsburgh teams started out there at San Bernardino, where the Pirates trained, and his son, Joe L., came East as GM to lead the Pirates to three great World Series championships.

There has been no spunkier Pitt team that overcame more obstacles or greater odds than the '32 Panthers. Never mind that they were blown out for the second time by a fumble, interception and three fourth-quarter touchdowns, 35-0, by another great Trojan team sparked by Cotton Warburton. The loss was anti-climatic. The nation still loved 'em. Only Colgate sent flowers.

Pitt fans remembered Bobby Hogan intercepting an Irish pass followed by Mike Sebastian, the Sharon Express, roaring 40 yards on a reverse for the first TD and Ted Dailey applying the clincher with a 36 yard interception run. The very first win over the Fighting Irish. How sweet it was!

That was a team loaded with All-American talent and the birth of the two-team system that was to propel Pitt to the heights.

Tailback Heller was brilliant despite the loss of his top receiver, Reider, who was injured early in the season, and made every All-American team; Skladany grabbed two 50-yard passes against Army and Harvey Rooker choked off the last desperate drive near the goal in a game the Cadets dominated. Skladany (two times), Hartwig, George Shotwell and Weinstock went on to become All-Americans. No fewer than five on that team.

The 1933 debut of a team touted for national honors was a shocker. For 56 minutes a gritty Washington & Jefferson team refused to believe the Panther credentials and fought the heavily-favored Panthers to a standstill.

Then, Weinstock booted a 30-yard field goal and Howie O'Dell, the all-time quick-kick artist, threaded his way through the Prexies for the only TD in a 9-0 squeaker.

Pitt introduced a Panther cub mascot named Jock at Navy and that seemed to help in a 34-6 romp while the Panthers managed to choke off the whirling-dervish running of Buzz Borries by clipping him out of bounds.

That set the stage for the first Neanderthal struggle for the national championship with Bernie Bierman's Golden Gophers. It was a titanic struggle of brawn against brawn in Minnesota.

Pug Lund won it with an underhand toss to Tanner of 14 yards, while Weinstock booted a field goal in the 7-3 blockbuster. Pitt fumbled it away — coughing up the ball twice within less than five yards of the end zone. It was the only loss in nine games.

Favored for the first time against Notre Dame, the Panthers bounced back the next week in rain-drenched South Bend before 20,000, the smallest crowd in this fierce series. Demoted sub Sebastian galloped 75 yards in a 19-0 first half mud bath. The Irish threatened just once, Ormiston intercepting to stop that, while absorbing their second-straight loss to tie the series.

The Panthers maintained their hex over Nebraska, 6-0, with O'Dell quick-kicking the Huskers into the hole and Sebastian in high gear — refusing substitution on being kayoed three times.

It was the year of atonement for Pitt in 1934, laying it on Southern Cal as repayment for two Rose Bowl poundings, but the big buster was a disheartening loss, you guessed it, again to Minnesota for the national title.

No greater drama has unfolded than this battle of the monsters of the Midwest and East before a tense crowd of 65,000 in Oakland.

The Panthers had rambled over neighboring W&J and West Virginia, and the Trojans, by the substantial margin of 20-7.

Pitt came up with a surprise passing attack, featuring a lateral from Weisenbaugh to Mike Nicksick (Nixon), and an aggressive defense. This time the Howard Jones Boys made the fatal miscues, a fumble recovered by Miller Munjas and blocked kick by Verne Baxter led to two Pitt scores. Baxter also made a sensational catch of a Hub Randour pass for the clincher.

Comedian Joe E. Brown and actor Regis Toomey, College '21 alumnus, flew in to provide the Hollywood entertainment at halftime.

That set the stage for the classic battle with the Golden Giants from the corn and wheat fields of Minnesota. Baxter added to the pre-game drama by disappearing the day before the game which made eight-column headlines on Page One. He was found wandering in Schenley Park, suffering from amnesia, the result of a blow in the Trojan game — and unable to play.

Outweighed 20 pounds a man, Pitt charged out in its white jerseys, which Jock considered lucky, gold pants and blue helmets. Thousands of fans who couldn't get into the packed Stadium rimmed the surrounding hills for this early showdown for the national title and revenge for the tough loss at Minneapolis the previous year.

The white shirts held Lund, Tenner, Larson, Bengston, Widseth, Bevan, Kostka and Company without a first down until the final minute of the third period. Pitt was anchored by three All-Americans in the middle, possibly the best ever — Captain Hartwig, Ormiston and Shotwell, a skinny 168-pound string-bean who looked like Abe Lincoln.

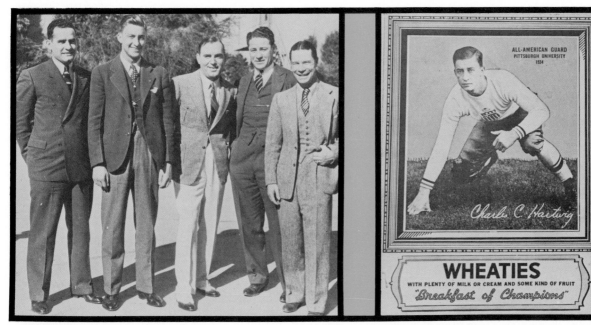

MOVIELAND — During a West Coast trip to participate in the East-West Shrine Game, Pitt performers, left to right, Miller Munjas and Charley Hartwig, along with Izzy Weinstock, second from right, visit with movie stars Pat O'Brien and Joe E. Brown.

WHEATIES HERO — Charles C. Hartwig was a national hero, as indicated by his appearance on the Wheaties cereal box. Better yet, how about "free silverware" — that's really a sign of the times.

READY FOR WAR — Combat-ready 1934 seniors include, left to right, George Shotwell, Harvey Reeler, Frank Kotz, Karl Sieffert, Captain "Doc" Hartwig, Izzy Weinstock, Bob Hoel, Heinie Weisenbaugh, Ken Ormiston, Stan Olejnizak, Miller Munjas, Mike Nicksick. Nicksick became Mike Nixon, an NFL coach.

Pitt tacked seven points on the board late in the second quarter, with a startling 64-yard run engineered by fullback Weinstock, considered by many to be Pitt's best ever. Izzy broke through Minnesota's All-American tackle Ed Widseth, flipping the ball to Nicksick who scored a TD.

Then, in the final minute of the third quarter it happened. Sophomore Bobby LaRue grabbed a punt on the dead run and the ball was ripped out of his arms by Gopher All-American ends Tenner and Larson.

From the Pitt 48, the Gophers, powered by Stan Kostka, huge (230) reserve fullback, cracked the Pitt line. On the first play of the fourth quarter, fourth and two, another sub, Alfonse, cut inside the Pitt right end where Baxter normally played, a third-stringer unaffectionately known forever as Alice for his savoir faire of wearing white tie and tails at dances, for the tying TD, 7-7.

After a breather with Westminster, viewed by only 1,500 drowning fans in New Castle, Pitt played to its third sellout Stadium crowd of 63,000 and rang Notre Dame's bell, 19-0. The highlight, Weisenbaugh's 42-yard interception return of a pass by Bill Shakespeare — the passer not the poet — to set up the final score. It was one of the worst Irish defeats, giving the series lead to the Panthers.

Nebraska was next on the chopping block, 25-6, in Lincoln. Then Pitt pounded an undefeated Navy team, 31-6, in the battle for the Eastern championship. But only after a shaky 13-6 first half and the Panthers have yet to tackle Buzz Borries, containing him only by clipping him out of bounds.

It was Braven Dyer, of the Los Angeles Times, who typed the tribute to one of Pitt's greatest teams: "Pittsburgh's pugnacious Panthers played the Trojans off their feet . . . a triumph that was more convincing than the 20-6 score."

There were two minutes to play, score tied at South Bend, when Marty Peters swung his leg, missed the ball but got enough of the turf to lift the ball almost straight up. Thus avoiding the outstretched arms of Pitt rushers.

The ball wobbled down from the sky, scraping the back of the cross-bar for a 9-6 Notre Dame decision. It was the only Pitt loss in the 1935 rebuilding year and the only Irish victory in a six-year stretch with the Panthers.

It was the first and only field goal Peters tried and kicked in his college career — a great big one. Thus, Pitt for the fourth straight year was denied an undefeated season and the national title by a single loss — Minnesota and Southern Cal accounting for two disappointments apiece.

However, this was the year of a bumper sophomore group who were to lay the foundation for the national titles ahead — Frank Souchak, Tony Matisi, Frank Patrick, Don

Hensley, George Delich, Dante Dalle Tezze.

Line Coach Bill Kern recalls one of the pivotal plays was a loose Irish fumble Delich tried to run with. "Never forget you are just like me — a dumb tackle — and always fall on the ball, not run with it," Kern barked. The other play that back-fired, he recalled, was a Pitt punt that took a crazy bounce back to the point where it was kicked.

A second-straight win over Southern Cal in the finale, 12-7, evened the series and paid back two Rose Bowl defeats. Pitt drove 81 yards for the decisive TD and on five occasions stopped the Trojans within three yards of the goal. Souchak intercepted a pass, pitching the ball to guard Biff Glassford to set up the other Pitt score.

In between USC and ND there were two scoreless ties with Carnegie Tech and Fordham, the first of a never-ever-again "Goose-Egg Series" of three pointless, but classic struggles of irresistible forces.

Ave Daniell wasn't much of a football tackle at Mt. Lebanon High, coming out for the team mostly because he was the biggest kid in town and wanted to be with the other guys.

The round-faced, amiable redhead, resembling and known as "Lil' Abner," and not much over 200 pounds, became a rare, if not the only, Walk-On All-American and successful in three fabricating and aerospace industries.

"Lil' Abner" was a thinking man's tackle in the rise of the 1936 Panthers from the depths of a stunning loss to Duquesne to a blitz of heavily-favored Washington Huskies in the Rose Bowl. And a long-sought national title that had eluded them by a whisker for so many seasons.

Dr. Jock paid him this tribute: "One of the smartest tackles Pitt has produced — he had no bad habits and learned how to play his position the right way."

ROSE BOWL BUNCH — While preparing for the 1936 Rose Bowl, in which Pitt beat Southern Cal, 12-7, this fearsome four-some frolics for photographers, from left to right, Bill Glassford, Ave Daniell, George Delich and Tony Matisi.

Daniell, whose brother Jim was also an All-American tackle for Ohio State and captained both the Cleveland Browns and Chicago Bears pro teams, repaid the honors and business education he received by serving as one of the organizers and contributors to the present Golden Panthers to recruit players and return Pitt to championship status.

Seldom, if ever, has any team in one season climbed from the bottom to the top in such a topsy-turvy fashion as the '36 Panthers.

This was the crazy year that Duquesne beat Pitt, then the next week the Dukes lost to West Virginia Wesleyan.

—Photo from University Archives

ROSE BOWL BOUND — In the 91-year history of Pitt football, only nine Panther teams were considered national champions. This was one of them. Here, the 1936 club prepares for the Rose Bowl in Pasadena, the Panthers' fourth and final appearance in that game. The line, left to right, included Fabian Hoffman, Averell Daniell, Al Lezouski (Leeson), Henry Adams, Bill Glassford, Tony Matisi and Bill Daddio. Backfield, left to right, Curly Stebbins, Vince Stapulis, John Chickerneo and Marshall Goldberg.

BLOCKING BOBBY — Bobby LaRue (21) gets out to block for Biggie Goldberg (42) who aims to pass at Pitt Stadium.

Wesleyan in turn lost to St. Vincent and Pitt pounded Notre Dame to make St. Vincent the "round-about national Champion" by comparative scores — some 60 points better than the Fighting Irish.

To take it in order, Pitt met its first big test in Columbus, taking on an Ohio State team that had destroyed New York University's Rose Bowl hopes, 66-0.

The game was played on a bright Columbus Day, Oct. 12, made to order for the razzle-dazzle offense of Coach Francis "Close the Gates of Mercy" Schmidt. Presidential candidate Alf Landon was the guest of honor, seated in a box on the 50-yard line where they always seat dignitaries so they can't see the game. When he was introduced before the kickoff the roar was deafening.

But that was nothing compared with the ovation given Jumpin' Joe Williams, who had scored six TDs against NYU the previous week, on entering the game late in the second quarter when the Buckeyes moved across the midstripe for the first and only time.

Jumpin' Joe tried a reverse around Souchak's end. Boom. Then a double reverse around Daddio's end. Boom. Then a triple reverse around Souchak. Boom.

It was fourth down and 37 to go. And that was the end of the Buckeyes and Jumpin' Joe, who had been pumped up as Superman — even before the real Superman — by New York columnist Joe Williams (no wonder he liked him) off his shrinking of NYU's Violets in the Polo Grounds.

Ohio State was held to 77 total yards. Curley Stebbins swept off tackle for the only score, 34 yards behind perfect blocking, in the 6-0 game.

But the next week, Oh My! The rains came in a tidal wave at Pitt Stadium. But George Matsik, a reserve halfback who ironically came from the same hometown of Ambridge as Pitt star quarterback Johnny Michelosen, buried the Panthers by slithering 73 yards for the only score — while Linebacker Mike Basrak ripped the ball out of Leo

Malarkey's arms with a crunching tackle near the goal to end Pitt's only threat. First downs: Pitt 11, Dukes 3. Too bad. They don't count in figuring the final score.

This shocking first-time loss to their hometown rival Dukes was typical of a season of so-called upsets. Or were they set-ups?

What the nation's football buffs didn't know was that Duquesne had a very tough team that was on its way to yet another stunning upset of Mississippi State in the Orange Bowl and a long string of victories in the years ahead. And that Basrak would become an All-American and All-Pro (with the Steelers), and that Halfback Boyd Brumbaugh and others were as fine as any players in the game.

The Panther comeback was ignited by a remark by George Musulin, a reserve tackle who would be shot down behind enemy lines in Europe during War II. It was the first day of practice after the loss. Sutherland strode across Trees Field past a group of Pitt players, Musulin moaned, "I'm so damn mad losing to Duquesne that I'm gonna stop drinkin' that Duquesne beer."

Jock smiled a rare smile — he was all business, no levity on the football field. The players roared and the agony of defeat had been broken.

Pitt rebounded to thrash Notre Dame, 26-0, before a new record Stadium crowd of 70,244, with long runs on a pass caught by Fabian Hoffman and an interception return by Johnny Wood cracking it open. The Irish came into the game undefeated, and suffered the worst loss in a decade. When did anyone outgain the Irish 399 to 90 yards?

The Panthers rolled into the Rose Bowl for the fourth time, the only Eastern team to play in more than one Rose Festival. They were determined to avenge three Rose losses, the Duquesne debacle and the second successive scoreless tie with Fordham's Seven Blocks of Granite.

In previous trips they had always been well received by the press — but not this time. Their loss to the Dukes was

GRIM GROUP — The Pitt bench in 1937 battle.

suspect and there were nasty columns about "Why Pitt?" and the three previous "Rose El Foldoes!" This made Washington an overwhelming favorite.

However, a record crowd of 87,000 unbelievers showed up to see Pitt slam the door on the unbeaten, high-scoring Huskies, 21-0.

Every Panther was a star that day, beginning with Goldberg's early dash around end, Hensley's interception of a Hinky Haines pass to avert a Husky threat and ending with a 71-yard interception score by Daddio.

Like Ohio State, Notre Dame, Fordham and Nebraska had discovered earlier, Washington's vaunted attack was blunted — a total of 145 yards gained and four killing interceptions by an unrelenting and fierce Panther defense.

What can you do for an encore after you've climbed the Rose Bowl and national championship peaks?

You can come back with much the same squad, an even better record, win all the national honors and become the first and only squad ever to thumb its collective nose at the Rose Bowl.

That was Pitt '37. Two teams of almost equal strength. Either one could beat the hell out of you or, if you happened to have Fordham's Seven Blocks of Granite, at least shut you out.

If Pitt's first team didn't beat you, the second team would — alternating quarters, with substitutions when needed. Goldberg, Cassiano, Stebbins at halfbacks; Patrick and Stapulis at fullback; Michelosen and Chickerneo at quarterback; Souchak, Daddio, Hoffman at ends; Deitrick, Matisi and Merkovsky at tackles; Lesouski, Petro and Walt Raskowski at guards; Hensley and Adams at center.

While the "Dream Backfield" the next year gained the notoriety of the legendary "Four Horsemen," this was the real "Dream Team" or "Nightmare Express" to opponents. Because Goldberg played out of position at fullback to

make room for Cassiano at left half in '38 and the '37 wrecking crew was a lot deeper at every position.

In the first big test, Goldberg rambled 77 yards on the second play of the rematch with Duquesne, once again in a sea of mud and rain. That was enough to wrap it up, 6-0, and repay the Dukes for that '36 shocker.

Next was Fordham. Nowhere in the annals of football can you find major teams playing three successive scoreless ties. Sounds deadly, but that's what happened — and they were classic matchups.

That third game with the celebrated "Seven Blocks of Granite" — anchored by Alex Wojciechowicz, Ed Pierce and Vince Lombardi, and coached by "Sleepy" Jim Crowley, the former Horseman from Notre Dame, had everything but a score.

FORMER ALL-AMERICANS Ernie Nevers, left, and Claude "Tiny" Thornhill served as assistant coaches at Stanford, and Thornhill, an All-America tackle at Pitt in 1916, succeeded Pop Warner as the Indians' head coach in 1933.

PITT'S DREAM BACKFIELD. The Pitt Panther quartet working behind a formidable line, which struck terror into opposing collegiate defenses throughout the 1938 campaign. No. 21 is right halfback Curly Stebbins, quite a man on Jock Sutherland's deep reverse. Second from left is quarterback, No. 15 Johnny Chickerneo, rugged blocker and expert punter. No. 42 of course, is All-American Marshall (Biggie) Goldberg, the Elkins Express. No. 43 is Dick Cassiano, who stepped into the tailback spot when Sutherland switched Goldberg to fullback.

Pitt actually scored a touchdown on a Goldberg reverse without anyone laying a hand on him. But it was called back as All-American Tony Matisi was detected holding on the opposite side of the line, not at all involved in the play.

Fordham missed three short field goals and Pitt two, a masterpiece performance of defensive play and frustration. Pitt coughed up seven fumbles, giving the Rams chances for field goals as close as the 10. Pitt led with 11 first downs to the Rams 4, and in yards gained, 195-110.

All three of those scoreless games attracted capacity crowds of 55,000 to the Polo Grounds, and scalpers never had it so good with New York embracing Goldberg as a rare Jewish star.

The Panthers roared at South Bend the next week, packing Cartier Field with the first-ever capacity crowd, and beat the Fighting Irish at their own patented comeback game, scoring three TDs in the final quarter for a crushing 21-6 finish.

It was Goldberg lighting the fire again, with a long pass to Fabian Hoffman and then bulling to the one to set up the go-ahead score. Curly Stebbins capped a 66-yard march, waltzing the last 26 on a reverse for the second TD.

Then Stebbins intercepted a pass, Frank Patrick bulling 21 yards for the final tally.

Whenever did anyone hold Notre Dame to 97 yards and three first downs? This was a temporary break in a great series, Pitt won five of eight, and five of the last six, causing coach upheavals at the Golden Dome.

Next, Goldberg personally executed Wisconsin, coached by another Notre Dame Horseman, Harry Stuhldreher, with two scoring bursts. And Dandy Dick Cassiano flew 73 yards with a lateral in the 21-0 massacre of the Badgers, who gained just 13 yards.

Then, the undefeated Nebraskans rolled into the Stadium and the Panthers shattered their dreams of a national title, 13-7, before a new record crowd of 71,000 that overflowed into field bleachers.

Dana X. Bible's Huskers pulled a trick 60-yard reverse on a punt return to go ahead in the third quarter, but Pitt finally pulled it out in the fourth quarter with an 80-yard march and a fumble recovery drive of 33 yards.

Pitt's last challenger to an undefeated season was Duke. Under heavy tackling pressure in a muddy Stadium, the Blue Devil punt returner, Honey Hackney, fumbled twice in the first half inside his own 20.

Souchak recovered the first bobble, then booted a field goal. Ed Spotovich grabbed the second and Cassiano on the next play knifed 14 yards off tackle for the score and a perfect 10-0 ending.

Pitt was undisputed No. 1, invited to the Rose Bowl, but rejected the bid in an unprecedented team vote, 16-15. The reasons dated back to the 1936 Rose Bowl. Washington players received $100 for expenses, the winning Panthers nothing — for giving up their holidays and work income. The Pitt coaching staff dug into their own pockets to give each player $17 for spending money.

This was the spark that ignited the long smoldering feud of Athletic Director Don Harrison and Sutherland over policy, with Harrison telling him in Pasadena "I made you, now I'll break you." But it was only the tip of a new Bowman Code iceberg of reducing scholarships, recruiting and practice time, and retroactive disqualifications of fifth year red-shirts in an abortive effort to join the Big Ten Conference.

A sad event, just when Pitt had climbed to an all-time peak. It was to result in a prolonged fall to the depths of four decades of losing seasons, until the arrival of Chancellor Wesley Posvar and Athletic Director Casimir Myslinski decades later.

Harrison resigned after the season and Sutherland a year later when there was a continuing reduction of scholarships and recruiting without a corresponding reduction in schedules, saying: "I will never field a team that has no chance to win."

The 1938 Pitt team had a "Dream Backfield," rivaling the legendary "Four Horsemen" of Notre Dame. A blanket of white, later identified as snow by unbelieving North Carolinans, covered the field in Durham.

It was the last game of the season and the Panthers were making a last-desperate bid to retain their national title, against undefeated, untied, unscored-on Duke. Pitt had been upset by Carnegie Tech earlier, but still had a shot at the top berth.

The weather in Durham seemingly was more suited to the Northerners than the Southerners. Not so. It was made to order for the defensive-minded Blue Devils, and the toe of Eric (The Red) Tipton.

Kicking frequently on second or third down, Tipton kept Pitt continually in the hole with his pin-point placements. No fewer than 12 punts skittering out of bounds inside the 20 yard line — seven inside the 10, as close as the 1.

Until, finally, it happened. In the fourth quarter, Bolo Perdue blocked a Pitt punt and fell on it in the end zone. That's the way it ended, 7-0.

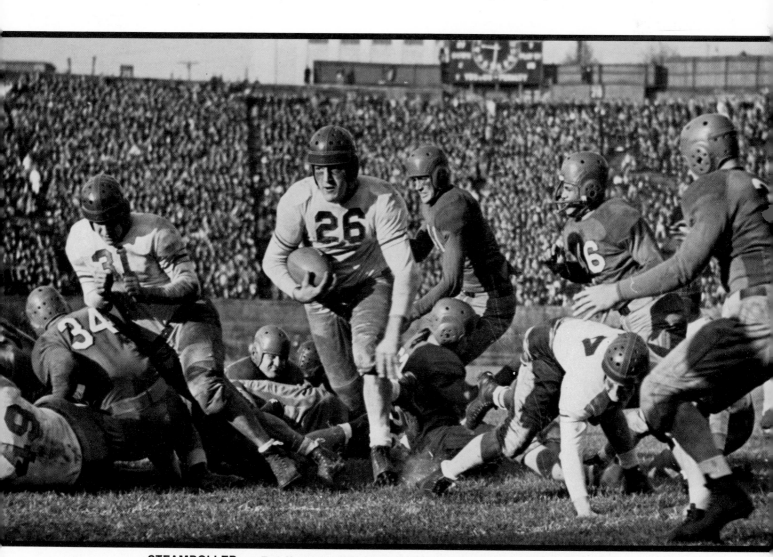

STEAMROLLER — Ted Konetsky (31) throws block that springs Ben Kish in 34-7 victory over Southern Methodist at Pitt Stadium in 1938.

Duke went to the Rose Bowl, Carnegie Tech went to the Sugar Bowl and Pitt went home.

The after game scene in the mud-splattered Pitt dressing room was heavy silence, broken only by players too heart-broken to pull off their uniforms, crying unashamedly. Not so much for the loss of a game, but for the loss of a coach.

It was Dr. Jock Sutherland's last college game, ending a 15-year Pitt reign as a national power, socking it to the best teams from coast to coast.

A few weeks earlier Pitt had been No. 1, with one of the greatest fourth-quarter explosions of 21 points that shattered three scoreless years with Fordham, 24-13. The all-time Stadium record of 75,867 cheering fans still stands.

Trailing 7-3, the "Dream Backfield" of Stebbins, Chickerneo, Cassiano and Goldberg, playing out of position at fullback to make room for Cassiano at tailback, struck back.

Daddio kicked a first quarter field goal. Then, Len Eshmont, with a Statute of Liberty long-gainer, sparked the Rams to a 7-3 lead shortly before half-time.

Pitt's great backs finally got it moving in the final quarter, Cassiano twisting away from two tacklers to end a 57-yard drive for the go-ahead score, 10-7.

After the kickoff, the Rams lost the ball on an ineligible receiver pass, giving Pitt possession on the 25. Boom. In six plays the Dream Boys took it in, Goldberg scoring.

Following the next kickoff, the Rams made a first down. Eshmont fumbled, Stebbins recovered and it was "All Goldberg" for the third touchdown in five plays. Marshall passed to John Dickinson for 43, rammed center for 4, circled end for 5, hit the middle for 9, then drew a mighty roar from the fans chewing up the last two yards on his patented off-tackle play.

Fordham registered a consolation TD on Eshmont passes against Panther reserves.

That explosive battle, coming on top of tough games with West Virginia, Pop Warner's Temple Owls, Duquesne, Wisconsin and Southern Methodist (Goldberg outpassed Matty Bell's aerial circus), plus the pressure of a 22-game winning streak, seemed to take something out of the Panthers for the annual city brawl with Carnegie Tech.

But no excuses. Tech had a strong squad, coached by two of Dr. Jock's sharpest disciples, and twice came from behind.

It began with a shocking 98-yard kickoff return by Stebbins. Tech came right back with a good kickoff return by Merlyn (The Magician) Condit and then a pass by Condit to George Muha in the end zone to make it 7-7.

Daddio kicked a field goal as the battle see-sawed. Then Pitt muffed a scoring chance after recovering a fumble on the Tech 17.

The Tartans fired back in the final minute of the half, intercepting a Stebbins pass. Condit's pass was deflected by Chickerneo and fell into the hands of Karl Streigel in the end zone for a heart-pounding end of the first half, 14-0.

That proved to be the end of it for Pitt. Two Tech scoring threats were stopped. The Tartans wrapped it up in the last quarter, taking advantage of a short Pitt punt from the end zone to the 21, and in five plays rammed it over, Muha taking it the last yard.

HISTORY-MAKING WEST COAST CARAVAN

FIRST TIME IN AIR — 1939 team made first airplane trip by any college grid team to Seattle where they beat Washington, 27-6.

In the final analysis, the Tartans closely outplayed Pitt and had a stronger squad that exposed the known weakness of the Panthers reserves in recording its most cherished win, comparable to their two big upsets of Knute Rockne's Irish.

Nebraska and Penn State were blown out, as usual, prior to the Duke Snowball, as Pitt closed out as tough and exciting a schedule as any team ever played, 8 and 2. For the first time, ironically, not winning a National, Eastern or City Championship.

Ignored in the 1939 pre-season national ratings for the first time since the Panther was a kitten, Pitt, coached by Charley Bowser, shocked even themselves by soaring to No. 1 with startling upsets in the first three games.

With only one member of the "Dream Backfield" remaining, All-American end Daddio and the rest of the Rose Bowl championship stars gone, Pitt made its first-ever trip by air to Seattle.

Nobody gave the Panthers a chance. Taking their cue from the air trip, they launched aerials of their own to shoot down a heavily-favored Washington team, 27-6. No one believed that score.

Emil Narick, now a sedate Judge of Common Pleas Court, flipped a TD pass to Joe Rettinger. Cassiano accounted for the second one with a pass and run. Ben Kish, who was part Indian, and became an All-Pro linebacker for the Philadelphia Eagles, caught a pass and bucked for two in the final quarter. Pitt completed 10 of 16 passes for 179 yards in the surprise attack.

Next, the Panthers chased West Virginia back to the hills, 20-0. This was followed by the greatest shocker of all on the strangest play of all at the expense of Duke and the McAfee brother halfbacks, George and Wes.

On the play that won the game, Wes McAfee caught a pass in the clear with John Dickinson trailing him. Dickinson, who became a leading surgeon, yelled: "Lateral! Lateral!" McAfee obliged and the ball fell in the arms of a startled Dickinson, who reversed his field and romped 47 yards to the Duke 10, setting up a Narick TD pass to Cassiano to turn the game around.

Cassiano twice caught George McAfee from behind in the open field with saving tackles and nabbed a second TD pass from Narick. Kish booted the clutch extra point, 14-13.

The Pitt bubble burst the following week against Buff Donelli's Duquesne Dukes, 21-13, followed by the first loss to Fordham in five years, the first loss to Nebraska in 18 years and the first loss to Penn State in 20 years.

The Panthers had one last gasp against Carnegie Tech. Edgar (Special Delivery) Jones, the most under-rated back in Pitt history, passed to Bob Thurbon for the only score, 6-0. Kish was the defensive hero, playing the last 20 minutes on a broken leg.

No Pitt team fought harder with less manpower and achieved more than the 5-4 Panthers of 1939. A fitting climax to the greatest decade until the present of the Golden Panthers. Let's see how they do for a full decade.

A 1961 REUNION — Stars from the '30s teamed up again. Front row, left to right, are Frank Souchak, Ave Daniell, Bill Kern. Rear, left to right, Bobby LaRue, John Michelosen, Marshall Goldberg.

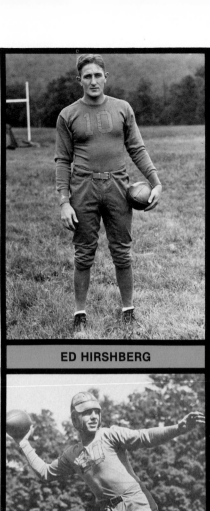

ED HIRSHBERG

RALPH DAUGHERTY

MIKE SEBASTIAN

WARREN HELLER

TED DAILEY

ROCCO CUTRI

ARNOLD GREENE

JOHN MICHELOSEN

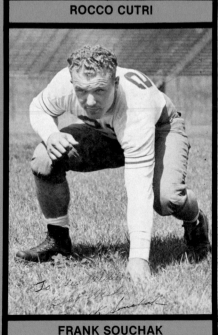

FRANK SOUCHAK

TONY MATISI

DICK FULLERTON

BEN KISH

AL LEESON

STEVE PETRO

BILL DADDIO

JOHN DICKINSON

DICK CASSIANO

EMIL NARICK

PITT RATED FIRST IN NATIONAL POLL

Associated Press List Shows 83 of 94 Sports Writers Voting for Panthers

By The Associated Press.

Mighty Pittsburgh, unbeaten since mid-season in 1936 and perennial Paladin of the East in intersectional warfare, is the nation's first football team.

Eighty-three of the ninety-four writers voting in The Associated Press gridiron poll chose Pittsburgh as the country's best eleven. The Panthers got 926 points on the final check-up of the first nationwide ballot of the season.

The emphatic thumping administered to Wisconsin by Pitt and Minnesota's narrow margin of victory over Michigan combined to give the Panthers a margin of 235 points over their closest rivals, the Golden Gophers, who tallied 691 points. Six writers chose Minnesota as the top team, three picked Texas Christian, while Dartmouth and California each had a single vote for fisst place.

The Leading Elevens

The first ten (first place votes bracketed, points scored 10, 9, 8, 7, 6, 5, 4, 3, 2, 1):

	Points.
Pittsburgh (83)	926
Minnesota (6)	691
California (1)	517
Dartmouth (1)	515
Notre Dame	500
Santa Clara	496
Texas Christian (3)	453
Tennessee	419
Duke	128
Syracuse	82

Second ten: Fordham 77, Michigan 48, Carnegie Tech 45, Oklahoma 40, Alabama 34, Vanderbilt 32, Baylor 31, Northwestern 23, North Carolina 18, Villanova 9.

Others mentioned: Arkansas 7, Oregon 6; Auburn 5, Iowa State and Boston College 3; Ohio State, Southern California, Louisiana State and Stanford 3, Tulane, Cornell, Columbia, Purdue, Idaho and Holy Cross 1 each.

Of the first ten only Pittsburgh (third), Minnesota (fourth), California (first) and Duke (tenth) were in the select circle a year ago when the first poll of the season was made, an indication of the rise and fall of football power in a year's time.

Two Out of Contention

Saturday's rash of upsets is reflected in the rankings. Cornell, supposedly Dartmouth's chief threat in the Ivy League, and Columbia, a dark horse which had gained plenty of fame by beating Yale and Army, are out of contention after rude smackings by Syracuse and Colgate.

Alabama ran into an improving Tennessee team and as a result is out of it in the South for the present. Northwestern and Michigan, ranking threats in the Big Ten, were stalled by Minnesota and Ohio State, after building up impressive early season records.

Of the unbeaten first ten only Minnesota, Tennessee and Duke appear to be safe this weke. The Gophers don't play, while the Vols meet the Citadel and Duke toys

Fordham and Offensive Show Fore

Pitt Coach and His Famed Backfield on Stadium Steps

Dr. John Bain Sutherland poses with the four ball carriers who have made his team the foremost eleven in the country, left to right, Harold Stebbins, senior in the School of Business Administration; Marshall Goldberg, senior in the College of Liberal Arts; John Chickerneo, senior in petroleum engineering in the School of Mines, and Richard Cassiano, junior in the School of Education

Pitt to Spurn All Bowl Bids

PITTSBURGH, Nov. 29.—The Pittsburgh football squad today voted against participating in any post-season football games, the United Press learned today. This eliminates Pitts as a possblity for the Rose Eowl game.

Pitt Grid Stars Get Top Ranking

NEW YORK, Sept. 1 (INS)—If you had to put your finger on one football player and one football team right now as possible standouts nationally next season you might as well take Marshall Goldberg, the halfbacking Jewish hillbilly, as the individual and Goldberg and the rest of the Pitt Panthers as the eleven.

There positively shouldn't be a better thrill-producer and player on the gridirons this year than Goldberg, and with that you can just aboue concede to Pitt a backfield which will be topped by few, if any.

Goldberg at fullback, Stebbins and Cassiano at halves and Chickerno at quarter will scale right around 200 pounds per man, and will be playing behind a real good line, aided and abetted by a flankman named Daddio. He figures to windup on some or all all-Americas.

That backfield will be showing the opposition a whole lot of everything, barring an epidemic of broken legs or other setbacks. They won't pass much, because the Panthers never do, but they don't have to with the kind of power they turn loose. They can pass, however, if they must.

The Panthers look like the nearest thing to the national champions that you can uncover with a quick glance right now, and ought to play the way right into the Rose Bowl if they care to, and will be reasonable at the last moment. They voted themselves out of it last season even before they received an invitation that would have been a mere formality. As it was, Alabama got the bid and, ultimately, a defeat.

Pitt figures on paper to be at least as good a ball club as it was last season, and many critics say it will be better, with the shifting of Goldberg from half to full, and a whole batch of replacements to step into any vacant spots.

It might be mentioned that the Panthers will have to be good to get by this season with a schedule that brings them against West Virginia, Temple, Duquesne, Wisconsin, Southern Methodist, Fordham, Carnegie Tech, Nebraska, Penn State and Duke.

However, against an assortment of foemen that looked equally strong last season the Panthers went undefeated and had their record marred only by a scoreless tie with Fordham, which should have lost. That probably will be taken care of all right by the Panthers this time, for the Rams no longer have the seven blocks of granite in the line. They may present a couple of blocks, but gone for good are Wojciechowicz, Franco, Babartsky, Druze and Woitkoski.

So tall, sedate DrD. John (Jock) Sutherland, the Panther coach, ought to have a victory in that game practically clinched already, regardless of where his team may wind up in the other contests, and

if this is so it ought to be a relief to him, for last season's scoreless tie, which spoiled a perfect record, was the second of two the clubs had engaged in in successive seasons.

At any rate, the Panthers look great by almost unanimous acclamation. Much san happen between now and the end of the season, but they ought to win in the East and if you must have a candidate at the moment for general recognition it might as well be those Panthers.

Dickinson Rates Pitt Top Eleven, Fordham Second

CHAMPAIGN, Ill., Dec. 11 (UP).—Pittsburgh's undefeated Panthers were adjudged the national football champions under the Dickinson system today and will receive the Knute K. Rockne memorial trophy offered by the Irish four horsemen.

Dr. Frank Dickinson, economics professor at the University of Illinois and originator of the Dickinson rating system, picked Fordham second and Dartmouth third.

PITTSBURGH IS FIRST IN FOOTBALL RANKING

Displaces California as Top Eleven, According to Associated Press Poll

By The Associated Press.

Pittsburgh's football power house, triumphant in the Rose Bowl last New Year's Day and seemingly ambitious to try it again, has displaced the University of California as the nation's No. 1 team.

The combination of Pitt's emphatic victory over Notre Dame and California's scoreless tie with Washington helped bring about the biggest shake-up so far in the national gridiron ranking pool conducted by The Associated Press.

Pittsburgh collected a majority of the first-place ballots, 31½ out of 55, and piled up a decisive margin on points, while California dropped to second place after leading the procession for three weeks. Alabama received more first-place votes than California in this week's balloting but was not supported strongly enough otherwise to avoid dropping a notch to third place.

Northeast Gains Power

The marked swing of football's balance of power to the Northeast, with five teams from this section in the first ten, is indicated by the following tabulation on a 10-9-8-7-6-5-4-3-2-1 basis, with first place votes indicated in parenthesis:

	Points.
1—Pittsburgh (31½)	509½
2—California (9)	449
3—Alabama (13)	422
4—Fordham (1½)	387½
5—Dartmouth	253
6—Yale	215
7—Santa Clara	166
8—Duke	159
9—Villanova	62
10—Minnesota	61

The second ten, with points: 11, Nebraska, 55; 12, Louisiana State, 52; 13, Baylor, 43; 14, Auburn, 30; 15, Rice, 29; 16, Colorado University, 23; 17, Indiana, 13; 18, Notre Dame, 12; 19, Holy Cross, 7; 20, Arkansas, 6.

Others listed were: Army, 2; Washington, Ohio State, Montana and Lafayette, 1 each.

Minnesota Back in First Ten

Minnesota, traveling a surprisingly zig-zag course, bounced back into the first ten after one week's absence. Duke and Villanova also moved into the select circle as the experts filled gaps left by Baylor, Nebraska and Ohio State. Baylor skidded from fourth place to thirteenth after its first defeat.

Nebraska's ranking at No. 11, a notch below Minnesota, marks one of this week's inconsistencies. Even though the Huskers lost some prestige in barely tying Kansas, the fact remains they beat Minnesota, which rallied voting support by trouncing Iowa.

Only two of the top ten, Alabama and Santa Clara, have records clear of either tie or defeat. Seven others have nothing worse than a tie on their slates, including the now famous and third successive deadlock between Pitt and Fordham. Minnesota has been beaten twice.

World-Telegram 1937 All-America

Selection by Charles E. Parker

FIRST TEAM

Position	Name	College	Home	Wt.	Ht.	Age
End	John Wysocki	Villanova	Wilkes-Barre, Pa.	183	6.00	21
Tackle	Tony Matisi	Pittsburgh	Endicott, Pa.	225	6.01	23
Guard	Joseph Routt	Texas A. and M.	Chapel Hill, Tex.	198	6.00	22
Center	Alex Wojciechowicz	Fordham	South River, N. J.	193	5.11	22
Guard	Leroy Monsky	Alabama	Montgomery, Ala.	198	5.11	21
Tackle	Albert Babartsky	Fordham	Shenandoah, Pa.	205	6.01	21
End	Frank Souchak	Pittsburgh	Berwick, Pa.	195	6.00	22
Quarter	Byron White	Colorado	Wellington, Col.	185	6.01	20
Halfback	Clinton Frank	Yale	Evanston, Ill.	193	5.11	22
Halfback	Robert MacLeod	Dartmouth	Glen Ellyn, Ill.	186	6.00	19
Fullback	Samuel Chapman	California	Tiburton, Cal.	190	6.00	21

SECOND TEAM

Pos.	Name and College	Wt.
E.	Bershak, No. Carolina	190
T.	Shirey, Nebraska	220
G.	Hooper, Cornell	198
C.	Hinkle, Vanderbilt	204
G.	Smith, Louisiana	210
T.	Mellus, Villanova	212
E.	Benton, Arkansas	193
Q.B.	O'Brien, Tex. Christian	150
H.B.	Goldberg, Pittsburgh	192
H.B.	Kilgrow, Alabama	178
F.B.	Davis, Indiana	198

THIRD TEAM

Pos.	Name and College	Wt.
E.	Sweeney, Notre Dame	190
T.	Gatto, Louisiana	215
G.	Lezouski, Pittsburgh	195
C.	Aldrich, Tex. Christian	210
G.	Zarnas, Ohio State	205
T.	Hale, Tex. Christian	215
E.	Holland, Cornell	198
Q.B.	Popovich, Montana	182
H.B.	Osmanski, Holy Cross	187
H.B.	Luckman, Columbia	192
F.B.	Lain, Rice	218

—These newspaper clippings were contributed by Fred B. Loeffler

PITT-NOTRE DAME
OCTOBER 25 1930

OFFICIAL 25¢

NOV. 27, 1930
25 CENTS PER

PENN STATE vs PITTSBURGH

PROGRAMS OF THE '30s

NEBRASKA vs. PITTSBURGH

P 25¢

PITT STADIUM

THE · PITT · PANTHERS · AND · THE · DUKES · OCTOBER · 17

25¢

PITT · DUQUESNE

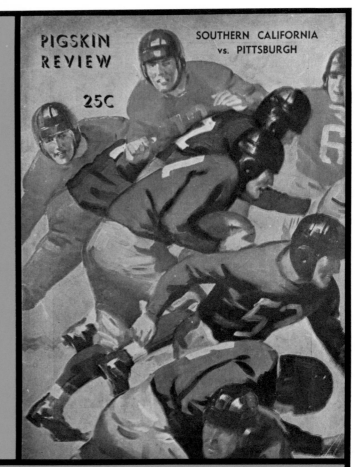

PROGRAMS OF THE '30s

—These programs were contributed by Bobby LaRue

Kissing Your Sister In Front Of 43,000 Or 45,000 Or 50,000 Fans

By Myron Cope

Myron Cope is a 1951 Pitt graduate and served as sports editor of The Pitt News during his student days. Now he is a sports commentator at WTAE Radio and TV.

Reprinted from 1978 Alumni News

If it is true, as the saying goes, that a tie is like kissing your sister, the men who in the mid-'30s played football for Fordham and Pittsburgh to this day hold the all-time American record for, well, simulated incest. Three straight times — 1935, '36, and '37 — they battled one another in the Polo Grounds, and the final scores were 0-0, 0-0, 0-0.

Jock Sutherland, a tall, grim man with a Scotch burr, coached Pitt at the time, presiding over a sort of thresher-type single wing offense that ground opponents to ribbons, all the while abjuring the forward pass as a frill for sissies. Through seven seasons, 1931-37, Pitt never lost more than a single game. Stocked right down to the third team with the toughest coal miners in Pennsylvania and West Virginia, the Panthers also could brag about a defense that during those seven years averaged six shutouts a season. The school's supporters trumpeted a battle cry that demanded, "Millions for defense, not one cent for faculty!"

As the ranking powerhouse of the East, Pitt decided to embellish its image by booking a series of New York appearances for exposure. Fordham seemed a likely opponent. The Rams, coached by Sleepy Jim Crowley, the ex-Horseman from Notre Dame, were coming into the big time and yet did not appear to have reached the point where they could handle Pitt. Crowley being a man about town, Broadway had adopted his team. Kate Smith, Mark Hellinger, and Ted Husing regularly journeyed uptown in carriage cars to participate in campus pep rallies on Rose Hill. Municipal enthusiasm for the Rams swelled. Altogether, a Fordham series struck Pitt as one that would pay satisfactory gate receipts while posing no particular threat to Sutherland's bituminous bulls.

November 2, 1935, the date of the first Pitt-Fordham game, drew near with both teams showing identical records — four victories and one defeat. But Pitt's defeat was by only three points, at the hands of Notre Dame. Bookmakers, who in those days did not bother to calculate point spreads, made the Panthers 2½ to 1 favorites. "According to all available information," a Pittsburgh newspaperman wrote two days before the game, "the Crowley line is nothing over which to become excited." The Crowley line, as it happened, was to become legendary as the Seven Blocks of Granite.

"We took it for granted we were going to win," recalls Bobby LaRue, a swift, compact Pitt halfback "and we played that way." University officials announced that 45,000 were in the Polo Grounds, although Frank Carver, then Pitt's press agent and later its athletic director, says the actual attendance was exaggerated by some 17,000. (In the two subsequent years, crowds of 50,000-plus were announced, though the truth was more like 43,000). Hyperbole was good business, for program advertisers

SEVEN BLOCKS OF GRANITE — Vince Lombardi, third from left, was a member of Fordham's famed cast.

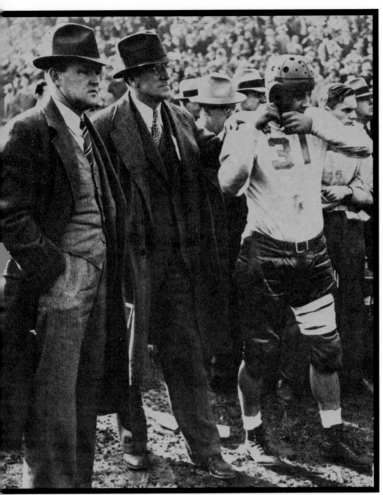

PITT BRAINTRUST — Bill Kern, at left, felt he was just as smart as Jock Sutherland when it came to coaching football. He questioned Sutherland's strategy in Fordham series. At right is quarterback Johnny Chickerneo (31).

were billed according to attendance. "Those were the good old days," sighs Carver.

The game was a dreary affair, distinguished only for its clean but brutal tackling. Between the 20-yard lines, the field was soggy; it may have been soggy inside the 20s, but neither team penetrated that deep to find out. Psychologically fat, the Panthers seemed unwilling to believe that Fordham's line could contain them. "It's just impossible," Quarterback Arnold Greene appeared to be thinking as he sized up a 3rd-and-18 situation and called for a smash into the line. In the end, Fordham outgained Pitt, 150 meaningless yards to 73, and the crowd, jubilant over a moral victory, surged onto the field and tore down the goalposts. This demonstration, plus a brief incident that occurred on the train carrying Pitt home, accounted for the entire weekend's excitement.

On the train, Sutherland and his first assistant, Bill Kern, fell into a disagreement over the Scotsman's strategy that day. "Do you think you know more football than I do?" Sutherland demanded.

"Yes," Kern answered. Thus did a beautiful friendship end.

The betting again was on the Panthers when they returned to New York in 1936. A week earlier they had manhandled Notre Dame, 26-0. Halfback Mad Marshall Goldberg, a sophomore sensation, had gained 177 yards. "In the open," wrote one journalist, "he travels with all the abandon of a typhoon on a holiday." By this time, however,

nobody doubted that the Fordham line was as tough as any in the land. Undefeated in four games, the Rams had not given up a first down to either Southern Methodist or St. Mary's of California. Blockers found it virtually impossible to move tackle Ed Franco, though he stood only 5-9 and weighed but 200 pounds. At right guard Vince Lombardi was, of course, tough and cunning. Crowley's game play was 90 percent defense. He instructed his linemen to concentrate on destroying the Pitt blockers before they crossed the line of scrimmage. Linebacker Alex Wojciechowicz, whose range was proportionately as wide as his name, would nail the ball carrier.

For two quarters the teams waged a bruising war that led nowhere. The second-half kickoff, however, sailed into the arms of Bobby LaRue, and he raced upfield through a funnel of Pitt blockers, emerging in the clear near midfield. Only one Fordham man, Andy Palau, stood in his path. "My God, with the New York press in the stands," says LaRue, "there was my chance to make All-America. I threw the guy a fake, a very nice hip fake that by all rights he was supposed to take. But he didn't. He was too dumb."

Late in the third quarter, LaRue again seemed in a position to score. Pitt had driven to the Fordham 3 and now faced fourth down. LaRue set himself to smash over his right side, between guard and tackle. "But there was a little mixup in our signals," he remembers. "I went in low and hard, but our guard, Bill Glassford, got his big bucket in the way." LaRue ploughed headfirst into Glassford's big bucket, then rebounded and started again. "Wojciechowicz lathered me," he sighs. "He almost tore me apart."

The game resumed its agonizing format. All the while, a substitute quarterback named Bob (Jerk) McClure sat on the Pitt bench wondering why his team kept trying to batter away at a Fordham defense that clearly was overloaded up front to stop the running game. Suddenly McClure heard Sutherland directing him into the game. Without consulting the coach, McClure immediately devised a plan.

He ordered the Panthers into a double wing, a formation that lent itself to the long pass. The quarterback, McClure in this case, ordinarily would throw the pass, but McClure reminded himself that Sutherland hated only two things worse than a pass — an incomplete pass and an intercepted pass. Prudently, McClure cast around for a back who would exchange positions with him and throw the ball. He selected left halfback Johnny Wood, a reckless mountaineer from West Virginia who punted barefoot and had a trick left shoulder literally chained to his side.

Deep in the double wing, Wood cocked his right arm as he saw his receiver race into the clear with ridiculous ease. Wood fired long. Alas, the ball ticked off the receiver's fingertips. Sutherland, possessed of a clear eye when it came to getting to the bottom of chicanery, jerked McClure from the game, which then ground on, death-like, to its conclusion.

"Next year," Pittsburgh columnist Chester L. Smith reported wishfully, "they are going to start the game on Monday morning and keep at it until somebody scores."

Actually, a third scoreless tie seemed an impossibility, for in 1937 Pitt fielded a juggernaut regarded by many as the school's most powerful in history. The best evidence was that John Michelosen and Johnny Chickerneo, the first- and second-string blocking backs, kept a man named Ben Kish on the bench. Kish was to play ten years of professional football. In New York Jim Crowley noted that his scout, Hugh Devore, had been so shaken by the sight of Pitt's offense that enroute home he lost his head and

MARSHALL GOLDBERG bolts through Fordham line in 1937 clash.

tipped a porter a quarter.

For the better part of the first half Fordham's line frantically managed to stave off Pitt's attack, but late in the second quarter Pitt stormed to the Fordham 5. There, the backfield lined up in left formation, with Curly Stebbins at tailback and Goldberg at wingback. Stebbins took the snap and started to his left. Goldberg, meanwhile, peeled out of the formation, gathered in a reverse from Stebbins, and swept deep around the right side. Pitt's famous deep reverse caught the Fordham defense moving in the wrong direction, and Goldberg raced untouched into the end zone. The play had been perfectly executed, except for one detail. On a meaningless patch of ground far from the action, Pitt's left tackle, Tony Matisi, was seen holding.

The touchdown nullified, Matisi screamed at the officials. A devout Catholic, he returned to the Pitt huddle and swore on the names of the saints and on everything holy that he had thrown a perfect block. "The next day," says Curly Stebbins, "I open the Sunday paper — the New York *News* — and there is the most beautiful picture of the most beautiful stranglehold you ever saw. Tony is in a crouch with his left arm around this Fordham guy's leg, hanging on to him for dear life, and the Fordham guy is standing up but sort of leaning, as if he's holding on to something. I can still see the whole scene. It reminds me of the flag raising at Iwo Jima." The Fordham player was Al Gurske. From Gurske's location on the field, says Stebbins, he could not have made the tackle had Goldberg been running 200 yards.

The clock ran out before Pitt again could thrust into the end zone, but in the second half the Panthers' big, swift backs went right back to thrashing the Fordham line. Stebbins ran brilliantly. Time and again, he knifed his way sizable distances. The only trouble was, he kept leaving the ball behind for Fordham to fall on. "I ran more yards without a football than anyone in the history of the game," Stebbins concedes. "It got to the point where it was just like passing the ball off to Wojciechowicz coming up the middle."

After his second fumble, Stebbins determined to make amends. Studying the Fordham offense, he drew a keen prognosis of the Rams' next move — a sideline pass.

"I read that play like a book," Stebbins says. "I was Johnny-on-the-spot for the interception. I had a clear field.

There wouldn't have been a chance in hell of anybody catching me, even if I would have walked. I grabbed that ball, took three steps, and fumbled."

Stebbins could not grip the ball securely because Jock Sutherland, a firm believer in hard work, had scrimmaged his team only two days before the game, and someone had stepped on Stebbins' left hand and broken it. To this day, Stebbins has a sizable lump on the back of his hand and his nose is twisted out of shape, owing to the fact that Sutherland teams rarely took the trouble to have fractures set. Stebbins makes no complaint. But he confesses that by the time he had committed his fourth fumble he began to have doubts about himself. He told Quarterback Michelosen, "Mike, I don't want to carry the ball. I can't hang onto it."

"Curly, I'm calling a play right now where you're going to carry the ball," Michelosen shot back. "If I don't, you'll lose your confidence."

"Okay," Stebbins said. He carried the ball and fumbled.

Stebbins' five fumbles plus three others made a total of eight for Pitt. Published accounts of the game vary according to the size of the reporters' hip flasks, but at least six of the fumbles were recovered by Fordham. One occurred at Pitt's 8-yard line and two others inside the Pitt 30; each time, the Fordham offense advanced the ball no farther than end Johnny Druze could kick it missing field goals. Once the Rams ploughed nicely through the Pitt line from the 28 to a first down on the 10, whereupon they astonished the crowd by throwing three passes — all incomplete. "They started to think," says Frank Carver, the ex-press agent, "and that's always dangerous for a football team." Jim Crowley, who became industrial commissioner for Lackawanna County, Pennsylvania, cannot remember which of his quarterbacks called those three pass plays, or why, but he is indignant at Carver's words. "You can't ever accuse any of my teams of thinking," snorts Crowley.

Having played a third time to no purpose, Pitt and Fordham had set a record for offensive ineptitude that in all probability will never be equaled. Crowley remembers that as he crossed the field and shook hands with Sutherland, both of them were mortified. "I would rather have been beaten 27-20 than have *this* happen again," Crowley earnestly told his rival.

Sutherland went home to Pittsburgh with a question

nagging at his mind. Why hadn't he yanked Stebbins from the game? The answer was that each time Stebbins had fumbled, Sutherland had told himself, "He can't possibly fumble again." Now Sutherland wondered if Stebbins had gotten all his fumble-itis out of his system. On the Monday following, Stebbins was undressing in front of his locker when he heard a Scottish voice bark, "Curly!" Stebbins turned just in time to see Sutherland flip him a football. He dropped it.

On the practice field that day, Sutherland arranged his squad in two long rows, each facing the other. He gave Stebbins a football, carefully handing it to him as he would an infant, and ordered him to run the gantlet. Sutherland admonished him that he had better not let anyone slap the ball out of his hands. Five times Stebbins went down the line. He emerged each time with the ball, but with his face bleeding profusely from the mouth and nose. "Some of those players must have hated me," Stebbins speculates, "because they sure as hell weren't trying to hit the ball."

Back at Rose Hill, the Fordham players, though sharing the ignominy of twelve scoreless quarters, had every right to feel proud of themselves. For three years they had dead-locked a team that unquestionably had the better talent — a marked superiority in running backs who hit into the Fordham line ferociously. "I played 60 minutes in all three of those games," says Ed Franco, the All-America Fordham lineman, "and I still have the bumps to show for it." Wincing at the prospect, the two teams met in 1938 for a fourth time, this time in Pittsburgh.

At last the logjam broke. In an action-packed contest, Pitt exploded for three touchdowns in the fourth quarter to win, 24-13. The fans, jammed into Pitt Stadium's aisles and temporary field bleachers, got more than their money's worth. There were exactly 75,857 of them there, according to an announcement from the box-office. "Actually," Frank Carver says, making a clean breast, "the crowd was only 68,918." The streak of ties had been broken, but the program advertisers' losing streak remained intact.

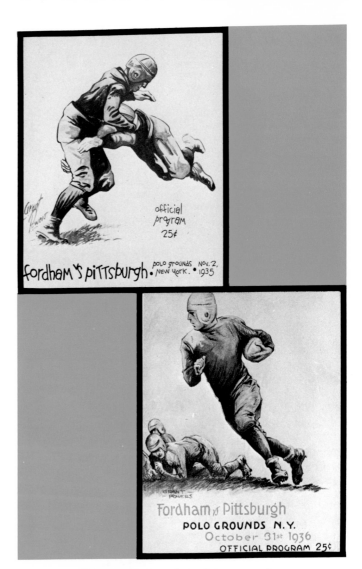

Program covers from famous series.

PITT STADIUM was filled to the brim for a fourth game with Fordham.

107

Marshall Goldberg

Marty Wolfson

MARSHALL GOLDBERG

Jock Talks About 'Biggie' Goldberg

"Goldberg Has It All"

By Dr. Jock Sutherland
The Pittsburgh Press

Oct. 26, 1937

Everybody wants to know more about Marshall Goldberg, Pittsburgh's remarkable junior and one of the finest backs I have ever seen.

Goldberg is a football player's football player. He is first on the practice field and he doesn't loaf while he's there.

Noted chiefly as a ball-carrier, Goldberg is an accomplished quick-kicker, passer and blocker. He kicked with his left foot and passed with his left hand when he reported at Pittsburgh, but has since learned to do both from the other side.

Goldberg is called "Biggie" because he was so small when he went out for high school football in his sophomore year. He weighed only 110 pounds. He scaled 185 pounds on his nineteenth birthday yesterday.

The University of Pittsburgh was not only the choice of Marshall, but of his family as well.

Goldberg learned to block in college. His high school coach wasn't concerned about Marshall's blocking. All he cared about was having his young luminary get his hands on the ball and running.

Most people agree that Pittsburgh schedules are tough, but Goldberg believes they should be harder. He reasons that he plays too little in games in which he really could run up yardage and scores. His ideal card would be Notre Dame, Army, Navy, Southern California, Minnesota, Fordham, Nebraska and Washington.

Goldberg has it all, including durability. He has been knocked out only once — last season, and he ran to a touchdown on the next play.

Pitt hopes Goldberg keeps up this year's pace insofar as his first play is concerned. Against Ohio Wesleyan he intercepted a pass for his first play and ran 55 yards for a touchdown. Against West Virginia he carried the opening kick-off back 78 yards. He ran 77 yards to a touchdown the first time he got his hands on the ball in the Duquesne game. He scored twice on Wisconsin, on a 65-yard run.

Goldberg comes from Elkins, in central West Virginia.

Marshall still is a country boy and a good West Virginian at heart.

In the heat of our Rose Bowl battle with Washington at Pasadena last New Year's Day, a substitute came into the Pitt lineup, and Goldberg asked him the time.

"A quarter past three," said the substitute, looking up at the clock.

"Let's see, that makes it a quarter after six in Elkins," said Goldberg.

Marshall's father, who takes in every game that it is possible for him to see, owns the principal movie picture theatre in Elkins. The family is very well to do.

There are four brothers, one a high school star this fall. Two older brothers are employed by the father. Marshall also formerly helped his dad, who right now occasionally has to go down the street to Elkins' other movie house to see his son in newsreels.

It is always open house at the Goldbergs because the boys were supposed to get along with people and to do things people did out in the world under proper conditions.

Marshall Goldberg himself says that he doesn't care to be rich, and doesn't expect to be. He hopes only to make a comfortable living.

He doesn't believe in working during the summer until he is through playing football. He swims, plays tennis, golfs, and goes to the movies. He is not a ladies' man. He is an exceptional, careful dresser.

Attaining stardom last fall, he had to become an after-dinner speaker, and he never avoided an engagement. Like blocking, he had to do it.

Marshall Goldberg learned to speak well in public. He'll do everything well that he tackles.

He's that kind of boy.

MARSHALL GOLDBERG, All-American in 1937 and 1938.

That's my boy! Sutherland has eye-to-eye chat with his celebrated back.

Blockers Made Marshall Goldberg A Great Running Star, Insisted Sutherland In His Pittsburgh Press Column

Watch Other Guys!

By Dr. Jock Sutherland
Head Coach, University of Pittsburgh

MARSHALL GOLDBERG

Oct. 28, 1936

It's seldom a sophomore football player makes the headlines as Marshall Goldberg has done this season. But then it's seldom that a youngster comes along as rapidly as this lad. He is only 18 years old, having celebrated his birthday last Sunday.

A year ago he was just a good halfback on an average Pitt freshman team that lost two games while winning three. Now he is a national sensation. You can't stop with Goldberg when it comes to handing out praise, however. Anytime any halfback starts to become famous, take a look at the men up front — or rather the men downfield. The best in the world needs interference and plenty of it.

Look at the great ball-carriers of recent years. For every open-field sensation there has been a well-known blocker. Red Grange had Britton. In the old days at Pitt, Tommy Davies had Tommy Holleran clearing the way; Gibby Welch had Jimmy Hagan; Ozzie Simmons, at Iowa, hasn't looked so good since Dick Crayne graduated; Ernie Pinckert, at Southern California, made Orv Moehler look very good; Red Cagle at the Army had Johnny Murrell, and Notre Dame's Marchy Schwartz had Marty Brill.

We can't point out any one blocker at Pitt to tie up with Goldberg. That hasn't been our system. All our linemen and backs are expected to block, both on the line and downfield. But because of the faith in Goldberg's ability to take care of himself in an open field, there has been a greater willingness on the part of the boys to get him out in the open.

Various men at various times have helped. There is a certain unity when the blockers realize that their efforts are not going to be wasted. Bill Glassford has come around from his guard post to make timely blocks. Johnny Chickerneo blasts away at ends because he knows that the man he's blasting for will repay him by picking up plenty of yardage.

Watch big Averell Daniell and Tony Matisi, our tackles. They block, too. What I'm trying to get across is that, at some time or other, on each of Goldberg's long runs, he has been aided by timely blocking.

This goes for all our halfbacks. Against Ohio State, it was Chickerneo and Bill Stapulis who opened the way for Harold Stebbins' touchdown run.

This isn't the usual cry that people make when they yell that anyone can run when they get good interference.

Goldberg has proved that he can make his own way, and that he is as dangerous when it comes to bucking as open-field running. Just because there has been no one man out of 10 running with him all the time doesn't mean that our blocking hasn't been there. It hasn't always been effective, and we're far from satisfied. But the boys are getting out in front.

GO, BIGGIE, GO! This is the sort of blocking Sutherland alluded to, as the secret to Marshall Goldberg's success. Frank Patrick (24) and Bill Glassford (10) provide escort here.

From "Colorful Coaches"

By Grantland Rice
In "The Tumult and the Shouting: My Life in Sport"

The days and nights I spent with "Hurry Up" Yost, Bob Zupke, Knute Rockne and "Pop" Warner will never be forgotten. Neither will the many hours I spent with Jock Sutherland, one of the greatest when he had full control at Pittsburgh.

Jock was never quite sold on the forward pass. He was a master at the running game and he didn't like to turn the ball loose in the air. He liked to feature ball carriers and blockers.

In certain ways, Jock wanted the center to be the best man on his team. "The running game," he said, "which is, or should be, the better part of football, depends on split-second accuracy and timing from center. If the ball gets to the runner a tenth of a second too soon — or too late — the running play may be spoiled. So in looking over my talent I pick a man for center who is never rattled or hurried or upset by anything."

I know that if I was in doubt in picking All-America talent, I was dead sure to get a good center from Pittsburgh when Jock Sutherland ruled the Panthers.

Jock's great Pitt teams rumbled and blasted out their yardage on the single-wing, unbalanced-line attack. When Jock had the horses, which was his custom, the Golden Panthers' attack was something to behold. Broken in spirit by the attacks on his taciturnity, dictatorial methods, and his habit of "too much winning," Sutherland left Pitt in 1938 and turned to the pros. On April 11, 1948, he died following a brain operation.

In his passing, I lost a friend, a comrade. The following day, I wrote the following in memory of "The Scotsman."

There's a fog now over Scotland, and mist on Pittsburgh's field;
There's no valiant hand to flash the sword or hold the guiding shield,
There's a big, braw fellow missing from the golden land of fame
— For Jock Sutherland has left us — and the game is not the same.

We hear the roaring chorus — and we get the age-old thrill;
But when a pal has left us, there's a gap that none can fill,
There's a shadow on the thistle and the Panthers' growl is low
— As the bagpipes send their message to the friend we used to know.

The laurel fades — the olive dies — the cheers are silent now,
No more the chaplet from lost years adorns the master's brow.
But here's to Jock, through fog and mist, beyond the final score,
— As we turn down an empty glass to one we'll see no more.

PITT PROS — Jock Sutherland speaks to former Panthers who turned pro with Brooklyn Dodgers, from left to right, Ben Kish, Steve Petro, Frank Kristufek and Dick Cassiano.

Everyone in Pittsburgh Was Jock's Friend

"No man ever cut it off so clean."

By Stanley Woodward
Views of Sport
New York Herald Tribune

April 14, 1948

Dr. John Bain Sutherland, the immigrant from Cooper Angus, Scotland, was buried in Pittsburgh today from Calvary Episcopal Church in the presence of his friends. The Doctor was a hard man to know, a myth rather than a personality to thousands of his fellow Pittsburghers. Yet people came from all over the country to see him buried. They filed through the church where he lay in state, thousands of people whom nobody knew. In the chancel to direct them were his old University of Pittsburgh football players: Johnny Michelosen, John Chickerneo, Marshall Goldberg, Dick Cassiano, Tiger Walton, Bill Kern, Bob Hoel, Ken Ormiston, Hal Stebbins, Mike Nixon, Frank Souchak.

His associates in high echelon football also came. George Halas and Ray Bennigsen, from Chicago; Bert Bell and Greasy Neale, from Philadelphia; Jack Mara, Jack Davies and Steve Owen, from New York; Mr. and Mrs. Gus Dorais, from Detroit; Legs Hawley, from Morgantown, W. Va.; Turk Edwards, from Washington, and others.

It was a great gathering of the football clans. All day the Doctor's friends milled through Art Rooney's offices in the Fort Pitt Hotel and those who didn't come sent wires or flowers or both.

Dr. Sutherland died Sunday from an inoperable brain tumor. He was picked up wandering in a muddy field in Wickliffe, Ky., last Wednesday. He was taken to the hospital in Cairo, Ill., and flown to Pittsburgh. There he was attended by Dr. J. F. Grunnagle and Dr. Harold L. Mitchell. Dr. Grunnagle performed an exploratory operation at 2 p.m. Saturday. A subsequent operation for removal of a brain tumor started at 7:30 p.m. The surgeons, discovering malignancy, gave up at 1 a.m. and Dr. Sutherland died at 4:15 Sunday morning.

He left Pittsburgh March 22, the day after his fifty-ninth birthday, on a combined vacation and business tour. The business involved was player scouting for the Pittsburgh Steeler professional football team of which he was coach and vice-president. His first stop was Coatesville, Pa., where he participated in a football clinic with Fritz Crisler, of Michigan. From there he was traced to Washington, Durham, N.C., Wake Forest, S.C., Atlanta and New Orleans. He was not heard from again until he was found in Wickliffe.

Rooney and other associates started to worry about him before this. The Doctor was in the habit of calling the Steelers' office frequently and his silence during the trip was unaccountable to his associates, Rooney, Ed Kiely and John Holahan. Michelosen, his chief coaching assistant, left him at Coatesville and heard nothing more from him. This was startling because Dr. Sutherland left dozens of loose ends, including the signing of Bob Chappuis, Michigan's great back, when he started on his trip.

The old Pittsburgh players who gathered at the church this morning agreed the Doctor had not been himself for

PRIZE PUPIL — Sutherland shows John Michelosen some football strategy.

six months. He had headaches. He stopped in the middle of his coaching lectures, forgetting to finish what he started. Only in retrospect do his friends remember this.

The devotion they had for him outlawed criticism. Johnny Michelosen, his quarterback at the university and his chief professional assistant, took over when the Doctor stopped short of the mark in his talks to the Steeler squad, thinking that was what was wanted, not suspecting the Doctor had reached the limit of his capacity.

No man ever cut it off so clean. Until a week before his death Dr. Sutherland ran his business. Tough, lean, six feet three, he was a formidable person to the end of his days.

Most people considered him forbidding. To your agent, he was a sentimentalist. He loved the University of Pittsburgh to which he came as an athletic scholarship man and from which he was graduated as an oral surgeon. When he and the university broke relations he was lost. He wasted a year coaching the New York Herald Tribune All-Stars.

He entered professional football as coach of Brooklyn, left to accept a commission in the Navy — he had been an infantry sergeant in World War I.

His work in this difficult job was spectacular. Using his accustomed stereotyped single-wing football, he lifted the Pittsburgh pros into the upper strata. Two years after he took over, the club tied for the Eastern Championship of the National Football League and it is incidental that they lost to the Philadelphia Eagles in a play-off.

Greasy Neale, coach of the Eagles, was here for the funeral. "Jock's popularity in this city is beyond belief," he said. "Everyone in Pittsburgh was his friend."

EMIL NARICK

By Chester L. Smith
The Village Smithy

Reprinted from The Pittsburgh Press

April, 1942

You will, of course, remember Emil Narick, the slim black-haired boy from West Virginia, who played his last football for Pitt in 1939 and turned out to be one of the slickest forward passers the Panthers have ever had. Emil was a right halfback all during his college playing days, and a good one, but it was when he started in to pitch the leather egg that he caught your eye. He was as cold as an Arctic wind as he stood there, no matter what the score or how many were piling in on him, and you sensed that here was a lad who had moved in and taken charge.

Narick stands up with Pitt's Gibby Welch, Warren Heller and Edgar Jones as a marksman with a football, but that isn't the story. More to the point at the moment is the note that came in yesterday's mail. Emil has gone to the wars — he is Cadet Narick of Squadron D, at Craig Field, in Alabama. When you help 'Keep 'em Flying,' you are doing your part to give him his wings. Emil is in the Air Corps.

Because he is a typical American, not long out of his teens, I think you will get a lift out of some of the things Narick has to say. There is none of the prodigy in him. He is cut to a familiar pattern. His coaches used to say that he gave them plenty of headaches off the field, but none when the game was on. One of them said once that "the only thing we worry about is whether he's going to turn up at 2 o'clock on Saturday afternoon." I think you get the idea; life was always something Emil enjoyed from 12:01 a.m. around to midnight.

It was characteristic of Narick that he produced when the cards were laid face up on the table. When he came back to the university in the fall of '39, there was only one member of the illustrious "Dream Backfield" of the previous season to pick up the baton — Dick Cassiano, at left halfback. John Chickerneo, Marshall Goldberg and Curly Stebbins had departed, leaving a chasm only slightly shallower than the Grand Canyon. Narick, who had understudied Stebbins for two years, was the right half. There was nothing else to it.

The opening game that season was with Washington, at Seattle, and Narick helped chuck his team to a 27-0 victory that knocked the critics cockeyed. That night a hard-bitten old codger, down from Alaska, collared Emil in the hotel lobby and insisted he bring the whole Pitt squad to his suite. "I just came in from the North and heard about this game," he said. "They were betting 2-to-1 on Washington, but I figured it couldn't be that bad, so I socked a couple thousand on you boys. Bring 'em all up, and I'll have the champagne. You can stay for a week if you want to."

Emil declined with thanks, explaining that there were training rules, etc., but he brooded all the way back to Pittsburgh. It would have been a swell party.

In his letter, he says he has been at Craig Field since late January. "We're working hard here," he adds, "and I like it better every day."

Even Before He Was A Judge, Narick Knew What Was Fair

"If in this way I can repay my obligation to my country, I'll be happy."

SERIOUS MOMENTS were shared by Emil Narick and Dick Cassiano, backfield stars on the 1940 Panther football team.

STARSTRUCK STARLETS surround Pitt heroes Emil Narick, left, and Ben Kish. They included, clockwise from left, Arlene Whelan, Susan Hayward, June Preiser, Jane Wyman and Joy Hodges. These aspiring young actresses were in Pittsburgh in 1939 for a stage show and posed for this picture at the William Penn Hotel.

Yes, and in '39 Pitt liked him better every week. It wasn't long after the return from the coast that the Duke Blue Devils dropped into the Stadium with an eleven that was cracked up to tear the Panthers to shreds, but Emil had other ideas. He tossed off a pair of touchdown passes, and while the Southerners put across two of their own, they neglected to make good one of the conversions and there it was: Pitt 14, Duke 13. Narick had nonplussed the master minds again.

"Our first period of drill is being devoted to learning the fundamentals of military life," he relates. "We usually drill in the morning and in the afternoon we have an exercise period. This is conducted by four physical instructors, who put us through calisthenics. Then we play games. Of course, my favorite is football. We play touch football. This keeps my right arm in pretty good shape, tossing passes, but I'm sorry to say the receivers can't compare with Dick Cassiano, Joe Rettinger, or John Dickinson, the boys who used to catch them so regularly at Pitt."

That's Emil from stem to stern. He didn't fancy it a bit when anyone muffed his passes, especially if he had theoretically hit the bullseye.

"I feel it is a pleasure," Narick concludes, "to be here, because I realize America has meant so very much to me in giving me freedom and liberty. Whether I ever return or not doesn't matter, but if in this way I can repay my obligation to my country, I'll be happy."

Go to it, Emil, Give 'em hell, and when you get back, look me up. We'll run down that sourdough from Alaska and put on a shindig that won't end 'til the sun comes up. It wouldn't surprise me if the old gaffer still has some of that gold of his riding on you.

DON'T GET TOO CLOSE to the future judge, else Emil Narick will stiff-arm you in the nose, or so it appears.

It Was Difficult To Field First-Rate Teams In War Years

By Jack Henry

"I was told to bring along my food ration book."
—Jimmy Joe Robinson

"We had big crowds rooting us on; the spirit was high."

—Bimbo Cecconi

Understanding the varied observations of quaint British actress Hermione Gingold is often as difficult as landing a blow against a puff of smoke. But on one occasion she achieved her aim at a double meaning by recalling, "I was bombed all during World War Two."

Pitt football partisans from the 1940's can readily identify with Hermione's remark since they spent practically the entire decade being bombed.

Sports and all other forms of show business quite naturally were demoted to second fiddle during the war years. The chilling effects continued even after the peace and in some instances never completely disappeared. What Franklin D. Roosevelt labeled "The War of Survival" had caught fire in Europe in 1939 and reached American shores two years later, triggered by the Japanese attack on Pearl Harbor. The guns eventually were silenced but, as the song suggests, the sad melody lingered on.

Pitt suffered the same problems as many other big-time schools during the war years — attendance declines, shortage of funds, transportation and schedule cancellations, the discontinuance of athletic scholarships and drastic reductions in recruiting. Some of the more fortunate colleges escaped the dragnet of trouble by using service trainees to play football, but Pitt was among those forced to survive with 17-year-old freshmen and 4-F's.

An added blow was that when the Pearl Harbor tragedy occurred, Pitt had not yet recovered from the malady known as the post-Sutherland blues. Jock Sutherland, a rare instance of a coach becoming a legend in his own time, had packed his bags and left before the 1939 season began. This mishap alone took more time to shake off than the seven-year itch.

Like his mentor, the innovative Pop Warner, Sutherland had mastered the formula for winning as evidenced by his acquisition of five national championships and a Pitt career record of 111 victories and 12 ties in 143 games. That sort of success made Pitt rooters part jubilant, part content and part smug. Obviously this made it all the harder to adjust to the 40's when the Oakland campus sometimes resembled Dunkirk without the boats.

Pitt has been in the football business since 1890 and if you prepared a highlight film covering that span the obvious temptation would be not to allocate much footage to the 40's. Following the departure of Sutherland the Panthers wore out four head coaches — Charley Bowser, Clark Shaughnessy, Wes Fesler and Mike Milligan — and came up with losing marks in eight of 10 seasons.

The patience of Milligan paid off with back-to-back 6-3 records in 1948 and 1949 to foster the hope that a turnaround in Pitt fortunes was about to occur. It finally did with bowl trips in the 50's, but not until the Churchillian warning of blood, sweat and tears had been experienced to the fullest.

It should be noted that occasionally there were some upbeat efforts in the troublesome decade. When you fight against odds for a place in the sun, you expect some blisters, but once in a while Dame Fortune can be induced to smile. It was at such times that Pitt followers relished Walter Hagen's advice to stop and smell the flowers.

That happened for example when Pitt produced startling upsets which embarrassed such worthies as Fordham, Penn, Ohio State and Penn State. In addition quite a few exceptional players managed to brush aside the obstacles and imprint their names indelibly in Pitt's Domesday Book.

One such case was the 13-0 triumph over Fordham in 1941, the blue ribbon achievement of Bowser's four-year reign. The Rams headed the unbeaten ranks at the time and Pitt's surprise party shocked the nation. Edgar (Special Delivery) Jones, perhaps the greatest Pitt player to be ignored by All-America selectors, was unstoppable that day in mutilating Fordham with his running, passing and interceptions.

Bowser, once a center for Sutherland here, had few opportunities to relax during his coaching tenure but the upset of Fordham put a smile on his face that wouldn't rub off. The back-to-back effort, success against Nebraska a week later, had him in ecstasy. Meantime the rash of favorable comments exceeded what had come his way when Pitt dusted off "Pitchin' Paul" Christman and his Missouri club in 1940. Christman, you may remember, later became a top-ranked television commentator.

Other victories which woke up the populace included those over Penn State in 1945, '46 and '48; the booby trap that was set for Ohio State in 1947 and the 22-21 nail-biter against the Penn Quakers in Franklin Field in 1949.

It required unusual players to rise above the Pitt won-loss chart in the 40's, but Special Delivery Jones was not the only one to carry the mail. Here is a notable list of accomplishments:

(1) — A special panel updated the Pitt All-Time football squad as recently as 1979 but such players from the 40's as halfback Jones, end Bill McPeak and guard Ralph Fife retained their original listings.

(2) — Fife and another guard, Bernie Barkouskie, won All-America berths, Ralph in '41 and Bernie eight years later.

(3) — Jones inserted his name in the Pitt record book for yardage on interceptions (132 for one game in 1941, and 224 for that season) and the figures still stand.

(4) — Lou (Bimbo) Cecconi completed TD pass to Nick DeRosa for 82 yards against Marquette in 1948 and it still remains a target for Panther tandems. Likewise Jimmy Joe

'Special Delivery' Carries the Mail

Acme Photo.

Edgar (Special Delivery) Jones, who sparked Pittsburgh's Panthers to the football season's most startling upset over Fordham in Pitt Stadium Saturday, is shown here on a typical first down foray.

High Spots in Week-End Grid Warfare

Pittsburgh, 13; Fordham, 0.

You had to see it to believe it. Out at Pittsburgh, however, there were people who expected it. These insiders knew that Pitt's de-emphasis was merely window dressing and that this year's club had as many good players as an average Sutherland Pitt eleven, and an exceptional back in Edgar (Special Delivery) Jones.

Frankly, they regarded coaching as the team's biggest drawback, and, as early as world series time, warned that once Pitt began to roll, in spite of Charley Bowser, Inc., it would be anybody's equal. Come the first week in November, Pitt barely lost to Ohio State and the next Saturday — well, there was the upset.

Jones, a terrific pro prospect who will be ready, willing and eager to play for bucks after June, paved the way for Pitt's first — and deciding — touchdown with the sort of pass that Bowser had yanked him out of the line-up for attempting under other circumstances. It was one of those scamper-hither-and-yon-before-you-throw things. Bill Dutton couldn't miss the toss when Jones finally got it off. It was that uncanny.

"The most amazing individual performance I have ever seen," said Jimmy Crowley of Jones' job of carrying 28 times for a net of 106 yards; toting seven times and passing once in Pitt's 70-yard march, to its first touchdown; kicking for an average of 38½ yards, and stepping 30 yards for a second touchdown after intercepting Steve Filipowicz's aerial.

The other heroes for Pitt were mainly linemen, concerning the best of whom Ed Franco stated: "If that Ralph Fife wasn't an All-America then there isn't any such thing. He made their reverses go. He was lead blocker. On defense he backed up his side of the line and piled up many of our outbacks that should have sent men into the clear."

Fordham's boys tried all the way but, statistic for statistic, they were outplayed as well as outscored.

LESTER BROMBERG.

Robinson still holds a premier spot with his 87-yard punt runback against Michigan State in '45, but our editor discovered, in researching this book, that Robinson returned one 90 yards for a game-winning touchdown that same season in a 7-0 victory over Penn State.

(5) — Fife and McPeak were chosen for an East-West booking and so were ends Stan Gervelis and Leo Skladany, guard George Ranii and fullback George Kracum. Halfback Ernie Bonelli played in the '44 Blue-Gray attraction and he and Kracum were involved in the College All-Star game. Cecconi was tabbed for the North-South rivalry and other Panthers to hit the limelight in the Blue-Gray matchup were center John Kosh, guard Fran Mattioli, fullback Carl DePasqua, along with Skladany and Barkouskie.

As far back as when Conrad Hilton roomed at the YMCA, peppery Chuck Meehan constantly told his coaching colleagues that Western Pennsylvania was the No. 1 football hatchery in the land. Since most of the standout Pitt players of the 40's were products of this area it would seem that Mr. Meehan was quite adept at keeping his ear to the ground.

Getting back to Bowser, he finally threw in the sponge at the end of the 1942 season and reported to the Navy. Along

OFF AND RUNNING — Jimmy Joe Robinson rips off a long gainer for Panthers. Today he's a minister on the North Side.

with headaches already mentioned he had fallen victim to the difficulty of operating under the Bowman Code ordered by Chancellor John Bowman to impose tough restrictions on varsity athletes. Former Pitt halfback Emil Narick, now a judge, once described Bowman:

"He was a very austere man and a Woodrow Wilson look-alike. He had vision on a grand scale, was serious in everything he tried and contended that suitable surroundings significantly affect student education and behavior. This fitted into his dream concept of the Cathedral of Learning."

When Bowser shuffled off stage, Pitt officials were determined to make moves that would erase the gloom over Charley's record of only 14 victories and a tie against 20 defeats. Most irksome was the fact that the 1940 rundown was Pitt's first losing season since 1912.

In the search for a successor the ballyhoo hit a peak that would have aroused the envy of Muhammad Ali. Finally it was announced that the new boss would be Clark Shaughnessy, a much-traveled and complex man who after years of chasing the rainbow had hit the jackpot when he coached Stanford to Rose Bowl glory in 1940. He did this by resurrecting the old-fashioned T-formation, adding the new wrinkle of a man in motion, and by the good luck of inheriting a backfield that featured Frankie Albert, Pete Kmetovic, Hugh Gallarneau and Norm Standlee, plus a wealth of competent linemen.

Eddie Beachler, then a sports writer for The Pittsburgh Press, greeted the newcomer with exuberance:

"It doesn't require a Gallup Poll to see that Pittsburgh has gone for Mister 'T' hook, line and sinker. Ask any kid

on the street and you will get a fair idea of the respect that everyone has for him. You can't fool the kiddies. The signing of Shaughnessy was the most popular job that Athletic Director James Hagan has done since he booted the Stanford Indians around in the 1928 Rose Bowl game."

Even the cagy Hagan, a onetime blocker for Gibby Welch who spoke only a trifle less than the Sphinx, was caught up in the hullabaloo. He explained:

"We went after the best man available and were lucky enough to get him."

Pitt fans were turned on and reported 58,000 strong for the 1943 opener against Notre Dame, a record for a season inaugural here. Unfortunately the Fighting Irish refused to cooperate and handed the Pitt team, which had five 17-year-olds in the starting lineup, a 41-0 shellacking. One observer, relating that Pitt used the much discussed T-formation, said simply:

"It was a case of T against TNT."

Shaughnessy brought in considerable talent to help him mold a winner. He signed Charles (Doc) Hartwig, Stan Olenn and Danny Fortmann for regular service and Sid Luckman for occasional visits. The cooks were competent but the broth failed to measure up. In '43 Pitt won only three times in eight games, four out of nine in '44 and only three out of 10 in '45.

Jimmy Joe Robinson, who had all the requisites to be a game-breaker and sometimes was, still recalls the Shaughnessy era. Now a minister on the North Side, he recently told sports writer Jim O'Brien:

"I have tried to put football behind me, but I find that every Saturday I still get the urge to be out there."

T-Time — Pitt head coach Clark Shaughnessy explains play to assistants Dr. Danny Fortmann, left, and "Doc" Hartwig.

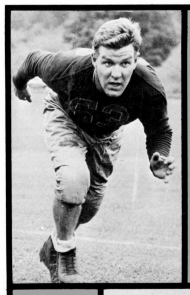

BERNIE BARKOUSKIE

Panthers produced a pair of All-Americans for the Forties.

RALPH FIFE

Jimmy Joe remembers Shaughnessy inviting him to come to Pitt and he was told to make certain to bring along his food ration book, which tells you something about that period. He adds:

"I was only 17 when I played for Shaughnessy, but I still recall vividly how hard he tried to produce a winning season. He featured what he called 'bang blocking' and he came up with such plays as the 'banana end', the 'Joe Louis left' and the 'Jack Dempsey right'.

"All I ever heard at that time was Sutherland, Sutherland, and more Sutherland. This put the heat on Shaughnessy right from the start. Then there was the time he got everybody upset when he switched our uniforms to red and white."

An oddity of the times in addition to Robinson's food-ration book was the constant switching of students from school to school to pursue special armed services training courses. An illustration of that was when in October of 1943 Bill Abromitis scored a touchdown for Pitt against West Virginia and the very next month a crowd of 21,000 saw Abromitis, then playing for Penn State, plowing over for a touchdown against Pitt.

The uniform change which Robinson mentioned apparently stirred up quite a fuss, but was not a dictatorial move by Mister "T". Elaine Kahn in a column for the Pitt student publication called "Kahnotations of Sports" reported the switch of colors was made by a committee which voted unanimously. I don't understand the fuss because unless my memory is playing tricks it seems to me Sutherland occasionally switched from the blue and gold to plain white.

In contradiction of Grantland Rice it matters not who won or lost, but who gets the blame. The string of Pitt setbacks meant that Shaughnessy got the blame and the handwriting was on the wall when he dropped six games in

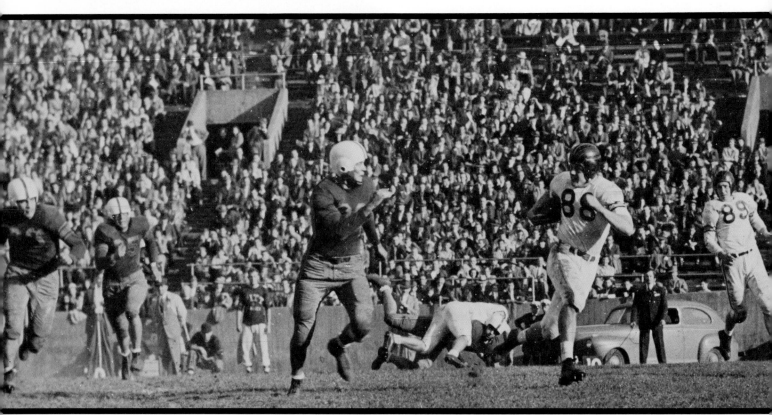

FUTURE STEELER — New Castle's Bill McPeak closes in for kill.

a row in 1945. The crowning blow was when the Panthers were held scoreless in consecutive outings against Temple, Purdue, Ohio State and Indiana.

Petitions for his ouster began to surface and 1945 was his final year here. Penn State fans may not have understood the basis for Clark's removal for they found him tough to beat. The Nittany Lions dropped their 1944 finale to Pitt, 14-0, a game in which Bernard Sniscak returned a second half kickoff 93 yards. In the 1945 closeout Pitt won again, 7-0, the only score being Robinson doing the specialty by returning a punt 90 yards into the end zone. Incidentally, one of the running backs during the Shaughnessy era was Pittsburgh's Herbie Douglas, who later won an Olympic Games bronze medal in the long jump.

A sure indicator in mid-1945 that Shaughnessy was being backed into the corner was the frequency of gags that were circulated. One was that Clark on the sidelines screamed to an assistant:

"Get Temenoff in there! Get Temenoff in there!"

When told that Temenoff already was in there, Clark allegedly demanded:

"Get his butt out of there!"

Then there was the anecdote that Shaughnessy diagrammed the perfect scoring play on the blackboard, but failed to note that he had 12 players on the offensive team. Press sportswriter Carl Hughes called the overload to his attention, much to Shaughnessy's chagrin.

After Shaughnessy, Pitt turned to a Youngstown product, Wes Fesler, as its savior. Fesler, a three-sport star with the Ohio State Buckeyes and an All-America end, stayed only one year.

He arrived in 1946 and took the town by storm. His season record was 3-5-1 but he had only a few critics. The feeling was that he had the qualities needed to establish a winning regime. However, the opportunity came for him to return to his alma mater as head coach, an offer he couldn't refuse.

Mike Milligan, a onetime Pitt line star by way of Aliquippa, was Fesler's chief aid in '46 and when Wes defected he stepped up to mark a return of the system of having a Pitt grad in charge.

Mike suffered visibly throughout a brutal 1947 campaign when he won only once in nine games. The solitary victory was achieved under dramatic circumstances and was simply more proof that truth is often stranger than fiction.

The victory was against Ohio State and a Hollywood touch was present since the Buckeyes invaded Oakland led by Fesler, who came to oppose his former players and brave the wrath of those who figured he had jilted Pitt.

Ohio State was a big favorite, but Pitt was the first to score when Tony DiMatteo punched his way to a touchdown from five yards out in the waning moments of the first half. In the third quarter the Buckeyes drove 63 yards to reach the Pitt two-yard line. The Stadium erupted when on fourth down Alex Verdova was nailed for a three-yard loss.

Five minutes later, Jimmy Joe went into his celebrated punt return act to reach the Ohio State 30 and short passes added 27 more yards. At that point DePasqua and Cecconi hooked up for a pass which cemented the 12-0 upset.

The long-awaited Pitt comeback became a reality in 1948 when Milligan and his now merry men posted a 6-3 effort. There was no early indication that this was to happen for in the first two games Pitt was humiliated by Southern Methodist and Notre Dame. But suddenly the Panthers became as popular as the guy who mails income-tax

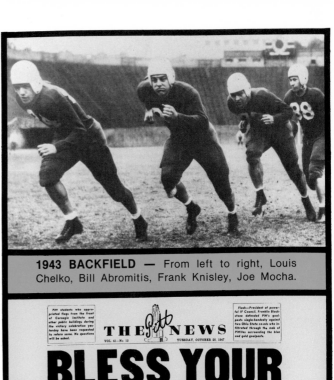

1943 BACKFIELD — From left to right, Louis Chelko, Bill Abromitis, Frank Knisley, Joe Mocha.

FRONT PAGE — 1947's only victory.

LEO SKLADANY — All-Star end.

BIG CATCH by Bimbo Cecconi (36) puts Pitt in better field position as part of a sensational one-man show as senior in 7-0 season-ending victory over Penn State in 1948.

CARL DePASQUA — Premier punter.

refunds by victimizing West Virginia, Marquette, Indiana, and Western Reserve in succession.

Ohio State interrupted the string with a 41-0 achievement as revenge for the 1947 loss. Pitt then showed its resiliency by bouncing back to jolt Purdue and Penn State. In the Purdue encounter Robinson stunned the Ross-Ade Stadium crowd of Boilermaker fans by returning a kickoff 100 yards.

But it was the 7-0 shutout of Penn State which turned Oakland into bedlam. With three minutes gone in the fourth quarter Woody Petchel's pass was deflected by Ralph Coleman into Nick Bolkovac's arms and he galloped 23 yards for the game's only score. Fran Rogel, later to achieve "Hey, Diddle Diddle" fame, then proceeded to rip the Pitt defense to shreds but Bolkovac stopped him one yard short of his touchdown objective. The setback knocked Penn State out of a bowl trip.

Milligan erased any fears that his 1948 record was a fluke by repeating the 6-3 number in '49. After squeezing past William & Mary, the Milligan Machine showed the two-year comeback was the real thing by dusting off Northwestern, the Rose Bowl champ, 16 to 7.

Even that spectacular exploit was overshadowed later when Pitt, making its first visit to Franklin Field in 17 years, edged Penn, 22-21, in a game which to this day I do not fully believe.

As I recall, Pitt went into the battle with the Quakers as an underdog but blasted its way to a 13-0 edge. The Quakers stopped turning the other cheek and roared back to move in front, 21-13.

All eyes were on the clock in the closing minutes when Pitt closed the gap to 21-20. Bimbo Cecconi on a punt run-back rambled 49 yards to the Penn 29. With 35 seconds left, Pitt scored, but the referees nullified it with an offside ruling. As a final touch Bernie Barkouskie impressed All-America selectors by blocking a Ray Dooney punt and Pitt came up with a safety for a 22-21 heart-tingler.

Cecconi, who roomed above Gate 3 of Pitt Stadium with such teammates as Robinson, Earl Sumpter, Flint Greene, Carl DePasqua and basketball whiz Dodo Canterna, rates the Penn game among the best of his many school memories. He adds:

"I am amazed at how much everyone remembers about the Pitt football happenings of the 1940's. We had good nicknames, but we weren't that great but many times we had big crowds rooting us on. The spirit was high and perhaps that was because school enrollment was up and the bad effects of the war were wearing away.

"At that time Pitt tuition was only $10 a credit hour. As I recall the players received tuition, room and $90 a month meal money. It was quite a period and all of us from that era talk over the old days time and time again."

Walt Cummins, currently the assistant athletic director at Pitt, is particularly qualified to sum up the 40's. In the first place he was a player here during the Charley Bowser days and then left to go into the service. He came back to Pitt and played for Fesler and continued as a veteran under Milligan. He then moved into administrative work alongside two of Pitt's finest athletic directors — Tom Hamilton, the Navy Hall of Famer, and Frank Carver, the Beaver

BOWSER'S BRAINTRUST — Head coach Charlie Bowser, center, is flanked by, left to right, assistants Arnold Greene, Al Leeson, Bob Hoel, Nick Kliskey, Mike Nixon and Bill Daddio.

squire. Cummins, who played quarterback, end, linebacker and tackle during his collegiate days, contends:

"We had many good players all through the 40's but our big problem was lack of depth. We could hold almost any team at bay for one half, but as the game wore on someone like a Buddy Young would come in to break our back."

There have been historians who point out that in some decades you could have slept all the way through and not missed a thing. That simply would not fit as an epitaph for the 40's. What happened sometimes wore your worry beads to a frazzle, but no one could claim it was boring.

HERE'S HOW WE'LL BEAT 'EM — Head coach Wes Fesler, center, shows assistants, Charles "Doc" Hartwig, left, and Mike Milligan some strategy.

DIFFERENT ERAS — Gibby Welch, left, an All-American halfback at Pitt in 1927, is welcomed into the Curbstone Coaches Hall of Fame by two standout running backs from the '40s, Emil Narick and Lou "Bimbo" Cecconi.

123

To Sutherland, A House Was Only As Strong As Its Base

By Arthur Daley
Sports Of The Times
New York Times

"He drew a respectful attention from his players. He was their champion."

Sept. 8, 1953

It was announced the other day that Dr. John Bain Sutherland would be formally installed this season in football's Hall of Fame. That's as it should be. There were gasps of dismay among the gridiron cognoscenti a couple of years ago when the original list was compiled. There was one glaring omission. Jock Sutherland, the phenominally successful Pitt coach for a decade and a half, had unaccountably been overlooked. This was akin to forgetting Ty Cobb, Babe Ruth, John McGraw or Connie Mack for a baseball Hall of Fame.

The dour Scot was a majestic figure of a man, physically and otherwise. He was tall, straight and spare, exuding power from a rawboned frame. His smile was thin-lipped and not frequent. To those who didn't know him he was a forbidding man. But the fortunate few who penetrated that hard outer shell found a warm and intensely human person. Perhaps he had fewer close friends than most men but the few he had worshipped him.

Even when he shifted from the collegiate ranks into the professional, he was not offered any welcome mat by his fellow coaches. Steve Owen, a hail-fellow-well-met, who calls everyone by his first name, always respectfully addressed Jock as "Doctor." Then the two roomed together for a week at the Sugar Bowl game. Sutherland dropped his mask of dignity and they became firm friends.

The outspoken Greasy Neale was much harder to win over. One day Sutherland joined those inseparable companions, Owen and Neale.

"You don't like me, do you?" said Jock to Greasy, a rare, mischievous twinkle in his eye.

"To tell you the truth, Doctor," said Greasy, "I respect any man in the football business. But I can't say that I like you."

Sutherland laughed his quiet laugh, vastly amused by Neale's painful honesty. But before Jock died five years ago, he even had won Greasy over to him.

However, it wasn't his personality which earned him recognition from the football fraternity as one of their "immortals." He earned that himself on the gridiron after a fantastic career. Jock had been born in Scotland and his mother sent him to live with relatives in Pittsburgh as the only way he ever could escape from a life of poverty. He was a 16-year-old boy, determined to educate himself and get ahead.

He took a job as a special policeman in a steel mill at night while he went through school in the daytime. On Saturdays he took part in the only sport he knew — soccer. Big and rawboned, looking much older than his years, he was invited to take a fling at American football. He played in the first game he ever saw and eventually became one of Pop Warner's greatest guards at Pitt. That's when he fell so madly in love with football that he never practiced dentistry despite a degree.

There have been few coaches with the insistence on perfection that Sutherland not only sought but demanded and got. Maybe he was a harsh taskmaster but he was an eminently fair one. As success mounted, not even his players begrudged him his ceaseless hours of drilling. If he didn't inspire the blind love that Knute Rockne won, he drew a respectful affection from his players. He was their champion who fought tirelessly for them, who encouraged them and who rejoiced proudly in every advance each made both during college and long afterward.

Jock attracted most of the brawny youths the Pittsburgh steel area had to offer. He always had the players, but he always had a team, too. He had it because he built with a scrupulous devotion to proper fundamentals. To him a house was only as strong as its foundation.

The fruits and the fancy stuff he scorned. The essence of his attack was the off-tackle play from the single wing he had learned under Warner. Deception to him was never as important as execution. So he was fanatical in his insistence that his players be well grounded in the fundamentals of blocking and tackling. Once they knew their jobs, the off-tackle play was virtually unstoppable. Thus did Pitt rank on top or thereabouts for year after year.

It broke his heart when Pitt was hit by a reform wave which split the university. So vast was Jock's popularity with students and alumni that he probably could have won his battle had he been willing to fight it out. But love for alma mater was too deep. He quit rather than risk an upheaval which might have done irreparable damage to the university.

So Jock moved into the professional ranks, bringing his perfectionist ideas with him. It took him a while to learn that the play-for-pay boys were so much better than the collegians that he had to plan accordingly. He refused to assign two men to cover Don Hutson, the Green Bay phenomenon. "No man can be that good," he said. Hutson murdered him, "Now I know," he said simply.

It was Sutherland who took a moribund Brooklyn team and lifted it to a peak never before attained in Flatbush. He even had made good in the toughest of all football competitions, among the professionals.

There was always a touch of grandeur to the doctor. He belongs on football's Olympian heights. It's nice to know that he formally has reached them.

Captain Tom And Johnny Mike Dominated Football In '50s

By Roy McHugh

"They didn't depend upon tricks of any sort to win ball games."

—The Owl

John Michelosen, a tried and true inheritor of the Jock Sutherland tradition, brought stability to Pitt football in the 1950s. The decade began with a new coach and a new system. One year later the new coach was gone. A comedy routine had developed, new coaches appearing on the scene with high expectations only to leave in the most precipitous way and be succeeded by the man who hired them: Athletic Director Tom Hamilton. At last in 1955 Hamilton gave the job to Michelosen and the effect was immediately all to the good: bowl teams in each of his first two seasons and better-than-.500 records in two of the next three.

Matched both times against Georgia Tech, the Panthers did not win either bowl game. Nevertheless, it was something to play in one. Nineteen years had gone by since the January first on which Michelosen quarterbacked Pitt to a famous Rose Bowl victory over Washington. Michelosen played on Sutherland teams that in 1934, 1935 and 1936 lost only two games. As a senior he was captain, becoming more and more Sutherland's clone. Once, the story is, when Pitt was protecting a lead against Notre Dame, running out the clock in the final minutes, a halfback broke loose and went all the way, 21 yards. Now Pitt would have to kick off — and give up the ball. Before the extra-point attempt, Michelosen, visibly unhappy, collared the offend-

ing halfback, "Dammit," he snapped, "the Doctor" — that was Sutherland — "won't like this."

Sutherland, for his part, considered Michelosen an extension of himself. He put him to work in 1938 as assistant backfield coach and when the blowup came, when Sutherland resigned as a protest against de-emphasis, they walked out together. Where Sutherland went as coach — to the Brooklyn Dodgers in the National Football League and then to the Pittsburgh Steelers — Michelosen went as assistant. It was by right of succession that the Steelers promoted him after Sutherland's death from a brain tumor.

As the 1940s ended, Michelosen remained, at 34, the youngest head coach in the NFL. Meanwhile, at Pitt, an earlier Sutherland disciple, Mike Milligan, had surprised everybody with a 6-3 season and wanted job security. He asked for a three-year contract but was willing to accept a two-year contract. Tom Hamilton offered him one year, take it or leave it. Milligan left it. And Hamilton then offered a four-year contract to Len Casanova, whose contract at Santa Clara had two years to go.

Was there ever a time when such minor technicalities made the slightest difference? In the 1920s, Casanova had been a halfback of some repute at Santa Clara. Neither that tie nor his contract kept him from coming East for a 20 percent raise.

Part of the new coach's baggage was the T-formation. Introduced at Pitt by Clark Shaughnessy and retained by Wes Fesler in a somewhat adulterated form, the T had disappeared during the Milligan years. Milligan, remember, had learned his football from Sutherland, that legendary

'50s FINEST — This 1950 lineup includes, left to right, Nick DeRosa, Bill Gasparovic, Mike Boldin, George Radosevich, Charley Thomas, Nick Bolkovac, Ted Geremsky. 　　　—Photo from University Archives

WEST COAST CREW — Head Coach Len Casanova, center, flanked by aides Jack Roche, left, and Herm Meister.

backs and none with more than average speed after the Marines took Paul Chess before the season started. We were fighting a police action in Korea, you may recall. Joe Capp, who scored two of the three touchdowns against West Virginia, went 56 yards for one of them and Bill Sichko had a 77-yard run and an 85-yard kickoff return in the opener at Duke, but there were games like the one with Miami, of which Jack Henry wrote in the Pittsburgh Sun-Telegraph: "Pitt could have rented its half of the field to the concessionaires." When Bestwick was not completing passes, Pitt had no offense unless his left-handed understudy, Bob Osterhout, was completing them, as he did in the last 15 minutes of the Northwestern game. Pitt scored 23 fourth-quarter points to none for Northwestern and still lost, 23-38. It was Osterhout's one moment of glory.

In 1950, the sun never seemed to be shining. The Panthers grew accustomed to playing in the rain and the mud and then came the big Thanksgiving Day snow. It buried Pitt Stadium, postponing the end of the season for a week. Even then, Pitt had to play Penn State at Forbes Field, where the grandstand roof had protected the seats. Repeating their Northwestern act, the Panthers scored 20 points in the second half to none for Penn State, but lost anyway when Nick Bolkovac, who held the all-time Pitt record of 44 extra points and hadn't missed one all year, missed one. Final score: Penn State 21, Pitt 20.

Casanova's first Pitt team was his last. He resigned the next year in July, forced to, he explained, because of his youngest daughter's health. She had never adapted to the Pittsburgh climate. Casanova himself, there is reason to believe, wasn't very crazy about it, either. Nor were Jack Roche and Herman Meister, the assistants who accom-

exponent of the single wing. But by 1950 the single wing was passe. In the NFL only John Michelosen still used it, at considerable risk to his career. Casanova, using the T at Santa Clara, had been 7-1-2 and 8-2-1 in his last two seasons, beating Kentucky and Bear Bryant in the Orange Bowl.

There was something else about Casanova. During World War II he had been a Navy commander. In the eyes of Tom Hamilton, the old sea dog, it was surely not the least of his credentials. In appearance, Casanova did not resemble the Latin-lover type his surname suggested. Rather, he had the man-of-distinction look appropriate to a board room: wavy gray hair, strong profile, level gaze. His antecedents were not Latin at all, but Swiss. Make allowances, if you will, for the fact that Switzerland shares a border with Italy.

Installing his T, Casanova needed a quarterback first of all, and he found one in Bob Bestwick, who was destined to break every passing record at Pitt, although not right away. Under Milligan, in his sophomore year, Bestwick had been a defensive back. He was not very tall — just 5 feet 10 — and he did not throw bombs. He did put the ball where the receivers were. One receiver, Chris Warriner, was not any taller than Bestwick and certainly couldn't run any faster, but he knew how to fake and shift gears. He ended up catching a lot of passes. At the same time, a lot of passes were being caught by Pitt's opponents.

Throwing them for Ohio State during the 1950 season was Vic Janowicz, an All-American. Throwing them for Miami was Jack Hackett, the Mighty Mouse from McKeesport. Throwing them for Notre Dame was Bob Williams. Bestwick actually outpassed Williams, 252 yards to 162, but a holding penalty against Pitt erased a touchdown pass to Warriner while Williams passed twice to Jim Mutscheller of Beaver Falls (in the years just after the war, the blue-chippers were getting away) for touchdowns that counted. And Pitt lost the game, 18-7.

Pitt that year lost eight games altogether, winning only from West Virginia. There were no experienced running

BOB BESTWICK

CHRIS WARRINER

LION KILLERS — The 1951 squad celebrates 13-7 victory over Penn State. See Alex Kramer, current administrative assistant to Foge Fazio, in the foreground.

panied him to Pitt from Santa Clara. Trapped in the Penn-Shady Hotel on what everyone supposed was the eve of the Penn State game the previous November, the three Californians watched the snow come down. Looking at one another, they shook their heads. But now escape had become possible; Tom Hamilton understood.

Commanding the aircraft carrier Enterprise during the final stages of the war, he had dealt with more pressing emergencies. In a wild mix of metaphors, Sun-Telegraph sports editor Harry Keck told his readers what Hamilton's intentions were:

"The athletic director has taken the bit by the teeth and will see what he can do about pulling the chestnuts out of the fire by doubling in brass as the coach."

He had been coaching off and on since his days in the Naval Academy backfield, first as a Navy assistant and for three successful years as head man. Pitt wasn't getting any neophyte.

And Casanova had left him some football players. There was Bestwick. There was Warriner. There was Billy Reynolds, a bandy-legged halfback from St. Mary's, W.Va., who had played both offense and defense as a sophomore and had intercepted seven passes. And there was Joe Schmidt.

Hardly anybody seemed aware of Schmidt, not even the sports writers, one of whom continued to misspell his name on occasion, substituting a "t" for the "d". Schmidt had been a two-way fullback who seldom carried the ball, but Hamilton used him only as a linebacker, and as a linebacker he was destined to be Pitt's first All-American of the 1950s and all-pro for eight years with the Detroit Lions. He's Pitt's only Pro Football Hall of Fame member.

Today Schmidt believes that if Casanova had stayed it would have made all the difference in 1951. "He knew football," Schmidt says, not implying that Hamilton didn't, but implying that Hamilton had other things on his mind. "Nothing against Tom. He did a good job under the circumstances. Tom was a motivator, a guy who tried to stimulate the players. He tried to build character, pride and so on But, looking back, I think he had too many problems, too many things to do besides coach."

Anyway, the Panthers lost their first seven games — to Duke, Indiana, Iowa, Notre Dame, Michigan State, Rice and Ohio State. All but three of those games — the ones with Iowa, Notre Dame and Michigan State — were close. Indiana beat them 13-6 on an 85-yard run by Gene Gedman of Duquesne and a 16-yard pass to Gedman from Lou D'Achille of Beaver Falls. For Pitt, Eldred Kraemer, a big blond freshman tackle from Minnesota who never had played high school football, intercepted a lateral pass and ran 49 yards. In the Iowa game, Kraemer blocked a punt. Against Michigan State, Bob Bestwick completed 26 passes for 345 yards, both Pitt records. The score of that game was 53-26, but the Panthers had not disgraced themselves. After a fiery speech from Hamilton, they were leading at the half, 20-19. Hamilton had been upset by articles in the Detroit newspapers referring to his players as "has-beens" and "nobodies."

Even in Pittsburgh there were doubters. On a snowy Nov. 17 the West Virginia game drew 9,800 fans. The Panthers won — something they hadn't done since the 1950 West Virginia game — and they won with ease, 32-12. Then they beat Penn State, 13-7. Every Bestwick-to-Warriner pass was breaking a record by now, and one for 32 yards scored a touchdown. The touchdown that won it, coming with only minutes to play, was a 16-yard sweep by Paul Chess, back from the Marines. The Panthers were looking better week by week. They had two rambunctious sophomore backs, Lou Cimarolli and Bobby Epps. They had a big, bruising sophomore end, Dick Deitrick. And in the Penn State Alumni Newsletter, Ridge Riley, ticking off reasons for the Nittany Lions' defeat, observed that "the thorn in their paw" was Schmidt. "We could not move him."

After Pitt went South to upset Miami, 21-7, ending the season with a 7-3 record, there was unrestrained joy. "At the final gun," wrote Jack Sell in the Pittsburgh Post-Gazette, "the happy Jungle Cats picked up Hamilton, who is no lightweight, stuck the game ball in his mitts, and carried him in triumph to the dressing room." There, Sell continued, they "put Captain Tom under a cold shower, clothes and all, and gave him a good dousing." A dignified, very formidable man, Captain Tom did not object.

"With material and spirit at an all-time high, the new coach will step into a soft berth," Sell conjectured. The

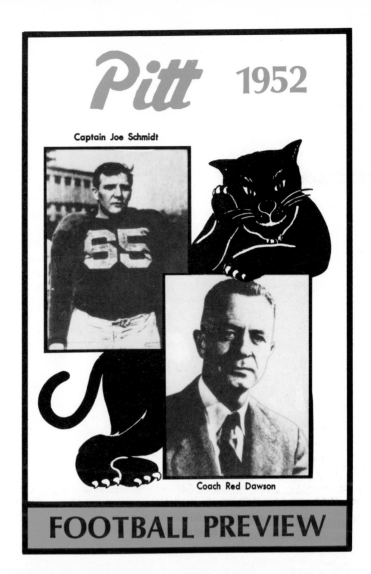

Captain Joe Schmidt

Coach Red Dawson

Pitt 1952

FOOTBALL PREVIEW

ALL ALL-AMERICANS — Pitt produced many All-America caliber football players through the years, including, from left to right, Dr. George McLaren, fullback, 1918-20; Ralph Chase, tackle, 1925; Bill Daddio, end, 1936-38; Eldred Kraemer, tackle, 1952-53; Dr. Tom Parkinson, fullback, 1929, and Bill Kern, tackle, 1925-27.

new coach turned out to be Lowell Dawson, known as Red, who had coached that high-scoring 1951 Michigan State backfield. Indeed there was good material. And Pitt won six games, while losing only three. But, soft berth or not, Dawson found lumps in the mattress.

Two of the three defeats were unexpected. After beating Notre Dame and Army, Pitt lost to West Virginia, 16-0. After beating Ohio State, Pitt lost to Penn State, 17-0. "Classroom troubles" finished Lou Cimarolli's season before it began. And when Joe Schmidt could play, he usually played hurt.

One of Schmidt's many rib, knee or shoulder injuries forced him to miss the Oklahoma game. On a blazing October day in Norman, with the temperature at 85 degrees, Oklahoma ran the Panthers ragged, 49-20. Notre Dame was next. Schmidt, recovered, would be in the lineup. At his request, or perhaps insistence, the coaches allowed him to give the pre-game locker-room talk, from which they were barred. Schmidt told the players, "Look, we're on our way to being a good football team. We're from Western Pennsylvania. Notre Dame has guys from Western Pennsylvania. They think they're better than we are. They've brainwashed themselves. Notre Dame has tradition. We don't. But we can beat them."

And they did, 22-19, leading all the way after a 78-yard touchdown run by Billy Reynolds. Schmidt, responding to his own oratory, made a 60-yard run himself with an intercepted pass. But late in the third quarter a Notre Dame lineman delivered a forearm blow to Schmidt's face — in 1952 only sissies wore face masks — and the result was an injury affecting even his spinal column.

He spent the next two weeks in the hospital while Pitt won from Army and lost to West Virginia. In the second game after his return he was "the best defensive player on the field, making a significant fumble recovery and at least a dozen vital saves" — the quoted material is from George Kiseda's Sun-Telegraph story — as Pitt crunched Ohio State.

With Bestwick and Warriner gone, Pitt depended on the run, not the pass. Reynolds alone outgained the whole backfields of Notre Dame, Army, Indiana, Ohio State and North Carolina State. Sometimes Pitt would shift from the

DICK DEITRICK — 1953 Captain

T to the single wing, pulling unwary or over-eager opponents offside. Says Schmidt (who played for four head coaches in his four years at Pitt): "Red Dawson had a good offensive mind. He was a pretty shrewd guy."

He was shrewd enough, anyway, to see trouble ahead. Pitt was back in the big time. The three sports writers covering the team — Kiseda, Sell and Carl Hughes of the Pittsburgh Press — agreed on that. Kraemer, the sophomore defensive tackle, had made the Look All-America team. "That boy's got everything," conceded Dawson. Deitrick, only a junior, was developing into a classic tight end, an intimidator of linebackers and cornerbacks. But the Penn State defeat had kept Pitt out of the Orange Bowl and it seemed to depress Dawson. His prediction for 1953 — "We may win three or four games, five at the most" — was close to the mark.

They were 3-5-1. The new rules eliminating free substitution proved bothersome. Forced to play both ways, many of the previous year's specialists were found wanting. Rudy Mattioli, Dawson's quarterback in 1952, couldn't play defense, so Henry Ford, who played defense superbly, and had played nothing else in his first two seasons, became the quarterback, sharing the assignment with Pete Neft, a sophomore. The only running back with adequate speed was Bobby Grier, also a sophomore, and he sat on the bench until the next-to-the-last game of the season.

Then in just 13 carries against North Carolina State, Grier ripped off 198 yards. With most of the fourth quarter left, and Pitt leading 40-6, Dawson took him out. In the press box, George Kiseda discovered that Grier could very easily break an all-time Pitt record. Warren Heller, in 1930, had rushed for 200 yards against Penn State. By the time

LEADERS CONFAB — Co-Captains Lou Palatella and Henry Ford of 1954 team talk with head coach "Red" Dawson.

LOWELL'S LINEUP — The one with the whistle is head coach Lowell "Red" Dawson, and the others, left to right, are Ernie Hefferle, Walt Cummins, Bob Timmons, Bob Friedland, Steve Petro and John Michelosen.

the word got to the bench, it was too late for Grier to return. N.C. State had the ball, and kept it for the rest of the game.

The Panthers' other victories were over Nebraska, 14-7, and Virginia, 26-0. Their one outstanding achievement, though, was a 7-7 tie with Oklahoma. For the second year in a row, they lost to their arch-rivals, Penn State and West Virginia. For the second year in a row, Penn State shut them out. Lenny Moore, just a sophomore, burned Pitt that year with a 79-yard touchdown run. Another big-name back, Paul Giel of Minnesota, ganged up on the Panthers all by himself. He rushed for 72 yards and three touchdowns, passed for 90 yards, quick-kicked 66, intercepted a pass on the goal line, and ran a punt back 65 yards to the Pitt five.

In 1954, having lost on the Coast to Southern California, 27-7, Pitt opened at home with Minnesota. A "So Long, Red" sign appeared. Minnesota no longer had Giel, but didn't need him. Five Pitt fumbles helped the Gophers to make it a runaway, 46-7. "So now Pitt is two games (and two defeats) down with seven to go in a schedule that is described in some places as suicidal and in others as murderous," wrote George Kiseda.

Mattioli had been the quarterback. A sophomore, Corny Salvaterra, replaced him against Notre Dame. "We switched to the T-formation on the Monday before that game," recalls Salvaterra. "I was told I'd be starting. I didn't sleep well that week; I'll never forget that." In a 33-0 defeat, no improvement was visible. On the following Tuesday, without warning, Red Dawson checked into Presbyterian Hospital. Dr. Richard Horn, assistant dean of the Pitt medical school, explained that the coach's trouble was a "heart irregularity," adding, "I don't expect him to be laid up much more than a week." As a matter of fact, Dawson never coached again. He settled eventually in Florida, where he was living in good health in 1982.

So with Dawson out of the picture, Tom Hamilton, the motivator, reappoints himself coach, and the moment could not have been more propitious. Pitt's next game is at home with Navy. The stage setting is marvelous, because Hamilton, in 1934, had coached a Navy team against Pitt (losing 31-7, Navy's only defeat that year). Informed that

LEAD THE WAY — Lou Palatella pulls out to block for Corny Salvaterra against West Virginia.

IRISH HEART-CRUSHER — Homestead's Billy Kaliden scores on keeper to beat Notre Dame, 29-26, in 1958 thriller.

Dawson is out and Hamilton in, Navy's 1954 coach, Eddie Erdelatz, groans. "Oh, hell!" says Erdelatz, prophetically. As in 1934, but not so decisively, an undefeated Navy team loses, 21-19.

Salvaterra scores twice, keeping the ball on the option play. Fred Glatz, a third-string end, recovers two fumbles and catches one of Salvaterra's passes for a 54-yard gain. Against Northwestern the next week, Glatz opportunely recovers another fumble and Salvaterra, with 39 seconds to play and the score 7-7, runs the keeper again for the winning touchdown.

Despite the presence of Ford, who can play anywhere, at left halfback, Pitt's offense is now geared to "the option without the option," so called, in which Salvaterra fakes a handoff to the fullback and then rolls out, at liberty to run or to pass. Most of the time, he runs. But with 2:22 left, his pass to Glatz from the four-yard line beats West Virginia, 13-10 (West Virginia's first defeat, by the way), and Pitt has won three in a row.

Hamilton gets the credit, and he deserves it. But a guard named Ed Stowe, cut from the squad for missing practice, reminds everybody that Dawson, "a great guy," had laid the groundwork. "It's just that he wasn't tough enough to

make you get out there and win," says Stowe revealingly. Tom Hamilton was tough enough, and he also resorted to old-fashioned uplift.

"When we played West Virginia," remembers Darrell Lewis, in 1954 a sophomore quarterback like Salvaterra, "we spent Friday night at the Summit Hotel in Uniontown. On the morning of the game, Hamilton lined us up in front of the fireplace in the lobby and read us excerpts from 'The Power of Positive Thinking,' by Norman Vincent Peale."

After WVU came Ohio State, the No. 1 team in the country. At Pitt's motel in Columbus, there wasn't any lobby; there wasn't any fireplace. "Hamilton put us in a stuffy bedroom," says Lewis. "He gave us the second chapter from 'The Power of Positive Thinking.'" This time the vibrations were negative: Ohio State 26, Pitt 0.

Against Nebraska, Hamilton started his second team, benching Salvaterra for Lewis, and Pitt won. But for the third straight year, Penn State held the Panthers without a point and they wound up the season 4-5.

Since 1952, relieved of his job with the Steelers, John Michelosen had been the defensive coach. Under Hamilton, who as Lewis recalls "would go around talking to people and let the assistants do the actual work," Michelosen was first among equals. Now he became the head coach officially. You could call it the start of an era.

Michelosen was the strong, silent type, a pigeon-toed Gary Cooper without the long neck. He lived by the rule of the self-confident or the stubborn: Never apologize, never explain. On the practice field, his head was always bowed. He appeared to be more interested in the grass just beyond his feet than in anything his players or assistants were doing, a misapprehension.

The Steelers (read: Art Rooney) had fired him for clinging to the single wing. At Pitt, he kept the split-T, having figured out a way to incorporate single-wing blocking. Since Red Dawson recruited by calf-size — it was said that he carried a tape measure — the material fit the system. There were people like Mean John Paluck, a 220-pound

CAPTAIN TOM'S TEAM — Rear, left to right, Bob Timmons, Tom Hamilton, Steve Petro, Steve Hoekef, front, left to right, Ernie Hefferle, Edgar Jones, Walt Cummins.

end, successor to the likes of Deitrick, Joe Zombek and Joe Bozek. In addition, Cimarolli was back. "He gives us much-needed speed," said Michelosen. And Joe Walton, who reminded the coaches of Chris Warriner, but had not done a thing as a sophomore, turned out to have Warriner's moves, plus an uncanny ability to hide from defensive backs in the end zone.

Of the first six passes he caught, five were for touchdowns, tying Warriner's record; of the 16 he had caught by the end of the season, eight were for touchdowns. Salvaterra did most of the quarterbacking, but Neft and Lewis played, too. Except when Lewis was in the game, the quarterbacks were as likely to keep the ball and run with it as to pass or hand off. Against Navy, Pitt tried only one pass all day, by Salvaterra. It was intercepted.

This excellent Navy team — George Welsh was the quarterback — keelhauled the Panthers, 21-0, a detour on their way to the Sugar Bowl in New Orleans. They arrived with a 7-3 record, their best since the Sutherland days. Oklahoma, the national champion, had beaten them, and so had mediocre Miami. Duke, with Sonny Jurgensen at quarterback, West Virginia, with Fred Wyant at quarterback, and Syracuse, with Jim Brown at fullback, had not. And in the last regular-season game, on snow-swept Mount Nittany, the team that lost by a shutout was Penn State, for a change. Jim Brown, in 12 carries, had gained just 28 yards against Pitt. Lenny Moore gained 10, in 13 carries, his worst-ever performance as a Lion. (It was still no excuse for the Steelers, who could have drafted him, to take a Colorado State defensive back named Gary Glick). Salvaterra ran with the ball only once against State — he'd been handing off a lot to Cimarolli — and went 62 yards for a TD.

In 1955, black people were Negroes. The Pitt fullback was a Negro — Bobby Grier. When Marvin Griffin, the governor of Georgia, heard about this, he said that if Grier played in the Sugar Bowl, Georgia Tech shouldn't, asking the state Board of Regents to back him up. "The South stands at Armageddon," he announced. "The battle is joined. We cannot make the slightest concession to the enemy in this dark and lamentable hour of struggle. One break in the dike and the relentless seas will push in and destroy us."

Even in the South, even with the Armageddon looming, his eloquence changed nothing. On the Georgia Tech campus, there was a three-hour demonstration. While police and state troopers stood ready with tear-gas grenades, hundreds of students marched on the state capital. There Rep. Muggsy Smith, a Georgia Tech graduate, promised them, "We are going to the Sugar Bowl." The students surged past him and past the guards at the door. They occupied the building for a while and then departed peacefully, burning effigies of Griffin as they returned to their dormitories. Three days later, the Board of Regents gave permission for Georgia Tech to play, but affirmed its opposition to "contests within the state in which the races are mixed."

Although New Orleans was a segregated city, the rules did not apply at Tulane University, where Pitt had arranged to be quartered. Grier ate, slept and practiced with the rest of the team. "Everything was great. I felt no pressure," he said in an interview many years later. The game itself, played at Tulane Stadium, tested his composure more severely.

Toward the end of the first period, from Pitt's 32-yard line, the Georgia Tech quarterback, Wade Mitchell, threw a pass to Don Ellis in the end zone. Mitchell had not yet com-

WELCOME BACK — Joe Schmidt, 1952 captain, and Pro Football Hall of Famer for Detroit Lions is met by Chancellor Wesley Posvar at Pitt half-time ceremonies.

pleted a pass. He was not to complete one all day. This pass, too high for Ellis, brushed against his fingertips. Ellis had no chance to hold it. But an official named Frank Lowry, pointing at Grier, who had fallen to the ground, called a penalty. Pass interference.

So Tech had the ball on the one-yard line and Mitchell banged it over for a touchdown.

That touchdown was the margin by which Georgia Tech won, 7-0. Late in the first half, Pitt drove to the one-yard line, where the ball was to go to Grier on fourth down. But Salvaterra "saw daylight," or thought he did. Instead of handing off to Grier, he went in behind him. Georgia Tech was waiting, and stopped the play.

The second half started, and Grier shook loose for the longest run of the game, 26 yards. It was not long enough. At the Tech 28, with one man between him and the goal line, he feinted in one direction and cut the other way. The defensive back was not fooled.

Pitt had one more chance. Late in the fourth quarter, on Tech's 11-yard line, Darrell Lewis called a running play. Up the middle went Ralph Jelic to the six. The stadium clock had stopped working and Lewis believed there were still 30 seconds to play. There was no time at all. The game had ended.

In the dressing room, Grier wept. He had not interfered with Ellis, he said. "I was in front of him, I couldn't have pushed him." Michelosen, his face expressionless, was sipping a Coke. As reported in the New Orleans Item, he "looked long and hard at a messenger who asked him for a statement for the press box. His brow furrowed in thought. 'Tell them it was a hard-fought game. And I'll wait till I see the movies of that pass interference to make my comment.'"

133

CORKY COST   BUGS BAGAMERY   RALPH JELIC   NICK PASSODELIS

TOM JENKINS   DARRELL LEWIS   BOB ROSBOROUGH   RAY DiPASQUALE

HERM CANIL   BOB POLLOCK   VINCE SCORSONE   CORNY SALVATERRA

The movies were inconclusive. Not so the statistics, which were one-sided in favor of Pitt. "They outmanned us, they overpowered us," said a Georgia Tech halfback, George Volkert. "When those Pitt guys hit you, you knew you were hit." The fullback said, "I get hit by this end, this Paluck, and when I'm pulling myself off the ground he's staring me in the face. He tells me, 'Look, fella, I'm Mean John, and if you come my way again I'm really gonna hit you hard.' Mean John's a good name for that guy."

There was talk about Georgia Tech's luck. "Sure we were lucky," agreed the coach, Bobby Dodd. "Pitt was as good a team as we met all year. All we can do against a team like that is play it close to the vest. We get that one score and we try to hold onto it. We give a lot of yardage. We try to keep you from getting that long touchdown run or pass. We figure after you've moved the ball a way on us we're gonna stop you before you can score. I hope we continue to be lucky."

They did. Twelve months later, in the Gator Bowl at Jacksonville, Fla., Pitt got the yardage and Tech won the game, 21-14. Pitt's regular-season record had been 7-2-1, with both defeats coming on the road.

The 1956 Panthers were not a high-scoring team — California had shut them out — but never until the Georgia Tech game did anybody tap them for as many as three touchdowns. Again they did a job on the supposedly unstoppable Jim Brown, holding him to 52 yards. Paul Hornung of Notre Dame, the Heisman Trophy winner, had to struggle for 59.

Syracuse lost to Pitt and so did Notre Dame. There were no easy Saturdays. The West Virginia score was 14-13 (favoring Pitt) and the Penn State game ended in a tie. At California, the Panthers were sluggish, but the 9-6 defeat at Minnesota was hard to take. Such were the substitution rules that they had not been able to get Bugs Bagamery or Darrell Lewis into the game to kick the extra point, and Salvaterra missed it. So with the game tied at 6-6 and five minutes to play, Michelosen, the conservative, gambled. On fourth and one at the Pitt 32, he went for the yardage, and sophomore quarterback Bill Kaliden fumbled the snap. Minnesota's Dick Borstad then kicked a field goal. On the subsequent kickoff, Joe Walton went all the way, 77 yards — the kick was short — but a clip seen by no one except the official who called it, and who never did identify the clipper, took care of that.

The next week against Notre Dame, Salvaterra lost a touchdown on a 56-yard run from scrimmage because of an obvious clip by — how did you guess? — Joe Walton.

Salvaterra was still keeping on the option without the option. In the final game of the season, with less than three minutes to play, it was Lewis who kept — and scored the winning touchdown against previously-undefeated Miami — but Salvaterra led the team in rushing and rushing attempts and threw enough touchdown passes to tie Bob Bestwick's career record of 15. Walton, still the phantom, caught six TD passes and made every All-America team.

"Slowly but surely," began a post-season review in The Owl, the student yearbook, "Coach Johnny Michelosen's Panthers are showing the nation that a team unversed in theatrics and sleight-of-hand magic tricks can play winning football. For the second consecutive year Pitt finished in the upper echelon of gridiron powers — and did it with a relentless, hard-driving ground attack and a sturdy defense."

Here the author answered the critics of hard-driving ground attacks (no one ever objected to sturdy defense). "Throughout the season," he wrote, "fans could be heard muttering that the Panthers didn't give the customers their money's worth. 'All they do is run off tackle and up the middle' was a common complaint." And a foolish one.

"This was the way the Panthers played. They didn't depend upon tricks of any sort to win ball games. They used talented material coached to perfection in the fundamentals — and it worked better than any razzle-dazzle that

THE THINKER — John Michelosen ponders explanation by halfback Jim Theodore over failed play.

GATOR BOWL BOUND — Joe Walton, head coach John Michelosen, Jim McCusker, Dick Bowen, Dale Brown and coach Jack Wiley whoop it up after it was announced Panthers were going to Gator Bowl in 1956.

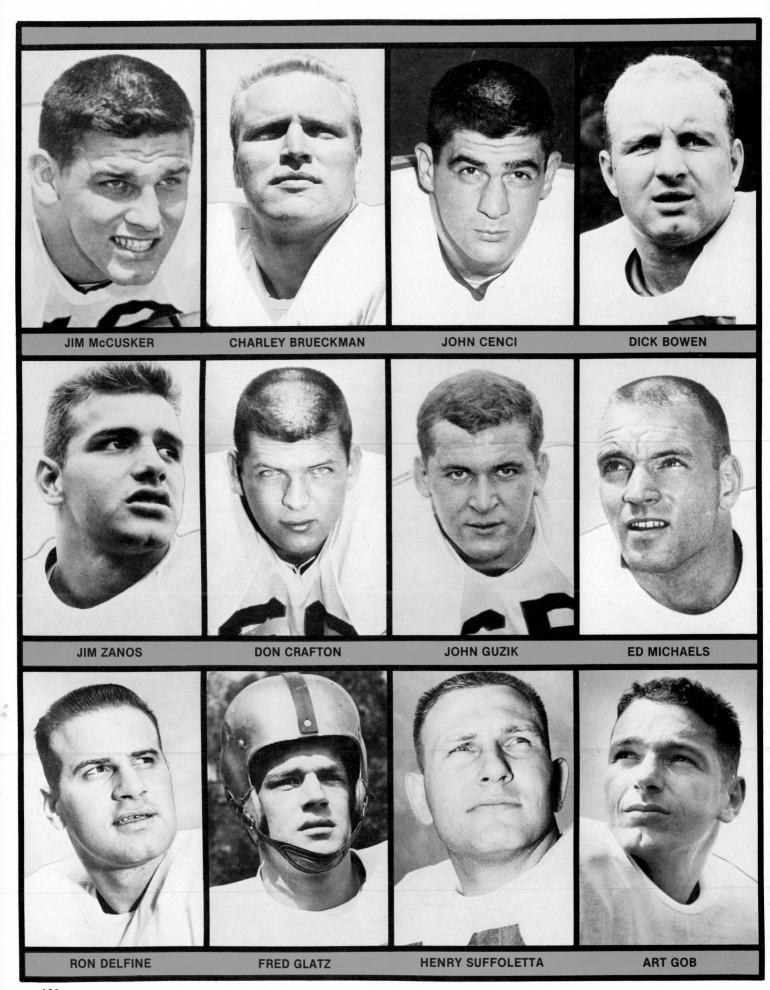

JIM McCUSKER   CHARLEY BRUECKMAN   JOHN CENCI   DICK BOWEN

JIM ZANOS   DON CRAFTON   JOHN GUZIK   ED MICHAELS

RON DELFINE   FRED GLATZ   HENRY SUFFOLETTA   ART GOB

numerous coaches have used at Pitt since Jock Sutherland left in 1938."

All true. But the Sutherland Age hadn't really returned. Pitt had a new chancellor, Edward H. Litchfield, whose values were those of the Ivy League. "Little things started happening," remembers Darrell Lewis, by 1957 a member of the coaching staff. "There was less recruiting money . . . more stress on eligibility . . . a rule against redshirting. They took away Ellsworth Center, where we practiced. The players had to eat with the student body. They'd get there late; everything would be cold. After Litchfield came, it was nip, nip, nip."

Still, there were more good seasons. Nineteen fifty-seven wasn't one of them. Oklahoma, in the opening game, stampeded Pitt, 26-0. Then, on successive Saturdays, the Panthers beat Oregon, 6-3, on a 22-yard touchdown pass from sophomore Ivan Toncic to Art Gob with 22 seconds to play; Southern California, 20-14, Gob scoring a touchdown after blocking a punt; and Nebraska, 34-0. But they ended up 4-6.

This was the team with the Five Jumbos. Myron Cope of the Post-Gazette gave them their name. In 1957 you could be a Jumbo if you were 6 feet tall and weighed 218 pounds, like Dan Wisniewski. Of the other Jumbos — Ron Kissel, John Guzik, Jim McCusker and Charley Brueckman — Guzik, 6-3, was the tallest and McCusker, 245, the heaviest.

The Jumbos were hard-hitting linemen. The Oklahoma backs were quick. Pete Dawkins and Bob Anderson of Army, a 29-13 winner over Pitt, were quick and powerful. Fran Curci of Miami, who looked as though he'd be squashed if the Jumbos could get their hands on him, was quick and deceitful, running with the ball when the Panthers expected him to pass. They expected George Izo to pass and he did, saving the game for Notre Dame with a throw that Aubrey Lewis caught for a 74-yard gain and a touchdown.

A footnote: As Myron Cope related this, during pre-season practice at Ellsworth Center, a sophomore named Norton Seaman, who was born in India, kicked a ball so hard and true that after clearing the crossbar it shot through a window without shattering the pane. Instead, it left "an oval-shaped hole the size of a football, the way Bugs Bunny runs through a brick wall." An impressed Michelosen announced that Seaman would do the place-kicking for Pitt. "He boots 'em with a soccer twist, you know," said the coach. "Then, all of a sudden," went on Cope, "Seaman became a sloppy kicker. He couldn't split the uprights from the two-yard line; his kicks spiraled off to the side with drunken indirection."

In the Oklahoma opener, Pitt had no need for an extra-point kicker. The following week, after the touchdown against Oregon, Seaman missed. He then disappeared until Pitt played Penn State. Ivan Toncic took over the extra-point kicking and did all right except in the 7-6 loss to West Virginia. With Penn State leading in the fourth quarter, 13-0, Pitt drove 74 yards for a touchdown and Toncic's kick was accurate. Now comes Bill Kaliden, passing to Dick Scherer for a touchdown, the play covering 45 yards, and Pitt can't get Toncic back in the game. So who kicks the point but Seaman, with the outcome riding on his soccer twist. In fact, he does it twice, the first attempt being ruled illegal because Pitt has five men in the backfield.

One of Michelosen's sophomores in 1957 was a center/linebacker named Serafino Fazio, called Foge. No doubt you have heard of him. Redshirting was still permissible in 1957 and Michelosen intended to redshirt Fazio, only

DICK (COMET) HALEY
Now Steelers' Player Personnel Director.

changing his mind in the Syracuse game when Charley Brueckman left the field with a separated shoulder. Sitting on the bench untaped and virtually unpadded, Fazio had to take Brueckman's place.

In the 1958 spring game, going 50 yards with an intercepted pass, Fazio looked like the best open-field runner on the team. Actually, Dick Haley was. Responding to his critics, Michelosen had gone to a pro-style offense with an end split wide, and Pitt opened the season in great style, beating UCLA, 27-7. A third-string end, Mike Ditka, blocked an extra-point try and caught a 16-yard touchdown pass from a third-string sophomore quarterback, Ed Sharock-man. Ditka, as we shall see, would be heard from again.

The Panthers won their first three games. Against Minnesota, they were one point behind with less than two minutes remaining when Bill Kaliden, on a quarterback sneak, pushed the ball across from the one-yard line. This was a big play. But Kaliden's biggest play — the most memorable play of the 1950s — came five weeks later against Notre Dame.

Eleven seconds were left and Notre Dame led, 26-22. Pitt had the ball at Notre Dame's five-yard line, fourth and goal. Kaliden, in the huddle, thought, "They won't be expecting us to run." He called his own play, a rollout to the right, making it appear, "for just a split second," that he might throw a pass. John Guzik, an All-American that year, was one of three blockers in front of him. Joe Scisly and Ernie Westwood were the others. At the extreme corner of the field, Kaliden angled into the end zone, almost stepping on the flag, and though George Izo completed a long pass to Red Mack on the first play after the kickoff, it was Pitt's game, 29-26.

Up to then, Pitt had lost only to Michigan State and Syracuse and had outplayed Army in a 14-14 tie. But the week after Notre Dame, the Panthers lost to Nebraska,

PRE-MED STUDENT **BILL KALIDEN** WILL BE OPERATING AT QUARTERBACK FOR **PITT** THIS SEASON....

AN ALL-AROUND ATHLETE.. BILL ALSO EXCELS IN BASKETBALL AND BASEBALL...

I'M JUST VERSATILE-- THAT'S MY DIAGNOSIS!

BILL NEVER FAILS!

...YET DOES EQUALLY WELL IN THE CLASSROOM (16 A's AND 3 B's IN HIS FIRST 2 YEARS.)

UNDER JOHNNY **MICHELOSEN,** **PITT** LOGICALLY RETURNED TO KNOCK-'EM-DOWN FOOTBALL...

I'M TAKING A STRONG STAND

...AND WOUND UP HIS FIRST COLLEGE HEAD COACHING YEAR IN THE SUGAR BOWL...

JUST LIKE GOING BOWLING!

...BECAUSE JOHNNY WAS BRED TO THAT BRAND AS QUARTERBACK-CAPTAIN OF THE '37 NATIONAL CHAMP PANTHERS!

whose only other victory all year was over Penn State, and then they lost to Penn State themselves, frittering away a two-touchdown lead. Their 5-4-1 record did not get them into a bowl game.

FEARSOME FOURSOME — The 1958 backfield included, left to right, Joe Scisly, Fred Riddle, Bill Kaliden and Dick Haley.

Tom Hamilton resigned the following June. After the break-up of the Pacific Coast Conference, California, Southern California, UCLA and Washington had formed the Athletic Association of Western Universities and were looking for a commissioner. Hamilton took the job. His prestige as an athletic administrator was enormous, going back to the early years of World War II when he organized the Navy's pre-flight training program and did more than anyone else to keep intercollegiate football a going concern. In 1949, when he came to Pitt, Chancellor Rufus Fitzgerald had given him a free hand. On matters pertaining to athletics, Hamilton made the decisions. With the arrival of Litchfield, that changed. Hamilton and Litchfield were too much alike — forceful, ambitious men accustomed to getting their own way. A power struggle which Hamilton couldn't win had been going on.

His successor was Frank Carver, the graduate manager of athletics. Litchfield's Ivy League bent, his "stress on eligibility," never alienated Carver, who believed that winning football teams and high academic standards were not antithetical. And Pitt, for a while, continued to win.

The 1959 team had its troubles. In the opening game, the

Panthers stumbled around against Marquette. They were behind in the fourth quarter, 15-13, when Mike Ditka, who already had caught a touchdown pass, suddenly reasserted himself. Self-evident though his ability was, as a sophomore Ditka had not been a starter until the eighth week of the season. Still, he caught more passes and probably made more tackles than any of the other ends. Football to him was serious business. His wide, somber face, small, tight mouth and cold, deep-set eyes conveyed the message to his teammates that it had better be serious business to them, too. There was the time a defensive back's mistake cost the Panthers a touchdown early in the game. "Let's get 'em the second half," the defensive back chirped as soon as the team was in the locker room, and it took the equivalent of a goal-line stand by the rest of the players to protect him from Ditka. Pitt won the Marquette game, 21-15, on two fourth-quarter plays by Ditka, who first blocked a punt and then got open a foot from the end zone for a touchdown pass from Ivan Toncic.

At Southern California the next week there were no touchdown passes from Toncic to anybody. Tom Hamilton, his allegiance still obviously with Pitt, watched the Trojans sack Toncic again and again. "They damn near murdered him," said Hamilton afterward, shaking his head. Pitt lost, 23-0, and was losing to UCLA in the fourth quarter, 21-6, when Toncic completed three touchdown passes in five and a half minutes. The last one, to sophomore Steve Jastrzembski, came with 31 seconds to play and gave Pitt the lead for the first time all day, 25-21. That was the way it ended. Then the Panthers shut out Duke, 12-0, and Michelosen was emboldened to observe, "The kids are shaping up."

Toncic, at this point, had thrown seven touchdown passes, three of them to Ditka. But there wasn't any running game. Then there wasn't any passing game. In successive weeks, the Panthers lost to West Virginia (whose defensive backs intercepted Toncic five times), to Texas Christian (a tackle named Bob Lilly played for the Frogs that year) and to Syracuse (Ernie Davis, wearing vinyl pants in the rain, slithered 25 yards for one of the Orangemen's five touchdowns).

Changes were called for, so Michelosen made them, getting Bob Clemens, Fred Cox and Jim Cunningham into the backfield together. Pitt's sports information director, Beano Cook, dubbed them "the C Boys." A popular variation acceptable to Beano was "the Three C's." By any name, they were good-sized backs, but not especially fast. Cunningham, though, was a bulldozer. He would carry the ball on play after play until the defense was bracing itself for up-the-middle stuff. Toncic would then fake a handoff and pitch out to Clemens or Cox. And one or the other, sooner or later, would break a long run.

Toncic threw just enough to pick up another touchdown pass, finishing the season with eight, a school record. Neither Boston College nor Notre Dame could handle the Three C's in the rain (although they didn't wear vinyl pants) and when Penn State fell, 22-7, Ridge Riley, echoing Grantland Rice in his newsletter, wrote that as far as he was concerned the CCCs stood for Catastrophe, Calamity and Chaos.

The Panthers ended up 6-4. Penn State's record, before the Pitt game, was 8-1, and the Lions had been invited to the Liberty Bowl. Their quarterback, Richie Lucas, was an All-American. But everywhere Lucas went, Ditka was sure to follow, knocking down everybody between them, and Serafino Fazio must have been doing something right because after the season his teammates elected him MVP. Meanwhile, there were the usual long touchdown runs by Fred Chaos (86 yards) and Bob Calamity (35 yards), while Jim Catastrophe played the role of decoy to perfection. "They were on me the whole game," he said. "I couldn't go anywhere. If I'd have run off the field, they'd have run off with me."

Catastrophe and Calamity were juniors and Chaos only a sophomore. The 1950s, ending with a bang, made the '60s look like something worth waiting for.

1959 LINEUP — From left to right in backfield, Curt Plowman, Fred Riddle, Ivan Toncic, Chuck Reinhold, and the line, left to right, Ron Delfine, Bill Lindner, Larry Vignali, Serafino Fazio, Norton Seaman, Ken Montanari, Mike Ditka.

Pitt Gets Back In Bowl Business

By Arthur Daley
Sports of the Times
New York Times

*"He's been carrying on a love affair all these
years with The University of Pittsburgh."*
—A friend of Jock Sutherland

Dec. 27, 1955

For the first time in nineteen years the University of Pittsburgh will be represented in a bowl football game when Pitt faces Georgia Tech in the Sugar Bowl on Monday. This fact has been generally overlooked as a result of the furor caused by the protest of the Governor of Georgia against Pitt's use of a Negro on its squad.

However, there is a feeling of sly satisfaction in this corner over the return of the Panthers to the bowl circuit. After all, it was the Rose Bowl classic of 1937 that precipitated the downfall of Dr. John Bain Sutherland as a gridiron coach at the Cathedral of Learning and left him a broken-hearted man until the day he died. Unusual, indeed, was Jock's attitude toward Pitt.

"Why is it that you never married, Jock?" someone once asked.

"Because," a friend answered for him, "he's been carrying on a love affair all these years with the University of Pittsburgh."

The heather of his native Scotland was still in his hair and the burr in his speech when Jock entered Pitt as an undergraduate. He'd never seen a football game but he was to become a great guard under the mighty Pop Warner. Then he became a great football coach. His Panther elevens were ranked near the top year after year and sometimes were acclaimed as national champions.

Dr. Sutherland was a tall, straight, austere man. His smile was frosty and his chill exterior did not invite familiarity. But those who were privileged to break through the cold crust found a warm, intensely human man and a loyal friend. Martinet and perfectionist though he was, his devotion to his players and his constant efforts to help them won their respect and then their affection.

It was this devotion to his players that led to the doctor's undoing. After three Rose Bowl failures, Pitt crushed Washington on New Year's Day of 1937. Most of his athletes were poor boys he'd rescued from a life in the mines by bringing them to college on athletic scholarships. So he gave them spending money for sight-seeing trips. When news of that generous gesture leaked out the holier-than-thou boys screamed like banshees.

The storm hit Pittsburgh and added to the growing feud between Sutherland and Don Harrison, the athletic director. The de-emphasis movement at Pitt grew stronger and Jock's position became untenable. No man ever resigned with more regret. The student body, which worshipped the dour Scot, went on strike. A defiant banner was hung outside the office of the Chancellor, Dr. John G. Bowman, formerly of Iowa. It read:

"We will trade our Iowa poison ivy for a wee bit of Scottish heather."

But the doctor had left Pitt and college football for good. Finding the professional game more challenging, he took over the coaching of the Brooklyn Dodgers and transformed that collection of misfits into a sleek and solid team. The outbreak of war prevented him from finishing the job in Flatbush.

Over-age and physically unfit though he was, Jock forced his way into the Navy with the relentless pressure and unstoppable power of one of his off-tackle plays. The doctor was a patriot and he got his commission. After the war he took over the coaching portfolio of the Pittsburgh Steelers. The Steelers played at Forbes Field in the very shadow of the impressive tower of the Cathedral of Learning. It wasn't quite being home but it made Sutherland fairly content.

If Pitt's decline as a gridiron power saddened him, Jock never showed it nor offered a comment. His football heroes of other years flocked around him at every opportunity. They were the doctor's "family" and he rejoiced in the success of each. Unfortunately he didn't live long enough to see Pitt's fortunes turn for the better, a slow but steady rise under the direction of Tom Hamilton, a sane and able administrator.

What would particularly thrill the old Scotsman would be the sight of Johnny Michelosen, one of "Jock's boys," in the coaching job. Michelosen is the link between the Rose Bowl game of 1937 and the Sugar Bowl game of 1956. Johnny quarterbacked the Panthers at Pasadena.

"Well done, lad," Sutherland might say to Michelosen, biting off the words in crisp fashion. Then the frost on that tall, unbending, dignified figure would start to melt as the glow in his eyes betrayed his inner satisfaction. He'd never even think that this was a delayed vindication of his own ideas. He'd just be proud that one of his boys had made good and that his beloved Pitt was back near the top again.

THE WEATHER
Cloudy and much colder tonight; Tuesday, fair and colder. Lowest tonight 20 to 25.
(Details Pages 2, 15)

Pittsburgh Sun-Telegraph

Complete Wire Reports by Associated Press and International News Service

7 ★★★★★★ STAR FINAL
CLOSING STOCKS

VOL. 24—NO. 33   24 PAGES   MONDAY, MARCH 6, 1939   THREE CENTS

JOCK SUTHERLAND QUITS PITT

THE HERO OF HOLDUP
★★★★★
He Tracked Bandits Down

Athletic Policy Assailed by Coach

Bandit Caught In Chase On North Side

Companions Escape After Victim Trails Getaway Car

A half-hour after three nervous holdup men left the employes in a Woods Run real estate office today, detectives arrested a 23-year-old boy who they said had confessed the stickup.

The suspect, thin, blond James Brunner, of Bridgeville, identified his two companions as only week-old acquaintances he had met in a North Side saloon, police said.

Hero in the capture was one of the holdup victims, Charles R. Frank, 25, of 3238 Bainton Street, who trailed the holdup car through North Side streets from his father's real estate office at 1439 Woods Run Avenue.

5 IN OFFICE AT TIME

Five persons were in the office when two strangers entered with drawn revolvers. They were Miss Laura Becker, 24, of 2806 Wadlow Street, North Side; Mrs.

Negrin's Foes Oust Cabinet In Revolt

BULLETIN

TOULOUSE, France, March 6.—(AP.)—Juan Negrin and Julio Alvarez Del Vayo, Premier and Foreign Minister in the deposed Spanish Republican cabinet, arrived here today by airplane.

MADRID, March 6.—(AP.)—A 'Big Six' defense council dedicated to an "honorable peace or a fight to the death" replaced today after a bloodless coup the regime of Premier Juan Negrin, who had held out for "resistance to the end" in the Spanish civil war.

(A dispatch from Hendaye, on the French-Spanish border, said that the probable effect of the new administration on continuation of the conflict was not apparent immediately, but that frontier observers believed the new council favored surrender to the Nationalists despite a proclamation of further resistance.)

Gen. Segismundo Casado, Military Governor of Madrid, seized power in a swift move. He

Navy Renews Plea for Guam Air Base

Vital to U. S. Defense, Admiral Leahy Tells Senators

By EDWARD B. LOCKETT
International News Service

WASHINGTON, March 6.—The Navy's No. 1 officer—Admiral William D. Leahy, chief of operations—told the Senate Naval Affairs Committee today that the nation's sea strategists believe it would be wise to fortify the Pacific Island of Guam.

Renewing the Navy's recommendations for $5,000,000 in Naval facilities on the tiny island close by Japan, Admiral Leahy urged the committee to include the Guam program in the $65,000,000 naval base bill now pending. The House rejected the Guam plan when it passed the measure.

SEPARATE BILL URGED

Admiral Leahy emphasized again and again that the proposed improvements on the island were

Roosevelt Adopts 'Definite Policy' To Aid Business

By WILLIAM S. NEAL
International News Service

WASHINGTON, March 6.—The federal government's gathering drive for the "appeasement" of the nation's private enterprise in an effort to stimulate recovery brought a series of important developments today.

The developments were:

President Roosevelt and his administration have adopted a "definite policy" of co-operation with business, Speaker Bankhead said after a conference with the Chief Executive and other congressional leaders.

A private luncheon, attended by Vice President Garner, was held by leaders in the Senate economy bloc which is determined to lift the tax load now being carried by business. Significantly, Bernard M. Baruch, the financier, addressed the Senators.

As a move to aid business, Senator King (Dem.), of Utah, introduced in the Senate a bill to repeal the undistributed profits tax so that "not a shadow of it will remain."

Senator Herring (Dem.), of Iowa, chairman of a special Sen-

Peace for Labor 'Ordered' By Roosevelt

By JACK VINCENT
International News Service

WASHINGTON, March 6.—President Roosevelt will flatly insist that the AFL and the CIO make peace, it became known today on the eve of the opening of the peace parleys he arranged between the two rival labor organizations.

The President, who will start

Resignation Accepted By Bowman

Condition Intolerable, Chancellor Told In Showdown

By HARRY KECK
Sports Editor

Chancellor John G. Bowman, of the University of Pittsburgh, today announced the acceptance of Dr. John B. (Jock) Sutherland's resignation as head football coach, effective immediately.

The chancellor made the announcement without comment by releasing his letter accepting the resignation tendered by the veteran coach on Saturday. Sutherland said upon the receipt of the letter from Bowman:

"I have no immediate plans for the future."

At a gathering with newspapermen at the P. A. A. shortly after noon, Dr. Sutherland denied he planned to accept a position as

---

OFFICIAL WEATHER FORECAST ON PAGE 2

Pittsburgh Sun-Telegraph

Complete Wire Reports by Associated Press and International News Service

FINAL HOME
Late News

VOL. 24—NO. 37   36 PAGES   FRIDAY, MARCH 10, 1939   THREE CENTS

STUDENTS ON STRIKE AT PITT

3 Hurt In Fire At East End Market

Chief Phelan Periled By Falling Glass On Penn Avenue

Three firemen were injured and two others—Fire Chief Nicholas Phelan and Battalion Chief William Kerr—escaped hurts in a two-alarm fire in the Giant Eagle Market at 5152-58 Penn Avenue early today.

Phelan and Kerr were standing in Penn Avenue when a plate glass window broken by a stream of water, showered glass around them.

FIREMEN INJURED

The injured firemen were Capt. Thomas L. Noonan, 55, of 610 Copeland Street, Hoseman Thomas Wilshire, 27, of 7247 Kedron Street, both of Engine Company No. 14, and Hoseman William Fowler, of 2857 Midland Avenue, of Engine Company No. 8.

Noonan was affected by smoke and Wushire and Fowler were cut by glass. They were treated at the scene by Dr. Daniel E. Sable and returned to duty.

Chief Phelan estimated the property damage at $8,000.

TRAFFIC TIED UP

Penn Avenue traffic was tied up more than an hour.

Slovak Rebellion Crushed by Czechs; Plea Sent Hitler

BULLETIN
International News Service

BUDAPEST, March 10.—A report that Bratislava Slovaks have appealed to Reichsfuehrer Adolf Hitler to intervene in their behalf with the Prague government was circulated here today.

By GEORGE LANGWEIL
International News Service

PRAGUE, March 10.—A Nationalist plot to bring about secession of Slovakia from Czecho-Slovakia and an "anschluss" between the autonomous region and the Nazi Reich was swiftly quelled today.

Dr. Emil Hacha, president of Czecho-Slovakia, dissolved the Slovak government, dismissing its members from office. Hacha then appointed Deputy Sivak as premier of a new Slovak government, with Premier Karol Sidor remaining in that post.

Military authorities at Bratislava and other Slovakian cities discovered the plot, engineered by supporters of the late Father Andreas Hlinka, former leader of the pro-Nationalist Catholic People's Party.

All former Slovakian ministers concerned in the Nationalist movement were reported to have been taken into "protective custody" on grounds that they had broken their "holy oath to protect the integrity of the country."

At dawn a Czecha mechanized division of troops moved into Slovakia, occupying public buildings and strategic positions at Bratislava and elsewhere.

Several hours later authoritative statements issued at Prague indi-

AFL to Offer New Plan For Labor Peace

Further Concessions To CIO Expected as Sessions Resume

Miners drafting pay demands — Page 2.

By JACK VINCENT
International News Service

NEW YORK, March 10.—President Roosevelt's labor peace conferences reached the crucial stage today even in face of reports the AFL was prepared to make a new concession to the CIO.

Tonight's meeting will be held in a New York hotel, a setting in contrast with their first two meetings, one in the executive offices of President Roosevelt, and the other in the Department of Labor in Washington.

Until now, it had been the President who kept the arbiters together. If, away from Washington and the personal influence of Mr. Roosevelt and Secretary of Labor Perkins, the committees can continue their peace talks, there will be some hope for peace.

AFL PEACE PLAN

A new ray of hope appeared with reports the AFL committee was drafting a peace plan recognizing the CIO's industrial unionism, with reservations, in certain

SIGN OF THE TIMES AT PITT
★★★★★★★
Protesting the Sutherland Resignation

U. S. Pact Ends Nazi's Trade In Brazil

By ROBERT G. NIXON
International News Service

WASHINGTON, March 10.—The United States has erected an "economic blockade" between Germany and Brazil, shutting the Nazi traders out of their principal South American market, through the new Brazilian-American economic and defense accord, compe-

Rally Charges Sutherland 'Squeeze Out'

Bowman's Regime Denounced for 'Bungling'

The planned student demonstration against the resignation last Saturday of Jock Sutherland, University of Pittsburgh football coach, got under way today.

Dental students were ready to lead the walkout, following a plan which Frank Scott, student football manager, said he had worked out with Leonard Levinson, sports editor of the Pitt News.

Protest signs had been prepared in advance for posting and for students to carry on parades through Oakland and the downtown district. In mass meetings and similar protest measures.

SIGNS OF WRATH

Signs read:

"Wanted—Spare time football coach. Must be stooge."

"Is the Panther dead?"

"Want a job? An opening for experienced yes-man at Pitt."

"Is Pitt a farce?"

"Million dollar stadium—no coach."

"Today we strike for the glory of Pitt."

"Arise, assert your rights."

The students charge Sutherland was "squeezed out" of the coaching position in which he guided Pitt teams to the heights. But leaders declared the protest was

Gator Bowl Brings Back Pleasant Pitt Memories

By Arthur Daley
Sports of the Times
New York Times

"The heritage was rich at Pittsburgh."

Dec. 28, 1956

When a tourist heads toward a certain bridge over the St. John's River on the outskirts of Jacksonville in Florida, his eyes inevitably are attracted by a pretty little stadium that cuddles among the palm trees on the right of the highway. This is the Gator Bowl, the youngest and least distinguished of the major bowls.

It could offer neither as much prestige nor as much cash on the barrelhead as the other New Year's Day football games. So it always finished fifth in a five-bowl race in regard to publicity and to desirability for television sponsors. The Gator Bowl obviously needed a gimmick, and the realistic zealots who control its destinies shrewdly devised one.

The Jacksonville spectacle was licked before it even started when it tried to compete against the Rose Bowl, Sugar Bowl, Cotton Bowl and Orange Bowl. Therefore the friends of the alligator said "Happy New Year" to the other bowls and moved their Gator Bowl to the Saturday before Jan. 1. That gave them sports page space and television channels all to themselves. The Gator Bowl has been moving with giant strides ever since.

The Gator Bowl has cornered a rip-snorting attraction in Pitt and Georgia Tech. These are two of the stronger teams in the nation and the Jacksonville operatives need not tug at their forelocks while kowtowing to their betters. The chances are that they're as good as anyone else in the bowl business.

This is a replay of sorts of last season's Sugar Bowl engagement when the Rambling Wrecks barely edged Pitt, 6 to 0, with the aid of a questionable pass interference penalty. But for the Panthers this game on the morrow becomes a reconfirmation of their return to the Big Time where they always belonged.

The University of Pittsburgh was as permanent a part of the football scenery as Notre Dame, Michigan, Ohio State, Southern California or Georgia Tech. This was the school that flourished under the coaching wizardry of Pop Warner and then under the genius of Jock Sutherland. The heritage was rich. But the eggheads at the Cathedral of Learning squandered that inheritance until Pitt became second-rate on the gridiron.

It took an admiral to refurbish the old family manse and restore some semblance of the graceful living of the Warner-Sutherland era. Tom Hamilton had been the driving force behind the Navy Pre-Flight program during the war and then the heroic skipper of the Enterprise. When this one-time Naval Academy coach retired with the rank of admiral, he dropped anchor near Schenley Park in Pittsburgh. As Pitt athletic director he turned into profitable channels his boundless energy, his talent for organization and his sound outlook on intercollegiate athletics.

There are enough star football players in the Pittsburgh area alone to staff a couple of dozen college teams. In fact, a couple of dozen college teams raid the Monongahela Valley annually and load their rosters with Pennsylvanians. Before Hamilton arrived, Pitt used to shoo away with a stick anyone who even resembled a gridiron performer. Tom stopped that nonsense and welcomed them as the neighbors they were.

Then he appointed Johnny Michelosen, a Sutherland quarterback during the days of glory, as head coach. Nor is that the only connection with the star be-decked past. Playing end for Pitt this year is everyone's All-America, Joe (Tiger) Walton, the son of Frank (Tiger) Walton, an All-America tackle for Sutherland a quarter century earlier.

Pitt has gone modern in its style of play to the extent that it uses the split-T, which Don Faurot invented and which certainly deserves to be named the Faurot-T. But Michelosen is as Scottish as Sutherland ever was. He hates to give the ball away. So the Panthers pass as sparingly as Jock's earlier teams. They prefer to grind it out.

Since this requires blocking, Pitt uses gang-blocking that is reminiscent of the single-wing Sutherland era. One ordinarily doesn't expect so much blocking out of the T. This naturally cuts down on the long-gainers — there are fewer blockers free for downfield work — but Pitt's short power plays crunch out the yards as inexorably as they once were crunched out by Marshall Goldberg, Dick Cassiano and Curly Stebbins of the Dream Backfield of some two decades ago. The blocking back for that trio? Michelosen, of course.

The Panthers are big and they have gained more than three times as much on the ground as in the air, although Corny Salvaterra, a roll-out quarterback who runs a lot, is a fair passer. Six of his thirty completions have gone for touchdowns.

Georgia Tech is smaller but faster, and it doesn't care too much for that new-fangled passing game, either. Wade Mitchell at quarterback is a master faker in the belly series and deft at pitchouts to the swift halfbacks.

The Gator Bowl not only is the first of the bowl games but it also may be the best. It never happened that way before.

But Not The Sugar Bowl . . .

AN APPLE A DAY didn't keep the press away. They wanted Bobby Grier to go over the controversial "pass interference" call that cost Pitt the ballgame in a 6-0 loss to Georgia Tech in the Sugar Bowl.

WHAT A LEMON — The Sugar Bowl setback left a sour taste in the mouths of Pitt's official party, from left to right, assistant coaches Steve Petro and Bob Timmons, athletic director Tom Hamilton, and head coach John Michelosen.

—Photos by Thomas C. Vrana

143

JOE WALTON

One Of The Smallest, But One Of The Best Tight Ends In The Game

By Dana Mozley
Of the New York Daily News

November, 1963

A s dearly as they love him, the New York Giants some-times make fun of their unsung hero of the last three seasons. No one else is allowed to, however.

"He's the only player in the league who wears Alder elevator football shoes," says Kyle Rote.

Wellington Mara, the Giants vice president, will add: "His only weakness is that he looks like he can't do it."

After Y.A. Tittle and Del Shofner and Don Chandler and Sam Huff and the other more noticeable athletes had their accolades, the talk had gotten around to Joe Walton. No matter how hard they try, the Giants' publicity staff can't make the ex-Pitt captain from Beaver Falls, Pa., out to be anything but what he is — the smallest tight, or close, end in the NFL. But, on one point, the publicists are right. Joe is one of the very best.

Because he is lacking in size, and in exceptional speed, and in color, Walton might be termed the best .270 hitter in the NFL. Although Tittle may concentrate on getting the ball to Shofner, he can almost always rely on Little Joe to come up with the big play, at the right time. He rarely misses.

There seems to be a fetish in the pro league right now that the bigger and stronger a tight end you can get, the better off you'll be. The Ron Kramers, Pat Richters, Mike Ditkas, Johnny Brewers and others are all 6-4 or 6-5 and weigh up to 250.

Except for the Pittsburgh Steelers' Preston Carpenter, who is supposed to spread only 190 pounds over his 6-1 frame, you can't find a small tight end anywhere.

That is, anywhere except New York. And Walton's actual statistics remain a mystery. One place in the special brochure that the Giants get out for press-radio-TV, Walton is listed as 5-11, 200. In another section, he is supposed to be 6-0, 205.

"If Joe is any taller than 5-9, I'm 6-9," declared Frank Gifford, "I'll give him about 190 pounds in weight. He's a little heavier in football uniform."

The darkly handsome Walton boasts about only one of his many feats. He refuses to keep it a secret that he still holds the intramural basketball scoring record at the University of Pittsburgh.

But he is genuinely modest, to the point, that he still fears every cutting period at camp. "Why, Walton is even worse than Joe Morrison," says Wellington Mara. "He begins to worry whether he'll make the first cut. Morrison, at least, won't get jittery until we're near the final trims."

"You know, I think Walton still believes what we all told him when he came to us from Washington," asserted Coach Rote. "He's married to a beautiful girl, Ginger (Miss Washington, D.C., 1959), who has fine talent as a singer. When we got her to sing as the feature of the first team party Joe attended, we told him then that he was strictly incidental to the trade. It was Ginger we wanted."

The Giant brass, however, wanted Walton. He was procured after four seasons with the Redskins (their No. 2

PRIDE OF BEAVER FALLS

Pitt people have always pointed with particular pride to Joe Walton, who has had an outstanding career in football and has long represented the University in an all-pro manner.

Walton was an All-American end at Pitt in 1956, and set a school record in 1955 for most touchdown passes caught in a season with eight — a remarkable feat because, in the Panthers' ultra-conservative offense, he caught only 11 passes altogether. He also set a career record for TD passes caught with 14 from 1954-56.

He came out of Beaver Falls to follow his father, Frank "Tiger" Walton (1932-33) to Pitt, and he did the same when he signed with the Washington Redskins, as their No. 2 draft pick in 1957. He was a topnotch tight end for four seasons with the 'Skins, and then three more with the New York Giants.

The Giants won three NFL Eastern Division titles with Walton as a starter. He was called by Y.A. Tittle "the best third down receiver in the game, bar none." In his pro career, he caught 178 passes for 2,623 yards and 28 TDs.

In 1982, Walton began his second season as the offensive coordinator and quarterback coach of the New York Jets, and received much credit for the improved play of Richard Todd. Before that, he had coached with the Redskins from 1974, and with the Giants from 1969.

Walton's records stayed on the books a long time at Pitt. Then Dwight Collins came out of the same Beaver Falls community in 1980 to catch ten TD passes in a single season, and, a year later, Julius Dawkins of Monessen snared 15 TD passes in one campaign.

Gordon Jones came to Pitt from North Versailles and set a career (1975-78) record for TD receptions with 21.

Even so, Walton will always remain on the minds of Pitt followers as one of their finest.

draft in '57), along with flanker back Jim Podoley.

"When we made the deal," Wellington recalled, "almost everyone though that Podoley was the one we really wanted. It isn't generally known, but we could have made a deal for Podoley, alone, in January 1961. It wasn't until July of that year that Podoley came to us, because it wasn't until then we could get Walton."

From his right end position, Walton does two things and does them equally well. He catches passes, and he blocks.

If the NFL kept records of passes thrown to and passes caught by its receivers — as is done in Canadian football — it's a very good guess that Walton would have the best percentage in the league. Just for instance, in the last three games he was 2-for-2 against the Browns; 5-for-5 against the Cowboys and 4-for-5 against the Browns in Cleveland.

"Not only does Joe have great hands," points out end coach Ken Kavanaugh, "but he runs exceptionally fine pass patterns.

"No one knows the personnel in our league any better. He could tell you everything about the strong side safeties. They're the ones he's usually running against.

"Though he doesn't have great speed, he does have good speed . . . good enough, along with what he knows of the personnel, to run a lot of deep patterns. There aren't many tight ends who do that."

Instead of allowing his size to be a detriment in blocking much bigger men, Walton makes it an asset. Because he is built lower to the ground, he is able to come off the ball from a much lower stance than other ends — and block lower and more effectively.

"Joe has a classic blocking stance," says Rote. "Straight back, and tail down." Adds Kavanaugh: "And he has awfully strong legs. That's where he gets his power. And, of course, you have to mention his enthusiasm. I've never seen anyone who likes to block more than he does."

Walton must either block the left linebacker or the left end. Ask him the toughest he has ever faced, and he'll quickly name Dan Currie, Packer linebacker, and Gino Marchetti, Baltimore end.

And, since both are in the other division, Walton won't even have to meet them this year — unless, perchance, Joe helps the Giants win another Eastern title, as he has already done twice.

"His only weakness is that he looks like he can't do it."
—Wellington Mara

"He's the best third down receiver in the game bar none."
—Y. A. Tittle

Hold That, Tiger, Joe Was Big Enough

"When your team loses, be prepared to take it." —Frank Walton

By Rudy Cernkovic
United Press International

Nov. 15, 1956

It's just the way the Tiger wanted it. Play it hard, clean and when you lose — be able to take it.

Joe Walton is playing football the way his dad wanted it. The Pitt end regards his role with the Panthers as a precious legacy. His father, Frank "Tiger" Walton, was one of Pitt's great tackles in the Jock Sutherland era.

The Tiger helped bulwark the rock-ribbed lines that cleared the way for the Panther backfields in the early 1930s. He played in the Rose Bowl in 1933 and the following season in the East-West All-Star Game.

Joe is equalling his father's gridiron accomplishments. He played in the Sugar Bowl last New Year's Day and is certain to be tapped for the East-West game.

Joe was a 135-pounder on a seventh grade football team when his father first saw him play.

After the game, the Tiger told his wife:

"Our Joe is too small for football. He better quit before he gets hurt."

Like his father, Joe prepped at Beaver Falls (Pa.) High School where he played with fierce devotion. When he was a senior, he was named All-Pennsylvania fullback.

After his high school career — when he always played with winning teams — college scouts sought out Joe.

Because his son had always been with a winner, Tiger took him aside one day and told him to prepare for defeat.

"Son, you haven't experienced defeat. But remember, when your team loses — be prepared to take it," he said.

When Joe finished high school, everybody took it for granted he would enroll at Pitt. But Lou D'Achille, a cousin who had starred as an Indiana University quarterback, induced Joe to visit the Hoosier school. Joe was impressed after a tour of the campus and decided to cast his lot with Indiana.

A few weeks before Joe was to enter Indiana, the Tiger developed an illness that was to be fatal.

"Dad never urged me to go to Pitt," Joe recalled. "He said I was to choose for myself. But deep down in his heart, he wanted me to enroll at Pitt — I sensed it. When I knew Dad was dying, I went to Pitt. I've never regretted it."

In September, 1953, Joe entered Pitt. Two days later, his father died.

The Pitt coaching staff, impressed with Joe's ability as a pass receiver and an open field runner, decided to convert him from fullback to end.

Last season, Walton was the nation's leading collegiate touchdown-pass receiver with eight. He has caught six scoring aerials in Pitt's first seven games this year to bolster his bid to repeat as the top scoring receiver.

Notre Dame coach Terry Brennan paid a tribute to Walton last Saturday when he admitted after the game that he had primed the Fighting Irish to point for Walton.

The 9-6 defeat experienced against Minnesota two weeks ago rankled the Panthers because of a disputed call. After the Gophers booted the winning field goal, Walton returned the ensuing kickoff for 77 yards and a touchdown that would have meant victory. But the score was nullified by a clipping call.

Pitt coaches, after studying their game movies, disagreed with the clipping call. Naturally, Joe was disappointed by the outcome.

But he recalled the words of his dad:

"The true test of an athlete is whether he can accept defeat."

A COUPLE OF JOES — Two Pitt All-America ends, Joe Skladany (1932-33), and Joe Walton (1956), get together.

HOLD THAT TIGER — Young Joe poses with pro football-playing father, Frank "Tiger" Walton.

'63 Season Stood Out Like Beacon In Stormy Sixties For Panthers

By Jim O'Brien

"They were the best guys you could put together . . . in so many ways."
—Bimbo Cecconi

The '60s were something less, as far as football at Pitt was concerned, or, depending upon one's point of view, they were something more. Charles Dickens might have described it as the best of times, and the worst of times. Then again, he didn't have to sit through it.

The 1963 team, with its 9-1 record and remarkable career achievement by its members, is a strong source of pride to Pitt people.

Only a few years later, however, the Pitt football program began a downhill slide. For three seasons, from 1966 through 1968, the Panthers posted a 1-9 mark each time out.

The '60s started on a struggling note, and ended in much the same manner.

The only other winning record posted in the period was the 4-3-3 mark in Mike Ditka's senior season of 1960, and the frustration of that fall was to set the tempo for the 10-year stretch. Even when the Panthers went 9-1 and were ranked third in the nation they did not get a bowl bid. But that's another story.

In short, it was a different decade. A difficult decade. A turbulent decade.

There was trouble in Southeast Asia from the start, and those of us who entered Pitt in 1960 always worried about when the war — or military action, as it was labeled — in Vietnam might worsen. We wanted it to be over, so other young Americans might come home, in truth, so we wouldn't be next. Instead, we heard of the killings, the maimings, and the disappearances of young Americans in alarming numbers.

There were student demonstrations throughout the land relating to Vietnam, to civil rights, to legalizing drugs. Hanoi. Little Rock. Mississippi. Space missions. Marijuana. Rock & Roll. These were all on the mind, and the lips of angry young people.

There are several events which stick in one man's mind from those student days in the early '60s:

• When Billy Mazeroski hit the home run over the scoreboard in left field to beat the New York Yankees when the Pirates won the World Series in 1960. That heroic homer, which turned the city upside down for days, was hit at Forbes Field, just across the street from the Student Union. Only a part of the outfield wall remains as a memorial. The Student Union has been refurbished.

• When John Glenn made America's first orbital flight in Friendship 7, and the astronauts became America's greatest heroes in 1962.

• When President John F. Kennedy was assassinated by Lee Harvey Oswald in Dallas in 1963. You heard about it as you passed by the University Shop. Then you went to the Student Union where everyone stood in shock around a television set. Where were you when you heard the news? Have you really stopped crying?

There were to be lots of highs and lows like that throughout the '60s.

Talking to people who were associated with the Pitt football program during those days brings it all back.

Lou "Bimbo" Cecconi was on the coaching staff at the start and the finish of the '60s, and can fully appreciate the "best of times, worst of times" tag.

He had been an outstanding football and basketball player from 1946 through 1950, following another war — one that was spelled with a capital 'W' and had Roman numerals after it — and he has always had blue and gold blood in his little but able body.

He still does, even after some difficult days at the end of his Pitt tenure, as he sits behind his desk at Steel Valley High School in Homestead, where he serves as assistant principal. He doesn't coach sports anymore.

"I had three kids graduate from Pitt, too, so it's my school in so many ways," he said, those large dark eyes still as sincere as can be.

He was an assistant under John Michelosen from 1958 through 1965, and he returned as an aide to Carl DePasqua from 1969 through 1972.

"As far as talent in football, the first part of the '60s was like a dream," continued Cecconi. "We had the best kids. They qualified in so many ways.

"I can look at the team photos, and I know every one of them, and there's something like 18 who are doctors or

SCREEN TEST — Head coach John Michelosen makes point while viewing game film with top assistants Carl DePasqua, top left, and Bimbo Cecconi.

"C" BOYS WITH BOSS — John Michelosen shows off his "C Boys" — Fred Cox, Jim Cunningham and Bob Clemens after a victory over Notre Dame.

dentists. They were good at football, and they were good at their studies. And they combined it with a helluva time. They were a wild bunch of kids in many ways, but they typified the ideal program. They had good times, they were super football players, and they accomplished their academic goals.

"They were the best guys you could put together. They may have champions now at Pitt, but they're not as well-rounded. We had the best guys you could have, and there were only 61 of them. Johnny Majors brought in twice as many kids in one year, but they couldn't measure up.

"Two years after John Michelosen was named Coach of the Year, he was fired and we all went. Then there was the collapse in the middle '60s when Dave Hart came in. Then we came back as coaches, and we thought we could do it because we were Pitt people, but we couldn't turn things around. We thought we had the blood in us to do it. We were wrong.

"So we were gone, too. Then the administration made up its mind about the kind of commitment that was necessary to put together a first-class program, and they went the other way. It's worked."

One of the quarterbacks Bimbo coached during his days as Michelosen's assistant was Jim Traficant, a tough, cocky kid from Youngstown. They had a disagreement in Traficant's senior season of 1962. Traficant complained then, "I made two mistakes in my life: the first one was coming to Pitt, the second one was staying."

Today, Traficant has changed his tune somewhat. He is the elected sheriff of Ohio's Mahoning County, working out of an office in his hometown. He has two master's degrees from Youngstown State University — in ad-

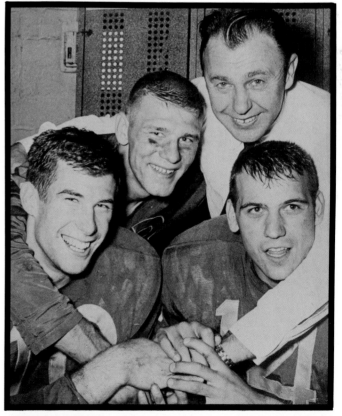

POINT-MAKERS in Pitt's 8-6 victory over UCLA in 1962 are hugged by Coach John Michelosen. Left to right, they are Paul Martha, who scored Panthers' touchdown, and Rick Leeson and Jim Traficant who collaborated on decisive two-point conversion.

LOOKING LIKE WINNERS are Pitt Coach John Michelosen and three Panthers who helped defeat Oklahoma, 13-9, in 1965, namely Kenny Lucas, Eric Crabtree and Mitch Zalnasky. Crabtree and Zalnasky both caught TD passes from Lucas.

ministration, and in counseling. He's worked for over ten years with youngsters in narcotics counseling and rehabilitation.

"No, I'm not sorry I went there," he says of his Pitt days. "I liked the people who were there. I probably could have had more fun somewhere else, but I came to an early awareness there that I had to work hard, on and off the field, and to tackle my schoolwork as well as everything else. I matured there, I think. And I graduated in four years.

"I thought Pitt was a good school. It was more of a commuter school in those days. When I was recruited, I was told they were going to pass. And I was a passing quarterback. I was not a gifted runner, so it was frustrating to quarterback a running offense and throw the ball three times a game. I probably could have picked a school that would throw the ball more. I'd have been happier in that respect.

"I remember one big thing, when we beat Syracuse at old Archbold Stadium when they had Ernie Davis and they were the No. 1 team in the nation. That was in my sophomore season."

That was in 1960. Pitt beat the Orangemen, 10-0. That was a strange season. Pitt finished with a 4-3-3 record, dropping 1-point decisions to UCLA and Oklahoma in the first and third games on the schedule, respectively. In between was a 7-7 tie with Michigan State, the first of three 7-7 ties that year. The others were with TCU and Army.

The Panthers beat Miami, West Virginia and Notre Dame, in addition to Syracuse, but were defeated in the finale, 14-3, by Penn State.

Pitt produced an All-America end that year in Mike Ditka, and the other flanker, Ron Delfine, was a fine one, too. Pitt had nine players drafted by the pros.

They had the much-publicized but underproductive "C-Boys" — running backs Fred Cox, Jim Cunningham and Bob Clemens — and linemen like Larry Vignali, Paul Hodge, Regis Coustillac, Dick Mills and sophomore Gary Kaltenbach.

That 1960 team was the start of something big at Pitt. The school came up with a great freshman class of athletes. Paul Martha was among them. From Wilkinsburg

and Shady Side Academy, Martha made his mark in a hurry, as a quarterback for a freshman team that went 6-0, for a freshman basketball team that was equally talented.

Those football players would produce a 9-1 record as seniors. The other four starters on that freshman basketball team were Paul Krieger, Brian Generalovich, Dave Sauer and Cal Sheffield, and they qualified for the NCAA Tournament as juniors and the NIT as seniors. It was a fine time to follow sports as a student at Pitt.

Ernie Borghetti was a big lineman who was red-shirted or held out of the 1960 season, which would have been his sophomore season. So he gained an extra year of eligibility. For awhile, it wasn't exactly a blessing.

The Panthers went 3-7 in 1961, with victories over Miami, Southern Cal and Navy, and Michelosen was hung in effigy in front of the Student Union. The next year, against another tough schedule, Pitt posted a 5-5 mark, with victories over Baylor, California, UCLA, Syracuse and Army, and defeats by Miami, West Virginia, Navy, Notre Dame and Penn State. Some good players in those years were Vignali, Cox, Kaltenbach, Steve Jastrzembski, Ed Clark, John Draksler, Tom Brown, and Ed Sharockman.

Then came the 9-1 season of 1963. That's what Borghetti remembers best. The Panthers won their first four, over UCLA, Washington, California and West Virginia, then got sidetracked by Roger Staubach and Navy, losing 24-12 at Annapolis, and bounced back to beat Syracuse, Notre Dame, Army, Miami and Penn State.

Martha and Borghetti were both named as All-Americas at the end of that season, Martha as a running back and Borghetti as a tackle. The other tackle, John Maczuzak, guard Jeff Ware and fullback Rick Leeson also got to play in post-season all-star games.

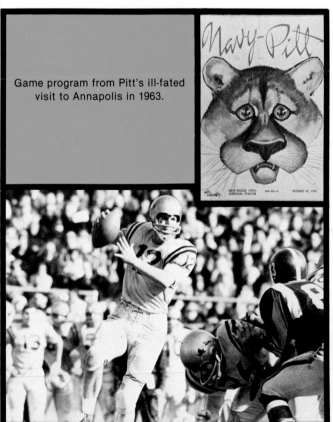

Game program from Pitt's ill-fated visit to Annapolis in 1963.

— Photo by Bill Jerome

ROGER THE DODGER — Roger Staubach was the biggest single reason Navy knocked off Pitt, for Panthers' only setback in 1963 season.

TOUCHDOWN TWINS — Panthers were blessed with two terrific running backs in the early '60s, Rick Leeson, left, and Paul Martha.

"A lot of things fell into place that '63 season," recalls Borghetti, who's a dentist today in his native Youngstown. "A lot of players on that team had been red-shirted like me. John Maczuzak, Ed Adamchik were also, and they were starting linemen.

"We had some disappointments in prior years, but it was just a great happening. We didn't get the bowl bid because of the assassination. We had a lot of success, but it ended on a disappointing note."

The final game with Penn State was postponed a week because of the death of President John F. Kennedy, and the delay kept the bowl committees from extending a bowl invitation to the Panthers. Pitt ended up empty-handed. "That was a shame," said Frank Carver, the athletic director at the time, "because Pitt would have given them the most entertaining bowl game of them all."

Borghetti said he got to go to the East-West and Hula Bowl. "That made it complete for me, but most of the other fellows felt even worse about not getting a bowl bid because they didn't go anywhere. It was almost a tragic ending to a successful season.

"I thought we were a better team than Navy, but we just beat Penn State and Syracuse, and we could have lost those. I couldn't have asked for more."

Borghetti injured his knee during the pre-season of his first year with the Kansas City Chiefs, and quit the sport to attend dental school at Tennessee.

He attends several Pitt games a year, and was at the 1982 Sugar Bowl to see the Panthers beat the Bulldogs of Georgia on that thrilling last-minute TD pass from Danny Marino to John Brown.

"It's tougher being a fan than it is playing," said Borghetti. "Sitting there in the stands . . . it really drains you. You worry more than when you were playing. They've really got it going now at Pitt."

Martha went on to play seven years of pro ball, six with the Steelers, and one more with the Denver Broncos as a defensive back. He became an attorney at the same time, and looks after the legal matters, among other things, of the Pittsburgh Penguins and the San Francisco 49ers for another Youngstown family, Edward J. DeBartolo Sr. and his son, Eddie Jr.

OUR LEADER — Chancellor Edward Litchfield called for more wide-open football for the 1963 season, and he got it.

"I wish we would have won a national championship," said Martha. "That loss to Navy was an accident, as I look at it. We played offense and defense in those days, and I would have liked to have seen how good we'd be compared to today's teams if we had specialized.

"But I loved my experience at Pitt. It prepared me for the real world in so many ways." It did even more for team captain Al Grigaliunas, who spent his childhood scratching for survival in a German concentration camp in Kaunas, Lithuania.

It took a little mischievous needling from Chancellor Edward H. Litchfield who said he wanted "wide-open" football. And Litchfield got what he wanted. The students waved empty wallets in the direction of his box during games at the Stadium and shouted, "Hail, Caesar!" It was all in good fun. Litchfield was a fine leader, and made you proud to be at Pitt.

"I'm glad we did so well this year," said Martha back then. "We played interesting football like Chancellor Litchfield wanted us to. His interest was a clue to our season."

Fred Mazurek was a junior quarterback on that 9-1 team. He came out of Redstone High School, where he had been the same sort of outstanding all-around athlete as Martha. Mazurek was a fine outfielder and hitter for Bobby Lewis' baseball team at Pitt, too.

Mazurek broke the school record at Pitt for yards gained in one season by passing for 949 yards and running for 646 for a total of 1,595, breaking Warren Heller's record of 1,338 set in 1931.

Upon graduation a year later, Mazurek married the coach's daughter, Sue Michelosen, and today they live in Clairmont, Calif., where Fred is an attorney and the director of corporate taxes for Avery International Corp., a com-

CURBSTONE COACHES CHAMPIONS — Head coach John Michelosen is flanked by his star offensive performers, Paul Martha, left, and Fred Mazurek, his future son-in-law, at annual Curbstone Coaches awards banquet at Roosevelt Hotel in 1964.

pany that provides labels for much of the merchandise one finds in supermarkets and such stores. Their son, a high school senior, is supposed to be quite a quarterback prospect.

"We had a quality program in the early '60s and we were student-athletes who went on into the professional world," said Mazurek. "Look how many became doctors and dentists and lawyers and engineers and teachers and businessmen we turned out. When you see what people have accomplished, that gives you real pride.

"I'm not saying this because he's my father-in-law, but there was so much unselfishness on the part of John Michelosen. His first concern was us as students of the University. Guys would be late or miss practice on a given night because of late labs, and no one gave them a hard time. We had coaches who were very interested in the players as persons, not just as tools to win a game. I have nothing but positive thoughts of my days at Pitt."

Rick Leeson was the fullback on that 9-1 team, and was second to Mazurek in ground-gaining. Today he's a dentist in Monroeville. "I enjoyed the football, and the school itself," he says. "The school couldn't have done more for us. They offered me a chance to continue my education. I paid for my dental school studies, but the loyalty of the school was unsurpassed. I know boys who got scholarships and didn't play a minute and came back for a fifth year and they were still on a free ride. When the school is loyal to you like that, I feel good about it."

In Mazurek's senior season, the Panthers took a pratfall, and finished with a 3-5-2 record. Pitt was 3-7 the following year — 1965 — and that brought about the firing of

ALL IN THE FAMILY — Fred Mazurek was a big man on the campus in 1964 when he courted the coach's daughter, Sue Michelosen. They later married and today they have a son who is a highly-rated high school senior quarterback in Clairmont, Calif.

Michelosen. Ray Popp of Monongahela was a good player on those teams, but there weren't enough like him.

Ed Assid and Phil Dahar, the team captain, were defensive ends on those last two teams of Michelosen. The defensive unit, that last year, was called the "Rahads," which is Dahar spelled backwards. And, at times, that's how they played. Pitt was searching, trying to come up with something like Paul Dietzel's "Chinese Bandits," but they came up with a Chinese puzzle instead. And Carver didn't feel that Michelosen and his staff could put the pieces back together again.

Assid and Dahar both became dentists — make that orthodontists, which means they can charge you more to straighten out your kids' teeth. Both are proud of their Pitt associations.

Dr. Assid, who has a chain of offices in the South Hills, said, "Football opened a lot of doors for us. Not so much the actual playing, but just being part of the program. I hardly played till my senior year. But people came to know us. After a few years, they don't remember whether you were an All-American or not. You get better as you get older."

Dr. Dahar, who has a flourishing practice in Greensburg, said, "I'm glad I played when I did, and at Pitt when I did. My dad died during my senior year of high school and I couldn't have gone to college without a scholarship. We wanted to win, but if we didn't it was no big deal. When I was a senior at Pitt, there were four of us in dental school. The program allowed for that. We were encouraged to study. I'm glad I played for whom I played. I wouldn't trade it for two national championships. I'm not sure you can trade on that ten years down the road."

Dahar often bumps into Kenny Lucas in Greensburg. Lucas lives there and operates the First Class Travel Agency, just around the block from Dr. Dahar's offices. Lucas also sells golf equipment in that region.

Lucas attends most of the Pitt football games, and remains good friends with many former teammates around the area. Lucas shared the quarterback responsibilities with Mazurek in 1964 and succeeded him in 1965.

That season, Lucas threw the ball more than any previous quarterback in Pitt history. "We were always behind and playing catch-up ball," he explained. "We had no choice but to throw."

Jim Traficant might have thrived under the circumstances, and, individually, Lucas loved it. He passed for 1,921 yards in 1965 which was the one-season record until Danny Marino erased it in 1981. Lucas got a lot of attention all of a sudden from the media when Marino moved in on his mark.

"I thought I was a pretty good quarterback," said Lucas, whose older brother, Richie, played the same position at Penn State and for the Buffalo Bills of the American Football League. "But Danny is a great one. And he's going to get better."

Lucas' favorite target was sophomore Bob Longo, who went on to become one of Pitt's most productive pass receivers. In a losing season, Eric Crabtree and Mickey Rosborough were other top receivers. Fred Hoaglin, the center, went on to a long career with the Cleveland Browns.

Hoaglin is a coach with the Detroit Lions these days, and Marty Schottenheimer, a linebacker for that 1965 team, is a coach with the Browns after a long pro career.

Dave Hart took over as the Pitt coach in 1966, and turned in three straight 1-9 report cards before getting canned with a year to go on his contract. He was a charming fellow, with a winning smile, and he could sell refrigerators to the Eskimos, but he couldn't win at Pitt.

He put together a young coaching staff, and most of its members all went on to become head coaches in major spots. One of them, Leeman Bennett, is the head coach of the Atlanta Falcons in the National Football League. Dave is the athletic director at Missouri, after a similarly successful stint as A.D. at Louisville. He was the right man for the wrong job at Pitt, it now appears.

Enough said about those three 1-9 seasons the better, but there were some quality performers along the way, including Harry "Skip" Orzulak, Geoff Brown, Denny Ferris, Jim Flanigan, Dave Dibbley, Bob Ellis, Dave Drake, Ed Gallin, Ed Whittaker, Frank Gustine, Jr. and Dave Havern.

There were much-ballyhooed freshman recruits each season — Ralph Cindrich and Lloyd Weston, for example — and a new slogan — "the new look" and "the year the Panther begins to growl" — but the end results were the same.

"We'll be 100 percent improved," Hart said before the 1967 season. "Of course, that may mean we'll only lose 20-0 and not 40-0." There were so many embarrassing losses. The worst came in 1968 when Pitt lost by 56-7 to Notre Dame, and the Irish let the clock keep running to end the game as quickly as possible. That signaled the end for Hart.

Havern, who hailed from McKees Rocks and was one of several standout quarterbacks to come out of that community, is a freight salesman for Wales Transportation today.

"We were in a no-win situation," said Havern. "They didn't de-emphasize it all the way; the schedule was still there. We were caught in between.

"Personally, I really enjoyed it; I got free reign, and I got to throw the ball a lot because we were behind so much. There was no pressure on us. Nobody expected us to win. I had Hart as a sophomore, and then I missed Carl DePasqua's first year — I was red-shirted — and came back for my final two seasons. Hiring DePasqua, I thought, was a step backward. It was an economic thing. One thing I learned at Pitt is that you have to spend a buck to make a buck.

"If they could have given Hart some backing and another year as coach, I think he would've won. It's interesting. A lot of people loved him — I thought the world of him — and other guys hated him. They thought he was the worst guy in the world. I thought he was the greatest; I'd have gone to war with him.

"Under DePasqua and Cecconi, there was a lot of humor and comic relief, but you had to feel bad in the end. You end up getting beaten by 40 points, and you wonder if you were that bad or not. You'd think, 'Maybe I should have gone to William & Mary.'

"It was like the Vietnam War. They sent us in and they didn't follow up on the commitment. They just left us out there. If they had only given those guys half the commitment they gave Johnny Majors."

The bottom line is that Havern has no regrets, not anymore. "Whether it was good or bad," he explained, "people still say, 'Hey, that's Dave Havern. He played at Pitt.' And that means something."

SOME STAFF — Dave Hart poses behind a football rather than an 8-ball with his first staff at Pitt, one that would endure the first of a string of 1-9 seasons. From left to right, Frank Cignetti, Bill Lewis, Dick Bestwick, Hart, Bill Neal, Jim Royer and Leeman Bennett. Cignetti became head coach at West Virginia, Lewis at Wyoming, Bestwick at Virginia. Hart became athletic director at Louisville and Missouri. Neal became head football coach and athletic director at Indiana University of Pennsylvania, Royer the player personnel director of the New York Jets, and Bennett became the head coach of the Atlanta Falcons.

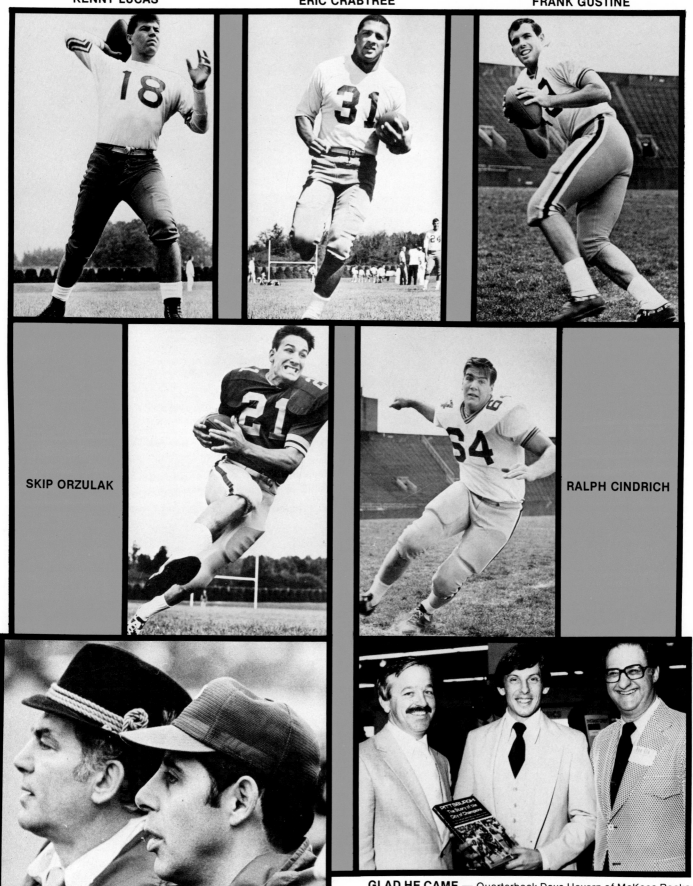

KENNY LUCAS

ERIC CRABTREE

FRANK GUSTINE

SKIP ORZULAK

RALPH CINDRICH

TRAGIC VIEW — After a promising start, things went badly for Pitt coaches Carl DePasqua, left, and Bimbo Cecconi at the end of the '60s.

GLAD HE CAME — Quarterback Dave Havern of McKees Rocks was a hero during some tough times in late '60s and early '70s at Pitt, but he's proud of the association, and proved it when he showed up to sign autographs at a book party at Kaufmann's to celebrate the publication of ''PITTSBURGH: The Story of the City of Champions,'' along with co-editors Jim O'Brien, left, and Marty Wolfson.

1960 LINEUP Front row (left to right): Ron Delfine, Bob Guzik, Larry Vignali, Andy Kuzneski, Rege Coustillac, Dick Mills, Mike Ditka. Back row: Fred Cox, Jim Cunningham, Dave Kraus, Bob Clemens.

1962 LINEUP Front row (left to right): Bob Long, Ed Adamchik, Ralph Conrad, Charles Ahlborn, Tom Brown, Gary Kaltenbach, Al Grigaliunas. Back row: John Ozimek, Rick Leeson, Jim Traficant, Ed Clark.

**1965
LINEUP** Front row (left to right): John Verkleeren, Ron Linaburg, Bernie Laquinta, Paul Cercel, Ray Popp, Jim Jones, Bill Howley. Back row: Bill Bodle, Fred Mazurek, Barry McKnight, Dale Stewart.

**1965 COACHING
STAFF** Front row (left to right): Bill Kaliden, Bimbo Cecconi, Steve Petro, Walt Cummins, Carl DePasqua. Back row: Joe Pullekines, Ernie Hefferle, Frank Lauterbur, Head Coach John Michelosen.

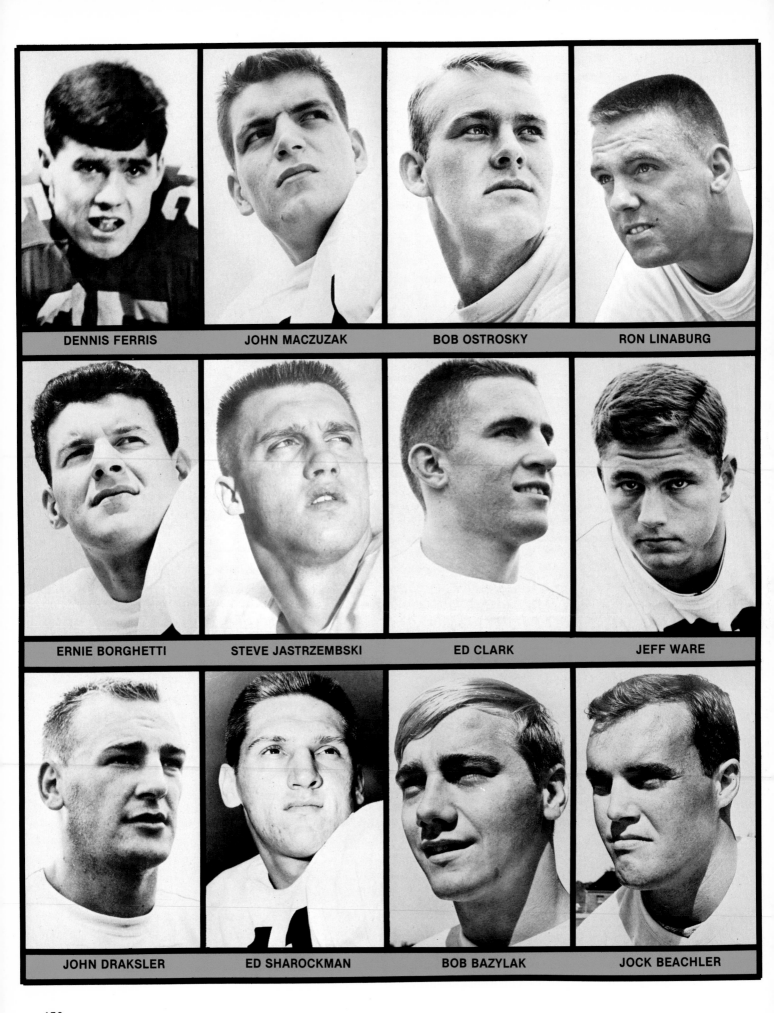

DENNIS FERRIS   JOHN MACZUZAK   BOB OSTROSKY   RON LINABURG

ERNIE BORGHETTI   STEVE JASTRZEMBSKI   ED CLARK   JEFF WARE

JOHN DRAKSLER   ED SHAROCKMAN   BOB BAZYLAK   JOCK BEACHLER

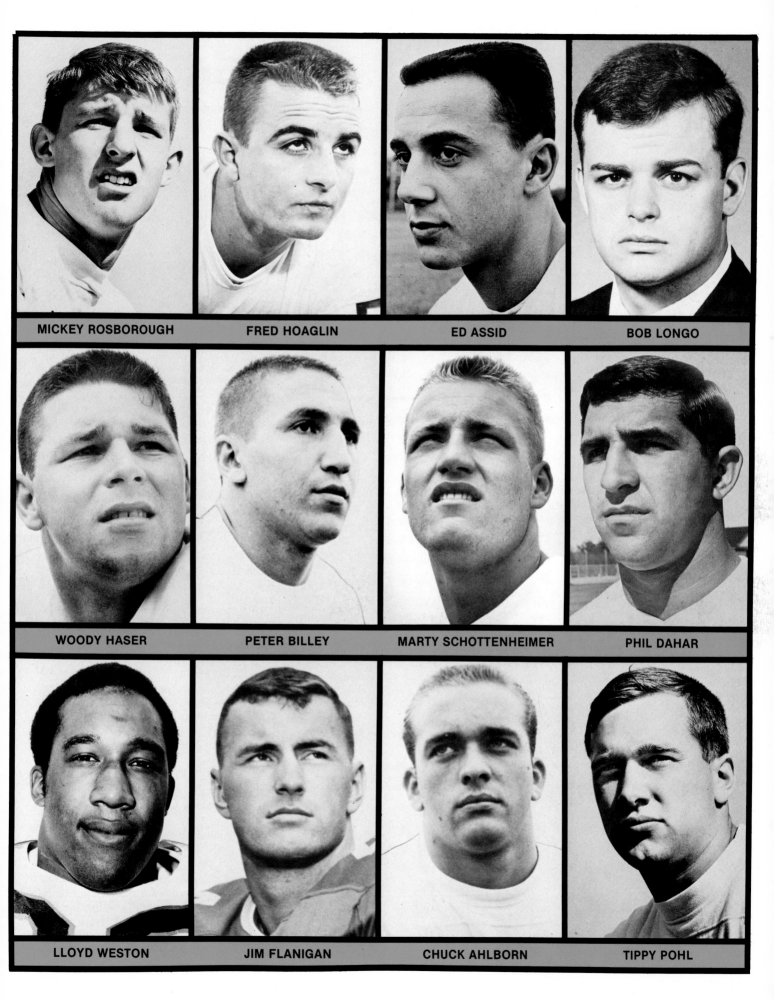

MICKEY ROSBOROUGH FRED HOAGLIN ED ASSID BOB LONGO

WOODY HASER PETER BILLEY MARTY SCHOTTENHEIMER PHIL DAHAR

LLOYD WESTON JIM FLANIGAN CHUCK AHLBORN TIPPY POHL

AL GRIGALIUNAS

Elena's Boy Captained
One Of Pitt's Finest Teams

"I'd climb back on the bike and try again."

By Jerry Izenberg
Newark Star-Ledger

Dec. 12, 1963

Mostly, the camp was a collection of flat, wooden barracks. It was in Bavaria, which is not the warmest place in winter, and for some there was daily despair because a man is supposed to be free and he is supposed to be able to carry his destiny in his two hands and he is not supposed to need permission to do it.

In Kempton, which was the name of this camp, the adults sat and waited and one day became the next and the next and the next and for the lucky ones the last day was the day the man came and told you that the next boat was yours.

The waiting was not a big thing for the children. Unlike the adults, Kempton and the places like it were what their young lives had been all about. There was no Little League in a Displaced Persons' camp. There was no Boys' Club and, certainly, there was no football. Still, they played.

"We didn't have organized games," Algis Grigaliunas recalled. "The closest thing was when we all went down and threw rocks at the German kids."

Algis Grigaliunas is 21 years old and this year he played end on the University of Pittsburgh's football team. He was also the captain and a football player is supposed to be all muscle and no head but Algis Grigaliunas majored in industrial engineering and he went through with a B average and the National Football Foundation gave him a plaque and a $500 grant for graduate studies.

For Elena Grigaliunas, it was the moment of truth. For Elena Grigaliunas, it is a long way from Kaunas, Lithuania.

Algis Grigaliunas was born in Kaunas, Lithuania, which was not a very important place and you have to wonder why both the Germans and the Russians wanted it badly enough to kill each other. They killed other people, too, and it was in Kaunas that the Russians killed Algis Grigaliunas' father. It was in Kaunas that Algis Grigaliunas' brother died of the fever and it was in Kaunas that Elena Grigaliunas persuaded a German sentry to let her through the lines with her baby, which was all she had left in Kaunas.

There were three DP camps in Algis Grigaliunas' life but he only remembers Kempton. By that time he was four years old and he remembers jumping off a beer barrel, which was the DP kids' equivalent of a playground, and he

These Panthers posted a 9-1 record. Front row, left to right: Eric Crabtree, Jock Beachler, Frank Novak, Ken Lucas, Fred Mazurek, Ken Perry, Carmen Sporio, Ronald Cimino, James Irwin, William Beck, James Gaffney, Bernard Laquinta, Robert Roeder, John Ozimek, Robert Sorochak. Second row: John Telesky, Rick Leeson, Gerry Cherry, Tom Black, Ray Conway, Dale Stewart, Jim Dodaro, Dan Picciano, Captain Al Grigaliunas, Ray Popp, John Cullen, Richard Dobrowski, Paul Martha, Barry McKnight, Bill Bodle, Marv Lippincott. Third row: Coach John Michelosen, Ed Assid, Steve Sisak, Mitch Zalnasky, Phil Dahar, Jim Jones, Glen Lehner, Tom Raymond, Bill Buchanan, Bob Guzinsky, Paul Kisiday, Joe Novogratz, Jeff Ware, Chuck Ahlborn, Dennis Bernick, James Hogan, the manager. Last row: Bill Howley, Tom Abele, Marty Schottenheimer, Bob Long, Gene Sobolewski, Tom Furjanic, Gabe Tamburino, Joe Kuzneski, Ernie Borghetti, John Maczuzak, John Jenkins, Fred Hoaglin, John Verkleeren, Ed Adamchick, Ron Linaburg, Paul Cercel.

1963 PITT TEAM

remembers that he was on the ground very still because there was a fractured skull and a broken wrist.

He remembers that he was in the hospital for three months and when he came out and his mother, Elena, spoke to him, he cried because he had forgotten how to speak Lithuanian. He remembers, also, that his mother did not like to speak about Kaunas and what happened there. He was too young to know why.

But when Algis Grigaliunas was eight years old, the man came and said "the next boat is yours" and Elena took her boy to New York and ultimately to Cleveland where a Lithuanian society had agreed to sponsor the Grigaliunases.

"My mother," Algis said, "had two professions. She was a nurse and she was a teacher but she couldn't get a job at either one and she had to go into manual labor. She worked very hard. She'd leave me at breakfast and she'd come home at six after running a punch press and one day there was a piece of her thumb missing because something went wrong."

Elena Grigaliunas worked as hard as she knew how to work, which proved to be very hard, because she wanted something for Algis and that meant that most of the day he was on his own.

But then Algis Grigaliunas had been on his own pretty much since the day he fell off that beer barrel in Bavaria. When he was eight, a neighbor in Cleveland gave him a two-wheeler bike. It was a big one. It was much too big for an eight-year-old. Algis Grigaliunas didn't know how to ride a bike anyway.

"I remember I'd get on and I'd try to ride it down the driveway and I'd fall off and then I'd climb back on and try it again." There was no father to hold the rear of the bicycle with comforting hands and there was no mother to run to with the bruises because Elena Grigaliunas was off running the punch press trying to make a living. But Algis Grigaliunas learned to ride a bike.

"I didn't especially care for football but when I was a freshman at Benedictine High School in Cleveland they had a football meeting and a man named Joseph Rufus, who was the athletic director, told us that if we got to be pretty good we could get a college scholarship," said Grigaliunas.

"So I became a football player. I knew my mother wanted me to go to college and I knew I couldn't afford it. I got to be pretty good. I got a chance to go to college."

"Why Pittsburgh?" a fellow asked. "What about the glamour schools?

"Well," Algis said, "at first I thought about the West Coast and all that kind of stuff and then I thought about my mother and I figured I owed it to her to go somewhere near enough to get home regularly."

Algis Grigaliunas went to Pitt and Pitt was very happy about it because while he was not a good enough football player to be drafted by the pros, he was a very good one at Pitt and he was the captain of one of the best teams Pitt has had in a long, long time.

He received his Red Blaik Scholar-Athlete Award and a lot of people said that this was a good thing for football because it proved the inherent good in the game. Possibly they are right. It proved, of course, that football does have a proper place in our campus culture.

Mostly, however, it proved something else. You water the seeds and you cultivate the ground and you need luck, too, but without the gardener, you don't make it.

Elena Grigaliunas had a green thumb.

From A Concentration Camp To American Gridiron Glory

CAPTAIN AL GRIGALIUNAS

161

PITT FOOTBALL — COMEBACK STORY OF THE '70s

By Jim O'Brien

"Coming up with a national championship at Pittsburgh was a rare thing. I may never have a national championship or go undefeated again. I'm not going to think that way, but one must face reality."

—Johnny Majors

"How'd I do it? Three things: excellent teammates, good coaching and The Good Lord."

—Tony Dorsett

"Coaches don't win football games. Players win games. Coaches don't go out there and line up."

—Jackie Sherrill

Those were the words of Johnny Majors upon leaving Pitt after a national championship season in 1976 and going home to become head coach at the University of Tennessee; of Tony Dorsett after the same sensational season when asked to explain how he had been the most productive runner in the history of college football and the winner of the Heisman Trophy, college football's most coveted award; of Jackie Sherrill upon being named to succeed Majors as the head coach of the Panthers.

Johnny Majors . . . Tony Dorsett . . . Jackie Sherrill. They are Pitt's answer to the Holy Trinity. They worked a miracle and saved college football in the City of Pittsburgh.

Who can forget Majors, the always-ebullient salesman with the penetrating hazel eyes? Or Dorsett, the effervescent, oh-so-confident kid who reminded you of the comedian Flip Wilson? They called him "The Hawk" because he could see out of the corners of both of his bright eyes at the same time. Or Sherrill, the slow-talking, low-talking coach with the long eyelids and thin lips who was the tough guy, the enforcer on Majors' staff, who went away for one year to become the head coach at Washington State University, and returned to Pitt to pick up where Dorsett and Majors left off?

They accomplished something that we may never see happen again. From the time Majors and Sherrill stood on Dorsett's doorstep at a housing project outside Aliquippa, where he had been a nationally-recognized running back at Hopewell High School, the Pitt program was on the upswing.

As John Pelusi, the starting center on the '76 team, said of Dorsett: "He's the sort of runner who comes along once in a lifetime and I'm so glad he came here in my lifetime."

Pitt won six games in Majors' first year, seven his second, eight his third, and went undefeated his fourth.

Majors, Dorsett and Sherrill put Pitt football on the map again, in the national rankings—the Panthers were No. 1 in all the polls in 1976—and made the Pitt football team a major part of the City of Champions.

"Sure we're part of it," said Sherrill as the Panthers prepared for the Fiesta Bowl at the close of the '70s, a decade in which Pitt went to a bowl game six times in the final seven years. "We use the 'City of Champions' in our recruiting pitch. We're close to the Steelers and Pirates, and our players know their players, and we share facilities from time to time. Young people like to come and play where there are winning teams, and a winning atmosphere."

Pitt pointed to the '80s with special pride, and the belief that another national championship was within its grasp. In 1979, the Panthers were led by a three-time All-America in defensive end Hugh Green, from Natchez, Miss., and Danny Marino, from Pittsburgh's Central Catholic High School, right down the street from the Pitt campus, who had a fabulous freshman season at quarterback. They posted an 11-1 record, and were ranked as high as sixth in the final national polls.

The Steelers still had their Joe Greene and Terry Bradshaw, but Pitt was holding its own with Hugh Green and Danny Marino.

The Pitt football program, four years after the departure of Majors and Dorsett, was still in outstanding shape. "It's tougher staying there," said Sherrill, "than getting there."

Well, Vince Lombardi said that, too, but Pitt is proving

OCTOBER 23, 1976 PITTSBURGH -VS- NAVY
THE DAY TONY DORSETT BROKE THE NCAA RUSHING RECORD

it can be done. It takes talent, hard work and dedication, and the people at Pitt have plenty of that.

Before Majors and Dorsett showed up at Pittsburgh, the Panthers had not played in a post-season bowl game in the previous 17 years. Sherrill was Majors' ace assistant back then, as he had been earlier at Iowa State University. Together, they wooed Dorsett to Pitt and away from Penn State and it was the start of a dynasty at the Oakland campus.

Russ Franke, a sports reporter for The Pittsburgh Press who covered the club during the period, offered this thought on the situation: "No single player ever carried a football team on his shoulders the way Dorsett did at the start of his career at Pitt. What happened here was one of the most dramatic comebacks ever seen in college football."

Majors, Dorsett and Sherrill gave college football a second chance in Pittsburgh. The three of them established and sustained—especially in Sherrill's case—one of the classiest and most successful football programs on a college level in this country.

Pitt's rise during Majors' four years as head coach was remarkable. The Panthers finished the 1976 season sitting atop the major-college polls for the first time since the Jock Sutherland era of the '30s.

They were the first Eastern team since the 1959 Syracuse team with Ernie Davis to be No. 1 in the nation. The odds against an independent other than Notre Dame winning a national championship are prohibitive, but Pitt pulled it off.

Pitt had endured nine losing seasons in a row prior to the arrival of Majors, Dorsett and Sherrill for the 1973 season. "I want to see guys with fire in their eyes," preached Majors. "Self-Image! Self-Image is so important!"

What is impressive about Pitt's rise to power was that it was sharing a city with the most successful pro football team in the land. There were many who believed the city wasn't big enough for both of them.

The pattern has been all too familiar in the last two decades. The growth of pro football has coincided with the decline of the college football game in big cities. New York, Chicago, Philadelphia, Miami, Detroit, Dallas, Atlanta and New Orleans have all been witness to the trend.

Apparently, Pitt was also suffering by comparison. It had not been so bad in the 1950s and early 1960s because the Steelers were such a pitiful football team themselves, never a legitimate contender and more often a basement-dweller and drawing below-par crowds by the National Football League's standards.

Chuck Noll was appointed head coach of the Steelers in 1969, the team was molded into a championship contender, and a new downtown stadium—Three Rivers Stadium, of course—was constructed at the confluence of the Allegheny, Monongahela and Ohio rivers. Suddenly, the Steelers were a hot item.

And that's where Majors came in. In 1972 the Steelers had reached the playoffs for the very first time; Pitt had lost 10 of its 11 games to reach an all-time low. The university chancellor, Wesley Posvar, had seen enough. He and Casimir Myslinski, the athletic director, were both West Point grads and they wanted a winning football program. They called for a new leader, a no-nonsense lieutenant—make that major—who could lead his troops to victory.

They brought in Johnny Majors—"We couldn't do any better than him," declared Myslinski—and Majors immediately let the local citizens know his approach to football. He compared football to war, and declared war on mediocrity as far as football at Pitt was concerned. "We want more guys who'll look you in the eye," he said.

During his first season, Majors was even moved to say, "We have the kind of schedule where if we recruit well enough and coach well enough, we can have a national championship at Pitt."

It seemed preposterous when he said it that first day of November, 1973, sitting in his office in Fitzgerald Field House alongside the 50-year-old concrete bowl where Marshall Goldberg and Bill Daddio and Curly Stebbins and John Chickerneo had led an earlier generation of Panthers to a Rose Bowl and national championship in 1936. Majors had some nerve then to talk about the possibility of returning Pittsburgh to that level of prominence, but confidence was one thing he didn't lack at the time.

On another November day, just three years later, Majors made good on his promise about Pitt football. Being No. 1 was not just an impossible dream. Those of us who were witness to the climax of the Majors-Dorsett era in Pittsburgh will never forget that fantastic Friday night, Nov. 26, 1976.

That was the night Pitt played Penn State in the final game of the regular season, under the lights at Three Rivers Stadium. It was a game that was changed from its originally scheduled time—the next afternoon at Pitt Stadium—so that it might be nationally televised. There were 50,360 in attendance for the finale.

GORDON JONES and TONY DORSETT signal Pitt's national ranking after Sugar Bowl victory.

It was a big game for my bunch, sitting in 40-yard line seats high in the stands. We were students at Pitt when the Panthers had their last outstanding football team prior to the arrival of Majors and Dorsett and Sherrill, back in 1963 when the Panthers posted a 9-1 record, losing only to Roger Staubach and a fine Navy team. Those were home-grown Panthers back then, such as Paul Martha of Wilkinsburg, Rick Leeson of Chartiers Valley, Fred Mazurek of Redstone, Ernie Borghetti from Youngstown, Al Grigaliunas of Cleveland. Even that team had a tough time against Penn State, winning the last game, 22-21.

The 1965 team was the last Pitt team to beat Penn State, and barely, by 30-27 at Pitt Stadium. That victory gave Pitt a 3-7 record that year, and was Johnny Michelosen's last game as head coach.

Pitt football was *so* depressed from 1963 to 1973. So it was with special pride that Pitt followers, alumni or anyone else, looked upon the Panthers against Penn State that Friday night at Three Rivers. None of the Pitt people were disappointed. Majors was more national in his recruiting missions, but his players, many with distant addresses, still represented Pitt.

At first, it was a struggle. Dorsett was limited to 58 yards in the first half—yes, that was a poor half for him—and the score was tied, 7-7.

It all began with the hiring of Johnny Majors as head coach in 1972: (l. to r.) the chancellor, Dr. Wesley Posvar, Majors and the athletic director, Casimir Myslinski.

At the start of the second half, Majors made a move. He put the Panthers in an unbalanced line, a formation he had used only 10 plays all season. Dorsett was the deep back in the I-formation. "I didn't think I'd see him at fullback," said Penn State coach Joe Paterno afterward.

The second half was all Dorsett and Pitt. Altogether, Tony gained 224 yards in 38 attempts—the seventh most productive outing of his star-spangled Pitt career—and the Panthers knocked off the Nittany Lions, 24-7.

With that victory, the Panthers blotted out ten years of bitter memories. During that spell, the Panthers had been whipped by Penn State by such scores as 48-24, 42-6, 65-9, 27-7, 35-15, 55-18, 49-27, 35-13, 31-10. Only once was it close, and Penn State outscored Pitt, 7-6, in that 1975 meeting.

"Beating Penn State was the biggest thrill of my life to date," said Majors afterward. "But right now there aren't enough words to express how I feel about Tony Dorsett."

Paterno expressed it even better than Majors that night. Talking about Dorsett, the Penn State coach commented, "He's the greatest football player we have ever played against at Penn State. In my 27 years here, we have played against some awfully good ones—Jimmy Brown, Archie Griffin, Bubba Smith and Greg Pruitt. But Tony Dorsett is the outstanding player in America; and it isn't even close."

It was the last time Dorsett and Majors would perform for the Pitt football team in Pittsburgh. They made it a memorable finale. For the record, this is what Dorsett accomplished:

• He finished with 6,082 yards to his credit, rushing for more yards in his career than anyone in the history of NCAA major college football. Near the end of the third quarter against State, he slipped free for 10 yards to become the first player ever to top the 6,000 yard mark.

• Became the first player in NCAA history to rush for 1,000 yards for four consecutive years.

• Scored 22 touchdowns his senior season to be the NCAA scoring leader, and 59 for his four-year career, tying him with Army's Glenn Davis in that department in the NCAA record book.

• Scored 356 points in his career for an all-time record.

• Established 12 NCAA records altogether, including a 5.8 rushing average in his senior season, and 29 Pitt records. He averaged 177 yards per game that last year. He ran for over 100 yards in every game and for at least 200 yards four times.

• He led the Panthers to the No. 1 national ranking and a berth against Georgia in the Sugar Bowl on New Year's Day.

No player in college football—at least in a long time—had turned a football program around like Dorsett.

Asked to assess his importance to the program, Majors said, "Could we have done what we did without Dorsett? I doubt it. This year, maybe. Over four years, never.

"As a freshman and sophomore, when we didn't have the help he has now, what Tony did for us then was unbelievable. He made Pitt a winner when, really, we didn't have the personnel to win."

Did he help recruiting?

"Yeah, he made it a little easier to recruit," said Majors. "High school kids like to play with a winner, and Tony showed them Pitt could win. That made it easier for some of the kids to decide to come to Pitt."

Three days after the victory over Penn State, it was announced that Dorsett has been named the winner of the Heisman Trophy as the outstanding college football player in the nation.

He was the first Pitt player to capture the award in its 41-year-old history. He had finished fourth in the voting the year before, which was the highest finish by a Pitt player since Mike Ditka—an Aliquippa area product like Dorsett—finished sixth in 1960.

One of Tony's teammates, Al Romano, a middle guard who gained All-America honors and finished runner-up to Notre Dame's Ross Browner for the Outland Trophy as college football's finest lineman, said of Dorsett, "Another thing that's important, he's a decent kid. And I'm awful proud to be on the same team with a Heisman Trophy winner. Week after week he gets all that ink and it doesn't affect him or us. We're all behind him."

Declared Majors: "He's the finest football player I've ever seen on the football field. I may never coach a player that good as long as I stay in the game."

Majors was named the College Football Coach of the Year after the 1976 season, repeating an achievement he had first attained after the 1973 season at Pitt.

A week after the victory over Penn State, Majors made an announcement most Pitt fans felt and feared was coming. He had accepted an invitation to return to his alma mater, the University of Tennessee, to rebuild its football team.

On Friday, Dec. 3, 1976, Majors resigned. He had two years to go on his contract at Pitt—it had been extended

ALL-AMERICA & HEISMAN TROPHY WINNER TONY DORSETT

after his first season—but he had to go. "I felt very comfortable here," he said. "I love Pittsburgh, and it's always hard to leave a place. But there are some roots I have there."

Majors had been an All-America tailback at Tennessee, leading the Volunteers to a 10-0 record in 1956, and finished second to Notre Dame's Paul Hornung in the Heisman Trophy balloting.

He became the Tennessee coach and athletic director in charge of football when he signed a six-year contract. It had a base salary of $50,000, and fringe benefits which brought his annual pay closer to $75,000.

His won-lost record at Pitt was 33-13-1. Only two previous Pitt coaches had fared as well. Sutherland's mark was 111-20-12, and Glenn "Pop" Warner was 59-11-4. Michelosen had been the only long-time coach with a winning record—56-49-7—before Majors made the scene.

"Very few people have experienced what I have these last four years," said the 41-year-old Majors. "I'd be an exceptional dreamer if I thought I could do it again, but I'm gonna give it my best shot. Heck, I'm young enough.

"Part of it is going back to where you were undefeated as a senior. That was Tennessee's last undefeated team.

"The people here have learned how to win—the players, the school, the boosters. I'm really pleased about that. I want to see them continue to win."

Myslinski made sure the Pitt people didn't look upon Major's departure as the signal to the end of an outstanding football program at the school. "We started with 15 Golden Panthers in 1971-72," said the athletic director, talking about the boosters' organization, "and now we're up in the thousands. Without them, we couldn't have got Johnny Majors or Tony Dorsett or what else we have. But we don't have to stop here."

Myslinski might also have mentioned that alumni contributions had quadrupled since 1972 to 1976.

Reflecting on his decision to leave Iowa State for Pitt, in the first place, Majors made this remark:

"I was coming to a city that I didn't think I would like, and it turned out that I loved it. When Mary Lynn (his wife) and I pulled out of our driveway at Ames for the last time, we didn't think we'd ever again experience the thrills of making a success out of something that had been in bad shape. But this, these four years in Pittsburgh, it beats it all."

Majors and Dorsett had finished their work in Pittsburgh, but they still had one more game to go, against Georgia in the Sugar Bowl in New Orleans on New Year's Day, 1977.

Dorsett had begun his four-year siege of the NCAA record books against Georgia in his first game as a freshman, when he exploded for his first 100-yard effort at Pitt. Now he was finishing up against the same Bulldogs, and he showed them he hadn't slowed up any in the four years he had been cracking college defenses.

Pitt beat Georgia, 27-3, and Dorsett set a Sugar Bowl record with 202 yards for a career total of 6,526 yards, if you count his post-season performances.

Georgia's Vince Dooley declared later, "The 1976 Pitt team was the most complete college football team I've seen. I knew they were good. But, until after they had manhandled us in the Sugar Bowl, I didn't realize how good."

Jack Butler, the Pittsburgh-born and bred head of the Blesto pro scouting firm, said of Dorsett that day, "He

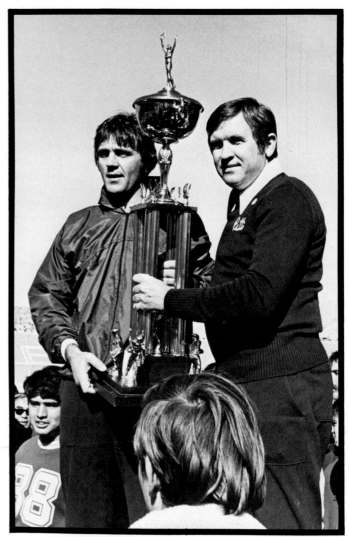

Jackie Sherrill and Johnny Majors display Championship trophy after Pitt defeated Kansas in the Sun Bowl in December, 1975.

runs like water." Butler said Dorsett was the best running back prospect since O. J. Simpson.

"He's just a great, great football player," observed Butler, who was once a great defensive back for the Steelers. "He's got such great movement, such great acceleration. He accelerates two or three times in one run. People worry about his size, but he's durable. He's put together. And he's a good kid, too."

Back home, there were others who shared Butler's enthusiasm for Dorsett. He was named the Man of the Year for the Dapper Dan Sports Banquet, the first collegian and first amateur athlete to win the award since it began in 1939. Majors had won the same award earlier.

On a national basis, Dorsett, in addition to his Heisman Trophy, also claimed the Player of the Year awards from the Walter Camp Foundation, Football News, Maxwell Club, Washington Touchdown Club and numerous other organizations.

He went on to displace Preston Pearson in the backfield of the Dallas Cowboys, and that was quite an achievement for a rookie because Pearson had four Super Bowl rings to his credit, two each as a member of the Cowboys' and Steelers' championship teams.

Meanwhile at Pitt, Dorsett's No. 33 jersey was retired. It was the only time in the 90 years of football at Pitt that a jersey has been retired.

MAJORS' MEN — Coach Johnny Majors stands behind his prize backs, from left to right, Robert Haygood, Tony Dorsett, Elliott Walker, Matt Cavanaugh and Bobby Hutton.

There were some other things that occurred in Dorsett's senior season that are worthy of recall.

In the next to the last game of the schedule, for instance, in a 24-16 victory over West Virginia, Dorsett scored three touchdowns. He taunted and angered the WVU players by wagging his finger to indicate Pitt's national ranking, and gained 199 yards in his final appearance at Pitt Stadium. On a late hit in front of the Pitt bench late in the game, Dorsett came up swinging, and was ejected from the game; otherwise he would have topped 200 yards a total of five times in his senior season.

In the game before that, Pitt beat Army, 37-7, to become the top-ranked team in the country when Purdue upset Michigan, 16-14. Dorsett again led the way, rushing for 212 yards and scoring three touchdowns.

The week before, Dorsett overcame a bruised leg, jammed elbow and poked eye to rush for 241 yards and two touchdowns, leading Pitt to a 23-13 victory over Syracuse.

This came the week after Pitt had won at Navy, 45-0, in a game in which Dorsett became the NCAA all-time leading rusher, breaking Archie Griffin's record of 5,177 yards. Dorsett rushed for 180 yards and three touchdowns that day. He broke the record set by the Ohio State All-America on a 32-yard touchdown run in the fourth quarter

"Every time I do something that a lot of people recognize," Dorsett said, "I'm going to take pride in it. And no matter how long or how much I've been into this game, I'll take pride in every record I set. I want to be known as No. 1, and I want to be known as that as long as I live."

It all began with the hiring of Majors, at age 37, back in 1972. Majors had compiled a 24-30-1 record in six seasons at Iowa State and guided the Cyclones to the only two bowl appearances in the school's history. The best season was an 8-3 record in 1971.

His theme at Ames was "Football is for winning and winning is fun."

Pitt was sure hungry for some fun in its football program. The Panthers' fortunes had taken a dip following the 9-1 mark in 1963 and reached the low mark with a 1-10 record in 1972.

Johnny Michelosen had been moved out after the 1965 season (3-7) and replaced by Dave Hart, an enthusiastic charmer who had coached Johnstown High School to a string of glorious triumphs and was a well-thought-of assistant at Navy when Pitt hired him.

Hart fell flat on his handsome face. His much-ballyhooed ballclubs had three straight 1-9 seasons before Hart was fired with one year remaining on his contract at Pitt. To replace Hart, who went on to administrative success at Robert Morris, Louisville and Missouri, Myslinski had sought some of the best known coaches in the nation. He nearly snagged some of them, but they all changed their minds in the end—much to Pitt's embarrassment—and remained right where they were.

In desperation, Pitt turned to Carl DePasqua, a former Pitt player from Williamsport and a former assistant on Michelosen's staff, to fill the void.

DePasqua rallied Pitt from three straight 1-9 seasons to a 4-6 record in 1969 and gave promise of better things.

Many people have forgotten, but Pitt got off to a great start in football for 1970, winning five of its first six games. Injuries to key players crippled the club, however, and it lost the last four games of the season to finish at 5-5.

There were some outstanding players on the Pitt team back then. They included defensive tackle Lloyd Weston, who had gained national attention playing for Pete Dimperio's team at Westinghouse High in the City League, and Ralph Cindrich, an All-America caliber but injury-jinxed linebacker from Avella, who would advance to the National Football League.

Besides Cindrich, there were three other prospects who would later play in the NFL, namely defensive backs Bryant Salter of South Hills High and Charlie Hall of Bala-Cynwyd, and center Bob Kuziel of West Haven, Conn.

In addition, there were ace receiver Steve Moyer of Pennsbury, running back Dennis Ferris of North Catholic High, tight end Joel Klimek of Seanor and Jack Dykes of Apollo. These were fine players.

There were two top-flight players from McKees Rocks, quarterback Dave Havern and fullback Tony Esposito. Havern had a weekly aerial circus show, connecting with Klimek and Moyer.

All sorts of good things were predicted for DePasqua's Pitt teams, but nothing came of it. Passing records were posted, but, alas, not winning records. The 1971 team finished 3-8 and the 1972 team went 1-10. DePasqua was fired Nov. 27, two days after a 49-27 season-ending loss at Penn State.

Majors came in to pick up the pieces at Pitt. The Panthers had been 16-56 since Michelosen's departure. They were 3-27 under Hart and 13-29 under DePasqua.

"I don't believe in making quick promises," said Majors the day his hiring was announced. "My job is to make lemonade out of a lemon."

Several days later, on a tour of the campus, he told students, "I know why they've lost here. There are a lot of things here that haven't been touched. The rust hasn't been wiped off in 20 years. This school has an attitude of losing."

Dorsett was the first player Pitt went after, and it was a combination recruiting effort by Majors and his top aide, Sherrill. Dorsett had been named to many of the high school All-America teams and had been timed in 4.5 for the 40. "He is," said Sherrill after Dorsett signed a letter-of-intent to attend Pitt, "the most complete high school football player I've ever seen."

Dorsett had narrowed his many choices down to Pitt and Penn State. "The chances of playing at Penn State right away weren't as good as they were at Pitt," explained Dorsett.

Dorsett was the fourth son of Westley and Myrtle Dorsett. Wes worked in the J&L Steel Works in Aliquippa. He thought his first three sons, Ernest, Tyrone and Keith, were all faster than Tony.

The youngest Dorsett stood 5-10 and tipped the scales at less than 160 pounds then, but grew into 185 pounds of pure speed and surprising inside power during his stay at Pitt.

Majors inherited some solid players who helped him at the beginning. There was some quality in the offensive line talent left him by DePasqua, and Dorsett started in the backfield with three other leftovers from the DePasqua program: a tough redhead in Billy Daniels, another quarterback from McKees Rocks, a solid blocker in fullback Dave Janasek and an effective wingback, Bruce Murphy.

The best of the defensive players Majors inherited were linebacker Kelcy Daviston of Duquesne, and tackle Glenn Hyde, who would later play for the NFL's Denver Broncos.

In addition to Dorsett, Majors and his staff brought in over 80 recruits their first time out. Majors knew he had to do something in a hurry. His recruits included a junior college All-America, Gary Burley of Grove City, Ohio, who anchored the defensive unit at middle guard.

The freshman class oozed with talent. There was Carson Long, an ace kicker from Ashland, Pa. From Florida came Cecil Johnson, a linebacker and defensive end, Don Parrish, a defensive tackle, and Arnie Weatherington, another linebacker. Pitt also picked up Jim Corbett, a tight end from Erie, and Al Romano, a middle guard from Solvay, N.Y. There was also a fine future quarterback in Robert Haygood, from Georgia, who'd go great later on with Dorsett in the Veer-offense.

Burley, Hyde, Johnson, Parrish, Corbett and Romano all developed into pro prospects while at Pitt.

Majors still had his doubts. His favorite question for those who approached him in his early days at Pitt was: "Do you think we can win?"

Once, he got caught in a snowstorm and couldn't keep a date to speak at a YMCA meeting at the William Penn Hotel here. Sherrill subbed for him, and said on April 12, 1973, "It'll take time, but Pittsburgh's the greatest sports city in the country, and the people are hungry for victory."

Even then, he knew.

Pitt tied Georgia, 7-7, for openers. In the third game, against Northwestern, Dorsett gained a school-record 265 yards in a 21-14 victory. Six weeks later, Notre Dame drubbed Pitt, 31-10, but Dorsett showed his stuff that Saturday afternoon, and gained national notice.

As a 19-year-old freshman, Dorsett had gained 209 yards against Notre Dame. No one in the history of the game had ever gained 200 yards against Notre Dame. It came on Nov. 5, 1973, almost a year from when Dorsett had played his final high school game at Hopewell. He broke the record of 195 yards set in 1952 by Oklahoma's Heisman Trophy winner, Billy Vessels. Going into that game, Notre Dame had the second-best defensive rating against the rush in the collegiate ranks. Dorsett spoiled that in a hurry.

Pat Livingston, the sports editor of The Pittsburgh Press, was moved to write that day: "Dorsett has the fawn-like grace and hidden power of a Gale Sayers or a Hugh McElhenny in miniature."

Pitt fashioned a 6-4-1 record that first year, and gained a berth to the Fiesta Bowl—Pitt's first bowl in 17 years—where the Panthers lost to Arizona State, 28-7. It was a start.

Majors received national Coach of the Year recognition for his first-year accomplishment, and Dorsett became the first freshman to make first-team All-America in 29 years.

When Majors talked about Dorsett, his legs would swing like a puppy dog's tail, as writer Vince DiNardo once described it, and his voice would suddenly go soft. "I have a lot of respect for Tony," Majors said then. "He was the first player I visited after taking this job. I'm impressed with his pride in being a great football player. He takes a lot of pride in picking up things right away and doing things the way they should be done."

It was a mutual admiration society. "I think Coach Majors is the best coach in the country," said Dorsett. "Look at the job he's done here so far."

TROPHIES PITT WON IN '76

Trophies won by the 1976 National Champion Pitt football team: (1) Grantland Rice Trophy from the Football Writers of America, (2) MacArthur Bowl from the National Football Foundation and Hall of Fame, (3) Heisman Trophy awarded to Tony Dorsett, (4) Cool Ray Cup for the Eastern Championship among the major universities, (5) Sugar Bowl Championship Trophy, (6) United Press International National Championship, (7) Lambert Trophy for the Eastern Championship. Missing is the Associated Press National Championship Trophy.

The two of them had only just begun. Majors and his staff brought in some more blue-chippers for their second season. They brought in five future pros in quarterback Matt Cavanaugh, running back Elliott Walker, wide receiver Karl Farmer and, closer to home, defensive tackle Randy Holloway of Sharon and defensive back Bob Jury of Library.

In addition, they pulled in center Walt Brown of Allison Park, guard Tom Brzoza of New Castle, defensive back Dave DiCiccio of Midland, and defensive end Randy Cozens, to name some standouts.

Dorsett got off to a slow start in his sophomore season. He was limited by a groin pull and a bad ankle. Pitt was 1-2-1 after four games before everybody got in gear.

Late in the season, when Dorsett was hurting, freshman speedster Elliot Walker went wild against Temple, running for 169 yards and four touchdowns in a 35-24 victory over the Owls at Pitt Stadium.

Pitt finished the 1974 season with a 7-4 record, but again lost the big ones—to Southern Cal, to Notre Dame and Penn State—and Dorsett slipped somewhat and failed to make first-team All-America. Pitt stayed home for the holidays.

Pitt was making progress, though, and Majors was happy. "Tony has had a lot to do with what we've been able to accomplish here so far," he said. "But I'm not going to say he's been the only reason. That wouldn't be fair to all the other great athletes here and all the hard work and sleepless nights the whole coaching staff has put in.

"Football is bigger than one man, and Pitt football is bigger than me or Dorsett. Everyone's hard work has gone into it."

Dorsett had the two greatest games, statistically speaking anyhow, in his junior season. You had to be at Army's Michie Stadium that Saturday afternoon of Oct. 18, 1975, to realize how super Dorsett was that day. Doc Blanchard and Glenn Davis never ran as well when they were Mr. Inside and Mr. Outside at West Point.

Dorsett's family sat directly behind our alumni contingent, and you couldn't help but share their delight that day. Tony totaled 268 yards—the best at Pitt up till that point—in a 52-20 triumph.

A month later, Dorsett was even more sensational against his favorite opponent, Notre Dame. He ran for 303 yards—his best day ever—on 23 carries against Notre Dame and added 71 more on passes from Matt Cavanaugh to lead Pitt to its first victory over Notre Dame in 10 years, 34-20. It was the first major win in Johnny Majors' career at Pitt.

It was especially pleasing to Dorsett. "When you're young and growing up," Dorsett said, "Notre Dame is Football, U.S.A. Everybody has a dream to go there."

Thank heavens, he went to Pitt instead.

Dorsett broke his own record against Notre Dame in near-freezing weather before a sellout crowd of 56,480 at Pitt Stadium. Pitt was warmed that day when they accepted a bid to play in the Sun Bowl in El Paso, Tex. The victory over the Irish gave them a 7-3 record.

Joe Paterno of Penn State personally scouted that game because the Nittany Lions had a break in their schedule.

"We've always known Dorsett was great," he said. "He's always been great. Not just today."

The Panthers lost their season finale, 7-6, to Penn State at Three Rivers Stadium.

Pitt perked up for its Sun Bowl appearance and clipped Kansas, 33-19. It was December 25, 1975, in El Paso, and afterward Jackie Sherrill announced to the squad that he was leaving Pitt to accept the challenge of the head coaching position at Washington State University.

Dorsett gave Sherrill the game ball. Some shed tears.

When Majors moved on to Tennessee, Sherrill was called back to Pitt. "Pittsburgh is my home," Sherrill said at the announcement of his hiring. "When I came here in 1973, I didn't even know what pigs-in-a-blanket were. Now I know all about holupki, pierogi, and bakklava. I love Pittsburgh, with its people and rich culture. I hated to leave in 1975, but I really wanted a head coaching job.

"It's good to be back. I'm very ecstatic, honored, and very happy to be back. Pittsburgh is a big part of my life."

Sherrill signed a five-year contract with Pitt, saying that "coming to the number one team in the country and sustaining that program is a big challenge."

Sherrill had come a long way. He wasn't a smooth-talker to match Majors, and at the University of Alabama he was a solid, but not spectacular, performer who played several positions. He was a team man. Sincerity was his strength. That and a willingness to work hard, and get the job done. People were comfortable with Sherrill.

One of Sherrill's prize rookies was Mark May, a 6-5, 270-pound offensive tackle from Oneonta, N.Y. "I came in for a weekend at Pitt," he says now, "and spent one night each with Tony Dorsett, and his two best friends on the team, Don Parrish and Cecil Johnson, and enjoyed myself. I thought Pitt was for me."

Sherrill got lucky in a hurry. When his staff was recruiting a running back named Ray Charles "Rooster" Jones in Pascagoula, Miss., they also discovered a defensive lineman named Hugh Green of Natchez, Miss. Green turned out to be a great one, Pitt's most spectacular player since Dorsett.

Pitt looked promising, especially with a senior quarterback like Matt Cavanaugh coming back to lead the attack.

The opener was against Notre Dame, just to make sure Sherrill knew he was back in the big time. Before a national TV audience, the Panthers took a 7-0 lead but Cavanaugh suffered a broken left wrist in the first quarter. On the play that snapped Cavanaugh's wrist and Pitt's chances for another national championship, the All-America quarterback completed a 12-yard TD pass to Gordon Jones.

Chancellor Dr. Wesley Posvar (left) and athletic director Cas Myslinski welcome new head football coach Jackie Sherrill.

J. C. WILSON   JEFF DELANEY   AL CHESLEY   DAVE LOGAN

GLENN HYDE   DON PARRISH   LARRY SWIDER   CECIL JOHNSON

Pitt ended up losing that game, 19-9, despite heroic defensive performances by Randy Holloway, Al Chesley and Dave Logan.

Pitt bounced back to win the next three games, 28-6 over William & Mary, and 76-0 over Temple, and 45-7 over Boston College before Florida tied the Panthers, 17-17, at Gainesville.

Gordon Jones, Elliott Walker and Freddie Jacobs were the big offensive guns. Cavanaugh came back for the Florida game and played well, though turnovers cost Pitt dearly. With Cavanaugh at the controls again, replacing Rick Trocano, the Panthers put on a five-game winning streak, defeating Navy, 34-17, Syracuse, 28-21, Tulane, 48-0, West Virginia, 44-3, and Army, 52-26.

Pitt's streak was stopped on a snowy day by Penn State—who else?—in the season finale, 15-13. State's Matt Millen thwarted Elliott Walker's attempt to score a two-point conversion.

Pitt went to the Gator Bowl and beat Clemson, 34-3. So Sherrill's first slate showed a 9-2-1 record. Not bad.

Sherrill suffered major losses from that squad, however, with a half dozen moving on to the pros: Cavanaugh, Walker, Holloway, Gary Silvestri, Bob Jury and J. C. Wilson. The Panthers had four first-team All-Americas in Cavanaugh, Jury, Holloway and Brzoza, and eight players were picked in the NFL draft.

But Sherrill still had some good ones coming back for his second season, in Jones, an All-America flanker, Hugh Green, an All-America defensive end, Jeff Delaney, a senior strong safety from Upper St. Clair, and Matt Carroll, a senior offensive guard from Norwood. Other standouts returning were the mammoth May, an offensive tackle,

Chesley, a senior linebacker, Logan, a senior middle guard from Pittsburgh's Peabody High, Steve Gaustad, a senior tight end from New Cumberland, and Dave DiCiccio, a senior defensive end from Midland.

Sherrill had a young team for 1978, but it registered a fine 8-4 record and accepted a Tangerine Bowl bid, where it lost to North Carolina State, 30-17.

Pitt won its first four games in 1978, defeating Tulane 24-6, in the opener as Trocano connected with Gordon Jones, while "Rooster" Jones, Larry Sims and Freddy Jacobs ran the ball well. The next time out, Trocano and Jacobs led the offense, and Chesley was a one-man gang on defense in a 20-12 victory over Temple.

Jacobs scored three second-half TDs in a 20-16 victory over North Carolina in the next contest. Pitt scored the first four times it had the ball to beat Boston College, 32-15, as Mark Schubert continued to boot field goals, and Trocano continued to find Gordon Jones open for passes.

Notre Dame interrupted Pitt, beating them 26-17 at South Bend, but the Panthers bounced back to beat Florida State, 7-3, the following week in a defensive struggle in which Green and Chesley starred.

Navy shocked Pitt in their next outing, 21-11, though Trocano threw for 275 yards, and Steve Gaustad grabbed 11 passes for 132 yards.

Pitt beat three long-time rivals in a row after that, edging Syracuse, 18-17, with Trocano coming through in the clutch; West Virginia, 52-7, with "Rooster" Jones running for 169 yards and two TDs, Trocano throwing for 146 yards and his backup, Lindsay Delaney, throwing for 72 more; and Army, 35-17, as Jeff Delaney picked off a fumble and ran 99 yards for six points, Trocano passing for 143 yards,

Pitt Had 1-2 Punch at Quarterback

RICK TROCANO
A competitor from Cleveland

and "Rooster" Jones running for 99.

Penn State stopped Pitt once again, 17-10, and the Panthers also came out on the short end in the Tangerine Bowl, bowing 30-17, to North Carolina State.

The record was 8-4, but Sherrill was hardly satisfied. He worked harder than ever, and he was a workaholic to begin with. "If you let him," said Jimmy Johnson, one of his former associates, "and if I didn't take him out once in a while and put a smile on his face, he'd work himself 24 hours a day and work himself into a grave."

Sherrill had to work hard because, from his second team, he was losing Gordon Jones, the best receiver in Pitt history, a dependable tight end in Gaustad; a starting center in Walt Brown; All-East offensive guard Matt Carroll; and five defensive stalwarts in Jeff Delaney, Logan, Di-Ciccio, Chesley and Mike Balzer.

Even so, Sherrill was looking forward to his third season. "I believe we will be a Top Ten team," he said at the outset of the 1979 season, and the Panthers played up to his expectations.

He came up with some fine freshmen, the best of whom was Danny Marino, perhaps the most sought-after prospect to come out of Western Pennsylvania since Dorsett. Marino, 6-4, 200, had been an all-everything quarterback at nearby Central Catholic.

Pitt opened at home against Kansas, and Trocano started at quarterback but split time with Marino. Sherrill was so anxious to get this great prospect some playing time. Marino's first pass was intercepted in the end zone, his second was nearly intercepted in the end zone, and, on his third try, he found Ralph Still in the end zone for a TD pass. Marino made things happen in a hurry. Pitt clobbered Kansas, 24-0, and another newcomer, fullback Randy McMillan, who'd been a great junior college rusher the year before, gained 82 yards in the first quarter and 141 yards altogether to give promise of big things to come.

The early euphoria for Pitt ended in a hurry, however, as North Carolina caught the Panthers napping the next week and won, 17-7. Pitt was still sleep-walking the week after and just managed to top Temple, 10-9, in Philadelphia.

Pitt beat Boston College, 28-7, with Marino coming off the bench and driving the Panthers to three of their four touchdowns. Trocano came back the next week and passed for 150 yards, and Marino came in and passed for an additional 120 yards, in a 35-0 victory over Cincinnati. Pitt had some 1-2 passing combination.

At Washington the week after, in a nationally-televised game, it was Trocano all the way in a hard-fought 26-14 win over the nationally-ranked Huskies. Anyone who watched that game won't soon forget the fabulous defensive showing of Hugh Green, or the running by McMillan, who gained 121 yards and scored two TDs.

The following Saturday at Pitt Stadium Pitt recovered from a slow start, and defeated Navy, 24-7. Trocano couldn't get anything going early against the Midshipmen, who had come into the game with the nation's top-ranked defensive unit. The Midshipmen had suffered many injuries to their ranks, but seemed capable of upsetting Pitt, especially when Trocano hurt an ankle on a quarterback keeper.

It took Marino, who had replaced Trocano, awhile to get going, and Pitt trailed Navy, 7-3, at the intermission. Marino drove Pitt to three TDs in the second half, and completed 22 of 30 passes for two of those touchdowns.

HUGH GREEN was the greatest defensive lineman in college ranks.

With Marino calling the signals, and firing at will, Pitt overcame Syracuse, 28-21, West Virginia, 24-17, and Army, 40-0, with the fabulous freshman hitting 17 of 30 passes for 272 yards and a touchdown in that game at West Point.

At Penn State, Marino commanded the Panther forces in a hard-fought 29-14 victory. Marino was 17-for-32 in the air for 279 yards and a touchdown, while McMillan ran for 114 more yards, and caught a 52-yard TD pass. Marino showed so much poise against Penn State, a perennial nemesis for the best of Pitt teams.

So Pitt had put together a 10-1 record, with only that nightmare in North Carolina still nagging at them, and accepted a bid to play in the Fiesta Bowl once again. Sherrill also announced that Serafino "Foge" Fazio would

be promoted to top assistant for the following season.

Marino and the Pitt offense were stymied most of the game by an aggressive and alert Arizona defense, but kept its poise and emerged with a 16-10 victory. Green had a great defensive game, and Marino passed for 172 yards and a touchdown, with McMillan picking up 81 more yards on the ground.

The three of them would all be back for 1980, and so would Sherrill. He said he intends to stay here.

"I can say it now and I'll say it again 10 years from now," he said. "I'll still be the coach. I'll still be in Pittsburgh. Even if I got fired, I'd probably open a hot dog stand here or something."

173

JOHNNY MAJORS

Johnny Majors is a modern-day "Music Man," college football's answer to Professor Harold Hill. Majors likes making the trumpets blare and the drums roll. He likes the TV shows and the media coverage. He likes getting into his twin-engine, phone-equipped Piper, and searching for new challenges.

He likes to build character, and instill discipline in his charges. In that respect, plus his penchant for flying his own plane—a zealousness also shared by Jackie Sherrill—he is a lot like Chuck Noll, the coach of the Steelers.

"A lot will depend," said Majors after his first few months at Pitt, "on the players' enthusiasm for our program."

Majors stood 5-10½, 180, but came across much bigger because of his boisterous, aggressive manner. He was more emotional and outgoing than Noll, but they both look at themselves as teachers.

"The fun of football is in the teaching," Majors once said. "I like to see a coach out there on his hands and knees, then jumping up to pat a guy on his back. As a football coach, I'm a Vince Lombardi fan.

"Lombardi had the two qualities that mean the most in coaching any football team. He was professionally tough, and he was personally emotional. And that's a heckuva combination.

"I was at Green Bay once when he was there and the thing that struck me was that they practiced like a good college team. Lombardi was a tough disciplinarian. His teams had to line up just so and run all their plays just so. But they ran them with the old man's emotion. It was very exciting to see how he stirred them up. You don't win football games with X's and O's. You win that way."

Coach Johnny Majors is flanked by his two top running backs— Elliott Walker (left) and Tony Dorsett.

JACKIE SHERRILL

Jackie Sherrill said he was glad to be back when he succeeded his old boss, Johnny Majors, after Pitt had won the national championship in 1976, but Sherrill felt he had some explaining to do about going away in the first place.

"I wouldn't have left Washington State for any other job except Pittsburgh," said Sherill upon his return. "Coming back to Pittsburgh was kind of special. My wife was from here, and I wasn't that far removed from the scene. I still had close feelings for the people here . . . Pittsburgh is what I consider to be my home."

His wife is the former Daryle Favro, who was a high school guidance counselor from Elizabeth, when they met soon after he arrived here the first time.

"The people in Pittsburgh are very honest people," said Sherrill, explaining his fondness for the place. "They're compassionate, yet they're tough, and I'm tough and like that, too. In five months, I probably met more people and became closer to them than I had in my whole time in organized sports. For a man just turning 29, it was a very important time. They gave me a home and they gave me a community involvement."

Johnny Majors, when asked to describe the role of a college coach, once remarked: "A coach has to be a salesman, a parent away from home, an academic adviser, a fund-raiser, a public relations man for the university . . . and a football coach."

Sherrill is all of those things, and then some. He not only sold Tony Dorsett on coming to Pitt in the first place, but he also talked Tony out of quitting school when he was a homesick freshman.

After five years on the job, Jackie Sherrill's record at Pitt was 50-9-1, and no other coach in the school's previous 91 years could claim that good a start in as many seasons.

"It hasn't been easy," said Sherrill: "There was a lot of pressure on me and my staff. What we have done the last five years has taken some of the pressure off.

"Though we haven't achieved the ultimate—winning the National Championship—it has been pleasing."

Coach Jackie Sherrill and Joe Pendry confer with QB Dan Marino.

PITT ALL-AMERICAS IN THE '70s

1973—1975—1976—TONY DORSETT

1974—GARY BURLEY

Tony Dorsett was hardly a one-man show at Pitt, though he received more publicity than anyone else. The Panthers may have put more talent on the field than anyone else in the country in 1976 when they won the national title under Coach Johnny Majors.

"After the material he had at Pittsburgh," opined Georgia coach Vince Dooley, whose team lost to Pitt in the Sugar Bowl at season's end, "there's not another school in the country where he could have gone and felt he had as good a team."

There were many members of that team who gained All-America recognition, and several who did not, but are now playing in the National Football League, like Cecil Johnson of the Tampa Bay Buccaneers, Don Parrish of the Kansas City Chiefs and J. C. Wilson of the Houston Oilers.

"We had a lot of great athletes," said Majors.

Pitt's first-team All-America honor roll during the '70s reads like this:

1973	Tony Dorsett
1974	Gary Burley
1975	Tony Dorsett
1976	Tony Dorsett
	Al Romano
1977	Matt Cavanaugh
	Randy Holloway
	Bob Jury
	Tom Brzoza
1978	Hugh Green
	Gordon Jones
1979	Hugh Green

1976—AL ROMANO

1977—MATT CAVANAUGH

1977—RANDY HOLLOWAY

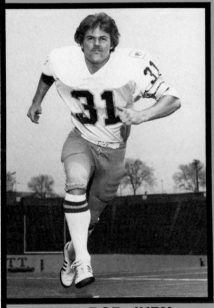

1977—BOB JURY

1977—TOM BRZOZA

1978—1979—HUGH GREEN

1978—GORDON JONES

177

This Decade Could Be The Best For Football In School History

By Bob Smizik

"The commitment has been made. We're at the point where success breeds success."
—Foge Fazio

Though the history of Pitt football is full of many seasons of rich success, some of them running together for years at a time, the 10 years of the 1980s may well prove to be the greatest in the school's history.

Though football is the most unpredictable of games, the foundation built in the '70s by first Johnny Majors and then Jackie Sherrill and which is now in the hands of Foge Fazio seems certain to maintain the Panthers at the highest level of football.

That the Panthers came into the '80s at that level can not be denied. They finished the decade of the '70s with an 11-1 record and went through the first two years of the '80s with the identical record. Such performances did not come by happenstance. There was much work involved in building the Panthers' fortunes.

The story of how Majors turned Pitt around when he arrived in 1973 is well known, but what isn't as well known is how the foundation of the '80s was built.

It all began in Majors' final days at Pitt as he prepared the Panthers for their national championship game with Georgia in the Sugar Bowl in 1976.

In the background, Sherrill, appointed only days earlier to replace Majors who was off to Tennessee after the Sugar Bowl, worked with an entirely new staff, one that included Fazio, and one that was picking up the pieces of a recruiting program that had turned somewhat sour in Majors' last two seasons. Pitt really hadn't recruited all that well in 1975 and 1976.

But 1977 was to be different. "We got our staff together and we turned them loose," said Sherrill.

"We worked like hell," said Joe Moore, who stayed on as Fazio's assistant head coach when Sherrill left for Texas A&M.

And what a crew they came up with. A kid from Mississippi named Hugh Green led the bunch.

"We heard he was good, but we didn't know how good," recalled Sherrill. And when did he find out! "About five minutes after the first practice started."

But it was more than Green. From New York came Mark May. "We thought we had a good one, but we were wrong," said Moore. "We had a great one."

NO. 1 TOAST — Pitt coach Jackie Sherrill offers a champagne toast to three of his players who were No. 1 picks in the 1981 NFL draft. From left to right, Mark May, Hugh Green and Randy McMillan were among the 11 Panthers selected on the first day of the draft in the best showing ever by one school.

Hugh Green Was The Greatest

NOBODY DOES IT BETTER — Pitt's Hugh Green holds up his trophy from the Maxwell Club in Philadelphia on Dec. 17, 1980, after winning its outstanding college player of the year award.

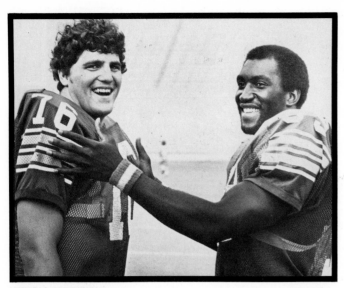

WHO'S WIDER? — Hugh Green, at right, measures shoulder span of teammate Bill Neill, who became a starter as rookie for the New York Giants.

From the South came Lynn Thomas, Carlton Williamson and Terry White, who were to form the nucleus of a great defensive backfield, and Rickey Jackson, who was to almost match Green, an all-time great, as a player.

Locally there were Benjie Pryor, Greg Meisner, Steve Fedell, Russ Grimm and Dave Trout. From the other side of the state came Bill Neill and Jerry Boyarsky. And from Ohio came Rick Trocano and Mark Reichard.

"It kind of hit us at fall camp," said Fazio, who was coaching the linebackers that year. "You see what's happening out on the field and it's hard to believe. There were so many of them who were so good.

"The next thing you know Trocano is starting the second game of the season, Trout is doing the kicking, Hugh Green is starting, Lynn Thomas is on special teams, Boyarsky, Meisner, Neill and Williamson are all playing. When the time came to put together a traveling squad for the third game of the season we said, 'Holy mackerel, we've got some players.'"

By the time the '80s rolled around they were already marked for greatness. When the season opened, 10 members of the Class of '81 were starting on what would be the best defense in the country and arguably one of the greatest of all time.

"Those guys did a lot for us even after they left," said Fazio. "They're gone but the attitude they developed among the younger guys is still here and it will continue to stay here.

"The 1981 team won a lot of games on tradition and winning attitude. In some cases they were playing a lot better than their own ability would carry them. They expect to be better because of the attitude and habits that were passed down to them."

Indeed, if ever there was doubt about the continuation of the Pitt program, the 1981 season erased it. The personnel losses were staggering from the previous season.

The defense needed completely rebuilt, the offense needed significant additions. But the new players stepped in without missing a beat, winning their first 10 games before being destroyed in the regular-season finale by Penn State, 48-14.

The loss sent the Panthers plunging from first to eighth in the United Press International poll. They had one last chance for redemption, one last chance to prove the first 10 games were not a fluke when they met second-ranked Georgia in the Sugar Bowl.

In an unforgettable game that left spectators and players emotionally drained, the Pitt defense swarmed all over All-American Herschel Walker to limit him to mere excellence and 84 yards as Bryan Thomas outplayed him while running for 129 yards and Marino and tight end John Brown teamed for a 33-yard touchdown pass with 42 seconds remaining to give the Panthers a 24-20 win.

The pollsters reversed their field and made Pitt the No. 2 team in the nation.

"I've never had a team give me more satisfaction," said Sherrill.

But even then Sherrill was thinking of leaving Pitt. There was an opening at Texas A&M that no man could refuse. The Aggies offered Sherrill a six-year contract, valued at approximately $250,000 a year, that renewed itself after every season. If ever they tired of Sherrill at College Station, it would cost them something like $1 million to get rid of him.

"It's the plum job in the country," said Sherrill in explaining his departure. "I'm going to miss Pittsburgh. The city has been good to me."

And so it was that the mantle was passed to Fazio, a Pitt man through and through. He played at Pitt in the late '50s and his term under Sherrill was his second as a Pitt assistant.

Fazio moved into a difficult situation. Sherrill left so much talent — players like Marino, tackle Jimbo Covert, split ends Julius Dawkins and Dwight Collins — that much will be expected.

But Fazio is up for the challenge.

"I feel confident that our program will continue to attract top-notch athletes and because of that we're going to be an exciting team," he said. "The commitment has been made. We're at the point where success breeds success."

SETTING SIGHTS on All-American status is Pitt's speedy Dwight Collins, a blue-chip wide receiver from Beaver Falls.

MUTUAL ADMIRATION SOCIETY — Penn State coach Joe Paterno is flanked by two quarterbacks who've competed against his team, former Arizona State star Mark Malone, at left, who is now with the Pittsburgh Steelers, and Pitt's Danny Marino during a Curbstone Coaches luncheon at Allegheny Club.

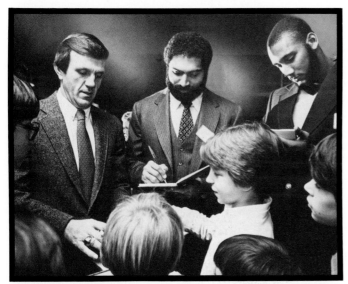

THREE'S COMPANY — Among the many local sports celebrities at the annual "sports night" of the Pittsburgh Press Club, were left to right, Pitt's Jackie Sherrill, the Steelers' Franco Harris, and Duquesne's Bruce Atkins at '81 affair.

SECOND GENERATION — Rich Bowen (12) of McKeesport's Serra High is one of the prize prospects of the 1982 recruiting class, and his dad, Dick Bowen, who coached the team, also played football at Pitt in the mid-'50s.

ON CUE — Greenfield's Sal Sunseri laughs aloud at one of Bob Hope's corny jokes during televised announcement of the Kodak All-America Football Team for 1981.

BIG BOY — Pro scouts were impressed with Bill Fralic as a freshman in 1981 season. It's no wonder. He is 6-5, 265, and the young man from Penn Hills starts at offensive tackle.

DANNY MARINO

COVER BOY — Pitt's senior quarterback from Oakland was on the cover of several national sports magazines at the outset of the 1982 football season. The kid from Central Catholic High School had a great shot at the Heisman Trophy entering the campaign.

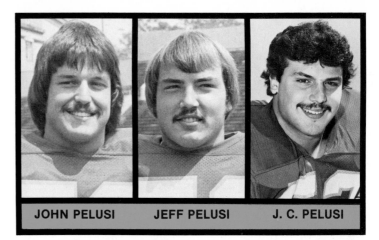

JOHN PELUSI   **JEFF PELUSI**   **J. C. PELUSI**

The Pelusi Family

To Pitt, With Love

The Pelusi family of Youngstown, Ohio, is a special clan, a close family with a fierce pride and winning spirit, and it has contributed much to the University of Pittsburgh.

John and Jean Anne Pelusi produced four sons, and three of them — John, Jeff and J. C. — have played football in a distinguished manner at Pitt the past 10 years.

Only Jimmy, now 26, did not attend Pitt. He went to Columbia where he played football and baseball and was voted the outstanding scholar athlete. He is now working toward his MBA at Harvard through a fellowship from General Motors Corporation.

The three who went to Pitt have been just as successful on and off the field. If Pitt is successful in winning a national championship in 1982, all three of them will have played on national championship teams.

J. C. — or Jay — is the starting middle guard on the 1982 unit. Like his other brothers, he also competed in basketball, baseball and track & field at Chaney High School. In addition, he plays golf and tennis. All the brothers ski.

Sports is important in the Pelusi household. John Sr. was a football coach at Chaney. All the boys started playing football in the first grade. Dad also coached Ed and Bob Matey at Chaney, and when Bob became an assistant football coach at Pitt he personally recruited three of the Pelusi boys.

"I'm thankful the boys are so close with each other," reports Mrs. Pelusi, "and with their mom and dad." She had more late suppers, dirty uniforms to clean and sneakers strewn about the house than she'd like to remember. "But it was worth it," she said. "The boys have all turned out well."

John, 28, was first team All-East and honorable mention All-American in 1976. He serves on the Board of Governors of the Pitt Golden Panthers as well as the board of directors of the Pitt Varsity Letter Club and the Alumni Council.

Jeff, 24, was first team All-East in 1979 and is a developmental design computer engineer in the nuclear research division of Westinghouse Electric Corporation.

J.C., 22, was first team All-East and an honorable mention All-American as a junior in 1981.

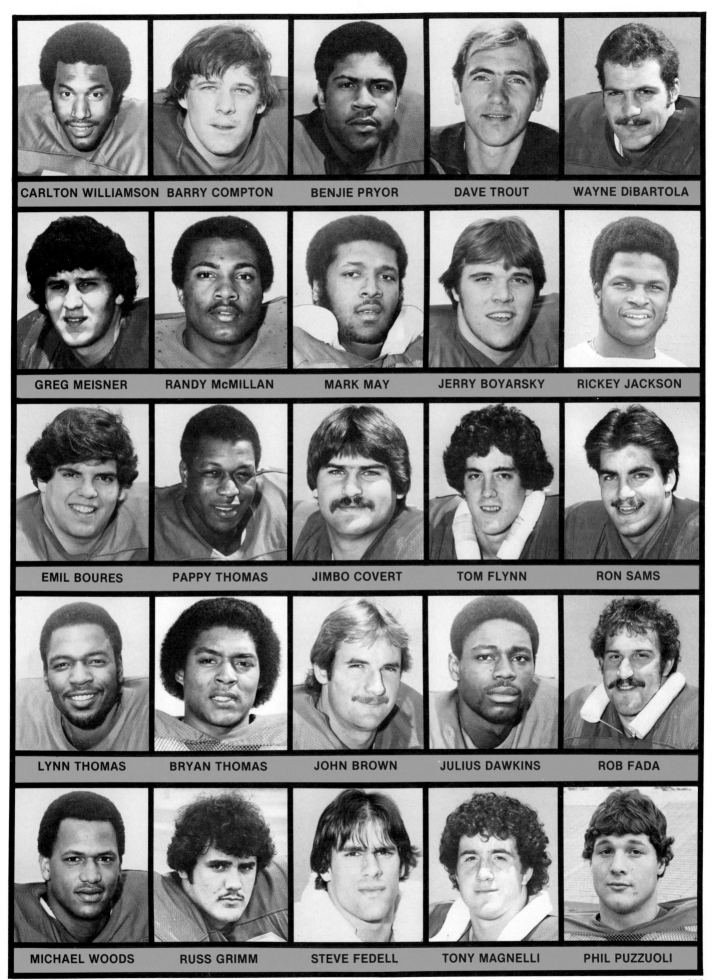

CARLTON WILLIAMSON	BARRY COMPTON	BENJIE PRYOR	DAVE TROUT	WAYNE DiBARTOLA
GREG MEISNER	RANDY McMILLAN	MARK MAY	JERRY BOYARSKY	RICKEY JACKSON
EMIL BOURES	PAPPY THOMAS	JIMBO COVERT	TOM FLYNN	RON SAMS
LYNN THOMAS	BRYAN THOMAS	JOHN BROWN	JULIUS DAWKINS	ROB FADA
MICHAEL WOODS	RUSS GRIMM	STEVE FEDELL	TONY MAGNELLI	PHIL PUZZUOLI

HERB McCRACKEN

Pop Warner's Quarterback Suits Up As 80-Year-Old

"I begged them to take me. I pestered them."

By Roy McHugh

Reprinted from The Pittsburgh Press

April 12, 1979

Can a 5-foot-8½, 165-pound defensive end play big-time college football?

They told Herb McCracken it wasn't possible. He proved them wrong.

But can a 5-foot-8½, 165-pound defensive end play big-time college football if he is 80 years old?

McCracken intends to try. Wearing the number 80 to correspond with his age — and cheating a little, he is two months shy of 80 — McCracken will suit up for the alumni-varsity game that concludes spring practice at Pitt a week from next Saturday.

The coach of the alumni, Dr. Darrell Lewis, has agreed to use him "for a play or two" — although not necessarily at defensive end. "I'll have to work something out," Lewis says.

In 1918, 1919 and 1920, McCracken was a quarterback, halfback or fullback when Pitt had the ball.

Lewis did not recruit McCracken. Nor did Pop Warner 62 years ago. Then, as now, McCracken was a walk-on.

"I begged them to take me. I pestered them," he said the other day from his winter-time home in Boynton Beach, on the east coast of Florida. There were reservations about his size, but at last the graduate manager of athletics, a man named Carl Davis, approved a tryout for McCracken (in those days college football was both less and more like professional football).

At Windber, where Pitt had its pre-season training camp, McCracken earned a scholarship.

He was a 60-minute player on teams that lost only two games in three years. Photographs show him to have been a resolute-looking character with well-developed neck muscles.

He took up coaching as the result of a casual conversation with a stockbroker friend who knew that the Allegheny College job was open. Then in 1924 Jock Sutherland asked him to join the Pitt staff.

McCracken grew up in Sewickley and he knew Sutherland well. "He was the town's night policeman when I worked on a mill truck as a kid," McCracken recalls. "I'd see him at 5 o'clock in the morning as I started on my rounds — a very fine, tall, silent man."

Born in Scotland, Sutherland had never played football. But, enrolling at Pitt as a full-grown adult, he took to the game at once. He was a guard, an All-American. By 1924, he had coached five years at Lafayette and his teams had held their own with Pop Warner's Pitt teams. Now Warner was moving on to Stanford, and Sutherland, the new Pitt coach, asked McCracken to be his assistant.

Instead, McCracken succeeded him at Lafayette.

There are football historians who have written that McCracken invented the huddle. It is not quite true. In 1896, for one game only, Amos Alonzo Stagg used the huddle at Yale. The Yalies were playing indoors that day, and because of the acoustics the signals could not be heard at the line of scrimmage. Bob Zuppke — Zuppke of Illinois — had begun using the huddle in 1921.

But to Zuppke it was only an occasional thing. McCracken made the huddle a basic part of his system at Lafayette after a telephone call before the 1924 Penn game from the conscience-stricken wife of an assistant Penn coach.

Penn had actually scouted Lafayette, she said, and knew all the plays — even the signals. In her mind, this was reprehensible behavior. McCracken, although not greatly worried, instructed his team to huddle on every down as a precaution. Lafayette lost 7-3, but McCracken liked the huddle so much he kept it — and he became a style-setter.

He coached until 1935. Against Pitt and Jock Sutherland, his record was perfect. Lafayette won the 1924, '25 and '26 games and then disappeared from the Pitt schedule.

McCracken had tough players from the hard-coal region of eastern Pennsylvania, recruited not by him, but by Lafayette alumni. With a partner, meanwhile, he had started a periodical called Scholastic Magazine, devoting nine months a year and eventually all of his time to the publishing business.

Scholastic Magazine and its various offshoots now have a circulation of 12 million. McCracken, retired, is still on the executive board.

He is also on Pitt's board of trustees. Alumni no longer in the full bloom of youth have played against the varsity — Dr. Dick Deitrick of the 1978 alumni squad was a two-way end in the early '50's — but McCracken will be the first trustee.

His weight remains what it always was — 165. "The quality," he admits, "is not as good." He runs and plays golf. His doctor, after a recent physical examination, pronounced him to be in "excellent" condition.

Asked what he did best for Pop Warner's team, McCracken replied, "Block and tackle." Will he block and/or tackle next week?

"I hope not. If the opportunity arises I might be tempted. It's a decision I'd have to make on the spur of the moment.

"But I won't do anything foolish," said McCracken sincerely.

JACKIE SHERRILL stands No. 1 among the all-time Pitt football coaches when it comes to winning percentage, just ahead of the legendary Jock Sutherland and Pop Warner.

ALL-TIME FOOTBALL COACHING CHARTS

Length of Service
(3 or more years)

Rank	Coach	Years
1.	Jock Sutherland	15
2.	John Michelosen	11
3.	Pop Warner	9
4.	Joseph H. Thompson	5
5.	Jackie Sherrill	5
6.	Charles W. Bowser	4
6.	Carl DePasqua	4
6.	John Majors	4
9.	Arthur St. L. Mosse	3
9.	Walter S. Milligan	3
9.	David R. Hart	3
9.	Lowell P. Dawson	3
9.	Clark D. Shaughnessy	3

Won-Loss Percentage
(3 or more years)

Rank	Coach	Pct.
1.	Sherrill	84.74
2.	Sutherland	84.73
3.	Warner	84.29
4.	Majors	71.74
5.	Thompson	68.18
6.	Mosse	66.67
7.	Michelosen	53.33
8.	Milligan	48.15
9.	Dawson	42.85
10.	Bowser	41.18
11.	Shaughnessy	37.04
12.	DePasqua	30.95
13.	Hart	10.00
	Pitt Total	**61.10**

Number of Wins

Rank	Coach	Wins	Losses	Ties
1.	Sutherland	111	20	12
2.	Warner	59	11	4
3.	Michelosen	56	49	7
4.	Sherrill	50	9	1
5.	Majors	33	13	1
6.	Thompson	30	14	2
7.	Mosse	20	10	1
8.	Duff	14	3	1
9.	Bowser	14	20	1
10.	Milligan	13	14	0
11.	DePasqua	13	29	0
		500	**318**	**36**

Charts compiled by Robert J. A. Pratt
Graduate School of Business
University of Pittsburgh

FOGE FAZIO

Some Master Plan Always Intended Him To Be The Pitt Coach

"I'm the guy who took Johnny Majors to meet Tony Dorsett."

—Foge Fazio

By Bob Smizik

When the telephone rang around 10 p.m. on the night of Jan. 18, 1982 in the Moon Twp. home of Serafino Dante Fazio, the man of the house had just walked in the door. He had, as was his frequent custom in the month of January, been out recruiting high school football players. The man on the other end of the line was a coach in the National Football League. He had a job to offer.

Serafino Fazio knew the offer might be coming and had given it a lot of thought. He was 42 years old and lusting to be a head coach on the college level. In his current job, as defensive coordinator and assistant head coach of the University of Pittsburgh, he was making little progress towards his goal. In recent years he had seen a drift in the thinking of athletic directors towards hiring pro assistants for head college jobs.

He was ready to make a move. Neither Maryland nor South Carolina had shown any great interest in him the previous month when they had openings. His mind was all but made up to leave Pitt.

"After the Maryland thing fell through (pro assistant Dick Nolan got the job), I felt maybe it was time to look elsewhere," says Fazio. "I felt I'd be in pro football in 1982. If Jackie Sherrill had stayed at Pitt, I'd be in pro football today."

But there were other movements afoot that made Fazio put off the pro coach. His boss, Sherrill, had been in Texas that day, interviewing for a job with Texas A&M. Fazio knew if Sherrill left, his chances of succeeding him would be excellent.

"I told the pro coach to give me some time on this," remembers Fazio. "There was something going on at Pitt and I'd get back to him in a day or two."

The pro coach had no problem with that.

When Fazio hung up, his wife told him of another call. Sherrill, she told him, had called from an airplane. She said Sherrill would return the call when his plane landed.

"I asked her," remembers Fazio, "if he said he was taking the job. She said he didn't say but he seemed excited. I said to myself, 'If he's flying back on a private plane and calling people on the telephone, he must be taking it. If he wasn't taking it, he'd be coming back commercial.'"

When Sherrill landed he called Fazio again. The news was good for both men. Sherrill was off to Texas A&M and

the best contract a college coach ever had. Fazio would be recommended as his successor. Less than twenty-four hours later, Foge Fazio, Pitt '59, was head coach of his alma mater.

The pro coach went off to look for a new man. Foge Fazio was back where some master plan had always intended for him to be.

From the beginning, Fazio was drawn to Pittsburgh.

His father, an Argentina native, emigrated from Italy to West Virginia some 50 years ago and took up work in the coal mines. It was seven years before he could call for his wife. A few years later Serafino, which means angel in Italian, was born.

He remembers life in Dawmont, W. Va. "We lived above the company store," he says, "and my dad worked in the mines. But one day there was a cave-in. My dad broke his leg. That was enough for him."

And Serafino Fazio was off to Coraopolis, Pa. and his destiny. Francisco Fazio bought a grocery store in Coraopolis and little Foge — so called because of his difficulty in pronouncing fudge — grew up with Western Pennsylvania football.

It was sandlot football against older kids with not much equipment. That's how he learned the game.

"I never played organized ball until I was in ninth grade at Coraopolis," says Fazio. His brother, Frank, was a senior and the starting center for Coraopolis. Foge was a linebacker and fullback, but he rarely played in that first year.

When the next season came around, Mrs. Fazio decided she didn't want her son playing football. "With my brother graduated she thought there would be no one to protect me. She wouldn't sign my permission slip," says Fazio. "But I got around that."

He was all-WPIAL as a linebacker as a sophomore and all-state by his senior year.

And now he was to get his first taste of recruiting. Miami, Indiana, North Carolina, West Virginia, Pitt and Penn State, in the person of a young assistant named Paterno, came around.

Though Jack Wiley and John Michelosen recruited him to Pitt, it was Joe Paterno who seemed to have the greatest impact on Fazio.

"He made many recruiting trips to our house," says Fazio. "It seems like every time he was in Western Pennsylvania he'd end up in Coraopolis. My dad would bring out the pepperoni and provolone and Joe would sit around and eat.

"My mother really liked him. But I guess I just decided to go to Pitt."

Not even the charisma of Paterno could take Fazio away from his destiny.

His career at Pitt, was good, but overshadowed by some of his teammates such as Mike Ditka, Ivan Toncic, Fred Cox and John Guzik.

The then Boston Patriots picked him in the fifth round of the American Football League draft. The National Football League did not pick him, but the Steelers tried to sign him.

"I guess I was flattered that Boston would pick me in the fifth round," said Fazio. He said no to the Steelers and went off to Boston.

He played briefly his first year and was cut the second. "I realized that I was a fringe player and I'd never do anything more than hang on, so I gave it up and went back to school for my master's," says Fazio.

Back to school and back to Pittsburgh.

Two years later he was teaching social studies at Coraopolis and helping with the football team. The next year he was a full-time assistant at Ambridge. He was hooked. He also played for the Pittsburgh Valley Ironmen.

"I had wanted to go to law school, but once I got started with football I forgot about it. Once I started coaching I seemed to like it. I enjoyed it and it came easy to me. I got along with the players and their families."

He was named head coach at Coraopolis in 1965 and compiled a 13-3-1 record in two years. And then it was off to the rounds that young men must make if they wish to become a head coach.

Boston U. was his first stop, where he was recommended by former teammate Ralph Jelic, whose son, Chris, will play for Fazio as a freshman at Pitt this fall. He spent two years at BU and another at Harvard before coming home to Pitt to coach under Carl DePasqua.

"There were a lot of handicaps," recalls Fazio. "The schedule was extremely difficult. Penn State and Syracuse had easier schedules at that time. Our facilities weren't like they are today. The locker room was the same one I dressed in when I was a player. There wasn't a weight room.

"But there was a lot of excitement and enthusiasm at first. We were taking over a program that had been 1-9 for three years and we won some games our first year (4-6). We were 5-1 the next year and then the bottom fell out." Pitt

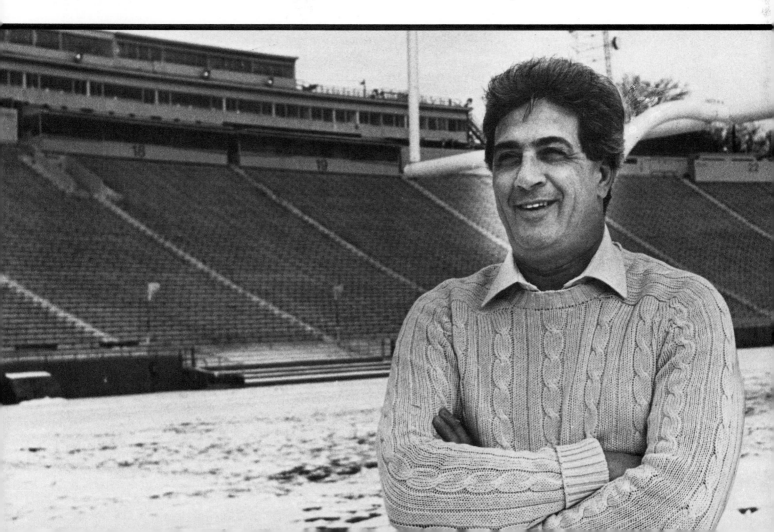

lost its last four games and though he would be around two more seasons, DePasqua was finished.

Fazio was only starting. When Johnny Majors was hired to replace DePasqua after the 1972 season, Fazio was kept on for awhile to help with recruiting.

"I'm the guy who took Johnny Majors to meet Tony Dorsett," says Fazio. "I drove him to Butch Ross' house (the Hopewell coach). I drove Johnny Majors all over Western Pennsylvania for about six weeks.

"I could see one thing. There was a new enthusiasm. You could see things would get done. Joe Avezzano (an assistant) brought in 10 guys from Miami in one weekend. We didn't bring in 10 guys by plane all year."

And as Fazio helped in the transition, a friendship was formed.

"Jackie Sherrill and I became pretty good friends," he says. "Jackie tried to talk me into staying. But Majors had just brought in so many guys I wasn't sure what I'd be doing. I might have been just an administrator or a recruiter or the coach of the defensive left guards.

"I didn't know if my talents would be used. If I stayed I might be buried as one of the good old guys."

Fran Curci offered him a job at Kentucky, but Fazio chose Cincinnati, where the program was decidedly less big-time. In four years at Cincinnati, Tony Mason developed a program and Fazio a defense, one that was nationally ranked.

When Mason left for Arizona, Fazio thought he might succeed him. Instead, Cincinnati chose Ralph Staub, who was fired four years later. Fazio tried for the Connecticut job, but there was a delay in naming a coach and in the meantime his old friend, Jackie Sherrill, called him from Pittsburgh.

Fazio went home as linebacker coach. A year later he was defensive coordinator and a year after that assistant head coach.

The grand design, one that Fazio will not acknowledge, was complete. The coal miner's son from West Virginia is the head football coach at Pitt, and if his journey is only now ended his work has only now begun.

He inherited a team that was almost certain to be ranked No. 1 in pre-season polls. Even though Fazio joked about how "when they see that a guy named Serafino Fazio is coaching Pitt they'll never rank us No. 1," the pressure most certainly will be on.

He is in an almost no-win situation. It was similar to what Sherrill faced in 1980, only more difficult. Pitt entered that season with such an abundance of talent that anything less than 12-0, in the eyes of many Pittsburghers, would have been a disappointment. Pitt finished 11-1 and unfulfilled.

The same is expected this season, except if Fazio pulls it off, people will say he did it with Sherrill's talent.

"That's something we just have to live with. I think it will motivate me and my coaches," he says. "I think our kids will be motivated by the fact that so much is expected from them."

NO. 29 — Pitt football coach Foge Fazio is flanked by Casimir Myslinski and Wesley Posvar at the announcement of his hiring as Jackie Sherrill's successor, and the 29th head football coach in Panther history.

TWO LEADERS — New coach Foge Fazio will miss leadership provided by former defensive captain, Sal Sunseri, who was taken in the 1982 draft by the Pittsburgh Steelers.

JOE TREES

"Call On Joe" Was A Byword

By Chester L. Smith
The Pittsburgh Press

May 21, 1943

Joe Trees died in his office in the Golden Triangle Wednesday afternoon known as a man who had made millions in oil, yet he had a background in sports which rivals fiction. As a young fellow he was a great football player; in his later years, when he was no longer able to take part in the more strenuous games of contact, he turned to hunting and fishing. In his 20's he was no man to be trifled with on the gridiron; by the time he had reached the expansive 60's and the retrospective 70's he was still able to pull a sure trigger and wield a seductive rod.

I remember a conversation with Mr. Trees 10 years ago or more when the snoopers of the Carnegie Foundation had publicized the awful fact that there were boys in this country who were actually getting their tuition and board in some of our best colleges and universities in exchange for their football talents. The Carnegie people had turned it into a first-rate scandal, intimating there was no fate too harsh for these youthful criminals. Mr. Trees' long and close contact with the University of Pittsburgh made him a likely subject to interview on the matter. He had seen football grow and prosper, and there had been stories about how he got his start. Some said he had been recompensed for his own activities in athletics at Pitt — which at that time was the Western University of Pennsylvania.

Mr. Trees listened attentively while I put the question to him and then chuckled.

"Shucks," he said. "I wouldn't give a nickel for a kid who wasn't worth subsidizing. I got my own education that way and I have helped dozens of them. I suppose I'm as big a subsidizer as there is anywhere. And they aren't going to stop me, either."

The story of Joe Trees goes back to WUP in 1889 when Bert Smyers, still an active attorney here, came to Pittsburgh from Bucknell Academy and organized the university's first football team. The WUPS played one game that fall — with Shadyside Academy — and were beaten. The following season they met Indiana State Teachers' College, and that's when Smyers, a 131-pound quarterback, got his first glimpse of precocious, red-headed 210-pound Trees, a tackle.

Quarterback Smyers thought he would like to have tackle Trees on his side instead of against him.

"How'd you like to come down to WUP?" he proposed. I couldn't afford it," Trees replied. But a scholarship and arrangements for board and room changed his mind.

"What happened to Joe Trees in the next few years sounds like a fable," Smyers declares. "I was working during the summers in the Union Trust Company, whose offices were in the same building as Standard Oil. We were anxious to get Joe a job that would keep him out in the open and in shape for football, so we persuaded the oil people to take him on as a tool dresser. That was how he got his start in the oil business. He began by investing $500 of his own and another $500 in a well near New Martinsville, W.Va. He would pike up a lease here and another there. Eventually, he ran that small-paying position, which was to keep him fit for football, into millions of dollars.

"I have never known a more sportsmanlike athlete, but Joe did encounter one man who never failed to rile him. It was after he had been graduated from the university and was playing professionally for the D.C.&A.C., and the fellow he hated was one 'Sport' Donnally, who played on the line for the Cleveland team. Joe's hair was not only red but thick and bushy, and 'Sport' had a habit of grabbing it in both hands when he thought no official was looking. That always meant a fight, and Joe would haul off and punch 'Sport' squarely on the nose. He was put out of many a game simply because he was goaded into retaliating."

Attorney Smyers recalls many members of that squad who became prominent personages in after years: Harry Evans, a treasurer for the Union Trust Co.; W. C. Gill, attorney; George Calvert, also a lawyer; Harry Calvert, a reporter for The Pittsburgh Press; Joe Sauers, whose father conducted a North Side Hotel. Others were Floyd Rose, now vice-president of Vanadium Alloys; Ted Boden; Dud DuBarry; Bob Brown, now manager of the Empire State Building in New York City; and 'Cowboy' House. There was no coach, and during the four years Trees, Smyers and others had to play every minute of each game because of a lack of substitutes.

Mr. Trees will never be forgotten at Pitt, not because he played on its varsity, but for his interest in the school, which was maintained until his death. "Call on Joe" was a by-word. He didn't fail once. If the band wanted to make a trip to a big game and lacked the funds, he would be there with his checkbook. He donated $100,000 toward the Trees Gymnasium, deeded the practice field to the school on which so many nationally-famous Panther elevens learned the rudiments, gave $75,000 to the building of Alumni Hall and bought $200,000 worth of stadium bonds.

Nor did he forget the college at Indiana, Pa., where he got his start. He was a perennial donor there, repaying a debt to "Aunt Jane" Leonard, his Indiana sponsor, who had given him the teaching position which made it possible for him to continue his education.

Those of us who dabble more or less continually in sports believe we knew Mr. Trees just about as intimately as those who met him in his many other activities, and we have a hunch that he was still "playing tackle" up to the minute he left us.

WALTER SARRAF

For Over 50 Years, He Knew The Score

"Other people talk about the all-time great games that they've heard about. I was there."

By Maria Sciullo
Reprinted from The Pittsburgh Press

Aug. 7, 1980

Walter Sarraf's record may not be listed in the Guinness Book, but it's still tough to match.

Until the 1979 season, the 75-year-old Mt. Lebanon resident had attended every Pitt, Steeler, Carnegie-Mellon, Duquesne University and high school championship football game played at Pitt Stadium.

Sarraf's remarkable streak started in 1925 — the year the stadium opened — when the Peabody High School senior got into the stands using his brother's Pitt student ticket. For the next 53 years, however, he played a more active role than spectator.

As a member of Pitt's freshman basketball team in 1926, Sarraf got the chance to help operate the stadium's two wooden scoreboards during football season. In those days, scoreboards were hand-operated, not electronic. Numbered metal cards were dropped into slots to indicate yardage, score and other information. It was a long tiring job.

"We also had to be very careful on windy days," Sarraf chuckled. "Sometimes the cards would blow out and hit the fans."

Members of the school's track and basketball teams worked the scoreboards until 1928 — months after Pitt won a national championship in basketball — when Sarraf brought in the Boy Scouts. The Scouts from Troop 100 had been ushering for three years and a dozen were needed for the new job.

Meanwhile, Sarraf moved down to the field with teammate John Cost, and the pair employed a Boy Scout trick or two in calling signals up to the scoreboard.

Fans marveled at the speed at which scoreboard information changed after a play was whistled dead. Most probably assumed that Sarraf and Cost were communicating with the scoreboard workers by way of telephone or some other device.

"No one could figure how we got the information up so quickly," said Sarraf.

The answer was simply they used semaphore. The hand-signals used by Scouts everywhere was the most efficient means of communication from sideline to scoreboard.

Sarraf would dress in white each week so that he could be easily spotted from above. A touch of the head or a bend of the arm must have made him look like a polar bear trying to spell P-I-T-T but, according to Sarraf, it was the fastest system in the country.

"You can go anywhere in the country today, and it's still faster than a computer," he said. "Now, there's usually 5-to 15- second lag after each play, but that's good enough because no one's doing any better."

Sarraf, a retired sales manager with Harbison-Walker Refractories, and his three brothers all went to Pitt. Two were chemical engineers, one a mechanical engineer, and Sarraf earned a degree in chemistry. After graduation, he continued working with the Scouts and remained close to the team.

"After I started work, in the afternoons I'd jump into my old Model A Ford and buzz out there to practice." Sarraf had his own locker in the Pitt dressing room for 50 years.

Electric scoreboards were installed in 1951 and the computerized boards used today came in shortly after Pitt won its ninth national championship in 1976. Sarraf remained on the field, but it wasn't until the 1969 season that he moved up to the press box to signal plays.

Having personally witnessed 53 seasons, Sarraf is an authority on the history of Pitt football. "Other people talk about 'all-star' teams and all-time great games that they've heard about," said Sarraf. "I was there."

It's a bit surprising that the one game among hundreds which Sarraf chooses as most outstanding was a Pitt loss. "Others come close, but it was the Pitt-Minnesota game in 1934 that had to be the most exciting," he said.

Pitt was coached at the time by the legendary Dr. John "Jock" Sutherland. The same 11 men played both offense and defense. Sarraf recalled that Minnesota Coach Bernie Bierman intended to wear down the Panther offense and hope for a defensive break.

"Throughout the first half, they just kicked on first down," he said. "They never ran a play. In the second half, they punted and Pitt lost the ball on the . . . 34-yard line, I believe. The final score was 13-7."

Sarraf is a smiling man who has Pitt football programs, field passes, newspaper articles and other memorabilia on file in his home. Most of the yellowed clippings are neatly mounted in a stack of large scrapbooks, the programs are stored by season in manila folders.

Most of the folders are filled with programs that include pictures of players and advertisements, but the single-page leaflets produced during the World War II years are simple and list only team rosters. Not only did the programs take on a different look during the war — one year the uniforms did, too.

Clark D. Shaughnessy brought the T-formation to Pitt in 1943, and two years later decided to change the Panthers' team colors to red and white. The former idea worked well, but the latter went over like a lead balloon. Soon Pitt was back to wearing blue and gold.

ELMER MERKOVSKY

ELMER MERKOVSKY — He Stood Tall

"I've got too much to live for to give up."

By Jim O'Brien

Reprinted from The Pittsburgh Press

Feb. 27, 1981

In the autumn of his youth, he was a fine football player. He was a big tough tackle who would take on anyone.

An all-star at North Braddock Scott High School in 1934, he set a standard of excellence and paved the way for a younger neighbor, Fran Rogel, to follow a few years later.

He went to Pitt and played for Jock Sutherland. He blocked for the "Dream Backfield" threw his body against Fordham's "Seven Blocks of Granite" in two of those three famous scoreless ties and, among his most cherished memories, performed in the '37 Rose Bowl.

He played for the Steelers for three seasons — 1944 through 1946 — under three different coaches. The first of those seasons was spent with the Pitt-Cards, a wartime combine of the Steelers and Chicago Cardinals. He weighed 240 then, and Art Rooney remembers him as a "steady, solid performer." Better yet, Rooney recalls him as "a good guy who always showed up at our Steeler alumni activities."

When Elmer Merkovsky quit the pro game, he went to work as a deputy sheriff in Pittsburgh. He had grown to 290 pounds and often was given the task of taking criminals to jail to start their sentences. No one was going to get away from him.

No one messed around with Elmer Merkovsky.

It is difficult to envision all these events in his lifetime when one sees Elmer Merkovsky sitting in a wheelchair in his room at St. Francis General Hospital in Lawrenceville.

His left leg has been amputated. As soon as he is strong enough to withstand another operation, his right leg will be amputated to the knee.

"It's kinda traumatic," he tells you. "It's a hard thing to go through." It's hard to say something in response.

Suddenly, all the solemn discussions with John Stallworth, Jack Ham and Calvin Sweeney of the Steelers about their foot operations and rehabilitation programs seem trivial by comparison.

Merkovsky, who will be 64 in April, said he weighed 260 last June and has lost 100 pounds since. Along with the amputation, he has suffered from just about every complication possible — stomach and liver ailments, fevers, jaundice — and the loneliness of his exile in the hospital. He has been in St. Francis since Oct. 18.

He is presently in an isolation unit because he has hepatitis. Visitors must don a hospital gown and wash their hands with an antiseptic solution upon entering and leaving his room. "Sometimes I go a little stir-crazy," he conceded with a smile.

Always the smile. It's still a winning smile and rivets one's attention. That and the gleam in his deep-set eyes He's cheerful.

"Geez, he's been in there a long time," said Art Rooney.

"I sent him a letter and had my brother, Father Dan, when he was still alive, say a Mass for him. I'll have to give him a call." And he has, according to Merkovsky.

Merkovsky came here from his home in Long Beach, Calif., on Oct. 16 to be inducted into the Pennsylvania Sports Hall of Fame. The affair was set for the following night at the VFW Hall in East Pittsburgh, where Merkovsky once worked at Westinghouse Electric.

He had been hospitalized last June, but had his doctor's permission to come here for the induction ceremonies. His left leg bothered him during the airplane trip here, however, and the pain grew progressively worse. By the time, he arrived here, he required a wheelchair to transport him through the airport terminal.

The next night, one of his six children, Bob, wheeled him into the VFW Hall to be honored.

Elmer entered the hospital the next day. He was told he had blood clots in his leg. Gangrene had set in and spread fast. "Your foot's dead," the doctor told him.

The days have been difficult for him ever since. Especially when he had fevers after the amputation. "There were times when I was like a wild animal in the intensive care unit," he says. His wife, Mildred, has been staying with her sister in East Pittsburgh and visits regularly. So does his daughter, Geraldine Stillson of Squirrel Hill, and her children call their grandpap on the telephone. One of his sons, Elmer Jr., played football at Pitt in the early '60s.

The father is soft-spoken, but a very strong man. He thinks his sports background has given him strength to handle all the adversity. "I think it helped," he said. "You just don't seem to give up. You don't get dejected as you might. You look forward to a different life — without your legs. But at least you know you're alive."

One of the doctors who looked after him was Dr. George Medich, the young man from Aliquippa who played football and baseball at Pitt, and is presently pitching for the Texas Rangers.

Before he left for spring training, Medich told Merkovsky, "Keep your chin up. You can do it. And when we come to play in Anaheim give me a call and I'll leave some tickets for you."

Merkovsky aims to give "Doc" Medich a chance to keep his word. "I've got too much to live for to give up," he said. "I want to see my youngest son graduate from Southern Cal; and my grandchildren call me and tell me they want me back. I've accepted what's happened to me. I got remorse about it, but I'd rather lose my legs than my life.

"There are a million things I can do, even if I'm in a wheelchair. The climate is so beautiful out in California. I'm looking forward to going fishing."

Postscript: Merkovsky had his other leg amputated soon after the above story was written. "One of his legs was taken off at the hip, and the other just below the knee," said his daughter, Mrs. Geraldine Stillson. "He was fitted for artificial limbs, but the therapist didn't think, at Dad's age, he'd be able to walk with them, but he fooled them. He's something else. He went back to California, and, before long, he was taking walks around the block. He learned how to repair musical instruments, and felt useful. He always told us courage wins out, and he was right."

SECOND GENERATION — Elmer Merkovsky Jr. came out of Wilmerding to letter as a tackle at Pitt in 1961.

ELMER EMBRACES his buddies back in 1938, from left to right, Al Leeson, trainer Herman Bearzy, and Marshall Goldberg. All three players later sent their sons to play football at Pitt.

Frank Carver Recalls His Days On The Hill

For nearly 40 years, he was a vital part of the Pitt sports scene, and he loved nearly every minute of it

relations Doc Carlson gained with opponents all over the country to move into major league scheduling in football.

* * *

In the spring of 1928, as an eager but awkward and slow high hurdler, I was awed by sharing a dressing room with Canadian Olympic pole vaulter Vic Pickard, and 155-pound hammer thrower Don Gwinn, who placed fifth in the Olympics, NCAA 440 champion Pete Bowen, Welch, who placed in the IC4A in the discus and javelin, Everett Utterback, a big point scorer with his sprinting and jumping ability, and Tiny Linn, an IC4A placer in the hammer throw.

* * *

One of the most popular men in Pitt sports history, Frank Carver served as athletic director at his alma mater from 1959 through 1968. He was the acting athletic director in 1948 before Capt. Tom Hamilton took over, and Carver served as graduate manager from 1949 to 1959. Carver was the sports publicist at Pitt upon graduation in 1931 through 1948, with a three-year hiatus for a stint in the military service. Carver enrolled at Pitt as a student in 1927, and competed in freshman track. "But I was too slow," he says somewhat sadly. He and his wife, Marty, live in retirement today in their beloved Beaver, Pa. home.

By Frank Carver

Trying to hit the peaks of Pitt athletic history from this far away in years makes me feel as if someone had asked me to climb the Alps. But I'm going to try by reliving, as best I can, my own impressions, beginning when I hit the campus in 1927.

There were two memorable football games in 1927, the 21-13 win over Nebraska, a Husker team that had no players from outside the state on its roster. They ran all over Pitt the first half, but we won on three long runs, a kickoff return of 100 plus yards by Gibby Welch, a pass from Jimmy Hagan to Welch, and a long run by Hagan. The other was a 0-0 tie with Washington & Jefferson, W&J's last gasp as a major team under Coach Andy Kerr.

* * *

That winter, 1927-28, the basketball team claimed the national title — there were no polls in those days — by winning all their games and compiling a 21-0 record, including four games on the road in five days against Big Ten teams. Incidentally, Pitt took advantage of the friendly

VIC PICKARD — Olympic Pole Vaulter

PITT STADIUM near completion in the summer of 1925.

The Pitt Stadium story has to be part of any tale on Pitt athletics. Urged by over-enthusiastic alumni, the University financed its construction costs ($2,125,000) with a bond issue. Ketchum, MacLeod & Grove got its start by doing the selling.

The original capacity was 65,000, although only Penn State and W&J filled 25,000-seat Forbes Field. To prepare for all eventualities, the foundations were laid to support a second deck for possible future expansion.

Only problem was that somebody forgot to get the schedules to match the capacity. Don Harrison became athletic director in 1927 and he beefed up the schedule within a few years, adding Ohio State, Notre Dame and Army. Even winning teams and improved schedules didn't draw the necessary gates, however.

I remember there were only 22,000 on hand to see Ohio State play Pitt when both teams were undefeated going into the fifth game of the 1932 season, and they played to a scoreless tie.

This was the Depression, and the $100,000 debt service was a major item on the athletic budget. Chancellor Bowman insisted it was an obligation which had to be paid and we did it every year until 1948 when it was refinanced. Bowman had learned his lesson. From then on, no new building was begun until the money was in the bank, which accounts for the fact that few, except the Cathedral of Learning, were built until Tom Hamilton got Pitt under the GSA.

* * *

A major item in the Stadium's cost was the 220 straight-away which demanded a tunnel at both ends, so that the finish was never seen by the few spectators who showed up for track & field meets. I heard it added another $100,000 to the cost.

There were a lot of great athletes who performed on that track, whether or not anyone was watching.

The 20s and early 30s were pressureless times. Frank Shea, who had been an IC4A champion in the 440 at Pitt, coached on a part-time basis.

He commuted from his home in Greensburg to his law practice in Pittsburgh, leaving his office every afternoon to climb to the old track house or Pitt Stadium. An omnivorous reader, he stuffed two books in his pockets, and read one going and the other returning.

Besides Pickard, Welch and Gwinn, his top performers were NCAA champion Pete Bowen in the 440, jumper Everett Utterback, who became a Pitt trustee, sprinter Ken Wibecan, and hurdler Eddie Knoblock, all holders of University records in their time.

* * *

What happened long ago, well, the word has come down to be half legend and half truth. The start of winning football seasons at Pitt began with the seduction of Joe Thompson from Geneva in about 1903. The Covies of that year had whipped Pitt twice that season, so several of them, including Thompson, were enticed to enter Pitt in 1904. The Panthers won all ten of their games that season as a result.

Thompson, a real honest-to-goodness hero of World War I, eventually became coach and brought his Pitt team through an undefeated, untied and unscored-on season in 1910.

EVERETT UTTERBACK

ARNIE SOWELL

Track Stars of Different Eras

There was another era in which wholesale transfers played a part, a few years earlier when players came from Kansas with the incoming coach, Arthur St. L. Mosse, who posted a 20-10-1 record from 1903 to 1905.

* * *

The outstanding hero in those early days was Hube Wagner, an end and fullback who captained the 1913 team and later became one of Pittsburgh's best-known surgeons, a medical director at U.S. Steel Corporation, a member of the Board of Trustees, and a member of the National Football Foundation Hall of Fame.

He outpunted the great Jim Thorpe, and played against Knute Rockne and Gus Dorais, but more to the point, he was the perfect embodiment of what a graduate of the University should be. I've maintained, and I lost my worshipping ability long ago, that in his case the man outshone the legend.

* * *

There was almost child-like innocence about the "professionalism" of college football in those days of few rules, no NCAA, no bowls, and no pot of gold at the end of the TV rainbow. What sins were committed were in the same spirit in which small towns were careless about the baseball players they collected when the occasion demanded extraordinary efforts to defeat a rival.

Perhaps the most successful when it came to acquiring worldly goods and the most interesting were the athletes of the period between Warner's good years and those of Sutherland, the post World War I era. I never saw them in football action, but I did come to know many of them, and hence this opinion.

There was Herb McCracken, a successful coach at Geneva, Allegheny and Lafayette (while at the latter, he whipped Sutherland, his predecessor, three straight times). He wound up a very successful publisher, helping to found Scholastic Magazine.

* * *

BETTER THAN THE LEGEND — Hube Wagner, left, is presented with National Football Foundation and Hall of Fame award by Senator George Murphy at Pitt Stadium ceremonies.

The Penn game at Philadelphia was the big one, except for Penn State and W&J, and our only real exposure to the Eastern press. There, the punts of Jess Brown had the folks at Franklin Field looking skyward all afternoon. On the same field, Tommy Davies ran wild, time after time.

He had his greatest game, however, in his final outing. As a single-wing halfback, when the formation was left, he teamed with the end to handle the opposing right tackle. Tommy wasn't very big — even for those days — and in this game had been roughly handled. He asked the ref to let him know when the game had only two minutes to go. At the appointed time, Davies took a healthy swing at the jaw of the tackle, and kept on going right to the dressing room.

* * *

There was a casual atmosphere about the sport. Charley Bowser, who later coached at Grove City, Pitt and Bowdoin, talks of the night before a Penn game when the bell captain at the Bellevue Stratford told him that Pop Warner wanted to see him. When Charley got to Pop's room, his coach told him that he was in a quandary about whether to start him at center or quarterback. That's hard to understand now, in a day when we've been sold on the theme that it takes five years to develop a quarterback.

The late Jack Sack, who turned out to be one of Pitt's greatest guards, and a very successful businessman, tells of reporting to freshman coach Andy Kerr when the uniforms were being handed out. He said the first question asked regarded one's playing background. Kerr wanted to know if you had gone to a prep school, Kiski or Bellefonte, for example, and if you did you could draw a full uniform. Jack had gone to Fifth Avenue High School, and he was given what was left, and it did not constitute a full outfit.

In this same group was Lou Mervis, a 200-pound tackle who missed making Walter Camp's All-America team because he wore another player's jersey in the Georgia Tech game, the one which Camp saw that year. It didn't stop him later from presenting the University with an academic building.

And All-America Herb Stein, another very successful businessman, and a member of the National Football Foundation Hall of Fame, was a member of the 1921 team.

* * *

In 1932, Don Harrison brought in Carl Olson, a very successful track & field coach at Froebel High School in Gary, Indiana. He was a delightfully supreme egotist, but a great coach, demanding and getting only the very best from his athletes as he developed some great ones: Olympian Herbie Douglas in the broad jump, Arnie Sowell and Charley Gongloff, NCAA champions in the 880 and javelin, respectively. Best known of all, of course, was Johnny Woodruff who won the Olympic 800 in 1936 to the chagrin of Adolph Hitler, and anchored 13 winning Class A relay teams in the Penn Relays.

Two fellows who competed in the relays with him on a regular basis bring back memories, too. The lead-off man was Frank Ohl. He had the heart of a street fighter for he never failed to grab the pole by the first turn, hitting into the pack with elbows akimbo, about as destructive as those Roman chariots with swords on their wheels. Al Ferrara was different, for he was possibly the slowest runner (other than me) in Pitt history. Fortunately, he was also the most determined for he never let anyone get by him.

* * *

FRANK OHL — "He had the heart of a street-fighter"

AL FERRARA — "Fierce competitor"

Wrestling's arrival at Pitt as a major sport was not greeted with applause by those who had hoped that Tom Hamilton would try to revive the basketball situation. They probably would have preferred to have wrestling start as a club sport. But Tom's selection of Rex Peery as coach precluded any such approach.

Rex is big-time all the way, a hell of a coach and individual, and wrestling was to be handled right. And it was. It must have been rough on Rex to see the early crowds — or lack of them.

I'm afraid I was a reluctant convert myself. It took awhile to appreciate two things about wrestling. I had never realized what real training for an athlete was like until I watched those wrestlers live on spit and chewing gum for four months, then pass up the chewing gum in order to drop a weight for the championships. And I never realized that the wrestling fan was, by far, the most knowledgeable spectator of all sports. Those folks could sit there and anticipate every move — and appreciate them. My years as president of the Eastern Intercollegiate Wrestling Association (EIWA) were a constant education.

* * *

Few people remember, and many would not believe, the difference in the football rules back then. You had to be tossed out of bounds to get the ball moved to the hash mark, which was closer to the sidelines then.

It meant if you were down within a few yards of the sideline you had to waste a down to get the ball out to where you could operate properly. If a forward pass fell incomplete over the goal line it meant the other side got the ball on its own 20 yard line. The second incomplete pass in the same series of downs drew a five-yard penalty.

* * *

Any tale of Pitt athletics would be incomplete without a description of the Pitt Stadium basketball arena. It went by the lovely name of a Pavilion, but it was better known to spectators and opposing players as the Icebox.

When the stadium was built the basketball floor was added as an afterthought. As a result, the playing floor was slightly under-sized and there were a half dozen or so huge steel columns that blocked at least a portion of the floor from all spectators except those in the first three or so rows on both sides of the floor. Wooden bleachers, with no backs, were erected over an exposed hillside from the floor to the roof.

Still, it was by far the roomiest arena in town. But not until the first visit by Notre Dame in 1932 was it sold out to its capacity of 4,000. The crowd that night exceeded all expectation, and only about half were able to crowd into the place, with people perched on railings and radiators. "Doc" Carlson always maintained that his sellout gave the Pittsburgh Yellowjackets their first sellout, too, for the rejectees, faced with a night out and nowhere to go, went to Duquesne Gardens to see the hockey game.

At any rate, when Pitt was having its good teams of the 1930s, sellouts were not uncommon, especially for Notre Dame, West Virginia and Duquesne dates. For visiting players, especially from the Midwest where larger field

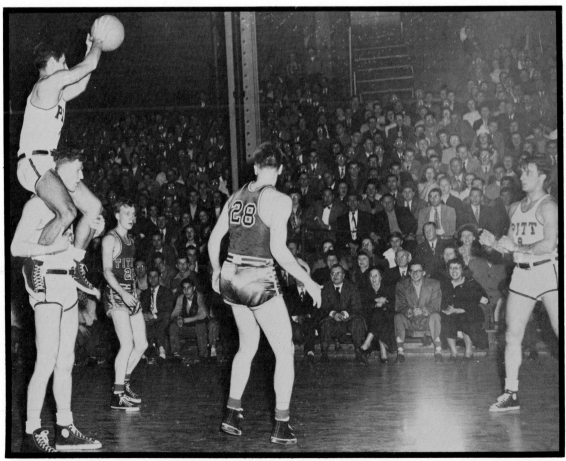

PAVILION PLAY — Bimbo Cecconi gets a boost from Ted Geremsky before he passes to teammate Dodo Canterna in game against Westminster before amused crowd in Pitt's old playpen under the Stadium.

houses were coming into style, the Pavilion was a shock to their systems. Not only was it small, but they had to dress in the visiting football team's locker room at Gate 3, and this meant a dash through the winter night before and after the game, and at halftime.

The Notre Dame series was the greatest and the most lop-sided. The Irish simply couldn't buy a win. I think Moose Krause, a monument on the South Bend campus, never played in a winning game against Pitt — six losses in basketball, three in football.

In one game, Notre Dame led by four points with 15 seconds to go, but Willie Kowallis and Tim Lawry tossed in hook shots from the corner to tie it, and Pitt ran away with the game in overtime. At South Bend one year, Notre Dame led by about ten points but the clock stopped and in what had to be the longest fourth quarter on record Pitt won in the last second. Coach George Keegan of Notre Dame threw the clock all the way across the floor at the end of the game.

Carlson's teams were known for their lack of height, and for coming from within a few miles of the Pitt campus. Charley Hyatt, who held all records until the coming of the one-handed jump shot, was barely six feet. Players the size of Paul Zehfuss, Willie Arture, Willie Kowallis and Tim Lawry, and Nate Apple were the norm, although two All-Americans of the period, Don Smith, a guard, and Claire Cribbs, a center, were slightly over six feet. For part of those years, the center jump was a fact of life, and the two-handed set shot from outside a must.

To compensate for lack of height, Carlson developed his famous ball-control offense, based on rifled passes and constant motion, known as the Figure 8. When opponents countered by going into a zone defense to take advantage of their height and Pitt's narrow floor, Carlson had his team stand outside and do nothing. I think one game with West Virginia was 3-2 at the half. Spectators tossed pennies on the floor.

* * *

For nearly two decades, an old frame World War I building played an important part in Pitt athletics. It was located on the hill where the Veterans Hospital now stands. It was next to the football practice field. Part of it contained one of the departments of the School of Engineering and Mines, the other the Pitt track house, and a not-too-luxurious athletic dormitory.

The track house had a steeply-banked cinder running track, not more than 12 feet wide, except possibly for the straightaway on one side which permitted a 40-yard dash. There were ten laps to the mile, and there was enough room in the center for a pole vault pit, a combination high jump and broad jump area, and a shot put ring. With the bamboo poles of the day, there was little chance of the vaulters hitting the roof.

"TINY TOUGHIES" — That's what Doc Carlson branded this young and undersized basketball team of 1943-44 that included, left to right, Nate Apple, Wally Zernich, Tom Ragen, Walt Jones and Bill Cieply, seen here dribbling across floor at Madison Square Garden before season opener with NYU.

My memory is hazy on the heating system which consisted of two smoky coal stoves. In these dirty, dusty surroundings, Pitt track coaches turned out a lot of fine athletes, and the dynamic Carl Olson went even further by getting the area high school coaches to form a Tri-State Track Coaches Association which held indoor championships in the track house, and drew teams from all over Western Pennsylvania and Eastern Ohio.

On the second floor of the engineering part of the building was the athletic "dorm." Pitt had no dining hall or dorms then and the scholarships had to be limited to athletes who lived within commuting distance.

These two large rooms were unpainted and didn't even have plaster walls. There were a few bunks and tables, similar to any Army barracks, which this had been. The heating was provided by two old gas heaters, the kind routinely condemned by building inspectors. The athletes should have died from asphyxiation had it not been for the fact that one of the windows had a number of missing panes.

This hilltop Hilton took care of the room problem in a limited way, but the athletes also had to eat. That was another problem.

A number of them had some help from home, and others got part-time jobs. One, now a very successful oral surgeon, got the job of opening up Todd's Lunch, a hole-in-the-wall Oakland eatery which catered to athletes. His 5 a.m. walk down the hill in the winter months had to be a continuous brutal experience, but Pitt has no more generous supporter today.

Carlson had a friend in the wholesale grocery business and about once a month he would provide a huge packing box full of canned goods and bread. Toward the end of each period, however, a lot of the young men were subsisting on bread and molasses until the new shipment came in.

Carlson got a lot of good PR out of his ice cream feeding, but this was a way he could get some nourishment into many of his players during the Depression.

I remember picking up one recruit, now an educator and a one-time Pitt trustee, at his home in Duquesne, stopping at Carlson's home in North Braddock for blankets, and delivering the young man to football camp where he had a job waiting tables to overcome his malnutrition.

Filling this boy's tummy became an obsession with Carlson, and he didn't win until after the final season when he took him to a place where one could eat all the chicken and waffles he wanted.

In one Depression year, Carlson bought overcoats for his whole team, some sort of a new material that was long on warmth, if short on style.

* * *

Edgar "Special Delivery" Jones may have been the most complete athlete in Pitt history. A word or two about Mike Sebastian, a Notre Dame nemesis. He broke the 1932

TRACK HOUSE — Over 200 athletes a week worked out at this converted World War I army barracks on a hill above the Stadium.

SPECIAL DELIVERY LINEUP — Edgar Jones, second from right, was one of Pitt's greatest all-around athletes, according to Carver. The others, left to right, are Earl Pressel, Ernie Bonelli, James Foley, and Ralph Fife on the '40 football team.

game open with a long run for our first win, and in 1933, at South Bend, he ran right down the middle on a simple power play for 60 odd yards and a touchdown.

Howdy Odell can't be overlooked. He was a tailback who weighed less than 150 pounds. He took the prescribed cut on the off-tackle play and hit the line expecting the hole to be open. This was a must under Jock Sutherland. The tailback was set about four yards deep and did not run for daylight. He ran for the hole, and it had better be there, otherwise a guard would have cleat marks on his back.

Odell, who later coached at Yale and, I think, Wisconsin and Washington, was a premier quick-kicker. He lined up about four-and-a-half yards back — he had to cheat a little — and he'd take one rocker step back, then forward and hit the ball a few inches south of the center's derriere.

With no free substitution, recruiting was more difficult in those days. Jock went for the best available athlete — a term Steeler coach Chuck Noll has popularized in more recent times. Centers and quarterbacks were linebackers, the fullback had to play defensive left halfback. When Pitt went to a 6-3-2 — quite an innovation, but it stopped Notre Dame — the fullback became an outside linebacker.

Some random recollections or reflections:

Camp Hamilton. The Department of Civil Engineering had a camp in the mountains near Windber. It was given to the school by A. R. Hamilton of the Berwind White Coal Company. The engineers had to spend a six or eight week session there, and sometime in "Pop" Warner's day it was used for pre-season training. Wooden huts eventually replaced tents, but at no time was it too luxurious. Veteran observers always maintained that the second intra-squad scrimmage at Camp Hamilton was the toughest game on the schedule.

Records. There should be two sets. One for athletes who, at the most, would have 27 games in their varsity careers — and play both ways — and another set for those today who can play as many as 44 regular season games in a four-year-varsity career.

Swimming. Pitt's swimmers were a homeless crew. From 1812 to 1950 they had Trees Pool, such as it was, but from then on they used the PAA, the Keystone Club (now Point Park), the YMHA and Frick School until the present Trees Hall pool was completed.

I have a special affection for the selfless men and women who officiated Pitt swimming and track meets: Vee and Art Toner, Alan Reidorf, Fletcher Hodes, Bill Croasmun and Bob Templeton, etc.

The first visit of the Army to Pittsburgh in 1931. The Corps of Cadets came via the P.&L.E. and marched through town that morning, causing a major traffic jam.

All-Americans. For the first four years as sports publicity director, I thought I made them. In 1934 we worked on our two guards, Doc Hartwig and Ken Ormiston and center George Shotwell. All made one or another of the various recognized teams of the day, AP, UP, INS, Rice, All-American Board (a Hearst creation), NEA, New York Sun, etc. All were linemen and the backs (some pretty good ones such as Bobby LaRue, Izzy Weinstock and Mike Nixon) yelled that if they hadn't run through the holes there would not have been any TDs. It was all in good fun, but I suddenly realized that it was not right. I never wrote the word "All-American" again in any press release. The result was that we had even more All-Americans in the remaining good years of the '30s.

In 1936 I pulled off a real PR coup. Either I or the printer left Marshall Goldberg's name out of the press guide roster. It was a mistake, sheer carelessness, but we made every newspaper and wire service in the country. Such is genius.

Baseball And Bobby Lewis
Synonymous For Over 30 Years

By Bob Smizik

"Classes come first. They come here to get an education."

—Bobby Lewis

When Bobby Lewis, who had had a distinguished career as a Pitt outfielder from 1949-51, was discharged from the Marine Corps late in 1954, he was not unlike so many other servicemen of that time in that he was unsure of what he wanted to do with the rest of his life.

His old coach at Pitt, Ralph (Sarge) Mitterling invited him to come back to help out with the team. Lewis figuring that he might some day succeed the 64-year-old Mitterling enrolled at Pitt to work on his masters and help coach the baseball team.

He and Mitterling, a former major leaguer who resurrected baseball at Pitt in 1939, were set to open the 1955 season when tragedy struck and changed the course of Lewis' life and of Panther baseball — the university's oldest sport, a game Pitt athletes were playing way back in 1869.

Mitterling suffered a major stroke on the Panthers first scheduled day of practice. He died 10 months later. Bobby Lewis was thrust into a job where some of his players, ex-servicemen like himself, were older than he was.

Lewis recalls a game in his first season against the Quantico Marines in Virginia. After it was over, he figured he'd go down to the American Legion for a beer. "When I walked in," said Lewis, "half the team was there and they were all drinking legally."

But Pitt baseball and Bobby Lewis were a match made in heaven. Lewis has become Pitt baseball. Except for his three years in the Marines, all of Lewis' adult life has been with Pitt baseball.

Doug Chambers, a catcher on the Pitt baseball team in the mid-60s and now a vice-president in communications at Pittsburgh National Bank, was shown a photo of Pitt's baseball team in 1890, and cracked, "Where's Bobby Lewis?" While Lewis has prospered in the job, putting good teams on the field annually and at the same time picking up high-level administrative duties within the Pitt athletic department, the baseball program has also come out of the deal a winner.

1924 EDITION — The Panthers posted an 8-3 record in 1924, with two wins over Penn State. Front row, left to right, Buck Snyder, Jakey Bohren, C. P. Carmen, Bob Irwin, Captain Steve Swetonic, Bill Parsons, Ira Hill, Monk Kelly. Back row: Manager Richard Harley, Nig Lauder, Alfred Schmidt, Jack Harding, W. J. Reagan, Edward Swisher.

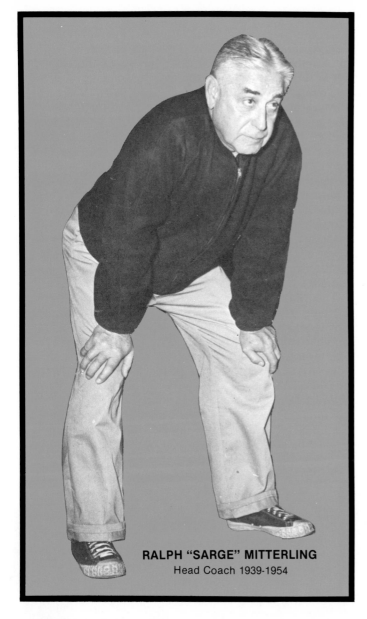

RALPH "SARGE" MITTERLING
Head Coach 1939-1954

most satisfaction from, he'd likely say Macha, who graduated in 1972 as Pitt's all-time home run leader with 14 and second in runs batted in with 64.

"Doc only came to us when he was going to pitch," remembers Lewis. "He'd take a day off from spring football practice and pitch. He wasn't real refined. He relied on his natural raw talent and his great desire. When he got into professional baseball, they worked with him and refined him. They gave him the other pitches. We never had much of a chance to work with him."

Though Lewis can take little pride in the athletic success of Medich, who was able to combine professional baseball with medical school, Medich is exactly the type of athlete who typifies the success Bobby Lewis has had at Pitt and the success the Pitt baseball team has had.

"I guess my ideas and the university's ideas are pretty much in line," says Lewis. "That's probably why I've been here so long. The idea is to get a degree. You can't let them forget that."

Sam Glass most certainly didn't forget it. Glass was a 5-4 catcher out of Alexandria, Va. who came to Pitt in 1964 because "my father told me to apply there."

Glass was cut from the freshman team by Lewis, but when a shortage of catchers developed he was called back. By the time he was a junior, Glass was starting. When Pitt went to the Riverside (Calif.) National Collegiate Baseball Tournament in March of 1968, Glass was something . . . walking to the mound to talk to Medich, who was 13 inches taller.

He was something at the plate, too, hitting .400 and making the all-tournament team. It was a feat that one notable player couldn't match. Phil Garner, then with Tennessee, failed to make the all-star team, and in his game with Pitt was hitless in four at bats against Medich.

But Glass scored more off the field than on it. He picked up a bachelor of chemical engineering in 1969, a masters in the same field in 1971, and a degree from the Medical College of Virginia in 1975. He did a residency in pediatrics in Richmond after his medical school and another residency in opthamology in Pittsburgh that he completed in 1982.

"I'm proud of my baseball career and what it did for me," says Glass, who went into private practice as an ophthalmologist in Ohio in the summer of '82. "We had a

"They come here to get an education," says Lewis, "and that has to come first. We don't take a lot of their time. We start practice at 4 o'clock and we have them out of here by 5:30. This is just an extracurricular activity like the band.

"Classes come first. I have a rule that no one misses a class. They can miss a practice to go to class, but they can't miss a class to go to practice."

In this day and age, when too many high school jocks look upon college as a means towards a career as a professional athlete and not as a way of getting a degree, it says tons about Lewis' Pitt program that his two most famous alumni — his only two players to make it to the major leagues, not only have degrees, they have them in prestigious fields.

George Medich, who has had a fine major league career with the New York Yankees, Pittsburgh Pirates and Texas Rangers, came to Pitt on a football scholarship and left as a professional baseball player and a physician. He became famous with the Yankees as Doc Medich.

Ken Macha, who had a brilliant Pitt baseball career, had brief major league flings with the Pirates and Montreal, is currently playing in Japan. Macha has a degree in chemical engineering.

If you'd ask Lewis which of the two players he takes the

GEORGE MEDICH
Still going strong

JOHN CARLISLE
1963 ace hurler

203

ANGELS IN THE OUTFIELD — Coach Bobby Lewis embraces two of his three outfielders, from left, Bill Kaliden, Nick Kartsonas and Herman Joy in late '50s.

bunch of guys who just loved to play. But we did more than play baseball. Every guy I played with graduated. On my senior team there are seven engineers, two dentists, two doctors and three others with graduate degrees.

"The trimester before we went to Riverside we had a team QPA of 3.25. We were kind of proud of that."

So was Lewis. But it hasn't been all academics. Lewis has produced two All-Americans in his tenure at Pitt — shortstop George Schoeppner, a second-team choice in 1959, and centerfielder Fred Mazurek, a third-team choice in 1965. Additionally, there have been eight all-district players — Schoeppner, Mazurek, Medich, Macha, right-fielder Corky Cuthbert (1963), shortstop Al Ricciuti (1963), pitcher John Carlisle (1963) and shortstop Joe Groetsch (1975).

Pete Suder, whose father was a major leaguer, was a standout for Pitt in the early 60s and another name that sticks in Lewis' mind.

Two of Lewis' teams made it to the district NCAA play-offs before being eliminated. The 1959 team, led by Schoeppner (.384), third baseman Jerry Matulevic (.297), outfielder Nick Kartsonas (.323), first baseman Ron Maser (.285), and pitchers Bill Hamilton (5-1), Dick Wirth (4-1), and Bob Conti (3-1), lost to Ithaca in extra innings of the district playoffs to finish the season 14-4.

The 1963 team, led by Cuthbert who set a Pitt record that still stands by hitting .492, Mazurek (.377), Ricciuti (.371), Brian Fisher (.315), Paul Martha (.271), Mike Supsura (.265), Carlisle (5-1), and Jim Sylvis (4-0), lost to Lafayette, 4-3, in the district playoffs to finish 18-3.

Mazurek, who was an outstanding quarterback on the football team, is a lawyer on the West Coast today. Martha is a lawyer who has a big hand in running the Edward DiBartolo sports empire. Sylvis has a doctorate in education and is teaching on the college level. Carlisle, perhaps the most talented pitcher ever to play for Lewis, is a doctor with the Navy.

He turned down an offer of between $50,000 and $100,000 from professional baseball to enter medical school after his undergraduate days.

"I have no regrets," says Carlisle, a cardiologist. "There were times when I was in medical school and it was a long afternoon in the lab and I'd think about it. But I don't any-more."

Carlisle is almost completely divorced from baseball. He was barely aware that Medich, another Pitt man, had been able to combine baseball and medical school.

Lewis adds to the 1959 and 1963 teams the teams of 1965, 1968 and 1981 as his finest. He won't, however pick the best.

Mazurek, hit .465 and lost the NCAA batting title by .001, was the star of the 1965 team. "He could run like the wind and he hit a ton," said Lewis. "He'd go four-for-five and come back to the bench and ask what he was doing wrong."

"Baseball wasn't a second sport to me," says Mazurek, now a corporate lawyer in California. "I thought I had a better chance to be a pro baseball player than I did a pro football player."

Other key players on the '65 team that finished 17-4 were third baseman Tom Beckett, shortstop Steve Kienzl, second baseman Steve Eiseman, first baseman Barry Wetzel and pitcher Lee Brueckel.

The 1968 team, which was 16-9, had an outstanding pitching staff, one that, surprisingly enough, was not dominated by Medich. Dave Welty, a lefty who was in the outfield when he didn't pitch, had perhaps the greatest year ever by a Pitt pitcher in 1967, compiling a 6-1 record with an 0.32 ERA that led the nation. His strikeout average of 14.6 also led the country.

Welty didn't live up to his previous year's record in 1968, but pitched well enough to get a contract from the Boston Red Sox after his career. Medich and Frank Gustine backed up Welty.

CO-CAPTAINS John Cioffi, left, and Al Ricciuti flank Coach Bobby Lewis in mid-60s.

ACE PITCHER — Dave Welty's statistics were sensational

Two outstanding Pitt players during the mid-70s were Don Seigle, a pitcher from North Catholic, and Pete Martorelli, a catcher from North Hills.

The pitching staff was the Panthers' strength in 1981, when they finished 25-8 team, the most wins ever at Pitt. Al Lachowicz, the ace, became a first-round draft choice of the Texas Rangers. He had a 7-3 record and was seventh in the nation with a 1.41 ERA. The No. 2 man on the staff was

FRED MAZUREK — Top Hitter

Larry Lamonde, who was 8-1 and signed with the Pirates after the season. Mike Luciow threw two no-hitters on his way to a 3-4 record and freshman Aaron Krause was 7-0. The team ERA was 3.20, eighth best in the nation.

First baseman Rich Kline was 20th in the nation in hitting with a .429 average. Shortstop Marc Massa batted .364 and outfielders Doug Steiner and Darrell Gissendanner .354 and .346. The team batting average was .302.

By now Pitt was playing all of its games on campus — at Trees Field — but it hadn't always been that way. The Panthers suffered a nomadic existence under Lewis, playing at eight different fields. They played at Pitt Stadium, where the right-field fence was so short a ball hit over it was only a double, West Field, Leech Farm, Wildwood Country Club, Forbes Field, Mellon Park, Schenley Park and Trees.

It is ironic that Pitt would end up at Trees because that was the name of the field where the sport was played in the early 1920s when the Panthers really got into intercollegiate baseball.

While a team known as the University Nine defeated Eckfords of East Liberty 21-20 in 1869, play was infrequent and rarely against college opposition. In 1870 the University Nine, records show, lost to a high school team, 21-15.

Baseball really took root in 1917 when Walter A. Blair was appointed coach. The Owl, Pitt's yearbook, calls the 1917 team, "the best that ever represented the university." Doc Carlson, the legendary basketball coach, was the second baseman on that team. Doctor William McClelland, later an Allegheny County Commissioner, was also a member of the team.

The 20s produced Pitt's first major leaguer, Steve Swetonic, a righthander who was 37-36 in five years with the Pirates. Tom Davies, the All-American halfback, was another fine performer on the Pitt teams of the early 20s.

Ira (Lefty) Hill, a pitcher-first baseman on those teams, remembers the era well. "We played all the local teams," he said. "West Virginia, Penn State and Bethany, which had a great team in those days.

"We played most of our games at Trees Field, but if we really wanted a big crowd, like for Penn State or West Virginia, we'd play at the Edgar Thomson Field in Braddock. When we went out there we'd get 500 or 600 people."

Hill was all set to sign a minor league contract with the Yankees when he graduated from Pitt.

"They wanted to send me to Atlanta," says Hill. "Carl Davis was the graduate manager of athletics (athletic director then) and when he heard that, he encouraged me to go to law school. I had won the outstanding student award at Pitt and Carl Davis was very proud that an athlete won that. He wanted to make sure I went into some profession."

Hill became a lawyer and practiced for 40 years before retiring from Reed, Smith, Shaw and McClay.

Baseball was dropped after the 1924 season because of the difficulty in finding a field. It was thought to be only a short lapse, but the sport didn't come back until 1939, when Mitterling, who had played a year with the Philadelphia A's, got the sport started again.

Andy Johnson was the top pitcher on Mitterling's first team and a year later Bob Malloy came along. Malloy was later to pitch parts of five major league seasons with the Cincinnati Reds and St. Louis Browns for a 4-7 record. Malloy won six games for the 1941 team that was 9-3.

The Panthers ran into field problems later in the decade. The 1947 season had to be curtailed so that the Civic Light Opera could use Pitt Stadium, thus ending the season on

STADIUM DIAMOND — Pitt resumed baseball in 1938 by playing at Stadium.

IRA "LEFTY" HILL — First Baseman 1920-1924

May 6. For several years afterwards the CLO took precedence over Pitt baseball.

There were some familiar names playing for Mitterling. Edgar (Special Delivery) Jones, the football star, played baseball and so did Sammy David and Dodo Canterna of basketball fame.

"We all loved the coach," said David. "He was great. The facilities really weren't very good, but we made the best of it."

Russ Kemmerer and Paul Smith, who were later to have major league careers, played briefly for Mitterling at Pitt in the early 50s.

"I didn't get to know Sarge until he was in his 50s, but he was some guy," remembers Lewis. "He had a dry sense of humor. And he was tough on the equipment.

"One day Sam Shapiro broke three bats and Sarge benched him. Sam said, 'But I'm hitting .345.' Sarge told him, 'I can't afford you.'

"If you hit a home run and cracked the bat when you came back to the bench you'd get a lecture on how to grip a bat."

But Lewis learned more than caring for the equipment from Mitterling and it is to Pitt's good fortune that he continues to pass along much of that to this day.

"We've had a lot of kids like Medich and Mazurek come over from the football program and play for us and they were all great athletes," allowed Lewis. "Joe Walton was a terrific baseball player, and used to lure major league baseball scouts to our games. Two other football All-Americans, Mike Ditka and Paul Martha, made a big contribution to our club. So did Billy Kaliden. And Frank Gustine. Now if we could just get Danny Marino to pitch for us ... He'd enjoy it, just like those other guys did."

206

Hall of Famers, All-Americans Emerged From Basketball Teams

By Jim O'Brien

"Pitt has had a great tradition. We're trying to get back to that."

—Roy Chipman

Soon after Roy Chipman became the tenth head basketball coach in Pitt's history, he learned a few things about the school's rich sports tradition.

"A lot of people didn't know who I was or any background on me, and they looked down on the fact that I was coming from coaching at Lafayette," recalled Chipman. "But I got some good letters of support. One man wrote, 'We know you'll do a good job. One of our greatest coaches, the legendary Jock Sutherland, came from Lafayette. And, hopefully, you'll do the same sort of job.'"

Chipman also became aware of Doc Carlson, Don Hennon and Billy Knight. "Especially Doc Carlson," said Chip-

man. "What a great coach he was . . . and his figure-8 continuity offense. Basketball at Pitt seems synonymous with him. Pitt has had a great tradition. We're trying to get back to that."

Actually, Chipman has gotten off to a better start than Sutherland or Carlson, or any other of his coaching predecessors at Pitt. In his first two seasons at the Oakland school, he has directed both of his teams to Eastern Eight playoff championships and the NCAA tournament.

The Panthers participated in back-to-back NCAA championships only once before, in Hennon's heyday (1957 and 1958) under Coach Bob Timmons, and Chipman is convinced the best is yet to come.

Pitt dropped out of the Eastern Eight after the 1981-82 season, and has cast its lot with the Big East, the fastest-growing league in the country with one of the best TV packages among the many conferences. There will be

ROY CHIPMAN — celebrates Pitt's first Eastern Eight title. **CLYDE VAUGHAN** (inset) helped him win second title.

207

greater national exposure and greater revenues in store for Pitt, and Chipman has been recruiting hard to be equal to the challenge.

Whatever Chipman has not learned about Pitt's basketball tradition, Joey David and his dad, The Rev. Sam David, can teach him.

Joe David grew up on Pitt basketball, and he couldn't be happier about the prospects of playing for the Panthers the next four seasons. He starred at Upper St. Clair High School and wanted to follow in his father's footsteps.

His dad, a priest in the Antiochan Orthodox Christian Church, came out of Bridgeville to play basketball at Pitt in the late '40s. He was a teammate of Dr. Hank Zeller, Dr. Nate Apple, Dodo Canterna and Bimbo Cecconi, among others. David was usually the leading scorer on the squad.

"Doc Carlson had as much pride in our academic achievements as he did in our athletic prowess," recalled Sam David. "I was fortunate to have some fine people as teammates. They were much older and they had been in the military service. One was Hank Zeller and the other was Nate Apple. They gave me so much encouragement."

He took his son, Joey, to the games at the Pitt Field House through the years. "I remember getting Billy Knight's autograph at one game," recalled Joey. This young man is something of a throwback, since he plans to enter medical school at Pitt. He wants to be a doctor.

There are a lot of doctors in Pitt's sports history, even if there has never been a Dr. J.

Dr. Sutherland and Dr. Apple graduated from Pitt's dental school, and Dr. Carlson, Dr. Zeller and Dr. Hennon graduated from Pitt's medical school. Chipman is called Dr. Chipman because he has a doctorate in physical education.

"I thought Carlson was quite a character," said Sam David. "His coaching methods were unique. When he arrived at practice, we put away the balls. All we did was run, or walk through his plays. One year we had as many plays as the football team.

"At first, I thought he was crazy. I didn't like him much. I'd been a big scorer in high school, and was used to having the ball. But he gave me an ear-beating in my freshman year about shooting so much. I came to respect him. I

CONGRATULATIONS FROM CHANCELLOR John G. Bowman are offered to, left to right, Nate Apple, Sam David, Bill Cieply and Doc Carlson after upset of Ohio State.

208

ALL-AMERICAN Charley Hyatt, center, had a ball on return to Pitt and meeting with squad from the '30s that included, from left to right, Skippy Hughes, Claire Cribbs, Russ Ochsenhirt and Charley Hughes.

didn't think he was a great, great basketball coach, but he was a great person."

Basketball, for all purposes, began at Pitt with Dr. Carlson, even though he was the school's sixth coach. He was preceded, in turn, by Benjamin F. Printz, Harry Hough, Wohlparth Wegner, Dr. George M. Flint and Andrew Kerr. Flint coached for ten seasons, the 1915-16 team being his best with a 15-2 record. Kerr was the best known coach, but that was because of his football coaching at several schools rather than his 12-8 record as Pitt's basketball coach during the 1921-22 season.

"Red" Carlson was among the many athletes who played football and basketball for Pitt in those pioneer days. Jimmy DeHart and John Loughran, the school's only letter-winners in four sports, were others, as were George McLaren, Andy Hastings, Ray Montgomery, Lloyd Jordan, Lou Mervis, Karl Bohren and Ralph Chase. One of those basketball teams was described in the Owl yearbook as another "Pitt team." An explanation followed: "To the uninitiated this means nothing, but to those who know, it means a team filled with fight; one that goes into battle giving all that it has, regardless of handicaps, for the glory of its alma mater."

Dr. Carlson became head coach, succeeding Kerr for the 1922-23 schedule, and stayed for 31 years. His career record was 367-248, and he was enshrined in the Basketball Hall of Fame in Springfield, Mass.

So was his best player, Charley Hyatt, who was a member of the charter class of the Hall of Fame.

Hyatt was Pitt's first All-American basketball player, and he rated the honor for three seasons (1928-30), and twice led the nation in scoring. He was a six-foot forward who could do it all. The Panthers had an overall mark of 60-7 during his varsity tenure.

During the 1927-28 season, Pitt won its first mythical national title by winning all 21 of its games, averaging a then phenomenal 38 points per game.

Paul Fisher, one of the few survivors, was a reserve on that championship basketball team, and a starting quarterback for the 1927 Pitt football team that went undefeated during the regular season, but suffered a 7-6 setback by

PIONEER PANTHERS — Pitt's first basketball team, that of 1897, included, sitting left to right, S. K. Hunter, Frank M. Roessing and Guy D. Wallace. Standing, left to right, are H. R. Hammer, C. S. Lambie, C. F. O'Hagan and H. G. Hammer.

Stanford in the Rose Bowl. Fisher was the only Pitt athlete to be on both squads.

The 77-year-old Fisher, who retired from Duquesne Light Co. in 1971, lives in suburban Bellevue today and attends all of Pitt's home football games, and several basketball games each winter. "I had Doc Carlson for four years," offers Fisher, "as freshman football coach, and for three varsity basketball seasons. I got along with Sutherland and Carlson real well, and they were both so different.

"One thing they had in common was that they always made sure we'd see things when we were traveling. Like Dr. Carlson took us out of the way in upstate New York so we'd see Niagara Falls. And Dr. Sutherland took us on a tour of the Hollywood movie studios before the Rose Bowl.

"We visited with 'Our Gang' kids, and Lon Chaney on the set of 'Laugh, Clown, Laugh,' at MGM. We posed for pictures with Douglas Fairbanks and Mary Pickford at United Artists.

"Those were great days. Charley Hyatt was just a good all-around player. And Marshall Goldberg played every bit as good as Tony Dorsett."

The Pitt basketball team won a second national title in the 1929-30 season, going 23-2 and losing only to West Virginia and Syracuse.

Dr. Carlson produced two other All-American basketball players in his day, Don Smith in 1933 and Claire Cribbs, in

1934 and 1935. Hennon gained All-America honors in 1957 and 1959, and Billy Knight in 1974, giving Pitt a total of five so recognized. Knight became the school's first All-Pro basketball performer, gaining the honor as a member of the Indiana Pacers of the American Basketball Association. After a merger with the more established National Basketball Association, Knight continued his pro career.

The basketball program marked its diamond anniversary during the 1981-82 season, and during those 75 years the Panthers have been represented in the NCAA and NIT post-season competition on many occasions, have traveled round the nation, and gained many honors and recognition for the University of Pittsburgh.

None were better than Dr. Carlson at sounding the praises of Pitt's athletic and academic programs. Some of his early players, Elmer Lissfelt, Lester Cohen, James and George Kowallis, to name a few, were storybook student athletes. Lissfelt, who tutored members of the basketball team on long road trips, was also a fine swimmer. He was named a Varsity Letterman of Distinction in 1965. George Kowallis later coached the freshman basketball team while attending medical school. "He was one of the finest boys — as a player and a coach — that I have ever met," declared Dr. Carlson.

As sportswriter Eddie Beachler wrote in a 1947 issue of "Huddle," a local sports magazine of the time: "Behind the

Two of Carlson's stars

LESTER COHEN　　　　**PAUL ZEHFUSS**

scenes Dr. Carlson gave even more. For 25 years, he has picked boys off the sidewalks of Pittsburgh and nearby towns, given them a 'Win 'Em All' philosophy ... thousands of gallons of ice cream and hot chocolate to build 'em up ... in many cases their first new overcoat or suit. And all of it paid for out of his own pocket.

"Dr. Carlson gave his boys even more than overcoats and ice cream. He preached an ambitious philosophy that spurred them into becoming doctors, dentists, teachers, lawyers, G-men, businessmen."

Dr. Paul Zehfuss, the only surviving starter from the 1928 national championship team, is still a practicing ophthalmologist in Alexandria, Va.

"It was an honor for me to play for Doc Carlson and on the same team with the great All-American player Charley Hyatt," said Zehfuss, who was known as "Poison Paul" in his playing days. "Some thought he was lucky, but I knew better. He was accurate in practice as he was in the games."

Dr. Zehfuss became Dr. Carlson's assistant in the Men's Student Health Service and was assistant varsity coach and freshman coach for seven years.

The center on that first national championship team was Jerry Wunderlich, and the guards were Stash Wrobleski and Capt. Sykes Reed. When Hyatt won the national scoring title in the 1927-28 season, Wrobleski was right behind him with 247 points to Hyatt's 292 points. Wrobleski and Reed had previously played together at Braddock High School. Dr. Carlson lived in Braddock in those days. No, he never went too far to recruit his players.

His second All-American, Don Smith, was born and raised in West View, and played basketball at Bellevue

High School. Smith was the star of the 1932 and 1933 Pitt teams. At 72, Dr. Smith was still practicing dentistry four days a week in 1982 at the Jenkins Arcade where he's had an office since 1964. Before that, he was in the May Building for 30 years.

"All that running Dr. Carlson made us do in his Figure-8 offense has paid off," said Dr. Smith. "My legs are still good. I'm standing all day and I have no problems."

Now at home in Whitehall, Dr. Smith said the road trips to the West Coast were special, too. "I had never been out of Pittsburgh before that," he said. "Things like that are important."

Mention Don Smith to Claire Cribbs and he comments, "He must have made a pact with the devil. Don Smith never gets old."

Dr. Carlson came by Cribbs, one of his all-time best, almost by accident. Cribbs had played high school ball in Jeannette, and upon graduation went to work for a year in a foundry in the Westmoreland County community. He continued to play basketball with Felders, a sandlot team.

"We went into Pittsburgh to play a game, and some guys from Doc Carlson's 1928 national championship team were on that team," recalled Cribbs. "I had about 20 points against them, and the next day Doc Carlson was on my doorstep.

"Sports gave me the opportunity to go to school during the Depression. When I went to Pitt, I stayed up at the Track House, and I went out for football for awhile. I was fortunate to get on a basketball team that had Don Smith on it.

"He was a senior when I was a sophomore (1933). I played center on that club, at 6-3. I played forward as a junior, and guard as a senior. Our team got taller, at least for those times. The big thrill was making All-American as a junior and senior."

Cribbs also recalled that his freshmen coaches were Dr. Zehfuss and Dr. George Kowallis. "They provided guidance beyond the basketball court," he said. "I wore corduroy pants with shiny knees, and an old slouch hat, and ate a lot of beans back then," said Cribbs, "but I was rich in so many ways."

In 1977, Cribbs retired as a school teacher after 42 years of service. He had been the basketball coach at Bellaire (Ohio) High School from 1949 to 1969.

Other standouts of the '30s were Willie Arture, Eddie Baker, Milt Cohen, Tim Lawry, Bus Albright, Al Wrobleski, Russ Ochsenhirt, Charley and Skippy Hughes, Rocco Cutri, and Ross Emrick.

Pitt made its first trip to the West Coast during the 1931-32 season, a 12-game road tour including stops at Purdue, Indiana, Kansas, Colorado, Stanford and Southern California.

Pitt and Duquesne began playing each other the following season. Chick Davies' Dukes proved too much for the Panthers, winning the first game of the city series, 26-25, before 4,000 at the Pavilion under Pitt Stadium. They filled the same facility again later that winter, with the Dukes taking the second game, 25-24, before a larger crowd.

During the 1934-35 season, Pitt posted an 18-5 record and won its third straight Eastern Intercollegiate Basketball Conference crown. Duquesne dealt Pitt one of its few losses, by 27-25, at the Pitt Pavilion, but the Panthers responded later in the schedule by ending the Dukes' 24-game winning streak, 35-34. In between Pitt defeated Fordham, 43-20, before 16,000 fans during a doubleheader

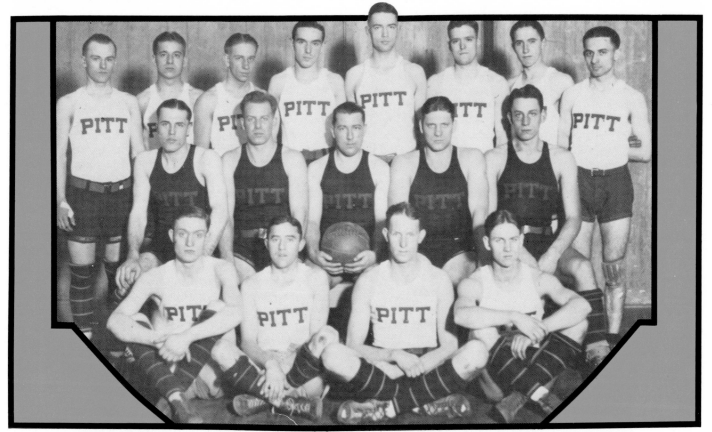

1925 SQUAD (Front row left to right) Joe Campbell, Cornelius Campbell, John McMahon, William McGill. (Second row) Wallace "Sykes" Reed, Elmer Lissfelt, Capt. William Parsons, Ralph Chase, William Rihanek. (Back row) Stanley Wrobleski, George Kowallis, Robinson, Ben Richman, Paul Brown, Ben Jones, Byron Baur, Mitchell Korbelak.

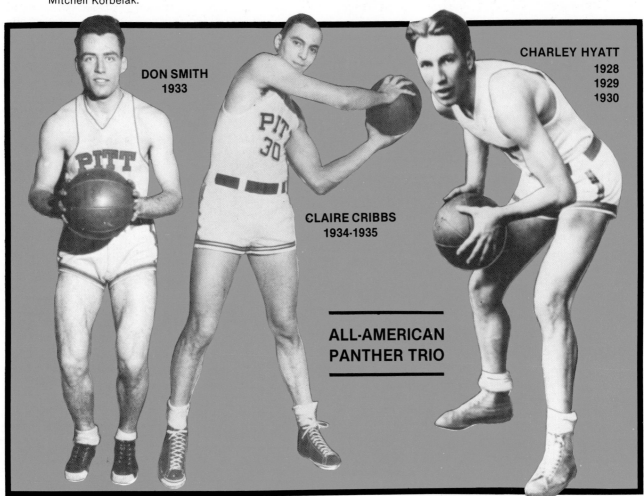

DON SMITH
1933

CLAIRE CRIBBS
1934-1935

CHARLEY HYATT
1928
1929
1930

ALL-AMERICAN PANTHER TRIO

at Madison Square Garden, and Notre Dame at the Pavilion, 26-22, and later by 27-25 at Notre Dame.

The Panthers were 18-9 in the 1935-36 season, and finished by playing in an Olympic Games playoff in Philadelphia, losing to the Temple Owls in the second game and ending whatever Berlin-bound ideas the Panthers may have had.

Highlight of the year was a comeback triumph over Duquesne, by 46-41. At the half, Pitt trailed by 25-16, but one of Dr. Carlson's celebrated "ice cream intermissions" did the trick, with Pete Noon and Bob Johnson showing the way in the second half.

Johnson, who captained the 1938 Pitt basketball team, became a successful sales executive with Rockwell Manufacturing, later Rockwell International, and then ACFI Industries.

Johnson grew up in Bellevue, but saw the country with the touring Pitt teams. "It was most helpful to me in later life," said Johnson, now living in retirement in St. Louis. "Traveling around the United States prepared me to talk to people. It was a great education. I wouldn't have gotten it if I hadn't played ball. It made it easier for me in business."

He remembered various trips. "We went to Kentucky once, and their coach, Adolph Rupp, told Doc Carlson that we should get out and see the horse farms around Lexington. We walked all around and they beat our tails that night. I remember Carlson storming, 'I'll never let Rupp do that again!'

"Doc always made you dress professional-like. He didn't let you get sloppy; he wanted you to make a good impression. He was big at promoting Pitt. We traveled by train, and he'd have us don our gold sweatshirts when we'd stop at a station and get on the platform and go through some of our Figure-8 plays. We'd attract a crowd, and they'd see 'PITT' on our shirts. So they always knew who we were."

Dr. Carlson used ten players that season, using two units, the way North Carolina's Dean Smith has done in recent seasons. Myles Zeleznick, who would later coach basketball at West Mifflin North High School, was among them, along with Bill Jesko, Frank Loucks, Ed Spotovich, Joe Garcia, Luke Rowe, Ted Roderick and Mike Radvansky.

Dr. Michael "Rags" Radvansky grew up in Duquesne and was a scrawny kid who Dr. Carlson provided with much personal care and attention. Radvansky also performed for Pitt's track & field team. Today, Radvansky is a member of the board of trustees at Pitt. He retired in 1977 after serving 10 years as superintendent of schools in West Mifflin.

"The thing that impressed me was the coach, Doc Carlson," related Radvansky after attending commencement exercises for Pitt's 1982 class at the Civic Arena. "Besides being interested in the coaching of basketball, he was concerned about our welfare. He stressed education. We never missed classes.

"Of all the teachers I had at Pitt — and I got my bachelor's, master's and doctor's degrees there — Carlson had to be one of the greatest teachers I had at the school."

Pitt won a fourth Eastern title, then dropped out of the group to go the independent route, and Pitt and Duquesne decided to call it quits after a long-standing, heated rivalry.

The high spot of the 1939 season was when Pitt

DOC CARLSON hosts his '48 team at his hideaway in Ligonier. Lineup, from left: Mort Lerner, Bill Cieply, Coach Carlson, Edward Latagliata, Dodo Canterna and Sam David.

established a team scoring record by beating Carnegie Tech, 73-42. Eddie Straloski topped Charley Hyatt's individual scoring mark of 27 points by scoring 13 field goals and six free throws for 32 points. That was two points shy of the city college scoring record for one game established by Tech's Mel Cratsley two years earlier against West Virginia. Cratsley was later the basketball coach and athletic director at Tech, then Point Park College, and continues working today as the ticket manager at Pitt.

With a record of 12-5, the 1940-41 Pitt team posted the best record in six seasons.

Sam Milanovich was convalescing at home in the summer of 1982 after a short hospital stay to repair an old basketball knee injury when he spoke about his days at Pitt. He retired in 1980 after having served as a superintendent for nine years at Cornell (Coraopolis when he first took the position) High School — Foge Fazio's alma mater. Before that, Milanovich was the superintendent at Aliquippa High School — his own alma mater, as well as that of many famous former Pitt athletes.

Milanovich had the distinction of being the team captain at Pitt for three years, from 1939 through 1941.

"One highlight was when I was a senior and we played in what was then the NCAA playoffs at Madison, Wisc. We beat North Carolina first, and then lost our next game to Wisconsin, 36-30. Another highlight was getting a chance to play in Madison Square Garden a few times. Our early-season tour of the Midwest by train was always something we looked forward to; we'd play four or five Big Ten schools."

Dr. Carlson had a succession of under-sized teams during his tenure, and he always gave them nicknames, such as "Rinkydinks," "Little Toughies," and "Busy Bees." Dr. Carlson said the "Rinkydinks are the little fellows with the big hearts." They included Paul Lohmeyer, Bob Artman, John Swacus, Tay Malarkey and Walt Jones.

Talking about the "Tiny Toughies," Dr. Carlson once said, "I don't inspire these kids. They inspire me."

Nate Apple, now a dentist in Harrisburg and a Varsity Letterman of Distinction, was a member of the "Little Toughies" from 1943 through 1946.

"I have had many reunions over the years with former teammates," Apple said. "Dr. Carlson would have been so proud to see that his philosophy of athletic scholarship and life — which he imparted so lovingly on those of us who were green kids from small towns and low income families — had borne fruit beyond his expectations.

"To us, Doc was a father figure, physician, psychologist and, more often not, clothier and food purveyor. He used to love those reunions of his at his summer home in Ligonier where 200 to 300 ex-Pitt basketballers, mostly physicians, dentists, engineers, architects, etc., gathered once a year to break bread.

"I realize it is a different world today and that Pitt athletics is big business, and an athletic scholarship is a ticket to the pros and big money, but if there were just a few Doc Carlsons around, wouldn't it be great to know that every one of the thousands who don't make it in the pros had that good sound education to fall back on, and somebody to impress upon them the golden opportunity they have as a recipient of an athletic scholarship?"

Hank Zeller had played four years at Washington & Jefferson, but was eligible — because of his military service involvement — to play another two years while attending med school at Pitt.

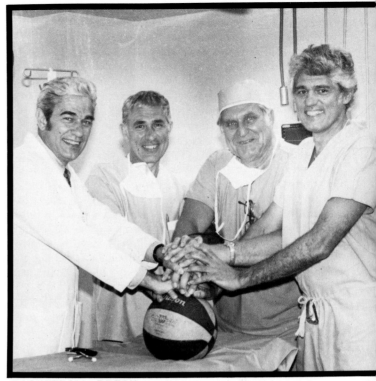

BASKETBALL BREAK — Four former members of Pitt's basketball team, all doctors today on the staff at Aliquippa Hospital, are (from left to right) Wally and Steve Zernich, Hank Zeller, and Mickey Zernich.

"I thought Doc did a helluva lot to open doors for me in Pittsburgh," recalls Dr. Zeller, now the chief anesthetist at Aliquippa Hospital. "I had been playing in the Muni League in Pittsburgh when Dr. Carlson called me to play for his team."

Dr. Carlson christened his 1944-45 team "The Phantoms." They included Dodo Canterna, Zeller, Carl Michalik, Nate Apple, Phil Marder, Tay Malarkey, and Frank Morris. Against Westminster, Canterna scored 37 points to establish a new college scoring record in Pittsburgh. Dodo didn't score a point in the first quarter and missed eight free throws, which made his feat that much more remarkable.

Other basketball players — "The Ice Cream Kids" — of that period were Sammy David, Bill Baierl, Alex Medich, Bill Cieply, George Radosevich and Wally Zernich. George McCrossin, a senior guard on the 1950 team, came within two points of establishing a new Stadium scoring record when he scored 35 points in a game against Grove City.

Pitt's basketball program wasn't going too well then, however, and the losses were more numerous than the victories. The lowpoint was the 1949-50 team that went 4-14.

Sammy David set a season scoring record with 390 points in the 1948-49 season, but Mike Belich, a 5-7 guard, topped that in 1950 with 415 points.

Starting with the 1951-52 season, Pitt began playing its home games at a new field house atop the campus. It also marked the beginning of the Steel Bowl Tournament which became the tip-off for each basketball season.

Pitt finished with a 12-12 record for the 1952-53 campaign, Dr. Carlson's final year as coach. Mickey Zernich was the captain of that club and its high scorer. He finished second only to the great Charley Hyatt with a three-year total of 845 points. Teammate Don Virostek finished fifth in the nation in rebounding.

That team was featured in LIFE magazine for using an oxygen tank on the sideline, a new wrinkle in Doc's long-time experiments with the fatigue curve.

Dr. Zernich is now the chief of orthopedics at Aliquippa Hospital. His older brother Steve is a general surgeon on the staff, and another brother, Wally, is a general practitioner. Along with Dr. Zeller, they often work together in the operating room. Think how Dr. Carlson would feel if he could see them working in concert today.

"I think that basketball-wise my coach was behind the times," says Dr. Mickey Zernich, who became president of the Pitt Varsity Letter Club in 1982, "but his promotion of academics was good for all of us.

"From our team, there's Don Virostek who's a dentist today in Vandergrift. There's Art Boyd, who was a Phi Beta Kappa, and became a general surgeon. There's Dutch Burch, a teacher. And John Kendrick owns his own business, and may be a millionaire. Dick Deitrick is an obstetrician. Academically, I'm very, very pleased with my days at Pitt, and that was my primary concern.

"But Dr. Carlson never recruited, he never went out of Pittsburgh to get a player, and that hurt our program," said Dr. Zernich. "He didn't think it was the thing to do. But everybody graduated. There was no such thing as not graduating. Everyone had a profession."

Dr. Carlson's successor, Bob Timmons, wasn't too keen on recruiting, either. He had hoped to become the head football coach at his alma mater, but was asked instead, by Athletic Director Tom Hamilton, to take over the basketball coaching reins.

Timmons, as low key a coach as you could find, was Pitt's basketball coach for 15 seasons — second only to Carlson in length. Carl Peterson was Timmons' Assistant.

Timmons might have gotten off to a better start than he did if Carlson hadn't recruited the wrong young man to be the first black in the Pitt program. Dr. Carlson couldn't make up his mind between Maurice Stokes and a young man named Ernie Bryant of Coatesville, Pa. Bryant left Pitt after his freshman year and never played varsity ball at Pitt. Stokes went to St. Francis of Loretto, put that school on the national sports map, and became an instant star in the NBA before being struck down by a disease.

"Imagine," Timmons reflects. "I would've started out with Stokes as a sophomore on my team."

Even so, Timmons managed to turn out some pretty good teams. Three times his teams went to the NCAA tournament, and once to the NIT.

The Panthers climaxed the 1956-57 campaign — the school's most successful in 20 years — by gaining a berth in the NCAA tourney. They beat Morehead State in their first post-season test, then bowed to both Kentucky and Notre Dame to finish with a 16-11 record.

Leading the Panthers that season, as they did for three seasons, were co-captains Bob Lazor and John Riser. Both Lazor, of Canonsburg, and Riser, of Washington, Pa., broke the existing Pitt career scoring records by netting more than a thousand points. Rounding out the starting five were juniors Chuck Hursh and Julius Pegues and sophomore sensation Don Hennon.

The following season, Hennon led the Panthers to a regular season mark of 18-6 and another NCAA appearance. But Pitt got knocked out in the first round by Miami of Ohio.

Hennon, a general surgeon today on the staff of several Pittsburgh area hospitals, broke Ed Pavlick's single game high of 40 twice, with 42 against Geneva and 45 against Duke. He also eclipsed Pavlick's single season record of 623 by a single point and, with yet another season still to play, broke Lazor's old career scoring record of 1175.

The team broke the Field House record of 98 points, set by Robin Freeman and his Ohio State teammates in 1955, by scoring 109 against Geneva.

With Hennon, who was only 5-9 but was picked on every All-American team in the nation, averaging better than 21 points a game, and Hursh doing most of the rebounding, and Pegues playing a great all-around game, the Panthers had their finest season in 23 years. They won eight straight, and played in the Holiday Festival at New York's Madison Square Garden.

Timmons once said of Hennon, the pride of Wampum, Pa.: "The thing that amazes me is his variety of shots. You know how a coach hollers in practice when he sees a boy take a poor shot? Well, with Hennon, you have to wait to see if the ball goes in before you holler.

"Hennon is like an Easter bunny. Once he finds the basket, everything goes in it."

Duquesne coach Dudey Moore compared Hennon to another great local basketball product, Dick Groat, who came out of Swissvale to star at Duke and with the NBA's Fort Wayne Pistons before becoming a full-time major league baseball player with the Pittsburgh Pirates. It was high praise, indeed.

Pegues graduated with an aeronautical engineering degree in 1958 and has worked at McDonnell Douglas Aircraft in his hometown of Tulsa ever since. He takes pride in being the first black varsity basketball player at Pitt, but even more in being the first black real estate developer in downtown Tulsa. He recently completed a 104-unit multi-family apartment complex there.

Reflecting on his Pitt days, Pegues offered, "I thought it was one of the most educational and delightful ex-

PITT FLOOR COACH Bob Timmons looks over the cream of his prospects as the Panthers prepared for the 1953-54 season. Left to right, kneeling, are Coach Timmons, Ernie Bryant, Bernie Artman and Dutch Burch. Standing are Joe Resutek, Ed Pavlick and Dave Duessel.

DICK FALENSKI   JOHN FRIDLEY   BEN JINKS

periences of my life. I really enjoyed my days at Pitt.''

He had been a standout player at Booker T. Washington High School. He said a local oilman, E. Alex Phillips, had been a pilot in the Navy for Pitt's Capt. Tom Hamilton. ''He thought I was a major college player, and directed me there,'' explained Pegues.

''The most important thing that I got from my coach, Bobby Timmons, was that no matter what the situation was, if you could keep a cool head, you always came out on top. He was a cool cookie. And he stressed the educational aspect at Pitt. I'm very glad I went there. It prepared me to meet challenges which I've faced since then.''

Timmons recalls Pegues once saying, ''An hour of prayer is often more important than an hour of practice.''

A reserve backcourtman on the 1957-58 team was Bill Shay, who has been so successful as the basketball coach at Allegheny Community College.

The Panthers started the 1958-59 season on a strong note, defeating Duquesne, 71-56 for the Steel Bowl championship, but slipped after that. They had to win five of their final six games to post a 10-14 record. Hennon didn't have a great senior season, but he still rewrote all the scoring records at Pitt.

There were some young players who impressed, notably sophomores John Fridley and Dick Falenski, and some solid juniors in Billy Mauro and Dick Mills. Fridley led the team in rebounding for three varsity seasons, Mills led the team in scoring in 1959-60 as a co-captain with Mauro, and Ben Jinks led the team in scoring with 13 points a game in 1960-61. But the records were mediocre, at 11-14, and 12-11. Football All-American Mike Ditka was a much-valued reserve in 1959 and 1960.

Pitt posted another 12-11 record in 1961-62, but showed terrific promise with four sophomores joining Jinks and sometimes Tom Maloney in the starting lineup. They were Cal Sheffield of New Brighton, who led the team in scoring with a 16.3 average, and Brian Generalovich of Farrell, who led the team in rebounding with a 9.2 average. Dave Sauer of Avonworth and Paul Krieger of Uniontown were the other sophomore starters. On that same squad was a gritty reserve guard named Tim Grgurich, who grew up in

Lawrenceville and was a three-sport star at Central Catholic High.

Generalovich impressed Purdue's All-American Terry Dischinger in the first road game. ''He's like a brick wall that smiles at you,'' declared Dischinger. Both Dischinger and Generalovich are dentists today.

Dave Roman, a transfer from Pitt's Johnstown campus, led the Panthers in scoring during the 1962-63 season with 15 points per game, and Krieger came up with over 10 rebounds a game, as Timmons' team went 19-6, gaining an NCAA tournament berth. They were bumped off in the first game, however, by NYU, 93-83. NYU was led by Happy Hairston and Barry Kramer at the Palestra in Philadelphia.

An unforgettable moment during that season was when Roman hit a last-second shot that seemingly beat West Virginia at the Field House, but it was nullified because Jinks had signalled for a timeout just before Roman released his shot. Pitt lost that heart-breaker, by 68-67, but came back soon after to win at West Virginia, 69-68.

Pitt posted a 17-8 record the next season and gained an NIT berth for the first time in the school's history. Sheffield led the team in scoring (18.5 ppg) and Krieger in rebounding (10.4). This time they were defeated by Drake, 87-82, in the opening playoff game.

The Pitt basketball program came apart at the seams after that. There were a few good players, such as Larry Szykowny, Bob Lovett, Daryle Ruby and Jim LaValley over the next few seasons, but not nearly enough. The Panthers failed to win more than seven games in any one season over a four-year stretch, and after a 7-15 finish in 1967-68 Timmons turned in his resignation.

''You get discouraged when you don't win,'' said Timmons. ''You put pressure on yourself, you coach harder, you like to win because you have pride in your coaching ability, but then you feel that maybe you're not doing the job. Maybe you're not getting across to your players.''

Timmons hated to recruit, which is understandable because it is a vile practice, but it had to be done, and he didn't have the stomach or desire to do it. So, at 55, he gave up the ghost. ''Coaching was getting to be no fun

BOB TIMMONS **BUZZ RIDL** **TIM GRGURICH**

anymore," he explained. "Recruiting is something that's become a big part of college basketball."

Buzz Ridl replaced Timmons, and that seemed strange on the surface. Ridl was a lot like Timmons — low key, mild-mannered — and his experience had been at Westminster, a small college program. But it had been a good small college program, and he always gave Pitt fits through the years. He was a good coach.

Ridl retained Grgurich as an assistant, and brought along Fran Webster to work with him. Ridl's first team, in 1968-69, went 4-20, by far the worst record in Pitt history. His program was so-so at best for four more seasons, with a 14-10 record the high mark. Kent Scott, Paul O'Gorek, Billy Knight, Cleveland Edwards, Pete Strickland and Mike Paul were the best of those teams.

Then Ridl struck it rich during the 1973-74 season. As a senior, the Braddock-bred Knight led the team in scoring and rebounding for a third straight season, averaging 21.8 points and 13.4 rebounds, and personally pushed the Panthers to the most successful season in the modern era with a 25-4 record.

After losing their first game of the season, the Panthers reeled off a 22-game winning streak — the longest in school history — and made it all the way to the NCAA Eastern Regional finals before losing to eventual champion North Carolina State, led by high-flying David Thompson. Pitt gained national prominence that year, rating a full-length feature in Sports Illustrated that focused on the homegrown aspect of the Panthers. All of them had played their high school ball within a short distance of Pitt.

Ridl went golfing with Webster the day before that big game with N.C. State, saying, "I felt I needed to get away from all the excitement of basketball for awhile." He also said, "I'd be surprised if we'd win."

Ridl was like that. He kept things in pretty good perspective. He'd say "Oh my" to express his unhappiness to officials.

The following year, with Kirk Bruce and Mel Bennett showing the way, Pitt posted an 18-11 record, and gained a second NIT berth, beating Southern Illinois at Madison Square Garden for openers, then losing to Providence the next time out.

Ridl retired after that season, his seventh at the helm of the Pitt program. "Coaching limits you," he explained, "and there are some things my wife and I would like to do. And you have to ask yourself, 'Do you have the energy and enthusiasm?' "

He returned to Westminster as athletic director.

Then Grgurich, an assistant since 1969, got the job. He had recruited such top players as Knight, Mickey Martin, Bruce, Jim Bolla, Lew Hill, Keith Starr and Tom Richards and, at 32, was eager to become the boss of his own program.

It took awhile for Grgurich to get his program off the ground. He went 12-15 and 6-21 in his first two seasons, before coming up with a winner, at 16-11, for the 1977-78 campaign.

Larry Harris, the highest career scorer in Pitt history with 1,914 points, led the Panthers in scoring, and freshman Sam Clancy from Brashear High of the City League led in rebounding that year. Terry Knight, Billy's kid brother, and Sammie Ellis were excellent contributors to the team's success.

Clancy became the school's all-time rebounder by leading the club in that category all four seasons, and was the main man as the Panthers went 18-11, 17-12 and 19-12 the next three years.

Grgurich got to coach Clancy only three years, quitting his job in frustration following a 65-63 defeat by arch-rival Duquesne in the finals of the Eastern Eight tournament in 1980. It was an ill-timed move that Grgurich may regret the rest of his life.

Bob Smizik, a sportswriter-contemporary of Grgurich, described him this way in a Pittsburgh Press account:

"He was a dead-end kid out of Lawrenceville, a bit of a hot-shot athlete at Central Catholic, a gutty, tough catcher in baseball, a hard-nosed defensive player in basketball. If there was a loose ball on the floor, Grgurich was usually going to get it. He took a minimum of talent and a maximum of all the intangibles necessary for success and made a fine career for himself at Pitt in the early '60s."

Grgurich was at Pitt for 20 years, over half his adult life. He was 36 when he quit. "He doesn't bleed blue and gold," wrote Smizik, "but he probably thinks he does."

When Grgurich gave up the job, he offered these thoughts: "Memories to me are the players who played for you and the successes they have on and off the court. To see a Billy Knight in the pros, to see a Tommy Richards making a successful life for himself, that's what's important to me."

Roy Chipman came in as the new coach. His record for three years at Lafayette was 60-28 and he had won two East Coast Conference championships. But he had to prove himself at Pitt, and he has done that and more.

He can coach, oh can he coach. Now if he can recruit as well, Pitt will really have something going for it.

"What we want to do," said Chipman, "is build the basketball team on par with the football program. I'm waiting to do the job — I can do the job."

Chipman's first club went 19-12, and his second rallied from an 8-6 start to finish with a 20-10 record. He won the Eastern Eight playoff championship both seasons, defeating Duquesne and West Virginia in the big games, and gained automatic NCAA berths both times. Dwayne Wallace and Darrell Gissendanner were senior co-captains of Chipman's second Pitt team, and they provided the leadership and spark, while sophomore forward Clyde Vaughan provided the scoring and rebounding necessary to win.

Chipman says the new football coach, Foge Fazio, is working closely with him in recruiting, and that he is optimistic that more area stars, like Joey David, will dream of playing for Pitt someday. And going to medical school. And being a real doctor, not just Dr. J.

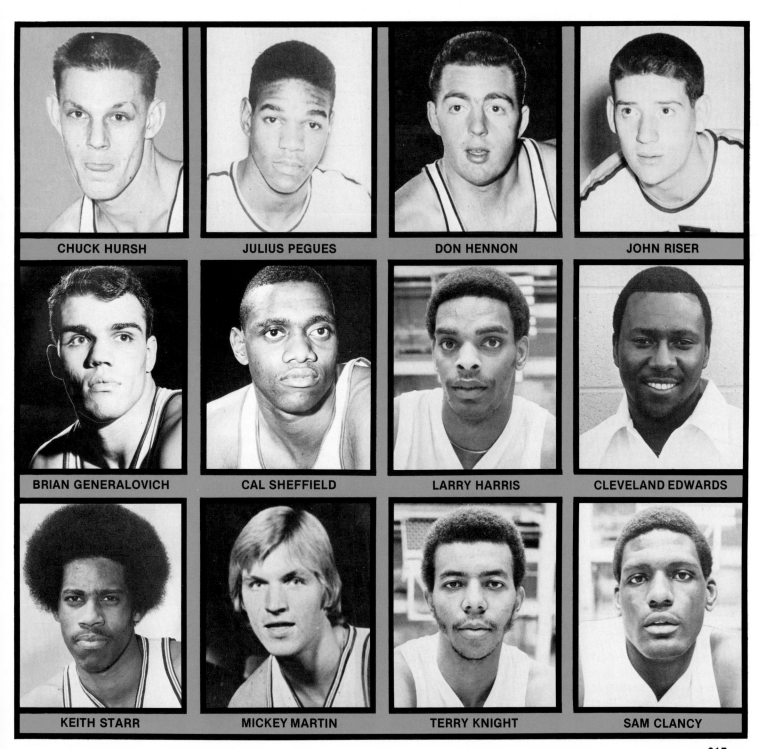

CHUCK HURSH JULIUS PEGUES DON HENNON JOHN RISER

BRIAN GENERALOVICH CAL SHEFFIELD LARRY HARRIS CLEVELAND EDWARDS

KEITH STARR MICKEY MARTIN TERRY KNIGHT SAM CLANCY

Boxing Began And Ended
With Jack Schricker in '30s

By Jim O'Brien

"It taught you self-reliance."
— George Dines

JACK SCHRICKER Showed the Way

Jack Schricker is the story of boxing at Pitt.

He was to the ring sport at the school what Jock Sutherland was to football, Doc Carlson to basketball, Carl Olson to track & field, Rex Peery to wrestling, Leo Bemis to soccer and Bobby Lewis to baseball.

He was the outstanding competitor on the freshman team when boxing was added to the athletic program at Pitt in 1930, and he was the head coach of the boxing team when the sport was dropped in 1939.

Pitt competed in boxing on a varsity level for one decade — during the so-called "Golden Era of Sports" when Pitt was a national power in several sports — and Schricker still has the letter from athletic director Jimmy Hagan advising him that Pitt was abandoning both boxing and wrestling as intercollegiate sports "due to lack of interest."

Schricker still takes exception to that. "I never did agree that lack of interest was the reason for dropping boxing," says Schricker. "Rather, there was a feeling in society that too many injuries were attributable to amateur, professional and college boxing.

"The depression of the 1930's caused many unemployed youths to turn to amateur and professional boxing in order to make a few dollars. Many of these new boxers were poorly coached and not too prepared physically, and out of shape for boxing. The result: many injuries and bad publicity."

It was a period, indeed, when Pittsburgh and Western Pennsylvania, in particular, spawned some of the greatest boxers in the sport's history. Pittsburgh was "The City of Champions" back then, too.

Between July 13, 1939 and Nov. 18, 1941, Billy Conn, Sammy Angott, Fritzie Zivic, Billy Soose — he had boxed for Penn State — and Jackie Wilson all won world boxing titles.

Schricker won his share of boxing titles, too. He captained the varsity team for three years, and was the 155-pound Eastern Conference champion as a sophomore and junior, and a finalist as a senior.

In his fourth and final year as coach, his team won its first Eastern Conference team title at Morgantown, West Va. "Things were real bright for future Pitt boxing teams," he recalls. "We had four freshman boxers who were better in their weight class than the varsity regulars."

Pitt entered a team in the nationals for the first time that year when they were conducted at Charlottesville, Va.

They were represented by Ralph Dorand, a 115-pound Eastern champion; Johnny Wargo (125), Captain Ralph Caruso (135), Jed Curzi (145), Ralph Bombe (155) and Paul Ashman (165).

After Schricker, Pitt's best boxer was Jimmy Giannati, a 135-pound champion from Uniontown who captained one of Schricker's squads.

The Pitt boxing team trained first at Trees Gym, then they worked out in a room just inside Gate 3 at Pitt Stadium, and boxed at the Pavilion, a gym located under the Stadium seats where the basketball team also played in those days.

College boxing competition consisted of three scheduled two-minute rounds.

The boxing team usually performed before or after the basketball team played at the Pavilion.

Francis "Cowboy" Siegel, a guard on the football team, captained the boxing team in 1933.

Several other fine football players boxed as well, including Warren Heller, 175-pound class, and heavyweights Arnold Greene and Ted Schmidt.

Schricker had never boxed before he entered Pitt, but he became a student of the sport. "I read everything on boxing I can find," he once boasted.

Boxing teams represented Pitt, Carnegie Tech, Duquesne, Washington & Jefferson, West Virginia, Bucknell, Penn State and Temple then. Tech hosted the first Eastern Conference championships. Pitt also competed against such schools as Syracuse, Army and Navy regularly.

Pitt boxed at Penn State before a full house of 6,500 but crowds of 1,500 were more common at the Pitt Pavilion. Pitt beat West Virginia, 4-3, in the first match there. Police riot squads were called out as a precaution when Pitt boxed Duquesne, but there were no incidents. The Dukes outduked the Panthers, 4-3, in that first meeting in 1930.

Imagine what it would be like today.

Schricker still has his scrapbook to spark memories of those days. He's retired now and he lives in Estes Park, Colorado, an area 70 miles northwest of Denver in the foothills of the Rocky Mountains where he and his wife, Sylvia, once vacationed and decided to come back and stay.

"There were seven elk in our backyard yesterday," said Schricker when we spoke with him, "and we've got big horn sheep and coyotes that come around, too. It's paradise out here."

Schricker came out of Carrick High School where he starred in four sports. He played on the baseball team at Carrick for six seasons, and the highlight of that long stay was pitching a no-hitter against Allegheny High. During the summers of his days at Pitt, he used to catch for the Pirates when Pie Traynor's teams played some minor league exhibitions. He even hit a home run over the wall in one such game. He was also a reserve running back on the Pitt football team.

But he never boxed until he came to Pitt. It was introduced as a varsity sport by Don Harrison, the athletic director at the outset of the '30s, and coached by Joe Orsini.

COACH JACK SCHRICKER, at left, poses with pugilists from Pitt's 1935 squad.

JIMMY GIANNATI Lightweight Champ

The first time Pitt ever competed against Duquesne in athletics, for instance, it was in boxing in 1930. Some say they have been at it ever since.

Schricker had a long stay at Pitt. He also helped coach the football team — as an aide to freshman coach Mike Milligan during Sutherland's reign — and he earned a bachelor's, a master's and a doctorate degree in education at Pitt. He was a principal for a long period in the Baldwin-Whitehall and Butler school districts.

The boxing sport produced another classroom success story as well. That was "Wee Willie" Davies, who was often referred to as "the uncrowned bantamweight champion of the world." Davies held the North American title for awhile, and was thought to be better than the reigning world champions, but couldn't get any title fights.

At age 28, Davies came up to Pitt Stadium one day in the summer of 1934, shortly after Schricker had been appointed boxing coach, and introduced himself. He said he had spoken earlier to Orsini about helping him to coach the team in exchange for an education.

"I knew nothing about the offer," says Schricker, "but I said I would check with Don Harrison, our athletic director, to see if he had any knowledge about having Willie assist with the boxing program."

During a subsequent conversation, Schricker and Harrison discovered that Davies had not graduated from high school. Undaunted, Davies went back to high school. He had dropped out in the middle of his junior year.

He went back to the same school district where his son was an elementary student. "What determination!" says Schricker. "In one year he was back to Pitt with his high school diploma, and we enrolled him as a full-time student. He became the assistant boxing coach in 1935.

"At the end of his freshman year, Mr. Davies applied for admittance to the physical education progam."

While being interviewed by Carl Olson, the track & field coach, Davies was told by Olson, "You're too small to handle high school classes; they will run all over you!"

Davies responded: "No they won't. What does size have to do with respect and discipline? Napoleon wasn't much bigger than me and he conquered the world!"

Enough said. Willie Davies was admitted to the physical education program. He later obtained a master's degree in education at Pitt.

A good deal of reminiscing was devoted to Davies when three former Pitt boxers got together for a round table discussion on the sport in the winter of '82 at "Froggy's," the Downtown restaurant-saloon where the sports photos and memorabilia covering the walls sparks such talk.

Dick Conti, a retired engineer and Varsity Letterman of Distinction, was there along with Dr. George Dines, a general surgeon, and Russ Vogel, former director of the Pittsburgh Parks & Recreation Department.

"Because Pitt was so good in football, and fairly good in basketball, we boxed and wrestled at the same level," said Dr. Dines. "We went up against the best teams."

This prompted a story by Vogel, a vociferous little fellow who still looks fighting trim. "We went out to Wisconsin when they were the national champions," he said. "That was the coldest winter ever up until this one, and we went out there by train. Boxing was big time there, and they had about 15,000 fans in the stands."

Conti entered the conversation: "The men in the first few rows wore tuxedos, and the women wore evening gowns. I never saw so many people in my life!"

Vogel continued his tale:

"Plattsburgh State boxed Wisconsin's 'B' team in the preliminary of a doubleheader program, and Wisconsin's fighters were knocking them out, one after another. And they kept carrying the Plattsburgh fighters on stretchers through our dressing room.

"Willie Davies said to me, 'Vogel, get ready!' I was our lightest fighter — I weighed 115 — and the first to go. I'm telling you I felt real lonely walking out there through that crowd.

"The ring was red with blood, with a white patch here and there. I looked in the bucket, and it was red with blood. Bud Moore, our trainer, tells me, 'Don't worry about anything.'

"I was going up against the first lefty fighter I ever fought, and he was a Golden Glove champion out of Chicago. The crowd was yelling, 'Bring on Pittsburgh!' There was this one little boy at ringside I'd met outside the building, and I'd let him carry my bag in. He was hollering, 'C'mon, Pittsburgh.' He was our only fan.

"This guy was good, but I stayed in there for three rounds, and lost by decision."

Conti came back, "I remember Schricker saying, 'We want to make a good showing against the national champs.' Well, we didn't disgrace ourselves."

Dr. Dines summed up his experience as a Pitt boxer, and the benefits from that experience in this manner:

"You were out there by yourself, and you had the possibility of getting hurt. It did something to you. It made you self-reliant. Afterward, there was such a feeling of relief."

RALPH DORAND 118-lb. Champ

PITT PUGILISTS learned a lot from "Wee Willie" Davies, at left. Those boxers included, front row seated, left to right, John Wargo, Ralph Dorand, Herb Turner, Jedio Curzi, Ralph Caruso. Back row, third boxer from left, Paul Ashman, George Lupinacci, John Neuner, Ray Bombe. The manager and two boxers next to Davies could not be identified.

Golf Began With Sam Parks Jr., Ended With A Budget Cut

By Pat Livingston

"Pitt has never taken the game too seriously. Maybe that's smart."

For whatever reasons, possibly the vagaries of Western Pennsylvania's inclement and exasperating springs, golf, a popular game at many U.S. colleges, never achieved major intercollegiate status at the University of Pittsburgh.

Yet the university has not been without its golfing graduates of notes, including a National Open champion who clawed his way to victory while the nation clawed its way out of the Great Depression of the 1930s.

While Pitt has been represented by golf teams since the 1920s — largely at the urging of Sam Parks, the man who won that Open title a couple of years after graduating from Pitt — to a large degree golf at Pitt has been a rather informal association of dedicated, self-motivated athletes who, linking themselves together because of a common love of the game, austerely represented the university as best they could.

"Sam Parks and I started the first Pitt golf team," recalls Jim Underwood, who was also on the Pitt swimming team. "We had no support from the athletic department, and we made our own matches and paid our own expenses."

Pitt, in short, has never taken the game of golf too seriously. And maybe that's smart. Maybe that's the way it should be.

Never, for example, had the Panthers employed a full-time golf coach. The closest they came to it was in the late 40s when Dave McCormack, a club professional at Shannopin Country Club, was persuaded to take on the Panthers as a voluntary, part-time chore.

Others who agreed to handle the assignment were assistant athletic directors, such as Clyde Barton, or a wrestling coach who had given up directing his own sport at the school, Rex Peery, who, many suspect, was more interested in getting himself out onto the fairways on a pleasant afternoon than he was in developing the type of nationally-rated NCAA champions he molded on the mat. Until Pitt gave up on fielding a golf team in 1979, Steve Petro, who played guard on Jock Sutherland's finest teams and has been employed by the university since, served the university as its golf coach.

In golf, the Panthers never achieved the stature of a University of Houston, which for years — until it was accepted into the Southwest Conference — specialized in the sport, or any of the schools of the Southern or Southeastern Conference which turns such prestigious tournaments as the North-South Amateur at Pinehurst into a hotbed of collegiate golf, a collegiate tour stop.

In truth, rarely were the Panthers competitive even with Penn State, a school which suffers similar handicaps try-

SAM PARKS JR. — As he appeared when he won U.S. Open Golf Championship with record 299 at Oakmont in 1935.

ing to play a temperate sport under intemperate climatic conditions.

Yet the Panthers' history in golf is not without its golden moments. From the day in the 20s when Parks' enthusiasm convinced the athletic department that Pitt was prestigious enough to have its own golf team, to more recent years, Pitt has attracted some excellent golfers to its concrete campus. They might not have been of the calibre of Arnie Palmer or Jack Nicklaus, of course, but as collegiate golfers several of them were pure standouts.

Some of Pitt's finest golf teams coincided with their top football teams. In the late 30s, when Jock Sutherland's snarling Panthers ran roughshod over the football fields of America, two of his All-America ends, Frank Souchak and Bill Daddio, were turning the Panther golfers — in the off-season of course, and after spring training at that — into the scourge of the Eastern links.

In their senior year, 1938, when the football players finally had a spring to themselves, Pitt's top three men on that team — Souchak, Barrett Melvin and Tony Kaye — won 27 of 30 matches as they paced the Panthers to an 8-2 record, perhaps the best in the school's history. Pitt's No. 4 man that year, Daddio, was capable of beating any one of his talented teammates on any given afternoon.

No one will ever know how far Souchak might have made it in golf. An ex-caddie from Berwick, Pa., the older brother of touring pro Mike Souchak, Frank, today a wealthy oil and gas man who winters in Carmel, Cal., and summers on Cape Code, gave up competitive golf upon graduation to concentrate on his career. Long after he had passed his competitive peak, in 1952, Frank Souchak ended up as a low amateur in the U.S. Open, finishing in the top five at Oakmont behind Ben Hogan and Sam Snead, the runaway leaders, hanging in there, a couple strokes behind, until the final round.

Sam Parks, however, remains to this day the Cinderella story of golf at Pitt.

Two football players who were fine golfers.

FRANK SOUCHAK   **BILL DADDIO**

Five years out of college and club professional at South Hills Country Club at the time, the only job he could find in those depression years, Parks had spent two years on the winter tour before winning it all at Oakmont. While legend today regards Parks as a rank outsider among U.S. Open winners, his victory was not a complete surprise. At least it was not to Clair Burcky, who was writing golf perceptively for The Press at the time.

In a story written prior to the district qualifier for the Open, which also was held at Oakmont, Burcky wrote:

"For the past two years, Parks has paced the qualifiers from this district, notching a 36-hole score of 145 at Oakmont and following with 146 last spring at Fox Chapel. He will be an odds-on favorite to lead the field again. And not a bad bet — at long odds of course — to win the Open."

A few years after winning at Oakmont — his 299 made him the first professional to break 300 over four rounds at the Hulton course, Parks gave up golf for a career in business. He joined U.S. Steel during the war years and retired as district manager for the American Steel and Wire Division of the corporation.

There were other good golfers at Pitt down through the years — even though most of them gave up competitive golf after graduation. On taking the coaching job at Pitt, McCormack recruited Bob Reilly, who at the time was one of the leading amateurs in the district. After losing their first two matches, Reilly got hot and sparked the Panthers to eight wins in their next nine matches.

The first Old Newsboys champion, Bill Baloh of Greensburg, went on to captain Pitt's team, and Ron Dermitt of Indiana, Pa., had a sparkling career with the Panthers, highlighting it with a runner-up finish in the 1961 Eastern Intercollegiates before losing the championship in a sudden death playoff.

SCORECARD CHECK — Sam Parks Jr., at right, reviews 18 holes with Fred Brand Jr., another top local golfer.

FEARLESS FOURSOME — Top golfers (left to right) include Sam Parks Jr., Jim Thompson, Ben Hogan and Ted Luther in 1941.

Gymnastics Program Points to Nationals In Sport's Renaissance At Pitt

By Norm Vargo

"Tom Hamilton is the man who believed gymnastics could go as a varsity sport here."
—Warren Neiger

Gymnastics is probably the most unusual sport in a world where sports come in all sizes, shapes and variations. If ever there was an individual sport, it has to be gymnastics.

Hanging in mid-air from the hoops, gliding through the air on the side horse, or dangling from the parallel bars, the gymnast is on his own all the way.

Unlike other sports which defy other human beings and their physical capabilities, gymnasts, perhaps, the best conditioned of all athletes, defy the natural elements as well as their opponents.

You could say that gymnastics has been "on its own" at Pitt from the time when then Athletic Director Tom Hamilton coaxed Warren Neiger to come in to organize and coach an intercollegiate program. And it's still sort of on its own under current head coach Dr. Frank D'Amico, who has enjoyed success, as his Panthers put together some of the best team records in the school's 30-year gym history.

Despite the prodigious efforts of Neiger, who's since given up coaching, and Dr. D'Amico, Pitt can claim only one NCAA champion in the more than quarter-century that has elapsed since the Panthers began as a club team. That's the inimitable Tom Darling who claimed individual National titles working off the flying rings in 1957 and '58.

"Tom Darling is one of a kind," recalls Neiger. "When Tom competed, he had no equal on the rings. Nobody could beat him. And he also performed on the high bar where he did pretty well. Tom took a turn at tumbling, too.

"Darling was a man you could built a team around. He was some kind of a gymnast, a rare find. His kind of dedicated athlete doesn't come along too often."

Darling also has the distinction of being Pitt's only All-American gymnast. He made it all three seasons.

Neiger fielded Pitt's first legitimate gymnastics team in 1954, playing a full intercollegiate schedule, which showed some of the national powers of the time — Army, West Virginia, Ohio State and Illinois. Pitt came out of its initial campaign with a dubious 0-5 record, losing to West Virginia twice along the way.

Neiger's "men on the flying trapeze" — as Panther gymnasts were called by Pitt athletes in that opening season — put on a good show. Neiger was satisfied. His program was off and winging.

"Some of the boys on that first team had never competed in gym events before," recalled Neiger. "They were competent, but woefully inexperienced. We were eager. It was a start, though."

Lack of scholarships led to a severe lack of depth through the early years, and proved to be a handicap for

WARREN NEIGER   TOM HAMILTON
They gave gym early boost.

Neiger. This situation would last into the late 1960's. There were times, Neiger might admit, that he wondered if gymnastics would ever succeed in Oakland.

Neiger credits Hamilton with rallying support from many sectors to keep gymnastics alive at Pitt.

"Hamilton is the man who believed gymnastics could go as a varsity sport here," says Neiger. "He used to stop and watch practice almost every day as he went to the squash courts in Fitzgerald Field House.

"He'd stop and talk with the kids, ask them how they were doing. Hamilton would ask me if I needed equipment, or if everything was working out. If I needed something, our gymnastics team usually could figure we'd get it.

"Hamilton was the best athletic boss a coach could ever have. He displayed an intense interest in the so-called minor sports, gymnastics among them. He's the guy who helped bring gymnastics to a peak, to achieve equality among the varsity sports here at Pitt. Without Tom Hamilton's interest and guidance, and understanding during the rough years, gymnastics might not have survived."

Neiger gave Pitt gymnastics its start. In D'Amico's five years at the helm, Panthers gymnasts have evolved into a top-caliber program, one of the better ones in the nation.

D'Amico became the Panthers' head coach in 1978 after being the assistant in 1976-77. Ken Lunz, who lettered for the Panthers four years as an all-around, was team captain and most valuable player as a senior, is D'Amico's aide.

D'Amico is the third coach in Pitt's gymnastics history. Ig Perez, who was a steady standout performer under Neiger, assumed the head coaching post in 1974. Neiger's final season as top man was 1973 making him a so-called "20-year" man among Panther varsity coaches at the time.

Although an era ended with Neiger giving up the coaching post, gymnastics has made strides although

SEVENTH BEST — Pitt's 1957-58 gym team finished seventh in NCAA tournament led by All-American Tom Darling of Philadelphia, left front row, and co-captain John Cacolice. Back row, Don Neeld (Dormont), Jim Mulvihill (Homestead), Dave Ruber (Pittsburgh) and Dave Hirst (Philadelphia).

things became a bit touchy during Perez' regime. D'Amico became well aware of this fact, as Perez' assistant.

"The level of gymnastics at Pitt has increased tremendously in the last few years," D'Amico pointed out enthusiastically. "We're at the point where our team goals could include a shot at making the Nationals . . ."

In fact, D'Amico's 1980-81 squad — which finished with a creditable 8-3 record — for the first time in Panther gym history Pitt put a national team in the NCAA championship meet in Nebraska. The team included Bob Besong and Dave Smith in floor and Franz Kratz in the vault.

Other members of the record-breaking team were Byron John and Jeff Litzinger. Litzinger was voted the MVP while Besong, Smith and Kratz earned All-East honors.

While gymnastics is enjoying a so-called "rebirth" at Pitt, Neiger's efforts cannot be overlooked. In addition to Darling's twin NCAA titles, Neiger-coached gymnasts claimed seven Eastern Intercollegiate Gymnastics League

FRANK D'AMICO
Present Coach

BOB BESONG
All-around ace

crowns and nearly a dozen EIGL second places. That's not bad for a secondary varsity sport at Pitt, or any other major university for that matter.

While D'Amico's gymnasts have a lock on Panther individual records, Neiger's proteges had their day in the limelight, too.

BILL SHENEFELT — Still rings was specialty for East McKeesport product.

EARL McCONNELL — Versatile gym star who came from Connelley Trade School to become Eastern champ in tumbling and floor exercise in 1962.

Pitt's individual marks are:

EVENT	SCORE	GYMNAST	SEASON
All-Around	53.2	Bob Besong	1980-81
Floor Exercise	9.45	Dave Smith	1980-81
Side Horse	8.95	Nooch Capini	1980-81
Still Rings	9.4	Bob Besong	1980-81
Vaulting	9.75	Bob Besong	1980-81
Parallel Bars	9.2	Alan Myers	1977-78
High Bars	9.4	Bob Besong	1980-81

Under Neiger, champions and runnersup included:

Tom Darling — 1956 EIGL runnerup — rings; 1956 NCAA runnerup — rings, 1957 & '58 EIGL champion — rings; 1957 & '58 — NCAA champion — rings.

Dave Hirst — 1957 EIGL runnerup, rings; 1959 EIGL runnerup, rings; 1960 EIGL runnerup, rings.

Jim Mulvihill — 1958 EIGL champion, high bar.

Don Neeld — 1959 EIGL runnerup, tumbling.

Earl McConnell — 1960 EIGL runnerup, tumbling; 1960 EIGL runnerup, floor exercise; 1961 EIGL runnerup, tumbling; 1961 EIGL runnerup, floor exercise; 1962 EIGL runnerup, tumbling; 1962, EIGL champion, floor exercise.

Edward Zamecnik — 1961 EIGL runnerup, still rings.

Dave Shidemantle — 1966 EIGL champion, long horse. 1968 EIGL champion, long horse.

Lowell Meek — 1970, 1971 EIGL champion, free exercise.

Some of Neiger's "highlights" during a fine coaching career:

- "Of course, Tom Darling's NCAA championships which have never been equalled . . ."
- "Then there's Dave Shidemantle on the long horse, who should've been an NCAA champion, too. But he had to settle for two EIGL titles instead . . ."
- "Lowell Meek came from a 2-8 team to go unbeaten two straight seasons and won the Eastern championship in free exercise twice . . ."
- "That first season of varsity competition, then our 1955 team which was Pitt's 'official' start in NCAA competition . . ."
- "The 1964-65 season which I feel was the crystallizing stage for Pitt gymnastics . . . we went 5-5 and Perez was a sophomore . . ."
- "Don Kasner becoming the first gymnast in Pitt history to win three events in an individual meet against Georgia Tech. He won side horse, high bar and parallel bars . . ."
- "Hirst going unbeaten through duals on the flying ring and breaking Darling's record . . ."

Neiger has some pleasant memories, but he declines to single out any gymnast as being his best. "Tom Darling is Pitt's only All-American and NCAA champion. I'd rather leave it like that . . .," he says. "Too many boys had much to do with Pitt gymnastics down through the years. It's a credit to all of them that the sport has survived some critical times . . ."

TOM DARLING — NCAA champion on flying rings in 1957 and 1958.

TOM DARLING

Even 30 Years Later, Tom Remains Darling Of Gym Sport

"Tom Darling put Pitt gymnastics on the national map."

—Warren Neiger

By Norm Vargo

Tom Darling is one guy who isn't afraid to admit he was a Pitt gymnast who was in the right place at the right time.

"Yes, I was fortunate to come into a brand new era of gymnastics when I arrived at Pitt," says Darling — Pitt's only NCAA champion and All-America in the 30-year-old history of the sport at the Oakland campus. "Every nationally-recognized gymnast of the time had graduated. Everything was there for me to reach my potential. I was comfortable with the situation. Certainly, you can say I took advantage of it."

Darling — now an executive for Nissen-Universal Corp. based in Annapolis, Md., — says he's "surprised" that he remains the Panthers' only gymnastics All-American, three-times, in fact, and Pitt's only NCAA champion after graduating more than a decade ago.

"Sure, I'm surprised that Pitt hasn't been able to produce All-American gymnasts," allows Darling, whom former coach Warren Neiger credits with putting the Panthers' gymnastics program on "the national map."

"Like I said, I was fortunate in that I came into a new program at Pitt with experience," recalls Darling. "Down through the years I thought Pitt would claim other champions. Some people came extremely close, but missed out for one reason or another."

Darling singled out some Pitt gymnasts whom he figures could've notched national individual titles. Gymnasts like Dave Hirst, who remains a long-time friend after being a classmate and teammate both at Pitt and before that at Lincoln High School in Northeast Philadelphia, and Jim Mulvihill, Earl McConnell, Lowell Meek and Ed Zamecnik.

"You could add Dave Shidemantle to that list, too," added Darling. "I've probably forgotten some others. Gosh, it's been so long since I've discussed Pitt gymnastics with people. It's hard to recall faces and names of the good ones."

Darling feels Hirst — who finished as the runnerup to Darling on the rings in 1957 — should've been a national champion. "Undoubtedly, Dave Hirst should've been a champion. He probably would've, too, but for injuries," reasoned Darling.

And Darling remembers Lowell Meek as probably the Panther gymnast who wanted a national title the most.

"Lowell wanted a title as much as anybody. Certainly, he has to go down as one of the 'hungriest' gymnasts ever to attend Pitt. Lowell, too, could've been a national champ had it not been for problems."

Darling explained those "problems."

"Yes, we had problems in those early years when Pitt was trying to get its gymnastics program going," said Darling. "There was little publicity in the sport unless you competed for a big school like, say, Penn State.

"We used to kid around that Penn State gymnasts always seemed to get extra points from the judges. They didn't have the sophisticated judging techniques back then as they do now.

"One reason I was able to win my first title and get national recognition was because I finished second in the NCAA rings my first season. People knew who I was the next couple of times around. That helped, just like the fact that all of the nationally-recognized people had graduated.

"I feel guys like Hirst, Meek, McConnell, Zamecnik and Shidemantle were hurt by lack of publicity. Nobody really knew who these guys were let alone that they represented Pitt. It wasn't fair, but in some cases gymnastic titles were judged by personality and such, instead of by effort . . .

"But that's changed, just as gymnastics has changed. I can see it happening.

"When I left Pitt, I took graduate work at Michigan State. After that, I was an assistant coach at the Naval Academy. During that time, I coached teams that competed against Pitt. I could see changes, and also internal problems that had cropped up."

Darling feels that these "internal problems" nearly ruined Pitt's gymnastic program. "It didn't help matters any," he declared.

Ironically, Darling credits Donna DeMarino Sanft — Pitt women's gymnastic coach — for sort of saving the boys' program. "Credit must go to Donna for keeping up the continuity when the internal problems threatened the boys' gymnastic program," he suggested. Without her effort, it's hard to say what might have happened.

"Pitt gymnastics survived to where the program ranks as one of the best in the country. I keep tabs on Pitt, and many other schools, because most of them use our equipment. That way, I see gymnastic people all the time," he added.

Darling feels a "special" significance for Pitt gymnastics.

"When I came to Pitt, Coach Neiger was still trying to build a gymnastics team. It was still in the club stages. I felt comfortable, though, because I had experienced a similar situation during my high school competition.

"It didn't take long for me to adjust. When we started to compete on the varsity level, I was ready. I repeat, I was more fortunate than most because I came in there with some experience. I used my experience to help others."

Darling feels Pitt gymnastics is becoming successful under coach Dr. Frank D'Amico because "homegrown" talent is staying home and going to Pitt.

"There was a trend where good high school gymnasts weren't even looking Pitt's way. They just didn't seem interested in going there. I mean, Pitt used to lose quality gymnasts to other schools. I don't mean locally, but some of the bigger ones around the country. I feel this trend has been reversed."

Hockey Team Made History
Mostly at Duquesne's Expense

By Jim O'Brien

"That game nearly killed me. Five years later they still wanted to amputate my leg."
—Dick Friday

The games with Duquesne University have always been the highlight of the hockey season at Pitt, going back to the so-called "Golden Era of Sports" in the late '30s when hockey was a recognized varsity sport at the school, and it is no different today when the competition is conducted on a club basis.

There was more rioting among the players and fans — the local police pointed to it on their schedule, too — in those earlier days at drafty Duquesne Gardens than there is today at the Civic Arena when these rivals clash.

"Fisticuffs and verbal brawls predominated from the opening faceoff to the final siren," wrote Bert P. Taggart in a Jan. 19, 1939 sports report of a Pitt-Duquesne ice duel.

There's another difference, declares Dick Friday, a forward for Pitt's "Might Mites" or "Dream Line" of the '30s. "The kids on the Pitt club team are bigger and better than we were," he said at a reminiscing session with former teammates at the University Club in the winter of '82.

Here's Pitt's hockey team for the 1908-09 season.
They were among the originals.

It has been generally thought by hockey buffs in this area that there have been two periods of hockey at Pitt: during a three-season span from 1936-37 through 1938-39, and the current club team that originated with the 1970-71 season, and is still struggling along.

In truth, our research has turned up a third period of hockey competition at Pitt. There was a team in 1906-07 that went 0-2, and another in 1908-09 that posted a 1-2-1 record, with a win over Penn, losses to Yale and Carnegie Tech, and a tie with Tech.

In 1909-10, a three-team league with Pitt, Tech and Penn State was started, but soon folded, with Tech holding a 3-0-1 record, Pitt at 1-2-1, and State at 0-2. State pulled out because the travel expenses to play at Duquesne Gardens were prohibitive. Dr. Milliken, a graduate of Toronto University, was the coach. He was, we are told, a man to be admired. But, alas, there was no student spirit, and the sport was dropped.

Pitt students actually started skating in 1894 when the first indoor rink — called the Casino — was built near the Panther Hollow Bridge in Schenley Park. Soon after, pro hockey got its start here, and Canadians were imported to play in a four-team league. That's right, Pittsburgh is the birthplace of pro hockey.

One of the game's early promoters here was a Canadian named Roy D. Schooley, and it was his son, Bob, who organized a hockey team at Pitt in the winter of '36. Young Schooley talked some other equally-addicted and ambitious students into getting up at 6 o'clock on a frosty morning for the first of similarly-scheduled workouts at Duquesne Gardens, once a streetcar barn and then the city's major indoor sports facility. The rink was located at Fifth and Craig on the edge of the Pitt campus.

They played just one game with an outside opponent that maiden season, an intra-city battle with Carnegie Tech that was played between periods of a Pittsburgh Hornets game at The Gardens. Tech won that first game, 1-0.

The second step came the following season, again solely on the initiative of the boys. They talked John Harris, a hard-nosed sports and showbiz promoter who operated The Gardens, into giving them ice time, and they formed the Ohio-Pennsylvania Intercollegiate Hockey League.

It was comprised of an Eastern and Western Division. Pitt, Tech and Duquesne comprised the Eastern end, and the Cleveland teams of John Carroll, Western Reserve and Fenn formed the Western part.

John Carroll compiled the best record in the West, and Duquesne had the best record in the East. Pitt was second. Duquesne and Pitt met in a best-of-three playoff, or at least that was the original idea, to see who would represent the East in the championship playoffs.

The Dukes defeated the Panthers, 3-2, in the first playoff contest on a Monday night, and the two teams met again two nights later — Wednesday, March 22, 1938 — in what

Pittsburgh's first indoor rink — the **CASINO** at Schenley Park, 1894.

a piece of stocking got in the cut. I developed phlebitis. It hemorrhaged for a month. Five years later, they still wanted to amputate my leg."

Friday, who was second in goal-getting only to Schooley on that squad, organized a 25th reunion of the veterans of that "longest game," and they got together on Feb. 9, 1963 at the Civic Arena. They played a pair of six-minute periods during the intermissions of the Hornets-Rochester game.

"That was almost as tiring as the original game," allowed Lovett. "We're talking about having another reunion, but the next time we're going to play it at the bar. We'll drink to it."

turned out to be one of the memorable "hockey happenings" in the history of Pittsburgh.

Pitt and Duquesne skated to a 1-1 tie that night in the longest hockey game ever played in this city's history. The game was halted, at the advice of an attending physician, at 1:55 A.M. after five over-time periods.

The teams had been on the ice for 1 hour and 56 minutes, or two minutes less than what would amount to three full games of 12-minute periods. There was one 10-minute overtime, and then four more 15-minute sessions.

Dr. Philip A. Faix, the Hornets' physician, said, "Further play might have had some serious effects on some of the boys. It was apparent from the way in which the attackers were going down when hit by a comparatively fresh defender and from the slow recovery of the players after being body-checked toward the end of the match, that nearly all the contestants were suffering from exhaustion."

Pitt had won only one of four games against Duquesne during the regular season, but they won the next two playoff contests to win the East title. They were knocked off in two straight games by John Carroll for the league championship.

Even so, that "longest game" experience is one that revives old aches and pains, as well as a great deal of pleasure, for those who were involved.

Friday and Walter Lovett and Taylor Brittain never tired of talking about it at a get-together at the University Club. Brittain brought along a scrapbook that had been put together by "a secret admirer" and given to him as a graduation present, and the yellowed newspaper clippings and photographs sparked many memories.

"I could have scored the game-breaking goal," offered Friday, "but it seemed like it was 3 A.M. and I tripped over my own feet. I just couldn't go it again.

"That game nearly killed me," he continued. "I fell and a guy stepped on me. His skate cut through my shin pad, and

BOB SCHOOLEY — He organized team sport at Pitt in '30s.

229

PUCK, AHOY — See the sailor cap on Duquesne's goalie, Alex "Sailor" Iungerich as he gets in the path of Pitt's fast-skating Bob Schooley during Pitt-Duquesne ice duel. Others, from left to right, are Dick Friday and Fran Fogarty, the former business manager of the Steelers.

College hockey was a hot item here in those days. Pitt, Tech and Duquesne played doubleheaders at The Gardens, and it grew to the point where they were outdrawing college basketball. Crowds averaged about 2,500, but there were some turnouts of 5,000 — mostly for the Pitt-Duquesne match-ups.

"We outdrew the Hornets," observed Brittain.

"We had all the cops there, too," recalled Friday. "The Pitt students and fans would be on one side, and the Duquesne students and fans would be on the other side."

At least for openers.

"We played them 13 times," said Brittain, "and we had fights half the time."

Pitt and Duquesne started competing against each other for the first time in boxing of all things, back in 1930, and it was the rioting that accompanied their hockey clashes, more so than the ones that occurred during basketball games, that led to a long rift between the schools, and a decision not to compete against each other.

One can understand the concern of school leaders after looking through some of the newspaper stories about those games between the Pitt and Duquesne hockey teams.

"With close to 4,500 wildly-cheering students and fans in the stands," wrote Bert P. Taggart in a 1939 story, "the Pitt and Duke tussle was productive of about everything but mayhem and manslaughter."

Claire M. Burcky observed:

"The long arm of the law and several Duquesne attendants were able to confine the brawling among the players. Not a spectator threw a punch, so sharp was the vigilance of the gendarmes."

In another war report by Burcky:

"The Panthers and Dukes met last night in The Gardens for the third time this season, and for the third time they stopped the game to put on a vicious brawl, punching with fists, slashing with sticks and kicking with knife-edged skates."

In that game, Pitt's Irving Artz slashed Duquesne's Walter McGill across the face. A Press photographer was manhandled by two Duquesne players. They knocked his glasses off, and whacked at his camera with hockey sticks.

"Fortunately, nobody was murdered," concluded Burcky.

Duquesne had the best team in those days, and won the regular-season title again for the 1938-39 season, and Pitt came in second once more. This time the title playoff series was reduced to two games, with the total goals deciding the winner. The Dukes won the first game, 1-0 and Pitt took the second and the title, 3-0.

"It's the same way today," said Lovett. "The playoffs mean everything."

Pitt again was clipped by John Carroll in the league's championship series.

John McSorley, who had captained the Notre Dame hockey team in his college days, coached the Pitt skaters during their two seasons of play in the Ohio-Pennsylvania Intercollegiate Ice Hockey League.

He owned several apartment houses, including the King Edward Apartments where he lived, and was a good friend of John Harris. That helped the Pitt team get in The Gardens, too.

Harris had selfish interests, as always, and kept 92 percent of the gate receipts, doling out two percent to each of the four schools for the doubleheader contests. This didn't sit well with Pitt officials, nor did Harris' insistence on running the league himself.

So Pitt pulled back on its assistance — the school had provided uniforms and picked up some other expenses, though the players had to buy their own skates — and the league folded. The guys who formed the team had graduated, for the most part.

Pitt didn't have a hockey team again until a freshman named Joe Testa founded a club hockey team in 1970. He did so with the help of Wade Welsh of the Alpine Ice Chalet, who coached the team through its first eight-game schedule in which it posted a 4-3-1 record.

Dr. Michael Sherman acted as faculty advisor for the team and stayed on for six years in that capacity. Len. C. Barcalow and Bob Montgomery coached initially.

The club, which made an unsuccessful attempt to attain varsity status, was the first champion of the Western Pennsylvania Intercollegiate Club Hockey Association, posting a 9-0-1 record in that circuit, and a 10-5-1 record overall in its second season.

They retired the Commissioner's Cup, emblematic of that league's championship, in 1975, after Pitt had gone undefeated through that spell.

"Then we took an independent schedule," said Jim Nelson, who has served as president of the Pitt hockey club since 1976. "We started playing Division II teams in New York, like St. John's and Wagner, and we've played Navy the past six seasons. We still play Duquesne and Carnegie-Mellon, and those are two intense rivalries."

The team plays Saturday afternoon games at the Civic Arena. Asked about his duties, Nelson said, "I do the same things Paul Martha does for the Penguins."

Edwin F. "Bud" Ellis graduated from goal-keeping to being an attorney.

PITT'S HOCKEY TEAM
1938 Champions Eastern Division Pennsylvania-Ohio League
Front Row (l. to r.) — Broida, Brittain, Ellis, Schooley, Lovett, Mangan;
Back Row (l. to r.) — Bennett, Cusick, Conick, Artz, Lowe, Kennedy. Coach John McSorley.

Leo Bemis Behind Soccer From The Start At Pitt

By Norm Vargo

LEO BEMIS — Soccer his baby at Pitt

"I'm a dinosaur ... just an old guy who's learned to make do."

—Leo Bemis

At Pitt, they spell soccer L-e-o B-e-m-i-s.

Leo Bemis is in his 30th campaign as Pitt's soccer coach. In fact, he's the only head coach the Panther booters have ever had. And his distinguished tenure makes him the undisputed "elder statesman" among the university's varsity athletic coaches.

Those who know Bemis, and his players, suggest that Bemis is perhaps the most optimistic and enduring coach at the university.

Certainly, Bemis qualifies as a legend of sorts.

Bemis came to Oakland during the summer of 1947, to complete his Masters Degree in physical education. He's been at Pitt ever since ...

"I'm a dinosaur," muses the bear of a man with a disarming grin, "just an old guy who's learned to make do and live with the situation. A guy like that, athletic directors leave alone."

Yes, Bemis has learned to "make do." Since he started soccer at Pitt in 1951 with a pick-up team that dueled Slippery Rock to a surprising 1-1 tie, Bemis has endured more "ups and downs" than a roller coaster.

Pitt's athletic program was still mired in turmoil during the early '50s. Tom Hamilton was on hand as athletic director, charged with the job of rebuilding the university's athletic program to the glorious stature it knew before World War II. Hamilton listened sympathetically to Bemis' urging that Pitt could field a soccer team.

Hamilton listened, and Hamilton agreed. But the time wasn't right. Soccer just didn't fit in yet. So, it was back to a club team in 1952 — and an 0-5-1 record. Bemis was far from upset, though. A year later, soccer was awarded varsity status.

Soccer had come full cycle from an intramural sport — Bemis doubled in brass as Pitt's director of men's intramural athletics — to varsity competition. Bemis' dream was now reality.

Dealing with reality has its pitfalls, Bemis soon learned. No scholarships. No feeder system from the scholastic sector. Not much of anything but desire, pride and a commitment to the university that soccer must succeed. That's all Bemis had to start with.

Relying heavily on boys he taught to play the game for the first time — and some players he lured to Pitt from Western Pennsylvania amateur ranks — Bemis forged Panther soccer. By 1965, Pitt already had the only six All-America soccer players in the school's history!

Jerome "Jerry" Bressanelli has the distinction of being the Panther's first soccer All-America, making it first in 1955 and repeating a season later.

CORKY CUTHBERT — One of the best, Cuthbert, turns to head upfield on damaged legs.

"Jerry was a great player," recalls Bemis. "His earning All-America honors gave soccer stature here at Pitt. We had something to brag about . . ."

Ronald Wyatt was the next Pitt soccer All-America, gaining recognition in 1958 and again in 1959. In '59, Wyatt was joined on the A-A list by George Zanicopoulus. Three seasons later, Paul Liberati became an All-America. In 1963, Dave Reichenbach made it, and in 1965, George Sommer was the last Panther booter to gain All-America recognition.

Bemis prefers to take a diplomatic approach when he's asked who are the top five players he's ever coached at Pitt. "Everybody had a part in making soccer the program it has been here," he says instead.

Pressed, Bemis leaned back in the chair behind his desk in the spartan office in Trees Hall that he calls "home" and pondered 29 years of Pitt soccer. The five players? It wasn't an easy task.

"Bressanelli has to be there. So does Sommer, and Reichenbach," offered Bemis. "Joe Luxbacher certainly was one of the best. And so was (Robert) 'Corky' Cuthbert. Let's see . . . that's about it."

Luxbacher still holds two Panther records. He scored seven goals against Edinboro State College in 1972 and is Pitt's leading career goal scorer with 35.

Other Panther recordholders are: Bob Cherry (1955) — most goals in a season, 17; Frank Bucci (1974-76) — most career shutouts, 14; Ron Goga (1957) — most shutouts, season, 6; Dave DeEmido (1969) — most assists, season, 12; John D'Amato (1954) — goals per game, 2.

"We've also had a number of boys earn All-Pennsylvania-Delaware-New Jersey recognition," says Bemis, clearly understating the fact that 42 Panthers had gained that distinction. Pitt's All-Pennsylvania-Delaware-New Jersey players are:

Vince Bartolotta (1964-65), Bressanelli (1955, 56, 57), Bucci (1976, 77), Fernando Carriquiry (1973), Cherry (1955), Donald Clark (1954), Michael Culhane (1954), Cuthbert (1961, 62), D'Amato (1954), William Eisinger (1957, 58), Fernando Fabregas (1958), Paul Griffiths (1955, 56), Sam Hazou (1955, 56), Jack Hester (1956), Harold Kipp (1957), Dennis Kohlmyer (1972, 73), Tsima Lekoma (1968), Liberati (1961, 62), Luxbacher (1972, 73), Andy McGraw (1962, 63), Gary Midock (1971, 72) and Robert Murdoch (1958).

Others are: Karl Nigh (1978), John O'Hara (1977, 78), Ted Phillips (1954), Reichenbach (1961, 62, 63), Art Richardson (1965, 66), Phillip Rogers (1954), Dave Shimpeno (1967), Irwin Siegel (1978), Peter Smith (1960, 61), Pete Snyder (1966, 67), Sommer (1964, 65), Ray Tarasi (1961), Gus Theofilos (1970), Eric Tiedtke (1980), Jeff Tissue (1979), Bob Trexler (1969), Chucho Valencia (1970, 1971), Wyatt (1958, 59), Norman Zanadelli (1955) and Zanicopoulus (1959, 60).

Through the years, Bemis has been one of the primary forces behind the growth of soccer in the Pittsburgh area. And he was instrumental in 'the development of the Western Pennsylvania Collegiate Soccer Conference in 1970. He's still an officer, serving in one capacity or another since the league's inception.

Bemis takes pride in the fact that most of his booters have never fit the "prototype" mold of an athlete — the one who always seems to do more on an athletic field than in a classroom. "As a coach, I never really thought that our players might be unique in the university's athletic scheme of things," said Bemis, "until one day back in the '60s. The Pitt Engineer called and asked permission to interrupt practice to take a picture of the engineering students who were on our team. I was amazed, I'll tell you, when more than three-quarters of the team turned out for that picture. That indicated the caliber of young people who were making our program.

JOHN O'HARA — Left school for Spirit

233

LAST ALL-AMERICAN — George Sommer in 1965

"Over the years, we've had players graduate and go on to be bankers, doctors, surgeons, politicans, corporation executives . . . the list could go on, and on. And there were some who went on to play professional soccer. Mark Nigh was the first to go with the Pennsylvania Stoners. Joe Luxbacher was with several pro teams, including the Spirit.

"Frank Bucci was a goalie with the Spirit and John O'Hara, who could have quite probably been a great college player here, captains the Spirit. Soccer players have gone on to great things. That's not only a credit to our program, but more so to the university . . ."

Thirty seasons of trying to promote soccer, find players and then trying to coax them to enter Pitt, find, then plead for, money to keep things together. Seeing it all about to fall apart, then somehow miraculously survive the hardest of economic times, Bemis has been through it all.

Bemis has categorized soccer at Pitt by decades.

"The '50s were filled with anticipation and some anxiety," recalled Bemis. "I can remember when I went to Hamilton, sort of hat in hand, almost begging him to consider giving soccer varsity status. It was agonizing to be rejected those first couple of years.

"But we got the green light. And we were fortunate — without the benefit of scholarships — to attract Bressanelli and others like Cherry, D'Amato, Wyatt and Zanicopoulus. I got $1,000 from Hamilton to start a varsity program. Not much, by today's standards. But, like I said, I had to make do.

"We got it off the ground, though. And that 1954 team — our first real varsity team — amazed everybody by turning in a spectacular 8-1 record. Grove City was the only school to beat us. On the plus side, we defeated Franklin & Marshall, Denison (twice), Slippery Rock (twice) and Ohio State, the Big 10 power of that era. We needed a great start. I think we might have even surprised ourselves."

Bemis grimaces as he recalls how he had to raid physical education classes, the football team, and any other place he could find a likely prospect to fill out a roster. "We took anybody who wanted to play," grinned Bemis, "soccer has always been a stepchild at Pitt for some reason. Kids weren't too sure they wanted to play soccer."

Bemis is a persistent sort, though. Out of a classroom came a rugged Irishman named Michael "Mickey" Culhane, a 29-year-old who needed an outlet to vent his unbridled energy. Culhane was good enough to make All-Pennsylvania-Delaware-New Jersey honors in 1954.

"Culhane was typical of the players we recruited in those early years," said Bemis. "He was in his late 20s when he came out. It didn't matter. He could have been an even greater player had he had the opportunity to play soccer earlier."

Almost a decade would pass before Bemis would have another Culhane-type Irishman playing at Pitt — Peter Smith, who learned the game in England. "We used to learn to play soccer from each other. That's where a guy like Smith helped so much," added Bemis.

Bemis likes to talk about raiding the football varsity for its kickers. "We got a few," he laughs, "Andy McGraw, Cuthbert and Ray Tarasi, all of them kicked for the football team. And they became great players for us, too."

In the 60s, Bemis thought he was seeing the light at the end of the tunnel. "We got three scholarships in 1961," related Bemis. "We got Reichenbach and Dave Shimpeno and they turned out to be excellent players. No, they were great players . . ."

Pitt made it to the NCAA playoffs in 1962 and again in 1965, only to lose to powerful East Stroudsburg, 2-1, on a late goal. "That game was played in Pitt Stadium. It was a muddy quagmire. But we had to play . . .," recalls Bemis, almost sadly.

Then Bemis' star, which began to soar to great heights, began to go down. "Money became tight. Soccer was again forced into the background," Bemis said. "I was looking to the '70s. The university was emphasizing sports and I thought we'd get in with it. But, it wasn't to be. We were a stepchild, again."

Cas Myslinski was now the athletic director. Again, a sympathetic ear was turned Bemis' way. Soccer would continue, but the budget wasn't big. Bemis was forced to find players in the classrooms and gym classes. By the skin of his teeth at times, Bemis made sure Pitt fielded a soccer team. A competitive team, at that.

"It runs in cycles," Bemis suggested. "I'm not unhappy here. I can't say I've ever been really unhappy. Frustrated, sure, unhappy, no."

Bemis vividly remembers his first Pitt team that played a strong amateur club, Beadling, on a snow-covered field that was lined off in black coal dust. He also remembers playing games and practicing at broken glass-laden Kennard Field in the Lower Hill. And he recalls dodging autos in Schenley Oval after practice. There were bad times, but there were also good times.

Memories of Pitt soccer, Bemis treasures them. He's 155-153-37 for his career. It's a good bet that Bemis can tell you something about every game Pitt played.

Highlights of the first 29 years. There were many.

"I guess the success we enjoyed in the 60s, and seeing soccer rise from a club team to a varsity sport, are the real highlights," Bemis says rather modestly. But there are others.

"The Stroudsburg playoff game will always stay with me, and so will the game against them, when we lost 1-0 to them at Oakmont," Bemis began. "Luxbacher's seven goals in a game has to rank in there. It was so easy. The Beadling game, I'll never forget."

How about great individual efforts?

"Again, there are many," nodded Bemis, his mind busy.

"I feel the greatest single game performance by a Pitt player was by Dave Shimpeno when we played Penn State and lost, 2-1. That was in the mid-60s and Penn State was a recognized national soccer power. Shimpeno — now the coach at Edinboro State College — scored our goal, but more important, he was all over the field playing like a man possessed. I've never seen anything to match it here."

Bemis recalls another gutsy effort, this one by Sommer — now a Swiss banker — in the '65 playoff game against East Stroudsburg. "Sommer had blood poisoning, but still played. He could have sat out, but he played. That was so unselfish . . .," Bemis said.

Where's Pitt soccer going? "Upward and onward, I hope," says Bemis hopefully. "I hope the '80s will bring a rebirth."

Pitt is still having success of sorts, although all-star caliber players are few and far between. The Panthers are enjoying success in the West Penn Conference where they notched the championship in 1981. Bemis still has a dream that he'll see the Panthers ranked among college soccer's elite before he's through coaching. "It can happen . . .," Bemis concluded, "under the right circumstances."

ALL-AMERICANS ALL!

JEROME BRESSANELLI
1956 and 1957

RONALD WYATT
1959 and 1960

GEORGE ZANICOPOULOS
1960

PAUL LIBERATI
1961 and 1962

Prince Put A Winning Smile On Pitt's Swimming Picture

By Eddie Beachler

"Swimming and diving are fun sports you can enjoy all your life."

Not many modern coaches attuned to the work-work-work syndrome would believe you can have fun and still win. That's what happened, however, during the Pat Corr era of Pitt swimming.

Not that Coach Corr was a funnyman. Far from it. He was a stickler for practice and discipline. It was just that, with swimmers like "Rapid Robert" Prince and the sing-and-swim quartet of the "Four Mermen," the Panthers were never without some waves of comedy and Eastern Intercollegiate Championships in the '30s.

"Rapid Robert," now a legend in swimming, broadcasting and toastmastering, scored both in and out of the Old Trees Pool — so named for millionaire oil wildcatter and benefactor Joe Trees, who boasted of being Pitt's first subsidized football player and sent the Pitt Band to the Rose Bowl in repayment.

On a bitter winter day, Prince arrived late — as usual — for practice in Trees, wearing a fur coat that was a mark of distinction on campus in those days of jazz, flappers, gold fish swallowers and stuffing guys in phone booths.

Coach Corr sternly chewed out Prince: "You're always late! Where the hell have you been?"

Prince flipped off his fur coat, revealing only swim trunks underneath, and informed the startled coach: "Hey, Pat, I'm ready!"

At the CCNY meet, "Rapid Robert" arrived with a cigarette dangling from his lips. Before Corr could admonish him for smoking, Prince yelled: "Here, Coach, hold this fag for me. I'll be back in 51 seconds." Which was close to Johnny Weissmuller's world record at the time in the 100 freestyle event.

Prince may be the best known of Pitt's swimmers because he's publicized his involvement through the years at so many sports banquets.

Prince, the original intercollegiate nomad who pursued an elusive diploma coast to coast, with stops at Stanford, Oklahoma and Harvard (law school), modestly admits "I never set any records until I reached Oklahoma and I paid my own way because I was an Army brat (son of a West Point officer)."

However, he saved his most celebrated performance for a high dive act from the balcony overlooking the Chase Hotel Pool in St. Louis when he was broadcasting Pirate games. He cleared a good 50 feet of concrete with his

BOB PRINCE — Swimmer and diver.

"Swannie" on a dare wager, noting "I'll do anything for twenty bucks."

Down through the years, 68 or so, Pitt has had more than its share of champions and championship teams. Short of Indiana, Ohio State, Princeton, Yale, Harvard and a few other powers, to be sure, but now rising fast on the national scale.

During the 1970s, under Coach Dick Bradshaw and the innovative development program of Athletic Director Cas Myslinski, the Panthers ruled as Eastern Collegiate Champions six consecutive years (1976-81), until they ran short of divers in 1982.

The men's team is coming on strong, with as many as eight qualifiers for NCAA in 1982; and the Pantherettes (lady swimmers) have made a big splash in a short decade, with more than their share of All-Americans.

Only one Panther has managed to grab an Olympic medal, Dr. Dick Rydze, and he is an adopted son — an NCAA national diving champion for Michigan from Mt. Lebanon, Pa. He won a silver in the 1972 Olympics. He was a daring diver, but not in the same sense as Prince.

DR. DICK RYDZE — Olympic medalist.

HEROIC RETURN — Anna Mae Gorman, left, a Pitt grad, gets welcoming parade along with Lenore Kight, upon return from competing in 1932 Olympics in Los Angeles.

Pitt claims him because he won it while attending Pitt Medical School. "I'm glad to be an adopted Panther," he will tell you. "I did all my practicing for the Olympics in Pitt's fantastic pool — it's the best indoor pool in the country."

Dr. Rydze had just come from the Pitt pool, located in the appropriately named Trees Hall, on a Sunday afternoon when he reminisced about his diving career:

"I was in the Olympics held in Munich when the Israelis were killed. It was hard to keep your mind on the Games with a terrible thing like that happening.

"I lost to Klaus Dibasi of Italy, who scored a record 504 points in the platform dive and the only diver to win the Olympics gold an unequalled four times. It was fairly close — he edged me by about six points.

"I still do a little diving for fun and am a board member of the Pennsylvania Special Olympics for Retarded Swimmers. I gave out the medals for the Western Pennsylvania Championships today and the kids were so happy."

Three more Panthers made it to the Olympics: Anna Mae Gorman-Lindberg (1932), who later picked up a B. S. in Social Work at Pitt; Angy Lopez and Orlando Catinchi (1980), who represented their native Puerto Rico.

Three Panthers have gained All-American honors: Stu Swanson (two years, backstroke); Jerry DeMuro, walk-on from New Jersey (distance free); and Pat Greenwell (diver).

Other NCAA qualifiers-Pitt record holders include: Sandy Pidgeon, another walk-on and son of Kiski Prep Headmaster; Jeff Trew, who succeeded despite injuries; Rick Carter, Ed Bergen, Ed La Noue, Greg Murphy, Geoff Emore, J. D. McCrillis, Jerry Zaleski, Mark Schuman, Mickey Termin, Dave Civis, Bob Greenwald, Orlando Catinchi, Scott Winkle, Scott Shearer.

In this same period, three Pantherettes achieved the feat of four-year All-Americans: Kathy Stetler (11 events), Suzanne Pulley (7 events) and Amy Jackson (7 events); thus, matching Tony Dorsett's achievement in football.

Stetler was Pitt's first woman national champion (50-yard fly) and Pulley won the J. Clyde Barton Award for academic-athletic achievement.

Some other A-A mermaids were Christy Elson, Patty Davis, Jan Ujevich, Sue Heon, Julie Terrell, Nancy Henry and Diana Firth.

Over the years, Panthers have climbed out of the pool to a wide variety of careers — dentists, doctors, lawyers, industrialists, union leaders. You name it.

It would seem to be fairly well established — the records are incomplete — that John T. Taylor, long-time secretary of the Allegheny Mountain Association and Mr. AAU, was

ALL-AMERICA WALK-ON Jerry DeMuro, right, talks swimming with Walt Young.

STAR SWIMMER James Underwood was honored as a Varsity Letterman of Distinction in 1967 along with Herb Stein, Elmer Lissfelt and Harvey Harman.

the first coach (1914-24) and J. A. Sweet, the first captain, who doubled as manager. Other pioneers were J. C. Hamilton III, Ken Lovejoy, W. W. Swope and W. H. McDiarmid, who presided as East Liberty Magistrate for many years.

Sue Taylor, the coach's daughter who succeeded him as AAU secretary and still was secretary in 1982 for what must be an AAU family record of some eight decades, recalls:

"In those days both men and women students had to swim one length in Trees pool to graduate. I helped Dad instruct the women and they were difficult because they didn't want to get their hair wet.

"Dad was U.S. swimming coach in the 1924 Olympics in Paris and coached Johnny Weissmuller to a gold, also Buster Crabbe in the 1928 Olympics in Amsterdam, and a U.S. women's team in the first Honolulu Championships in 1928."

Dr. Alan Kistler, one of a long string of swimmers to become dentists, claims the Pitt teams in the 1920s "were as good as there were anywhere in the country. We met all the good ones — Army, Navy, Syracuse . . . and only lost one or two away meets because you didn't get any breaks in scoring fancy diving and close finishes.

"The early teams were built up by swimmers from the club teams, such as Pittsburgh Natatorium, Soho Baths and the Braddock Y. Harry Taylor, son of the coach, was a one-man gang in 1918-19."

The late 1920s teams included Reginald (Pete) Bowen, a sprinter (1927) enroute to becoming a national sprint track champion; Dr. Elliott Brodie, a professional magician who pulled rabbits out of the hat when he wasn't pulling teeth; Dr. Harry Robb, a top college-pro football official; Buzz Wright; and Jim Underwood (1928 sprints), who sprinted to President and Board Chairman of Fortune 500 — Vulcan Industries, of Latrobe, Pa.

Dr. Homer Butts (1925 Captain), a rabid Panther all-sports rooter and dentist in that order, credits Pat Corr with being "one of the first real stars in distance events (1921-23)," he began coaching while attending Pitt Law School and built Pitt into an Eastern power with a half-dozen championships or runner-up finishes (1924-37) with very few tuition-only scholarships.

Russ Lindberg, stocky 1936 captain, was the dominating all-strokes star and holder of most of the Pitt and AAU records in that period, just a few seconds off Weissmuller's world marks.

Lindy was one of a number of Homestead Library AAU swimmers developed by Jack Scarry and steered to Pitt to fuel the championship drive. He married Anna Mae Gorman, Olympian member of Homestead Library's four-time national championship relays team, and their son Rusty later swam for Pitt.

Although earning BA and Master degrees in education, Lindy opted to become a steelworker in U.S. Steel's Irvin Works and climbed to secretary-treasurer of United Steelworkers Local Union 2227. He also has served as secretary of the Pitt Varsity Letter Club.

Lindberg has been a major force in the development of district swimming, as an AAU official and coaching the

PAT CORR — Distinguished coach.

1933-34 SWIM TEAM included (front row left to right) Schmieler, Geyer, Staweuk, Lindberg, Meyers, McQuillan, Hively. (Second row) Faust, Coach Corr, Jones, Lewis, Adelsberg, Denny, Hanna, Stinner, Madden, Lee, Ruhe. (Back row) McClayton, Crumime, Moore, Keck, Muzyk, Heid, Nelson, Chambers, Stiranka, Hoesett, Ballantyne.

first age-group teams of YMHA and Mt. Lebanon Aquaclub that spawned some 60 teams now producing a youth wave of outstanding swimmers.

Other Eastern champs of that period included divers John Carik and Dr. Harry Geyer, Herman Adelsberg, Bernie Lelake, Jack Hanna, Dr. Bill Lewis, Jim Lavine, Jack Riley, Tom Locke, Tom Anderson, Jack Denny, Ray Cogswell, Dr. George and brother Joe Schmeiler, Dr. Jim Patton, and Bill Ruhe, who went on to Annapolis and served as a Navy submarine commander in War II.

Onto the scene in the late 1930s came the "Four Mermen" — the greatest sing-and-swim quartet of Hymen and Milton Lederstein, Al Beacon and Al Slobodian. From the Hill District, they were teammates on Fifth Avenue High School's only City championship team and the Irene Kaufmann Settlement's Tri-State AAU Champs.

They were unbeatable in the relays, setting new records, and Milton Lederstein re-wrote the distance free marks, a superstar in his time.

As a team, this quartet sang, swam, joined the Army, entertained the troops and fought War II in Europe. Only to be broken up after the war when Hyman Lederstein married a French girl and became a leading fashion designer in Paris.

Ben Grady, a Michigan national diving champ, took over as Pitt coach for Corr who decided it was about time to be just a Pitt lawyer, from 1940 to 1966. He produced teams that won the Eastern championship seven times (five straight from 1952-56), were six time runners-up and the first undefeated team in 1948.

Some of the stars were Herb Cosgrove, Gus Wilde, divers Bill McQuillan and Bill Brown, Walter Nowatny, Dr. Richard Ames, Paul Brugger, Bill Grant, Mike Levine, Al Ciocca, Jim Zentgraf, Don Fanning, Ron Gainsford, Bill Furrer, Skip Monsein, Ed Robson, Ken Cooper, Charles Nance, Tony Sarsfield, Jerry Sollinger, Richard Rush, Joe Orloff, twins Ron and Rob Levine, Steve Ganong and Carl Warnes. Marty Kramer (1940-41) went on to become an Ar-

MILT LEDERSTEIN — Star on Pitt's swim team in the '30s. He was one of the most consistent winners on the Pitt varsity swimming team.

FOUR MERMEN — They swam together and sang together and joined the Army together. They were (left to right) Pitt swimmers Milt Lederstein, Hyman Lederstein, Al Slobodian, and Al Beacon.

1951-52 SWIM TEAM included (front row left to right) Coach Ben Grady, Tom Blosser, Walter Port, Bob Lepiane, Al Baran, Capt. Jim Zentgraf, Jules Melograne, Bob Gover, Bill Corr, Don Fanning, Al Ciocca, the assistant coach. (Second row) Charles Floyd, manager, Ronnie Gainsford, George Jennings, Jim Palmer, Dick Peterson, Fred O'Nions, Harry Piwowarski, John Marcosky, Roger McGill, trainer. (Third row) Macy Stein, Mervin Schrecongost, Gary Greer, Bill Furrer, Gerald Weiss, Charles Browne, Roy Kaupe.

my bomber pilot in Europe during War II and super star in the business world, climbing to President-Board Chairman of Gimbels department stores.

In the 1950s, a Pitt swim graduate, Jack Morris, went on to coach outstanding AAU teams at the Young Men-Women's Hebrew Association that scored in National Age-Group championship meets.

Pitt built its Olympic pool in 1962, designed by Coach Grady. But it wasn't until 1971, when Dick Bradshaw, graduate of powerhouse Ohio State, arrived that the swim program began to roll.

Bradshaw founded the Pitt Aquatic Club to develop young swimmers and provide a feeder program for both men and women varsity teams. Then, the next year (1972) he took over as head coach of both teams and Pitt was on its way up the national ladder.

The Panthers racked up their first undefeated season in 30 years in 1978 and Bradshaw moved up to the new position of Co-ordinator of Pitt Aquatics, Physical Education and Recreation Programs. Fred Lewis, 1970-72 distance champion and assistant coach, succeeded him as men's coach and Dave Belowich as women's coach.

Pitt now is moving into the Big East Conference with questionable manpower. Scholarships have been reduced from a dozen to half that number, but the Golden Panthers are mustering support. Pitt was picked as the site for the 1983 Big East Swim Championship.

As in other sports, and more so, swimming records are made to be broken. Coach Lewis points out "the kids today are swimming faster than Weissmuller when he was setting world records. Age-group teams are developing swimmers as early as six-year olds, plus weight lifting techniques like football, better nutrition, more pools, bigger bodies and daily practice."

The Pitt record and credits would be incomplete without citing the contributions of Vee Toner, the No. 1 lady sports chauvinist, and Emil Bonavita, a shot putter of considerable note. Toner was a tireless and persistent pioneer official in both swimming and tennis on the local and national level, along with being inducted as the only lady member of both the Curbstone Coaches (football) and Gus

DICK BRADSHAW Oversees swim programs.

TWIN TANKERS — Robert and Ronald Levine.

Fan Club (baseball), otherwise all-male, second-guessing Monday luncheon clubs when originally conceived. Bonavita, as Red Cross Water Safety Instructor, trained thousands and thousands of life guards and canoeists.

So, to put it all in perspective, the champs of the early years may be obscured by the times the kids are reeling off today. But the oldsters were every inch the champs, considering they had only the rivers, lakes and limited coaching — except for dedicated people working in other jobs — like the Taylors, Corrs, Scarrys, Lindbergs and others who coached part-time for the love of the sport.

One thing is sure. Unlike most other competitive sports that last only to the high school, college or pro level, swimming and diving are fun sports that you can enjoy and benefit from most of your life.

TREES POOL — One of nation's finest facilities.

PITT'S FANTASTIC OLYMPIC POOL has hosted a dozen major championship events. It has an 8-lane 50-meter course, 20-lane 25-yard course, electronic timing system, electronic scoreboard, diving complex of four boards and tower of three stands for events ranging from one to 10 meters, warmup pool and weight lifting room for training. The pool is in Trees Hall, appropriately named for millionaire oil wildcatter Joe Trees who donated the original Trees Pool-Gym in 1912.

Early Tennis Years Were Brightest During A Long Run In The Sun

By Paul G. Sullivan

"On the fine clay surfaces where the Cathedral of Learning now towers . . ."

The very first of a million or two tennis struggles that I have viewed involved two bigger, older neighbor boys, Russell Willison and Leon Arbach. They were playing hard — but for fun — on a clay court near my home in Shadyside, Willison with the sweeping top-spin drives termed "Lawfords" for the famous British racqueter who originated them, and Arbach with the chop-stroke that rarely wins championships, but has won many matches against players with fancier arsenals. As a matter of fact, I think Arbach had the edge that day, but I was then foggy on the scoring system and, too, on the score.

Somewhat later, I learned that Russ Willison was captain of the Pitt tennis team, but it wasn't until I began

TENNIS TEAM, 1907 CLASS — Captain Robert Weddell Bricker is in foreground, with Thomas Alan Miller, the manager at left, and James Roberts.

writing sports for the Pittsburgh Gazette Times in 1922 that I saw the Panthers in competition. That spring, on the fine clay surfaces where the Cathedral of Learning now towers, I covered the home contests of the varsity, coached by former Western Pennsylvania champion Dr. Tom Stephens and featuring small left-handers Jim Garroway and Shorty Cooper, through a season describable as satisfactory if unspectacular.

Meanwhile, before America's entry into World War I, there emerged, from Edgewood and the ranks of the Joe Duff-tutored Pitt football squad, wiry, tough Billy McEllroy, who parlayed speed of foot, a sharp forehand, and the invincible conviction that the power game was best into a sequence of triumphs that carried him to the West Penn title and to a five-set final loss to the great R. Norris Williams in a major tournament in Buffalo.

Those two pioneer tennis players — Willison and McEllroy — did themselves and their alma mater proud in after life. Willison became a respected real estate and banking executive and McEllroy received a Pitt medical degree, volunteer-coached the tennis team for a decade or so, and served a distinguished term as dean of the Pitt Medical School. More importantly and to my personal knowledge, both proved topflight men.

Over the past half-century, Pitt has scattered a score or more of especially formidable tennis players through its annals, but Pitt tennis hit its peak in the middle 1920s when, in the happy fall of 1924, Dave and John O'Loughlin arrived as freshmen from Westmont, near Johnstown, and Byron Baur enrolled from Erie. In the same draft, Jack Lauler entered Pre-Med from Duquesne Prep and not long afterward Henry Bourns transferred from Carnegie Tech.

Dave O'Loughlin had been National Boys' champion in 1922, and in 1923 he had fought the renowned George Lott, then National Junior titleholder, to five sets in the final of the National Junior Clay Court championship event at Indianapolis. Baur and John O'Loughlin were potent enough that Coach Stephens might have picked his number one man blindfolded without risk of weakening the head of his lineup, while Lauler and Bourns, alternating at No. 4 singles and in the doubles, rounded out a force that no district opponent could rival.

Following a perfect freshman campaign in 1925, the O'Loughlin-Baur-Lauler-Bourns troop whipped into its 1926 varsity debut by sweeping all 13 of its matches with every district foe plus West Point, Rutgers, Syracuse, Colgate, Bucknell, and Dickinson from the East. No victim, except the Alumni, amassed more than two individual victories in a team match, while five, including West Point, Colgate, Syracuse, Bucknell, and Allegheny, were shut out.

Regrettably, that powerful Panther array fell to a 5-4-1 record in 1927. Loss of their home courts to excavators for

DR. WILLIAM S. McELLROY

THE REAL McELLROY — As Billy McEllroy, he captained the Pitt tennis team in 1971, and later coached the team in the '20s and '30s, before becoming, as Dr. William S. McEllroy, dean of Pitt's School of Medicine. As player from Edgewood, front row left, he sat with teammate Herbert Lytel. Standing, left to right, were Charles Gaut of Irwin, the manager, and Walter Flood of Pittsburgh.

the Cathedral of Learning sent the unconditioned netmen off to an opening setback at Ohio State. Came then a jolting 3-3 tie with Dickinson and reverses at Navy, Penn, and Yale.

The disappointments of '27 were followed in 1928 by Dave O'Loughlin's withdrawal from sport for his first rugged year in Med School, so that neither then nor ever since did a Pitt tennis crew attain the memorable peak of those splendid sophomores of 1926.

Of the O'Loughlins, John, the eldest, was the steadiest off both forehand and backhand. His tremendously effective game was developed as a foil for the terrific forehand drive of middle brother Dave. John's service, overhead, and volley were more consistent than menacing, but off the ground he handled everything thrown at him and he played each point as if it were for win or lose. He was alert to pounce on medium-short returns to force his way to the net where, like the immortal "Little Bill" Johnston, he seemed invariably to be in position to put the ball away simply because his tactic induced weak enemy returns. He was equally rough two decades after becoming a successful dentist.

Year in and year out, point in and point out, Dave O'Loughlin's forehand drive was as hard and deep as any

I've seen or failed to cope with. "Big Bill" Tilden taught him the basic stroke and Dave adapted it to near perfection to his stocky build that allowed him maximum power in meeting the ball close to shoulder-high at the top of its natural trajectory. Dave, who became a fine surgeon in the obstetrical and gynecological fields, stayed with victorious tennis until his sudden death in 1955 not long after winning his fifth West Penn singles championship more than a quarter-century after his first.

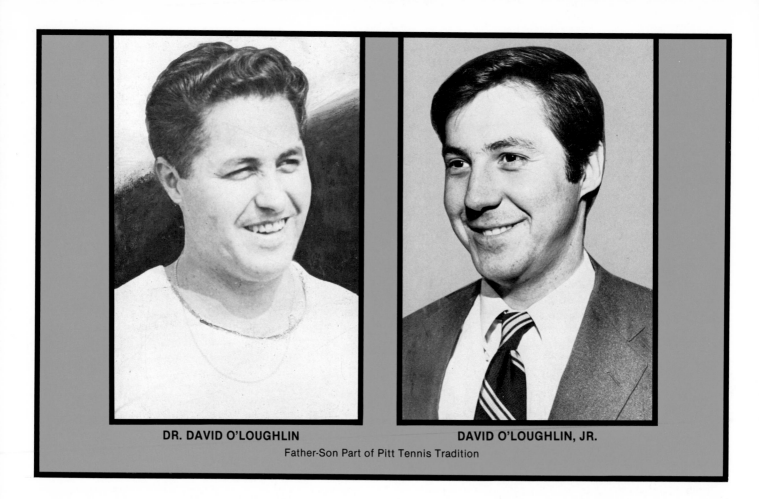

DR. DAVID O'LOUGHLIN   **DAVID O'LOUGHLIN, JR.**

Father-Son Part of Pitt Tennis Tradition

There was also a third Panther O'Loughlin. Youngest brother Billy, who arrived on the campus to help fill the void created by the loss of Dave and John, was another forehand slugger despite a frame packing scarcely 100 pounds — sometimes less! Like Dave, he hit for murder and no way would he concede superiority to his family elders. He was a recognized factor in junior tennis at home and nationally and though his varsity years were less scintillating than his brothers, he won more than his share.

Still a leader of the Erie Bar and a prime figure in the tennis colony of his area, Byron Baur is recalled at Pitt as a player who achieved Western Pennsylvania title stature as a young man with a variety of weapons employed intelligently to maximum effect. He was crisp and sharp with all the standard shots, but his real strength lay within himself: indomitable determination, total concentration, and confidence regardless of the opposition. "By" Baur never beat himself, never fell into streaks of needless errors. He was a member of the memorable trio of '26.

Besides 1926, Pitt's most notable net seasons may have been 1925, the senior campaign of Arnold Silverman, first of several crack young men from Baltimore to blossom at the university; 1939, when indefatigable Joe Kristufek from McKeesport paced a well-balanced squad; 1949, the heyday of powerful Johnny Lohstoetter and Stan Weil; and 1972 in which veteran Gary Schwartz captained freshmen Joe Kantor, Tom Currant, and George Dieffenbach to the Panthers' most impressive latter-day record.

The 1925 outfit went undefeated, its nine wins dimmed only by two ties with a formidable W. & J. foe featuring basketball sharpshooter Stump Friedrichs and a draw with surprising Bucknell. No. 1 ace Silverman lived by the chop and the slice — and he lived well indeed by them. He was a

likely victor at the head of the line-up and in an era of only four singles and two doubles to the match, a consistent winner atop the singles was a whopping percentage of the battle.

Dr. Billy McEllroy had succeeded Dr. Stephens as volunteer coach as the 1920s waned and by 1939 he had passed the baton to Dr. Dave O'Loughlin. Kristufek, a cross-country competitor, could run all morning to warm up for all afternoon. His stout legs carried him and a good part of the '39 tennis team to an 11-2 mark for an eminently gratifying spring performance with abetment of Frank Harmuth, Ed Goedhring, Bob Burns, and a sound sophomore supporting cast. Kristufek, by the way, would soon distinguish himself as a World War II Navy bomber pilot with one of the lengthiest tours of combat duty in the annals of the Pacific.

Dave O'Loughlin held the post-war helm to steer the Lohstoetter-Weil 1949 crew to 11 triumphs against two reverses. Blond, husky Lohstoetter mounted the diversified guns of the "big game". His service leaped at you, his forehand smoked, his backhand streaked or spun, and his overhead and volley were lethal. On the district varsity front, he had no takers; in the open events, his few setbacks were accomplished mainly by such guile and artifice as change of pace and spin and the crafty delivery of junk. He was a player after Dave O'Loughlin's own heart. Ohio State early and Penn State late stopped the '40 force, but ran for their lives to do it.

Coach Fran Webster's 1972 team turned in an astounding 11-2 achievement in the wake of probably the all-time Pitt tennis low point of 13 defeats in the 15 contests of 1971. With Schwartz lending experience and balance to the largely yearling '72 line-up and the Kantor-Currant-Dieffenbach axis contributing sustained punch, the season was notable for its sequence of happy decisions that a less resolute approach would have blown. Remarkably, the brace of beatings were beauties — 9-0 to old nemesis Bucknell and the same scouring to Kent State!

It is interesting and surely fair to chronicle that in the seasons between the glory years sketched above, a considerable batch of excellent, even brilliant, Pitt tennis redoubtables enjoyed impressive days in court. Most outstanding of these was Eddie Jacobs, a nationally reputed southpaw, who arrived from Baltimore to overlap the final year of the tenure of Dave O'Loughlin after Dave's sit-out season while acclimating to medical school.

The 1929 team, however, despite availability of such talents as Jacobs, O'Loughlin, Lou Levin, Milt Cohen, Morton Baker, Gyp Wunderlich, and Tom Hadden, proved unable to put it together for better than a 7-5 record, punctuated by losses to Notre Dame, Penn, Swarthmore, Georgetown, and Navy. Jacobs, subsequently chosen for the United States Davis Cup squad, owned excellent weaponry all around, but his Pitt years were not productive of historic team results.

In the early and mid-1930s, several strong, well remembered Panthers shone individually on teams with no better than modest over-all accomplishments to prove two propositions: first, Pitt dominance of the home scene and, second, the fact that college tennis in the Pittsburgh area has never generated enough top-to-bottom class to challenge effectively the eastern and western court giants favored by proximity to bottomless talent pools and often by jet-pressured recruiting.

Eddie Jacobs was followed by his right-handed, somewhat less gifted kid brother Bill, whose nicely rounded style stoutly pulled its weight in the boat along with the blasts of Billy O'Loughlin. Nat Ganger, a clever, tenacious Clevelander, sliced and volleyed to assure critical wins that kept team totals on the upper side.

But special accolade must be reserved for three products of the West Penn junior development program: Eddie Alcorn from Dormont High School, Paul Steele of Shady Side Academy, and Bobby Madden, son of Pitt's Law School dean, J. Warren Madden, whose elder boy, Joe, likewise added materially to Panther potency.

Year in and year out and for three decades after graduation, Alcorn stacked up numerous victories with an upper-moderate paced forehand that raked opponents to distraction. An also moderate, well-placed service and a consistent, sliced backhand completed Eddie's armament; he had small taste for the net environs and little need in most situations to worry about getting there.

Steele, today an esteemed orthopedic surgeon practicing in the wake of an illustrious father, and also the Steelers' team doctor, was one of the smartest tennis and squash racquet players ever turned out in Pittsburgh. He overwhelmed no one and fed problems to every one. Medium-sized and sturdy, he exploited the three famous Tilden variables: pace, length, and spin. I watched him, maybe a dozen years out of Pitt, pick Johnny Lohstoetter apart in the latter's best tournament season. In addition, his steadiness, accuracy, and sharp net play rendered him an ideal doubles partner.

Madden was the sharpshooting flash par excellence. His shots were classic. His hard-hit serve mixed spin and slice, his groundstrokes were sound, brisk, and well angled off both sides, and he dearly coveted the net, to which he regularly advanced under authoritative service.

Let me wind up with acclaim of two latter-day Pitt tennis standouts. Dave O'Loughlin, Jr., now a lawyer and civic figure, honored his revered parent by registering 10 singles wins to one loss in 1962, while his teammates, Joe Brown, Jr., racked up nine and two. Without his dad's blistering power, Davy unloads all the shots with sound court sense and the family competitiveness. Brown, an uncompromising flat blaster, forehand and backhand, lacked only mobility in his quest for pre-eminence. Joe had the psyche and a dash of the ground equipment of Ellsworth Vines, which is to proclaim it all of a congenital hitter.

The current team is coached by George Dieffenbach, a former member of the team.

In seven seasons, his teams have posted a record of 48 wins and 44 losses. The team went 7-7 in the spring of '82, with Steve Berkovitz of McKeesport the team MVP with an 8-5 singles record. D. J. Mariano was 9-4.

Dieffenbach, who is from Williamsport, was one of Pitt's finest players, achieving a 32-13 record in singles, and 24-20 in doubles under Coach Webster. He is now pursuing a Ph.D. in Pitt's School of Education.

He also coordinates women's tennis at Pitt. "Our goal is to develop, improve, and make each program competitive," said Dieffenbach.

So that's my freehand sketch of Pitt tennis. More could have been said, but at least, I think, what has been said should have been said. The writing has aroused pleasant memories for the writer.

JOE KRISTUFEK & FRIEND — McKeesport's Joe Kristufek, who competed in three different sports for Pitt in late '30s and captained the tennis team, now operates indoor tennis facility in Grosse Pointe, Mich., where he was host to international tennis star Bjorn Borg.

Track & Field Teams Took Honors In Every Respect Through The Years

By Bob Smizik

"I knew if I got a good education I'd make it in the world."

— Herb Douglas

Aside from football, and possibly basketball, no athletic program has brought more national glory to Pitt than track, a sport that never really caught on with the public in Western Pennsylvania but one that took the Panthers to the heights.

The big years for Pitt track began in the mid-1920s under Frank Shea, who himself had been a star Panther runner and later an Olympian, and continued onward and upward when Carl Olson was recuited out of Indiana high school circles to succeed Shea in the early 30's. Under Olson, Pitt track was a national power, producing countless IC4A titles, several NCAA champions and two Olympic medals.

When Olson stepped down, forced out by age, Pitt track never again was the same. Though there were still many individual successes, and another Olympian, budgetary restrictions turned a national program into a regional one.

Track began at Pitt somewhere around the turn of the century, but didn't approach a big-time status for another 20 years. Jock Sutherland was the captain of the 1917 and 1918 teams, at which time Shea came on the scene to help vault the Panthers into national prominence.

An Irwin native, Shea won the AAU championship in 1917 and three years after that was a member of the Olympic team, competing in the 440-yard dash. The famous Andy Kerr was coaching the track team in 1921, but two years later he gave way to Shea, who was studying to be a lawyer, and Pitt was on its way.

Gibby Welch, the all-time football great, was an early Pitt track hero. Welch scored 71 points during the 1926 season competing in the shot put, discus, javelin and broad jump. During that season Welch broke Sutherland's discus record with a throw of 141-8 3/8. Welch also set the Pitt javelin record.

Teammates of Welch, as Pitt began to get national attention, were pole vaulter Vic Pickard and hammer thrower Don Gwinn.

Pickard was captain of the Canadian Olympic team in 1928. Gwinn represented the United States the same year. Quarter-miler Pete Bowen was considered a prime candidate for the U.S. team, but injured his back the night before the trials. A top sprinter on the team was Ken Wibecan.

The late 20s brought Everett Utterback to the Pitt campus and this was to begin one of the great success stories of Panther athletics.

Utterback, a black man, was a baseball player in his native Mayfield, Ky. and it was a strange road that brought him to Pitt.

"I had never even seen a track meet until I left Kentucky," said Utterback. "I went to Lincoln University for one year but had to drop out of school for lack of funds. I went to New York to work and in my free time played some baseball. One day I was shagging balls and a guy watched me and asked if I wanted to try out for his track team."

The guy was Hunter Johnson, a former Pitt trainer. When he saw what Utterback could do he sent him off to Pitt where a track scholarship awaited him.

"I guess they'd call me a decathlete today," said Utterback. "My best events were the broad jump and the hop, step and jump. But I also competed in the 100, 200, high jump, pole vault and shot put. In dual meets I'd usually win the dashes, the long jump and the pole vault. Sometimes I'd win the high jump, too."

Utterback, who later became a lawyer and Pitt's first black trustee, remembers his Pitt days well.

"Pitt was a different type of place then," he said. "It was bigoted and discriminatory. A black fellow had a real difficult time back then. When you went out of town to compete you often couldn't stay at the same hotel with the rest of the team. But Coach Shea settled that in a very neat way. He'd register the entire team and then come out and give me a key."

In 1931, when Shea appointed Utterback captain of the track team — thus making him Pitt's first black captain — there was an uproar on campus.

As Utterback remembers it, "The athletic department didn't want to ratify my appointment. They put all kinds of pressure on Shea to appoint someone else and he wouldn't do it. The Pittsburgh Courier and the NAACP got into it. There was quite a lot of publicity and finally Shea decided to send out ballots and let the team vote.

GOOD OL' DAYS — Ray Tinsley pole vaulting at Schenley Oval.

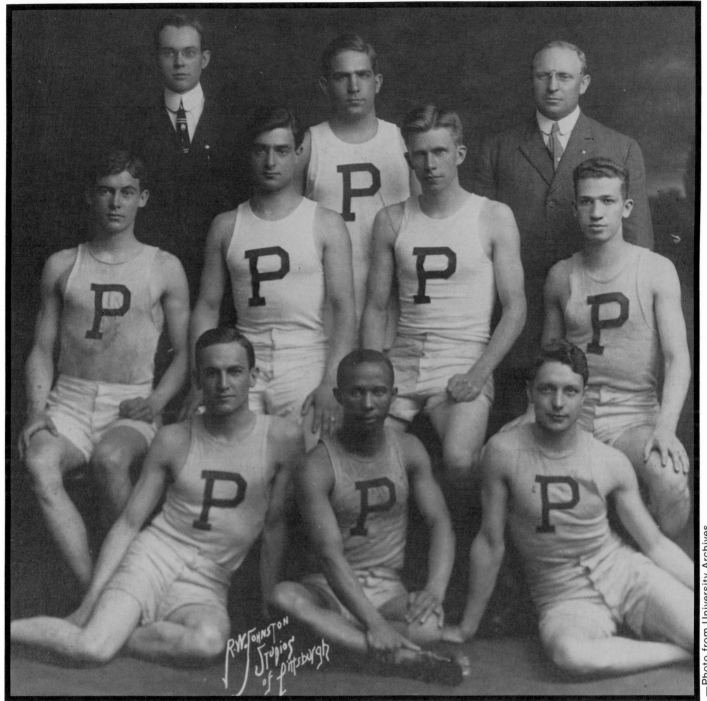

THOMPSON'S TROOPS — Col. Joe Thompson, rear right, and his 1911 track team.

"According to Shea, I was unanimously elected captain of the team."

Shea was gone two years later and Utterback thinks to this day that he was pressured out because of the racial issue. Others, however, say that Shea, a part-time coach, wanted to devote more time to his law practice.

Utterback gets a chuckle out of the event that followed Shea's departure.

"They went to Froebel High in Indiana and brought in Carl Olson," he said. "He brought half of his black track team with him. He turned out to be just as liberal as Shea."

Shea left his mark at Pitt and on the men he coached. "He insisted that you conduct yourself in a gentlemanly manner at all times," said Woody Harris. "His main concern was to make a gentleman out of you."

It worked with Harris, who never put on a track shoe until he came to Pitt and who only went out for the team to get out of a swimming class. After a fine Pitt career, as a long jumper, high jumper, pole vaulter and sprinter, Harris became a dentist and still practices in the Ambridge area.

It was during these years that Pitt began what was to become a successful trek to the prestigious Penn Relays. "On paper we had the best relay team in the world," said Harris, who grew up in East Liberty. "Our times were the best. But something always happened and we didn't win."

That was to change under Olson, a driven man who drove his athletes even harder.

"He wouldn't accept anything but your best," said former Pitt Athletic Director Frank Carver.

247

JOHN WOODRUFF — Pitt's only Olympic gold medalist

By the mid-30s Olson had molded a phenomenal relay team, one that won 13 Penn Relay championships.

The key to Olson's relay teams was John Woodruff, the great Olympic half-mile champion.

Herb Douglas, who won the bronze medal in the broad jump in the 1948 Olympics and who is a real student of Pitt track history, knew those relay teams well.

"They didn't have a real fast team but they didn't have to with Woodruff running last," said Douglas.

What they lacked in speed, they had in heart.

Frank Ohl opened up for Pitt and won eight Penn Relay championships in his three years. "He brought the baton home first every time," said Carver. "He was short and he didn't mind going into the pack at the first turn. He went in with his elbows spread wide."

Al Ferrara ran second on many of those championship relay teams. "I used to kid him and say he was the slowest man in Pitt track history," said Carver. "But he wouldn't give up the lead."

Claude McKee and Larry Tregonning often were third and responsible for giving the baton to the great Woodruff, who either opened up a large lead or caught some less talented individual from behind.

Olson always had great sprinters around. Dick Mason and Art Thomas, both graduates of Pittsburgh's Oliver High, were IC4A champs in the 30s and Orville Fleming, now a doctor, was another excellent sprinter as were Bill Carter and Hap Stickel, who later coached at Army.

A team of Carter, Stickel, Al Peretic and Bob Smith won the Millrose Games mile relay with a time of 3:25.5 in 1942.

Olson's next truly great performer was Douglas, who came to Pitt on a football scholarship in 1946 but who was already well-known to Olson.

"I went to Xavier (New Orleans) for my first year of college in 1941," remembered Douglas. "and we won the 440-yard relay at the Penn Relays. Pitt was the team that finished second."

Douglas scored a touchdown against Notre Dame the first time he carried the ball, going more than 50 yards for the score, but once they saw what he could do in track there was to be no more football for him.

Douglas won IC4A titles in the indoor and outdoor broad jump and in the 100-yard dash in his first year at Pitt. He continued to win broad jump titles but never again won in the dash at the IC4As. He also won three AAU broad jump championships. He took a second in the NCAAs as a sophomore but did not compete the next two seasons because of illness and injury.

It was the injury, a pulled muscle, that made a lot of people think Douglas wouldn't make the Olympic team. One of those people was Olson.

"I'd always had a personality clash with Olson," said Douglas. "I loved the guy for what he did for track, but we had trouble getting along. He was never technical enough for me.

"I'd run a race and not do well and the first thing he'd say to me was, 'What happened?' I would say to him, 'You tell me what happened.' "

When Douglas pulled his muscle in 1948, he had to drop out of the IC4As and the NCAAs. "Olson counted me out," he said.

"He'd go up to Schenley Oval every day with Clarence Doak (an Olympic candidate in the intermediate hurdles) and leave me back at the stadium to work out on my own.

"I was having trouble with my form so I went to see Ben Grady, the swimming coach. He worked with me every day, bless him. We really got together and hit on a method to get me higher, like a diver — that took me to the Games."

As for Olson, he was, according to Douglas, "too embarrassed to talk to me."

In later years Olson and Douglas patched up their mini-feud. "He was a great coach and did ever so much for track in Pittsburgh," said Douglas, a vice-president with Schieffelin & Co., a wine and spirit importer in New York.

FIELD STARS OF THE '30s

EMIL BONAVITA   CHARLES GONGLOFF
At Old Trees Field

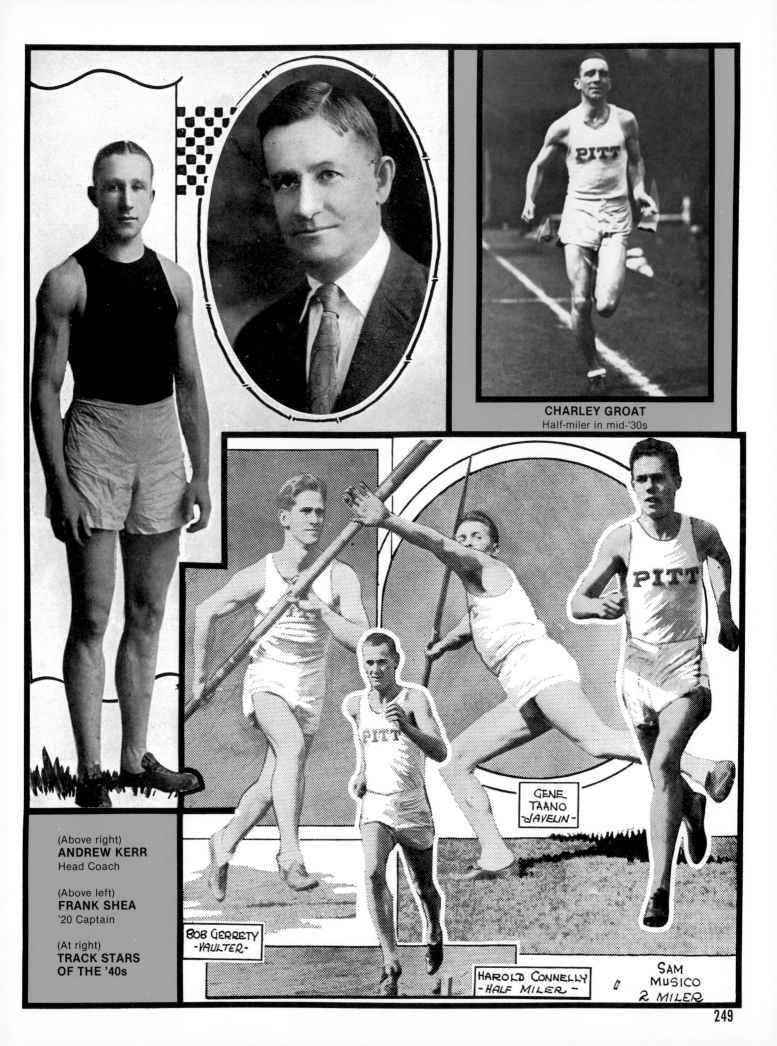

CHARLEY GROAT
Half-miler in mid-'30s

(Above right)
ANDREW KERR
Head Coach

(Above left)
FRANK SHEA
'20 Captain

(At right)
TRACK STARS
OF THE '40s

BOB GERRETY
-VAULTER-

GENE
TAANO
-JAVELIN-

HAROLD CONNELLY
- HALF MILER -

SAM
MUSICO
2 MILER

249

CRACK RELAY TEAMS — 1941 relay team included, left to right, Bill Carter, Larry Tregonning, Del Anderson and Harold "Hap" Stickel.

Coach Carl Rees poses with gun over Pitt's one-mile relay team that included, left to right, Zinnerford Smith, Jay Moody, Vince Wojner and Mel Barnwell.

Douglas cherishes his track records and his Olympic medal, but he cherishes his education even more. "All I wanted was a good education," he said. "I knew if I got a good education I'd make it in the world."

Olson had dozens of excellent athletes in his years at Pitt. Javelin throwers Charley Gongloff and Gene Taano are two and sprinter Herb Carper and half miler John Wilson two others.

The magnificent Arnie Sowell, an Olympic half-miler, took Pitt back to the heights in the 50s, but by the time Olson left, the track program had started downhill. Pitt could no longer compete with the major track powers. The money wasn't there to keep the program big time.

Carl Rees, his assistant, succeeded Olson in 1959 and stayed through 1966.

Sprinter Bill DelVecchio, an oral surgeon today, was probably the most outstanding performer of Rees' era. He finished fourth in the 100 yard dash in the NCAA championships, coming out the bottom man in a four-way photo finish.

Mel Barnwell, another sprinter, finished fifth in the NCAAs and Dan Kanell, an orthopedic surgeon today, placed in the discus.

Joe Friend and Luddy Hayden, hurdlers who also competed in the broad jump and relays, were key men for Rees' teams in dual meet competition.

Ill health and a decision to change philosophy away from dual meets and to relay competition, caused Rees to give up the job in 1966. Jim Banner, who ran for Olson in the late 40s and early 50s, and who assisted Rees from 1961-1964, was his successor.

Pitt track picked up under Banner. He brought in Jerry Richey, who became the youngest runner ever to break the four minute barrier in the mile and who won an NCAA championship at two miles. Richey, a lawyer today in the firm of Buchanan, Ingersoll, Rodewald, Kyle & Buerger, also anchored a distance medley relay team that set a world record of 9:39.7 and won an NCAA championship. Other members of the team were Ken Silay, Smitty Brown and Mike Schirko.

Bryant Salter was a football standout but also an All-American in track in the high jump and triple jump.

"If he hadn't played football and could have concentrated on it, he would have been a great decathlon man," said Banner.

Javelin thrower Dan Kouvolo was another great under

| EVERETT UTTERBACK | FRANK OHL | BILL REA | HERB DOUGLAS |

LONG JUMPERS

CARL OLSON　　　　**CARL REES**　　　　**JIM BANNER**　　　　**MIKE AGOSTINELLA**

Banner, but there could be no athlete in Banner's time who accomplished more than Bill Rea, an eight-time IC4A champ and a seven-time NCAA All-American in the long jump.

Rea was a world-class performer who had Olympic aspirations. Trying out for the 1972 Olympic team, Rea was in third place with a jump of 26-1. "He had a jump earlier of 25-10," said Banner, "and he took off a foot behind the board."

Rea looked like a sure shot to make the team. But in the closing stages of the event was beaten out by a jump of 26-1½.

He lost his spot on the Olympic team by a half-inch.

Banner and Rea talked afterwards. "I don't know what a coach says to an athlete at a time like this," said Banner.

To which, Rea replied, "I'll tell you what an athlete says to a coach: I'll be back in four years."

It would be a great story to say that he was, but he wasn't. Dental school studies kept him from devoting full time to his practice.

But it's a greater story to say that he was back eight years later. The competitive fires burned deep within Bill Rea. Though the American team was boycotting the 1980 Olympic Games, he was eligible for the Austrian team, hav-

ing been born in that country while his father was serving in the military.

Rea put his dentistry aside and went back into full-time training, competing throughout Europe. When the 1980 Olympics were held in Moscow the American team was home but one American was there.

Bill Rea didn't win a medal for Austria, but his story is an incredible one.

Banner left to become athletic director at Carnegie-Mellon in 1975 and was succeeded by Mike Agostinella.

Agostinella has produced three NCAA All-Americans, quarter-miler Karl Farmer, triple jumper Larry Kinney and half-miler Darren Garren. Distance runners Mel Boyd and Dave McDonald, miler Nick Martin and high jumpers Dan Goodyear, Keith Taylor and Tim Riley are other standouts who performed for Agostinella.

The track program today is dramatically different from the days of Shea and Olson.

"We concentrate on middle distance events," said Agostinella. "We haven't had a dual meet in four years. We don't actively recuit people in the fields events. In our situation you have to pick an area and go in that direction. We picked the area where we thought we had the greatest tradition."

DAN KOUVOLO　　　　**DAN GOODYEAR**　　　　**ARNIE SOWELL**　　　　**GARY MECKLEY**

POINT-GETTERS

BILL DELVECCHIO

BRYANT SALTER

WES KING

MEL BARNWELL

JIM DONAHUE

LARRY KINNEY

DAN KANELL

KARL FARMER

STEVE HEIN

ARNIE SOWELL

"He was a good-will ambassador for Pitt at the Olympic Games."
—Carl Olson

ARNIE SOWELL . . . one of the greatest middle-distance runners in the world.
He was the pride of Pitt and Schenley High School.

By Jim O'Brien

arl Rees re-wound the film reel in a dimly-lit room at Pitt's Trees Hall physical education complex atop Cardiac Hill. He wanted to watch, just once more, the film of Arnie Sowell finishing fourth in the 800 meter run at the Olympic Games in Melbourne, Australia in November of 1956.

It's a result that still causes Rees, who was the assistant to Carl Olson with Pitt's track and field team at the time, and anyone who closely followed Sowell's collegiate career, to shake his head in disbelief.

"Arnie Sowell was one of the greatest runners who ever lived," remarked Rees, who later became the head coach of the sport at Pitt, and remains a physical education instructor there today. "He had such great range. He could run from a quarter to five miles. Nobody did it all as well."

When needed, Sowell could also be called upon to compete in the high jump or long jump, if it meant more points to the Pitt total in a dual meet. He anchored all the key relay teams for the Panthers.

At nearby Schenley High School, Sowell had been a hurdler and high jumper on the track team, and an outstanding swimmer.

He turned to track, in the first place, because he couldn't beat one of his buddies in swimming at Schenley, and once he switched sports he excelled. He was a natural. Once he realized just how good he was he dreamed of running in the Olympic Games.

Sowell was regarded as one of the greatest middle-distance runners in the world. Going into the Olympic Games, he was co-holder of the world's 1000-yard run record at 2:08.8 minutes, had been the 1C4A half-mile champion the past three years, and the NCAA and National AAU half-mile king the previous two seasons.

His main competition was Tom Courtney of Livingston, N.J., who ran for Fordham. Sowell had beaten Courtney many times, but mostly indoors. Courtney had his number outdoors, however, and beat him in the Olympic Trials. So Sowell was seeded second behind Courtney in the handicapping for the 800 meter run at the Olympics.

In "Chariots of Fire," the inspirational English movie — about two Olympic athletes — that won the Academy Award as the "best movie" for 1981, nothing goes wrong! Nobody gets injured or kidnapped or broken-hearted before the big games.

Sowell shared the ambitions of the real-life athletes depicted in that movie, Eric Liddell and Harold Abrahams, who "ran with hope in their hearts, and wings on their heels." Said Sowell: "The Olympics are all you hope for . . . and more."

But everything went wrong for Sowell. After he qualified for the Olympics, Sowell took several weeks off from his training. He took a job at a recreation center in The Hill, and sprained an ankle playing basketball with the youngsters.

"He wasn't able to train and condition himself properly prior to the Games," recalls Rees.

"Then it turned up a cold and rainy day in Melbourne, and they were running on a crushed-brick track. A light guy like Arnie — he only weighed about 135 pounds, and he was 5-11 — was at a disadvantage on a wet, heavy track like that. It's the same way in a horse race, I'm told."

Sowell set the pace until the stretch run, but he finished fourth. "A blanket could have covered all four men at the

DYNAMIC DUO — Sowell sprints by Tom Courtney in one of their countless head-on duels.

finish line," wrote Les Biederman of The Press. "But Sowell was fourth. It was a heart-breaking effort for the 21-year-old Pitt star."

Upon his return to Pittsburgh, Sowell said, "I ran the race I planned just the way I figured it out. I wanted to set the pace and I did. I felt when the time came in the stretch to call on something extra, I'd be ready.

"But this time, when I called on my reserve, it just wasn't there. I have no regrets. I ran the best I knew how and it simply wasn't good enough.

"Many people now are critical of me for setting the pace but they weren't critical of me when I was winning back here. I'd rather lose a race in exceptional time than win a slow one. If we ran this race again tomorrow, I'd run it the same way."

Courtney caught Sowell in the stretch and proved stronger at the finish. Courtney captured the gold medal.

Following the Olympics, Sowell beat Courtney at least eight straight times on indoor tracks, including a record-breaking effort at 880 yards in the Millrose Games at Madison Square Garden in February of 1957. But Sowell

lost all five races they ran outdoors the previous year, including the biggest race of them all at Melbourne.

"I had to admire him for what he did," says Courtney now. "It was a mistake to run the way he did, but he decided to go for it. He could have finished second, I'm sure, but he wanted to win. He made a valiant attempt. I think it was worth the try."

Courtney resides in Sewickley these days, and commutes to his downtown Pittsburgh office where he's an investment counselor for Federated Investors, a money market fund.

Courtney recalls the race:

"I took the lead initially, then Sowell took over. He led most of the way. I had planned on sprinting the last 80 meters. With 140 meters to go, Sowell took off in a sprint.

"I knew that, at the pace we had been going at, there was no way he could sustain that pace. Then I thought, 'My gosh, here we are in the Olympics. I wonder if he could go all the way.' So I chased after him. After I went by him, he was tying up (muscles pulling). He had run his sprint, and I had run my sprint, and I was tying up, too. Then Derek Johnson, from England, came up on the inside and went by us both.

"Somehow, someway I was able to reaccelerate, though I was totally spent. I was able to catch Johnson and stagger across the finish line. I mis-ran the race, but I couldn't take the chance of letting Sowell go. Sowell was the man I had to beat; he was my competition."

Johnson finished second, with Auden Boyson of Norway third.

"It was a terrible track that day; it was so soft," recalled Courtney. "There's no question it had a more adverse affect on Arnie. He was 5-11, 135. I was 6-2, 185. He was better on the boards indoors because he was such a light runner, in weight and the way he hit the track. He had an effortless type of running style."

Their competition was a long and great one, and both gained entry into the Track & Field Hall of Fame.

"I first ran into Arnie in my junior year (1954) in the IC4A Championships," recalled Courtney. "At that time I had about 10 wins in a row and was regarded as the favorite. I always thought I had a great kick. Sowell went by me at one point in the race, as we went into the backstretch. I thought, 'I ought to go by him now. I'll out-kick him at the finish.' Well, I kicked and I couldn't quite catch him. That was the first of many defeats to Arnie Sowell.

"I remember being startled by that. At the time, he was a relative unknown. But I got to know him pretty well after that, and so did everybody else in the world. I had to revamp my training techniques to beat him, and by doing so I set Olympic and world records."

In 1979, Courtney joined Sowell and Lon Spurrier, another world class American half-miler on that 1956 Olympic team, for a reunion lunch in San Francisco. Sowell also recalls the get-together.

"I'm pleased with what I accomplished," said Sowell, who retired in 1979 after 23 years of military service as a lieutenant colonel in the U.S. Army, and resides in Pacifica, Calif., a suburb to the south of San Francisco. He's working now as a materials manager with Dalmo Victor, a firm that makes early-warning systems for military aircraft.

"I'm somewhat disappointed in not going as far as I had hoped to go. My goal was to become the Olympic champion, to be what Tom Courtney became. But we can only have one of them and he won," said Sowell.

PITT'S CRACK 2-MILE RELAY TEAM included, from left to right, Jim Moore, Wendy Harford, Perry Jones and anchorman Arnie Sowell.
—From the University Archives

LONELINESS OF THE MIDDLE-DISTANCE RUNNER. Arnie Sowell attracted as many as 50,000 for track and field meets in Los Angeles, and upwards of 20,000 in Philadelphia and New York. But few cared in his hometown of Pittsburgh. Judge John Brosky, at right, a former Panther track standout, always showed up and helped officiate the meets, along with Art and Vee Toner, and a few other similarly dedicated individuals.

Asked about the problems, with the pre-Olympics injury he suffered, and how the track surface wasn't in his favor, Sowell said, "I always worked as a recreation counselor each summer, and I got into a pick-up basketball game. I was going for a rebound and I came down hard and tore ligaments in my ankle. I was on crutches for awhile, and missed a lot of training. There was some question as to whether or not I could compete in the Olympics. Coach and

I kept it quiet, and I was able to rehabilitate myself enough for me to compete.

"I have no excuses. I didn't lose. I got beaten by Tom and the other guys. I could have done better. That Tom, though, I always said he could run a 1:49 in a hurricane. It made no difference, and he could do it running across a cornfield. I don't know where Tom got that kick to win that day."

It was one of the few stains on Sowell's record, and it

couldn't erase all his remarkable achievements at Pitt.

"He is," said Carl Olson, "a good-will ambassador for Pitt."

George Kiseda covered Pitt sports in those days for the now-defunct Pittsburgh Sun-Telegraph, and he *cared* about track and field. Kiseda crusaded for the sport, but to no avail. Only a few fans, friends and relatives turned out for track meets in Pittsburgh back then, and it's no different today. Sowell was a magnate and often the main draw when 50,000 turned out for a track meet in Los Angeles, and 20,000 in New York and Philadelphia, but he went largely ignored in his hometown.

Kiseda is still critical of Olson's training methods. "He was training Arnie Sowell the same way he had trained John Woodruff 20 years earlier," claims Kiseda, a Pitt alumnus who works today as a copy editor in the sports department of the Los Angeles Times. "He didn't adopt more modern training concepts, such as interval training. He thought you ran distance for endurance, and sprints for speed, and that was about it.

"Sowell was so good, there's no telling how great he could have been if he had been trained better. But Olson was a good man otherwise, and more than Pitt bargained for, considering they weren't that interested in track.

"It's amazing that, in a city that didn't care about track, and at a school that paid no attention to track, they had two of the greatest half-milers of all time — in the world! Woodruff was awesome. He did things that were astonishing. And, if Olson had adapted to modern training methods there's no telling what Sowell could have done."

Rees is too smart, and too diplomatic, to get into the middle of that controversy, and Olson is dead and can't defend himself. Let it be known, however, that Rees didn't always agree with Olson's methods.

Rees remembers Sowell single-handedly — or should it be single-leggedly? — beating Army in an indoor meet at West Point.

"They had so much more depth than us," recalls Rees. "But Arnie won the 600 and the 1,000, and scored in the long jump, and then anchored our mile and two-mile relay teams to victory. The amazing thing is that the relays were run right after each other — back-to-back — and Sowell still pulled it off. We had to win the last relay to win it, and we did. He did. I was one of the most amazing one-man performances I've ever seen in track."

Sowell was so versatile, a coach could use him in any of eight events, and as many as four or five, in any particular meet. Carl Hughes, who reported on Pitt sports back then for The Pittsburgh Press, often referred to him as "Amazin' Arnie" Sowell.

"Pitt has as close to a track superman," wrote Hughes, "as there is in the world today."

"One of the things that benefitted me as far as having Olson for a coach," says Sowell now, "was that he insisted I be a well-conditioned athlete. Maybe he didn't have all the modern techniques, but I think I accomplished as much as I think I could have under Coach Olson.

"Lloyd Duff was his assistant when I first got there, and he got me involved with interval training. Olson was very team-oriented, but Duff believed in developing an individual star, too. He believed that if somebody could

accomplish something special, he should be given every opportunity to do so."

As an 18-year-old sophomore, Sowell broke the school's half-mile mark set by Woodruff in 1939, establishing a new mark at the IC4A meet at Randall's Island in New York.

He broke Woodruff's 15-year-old record in that event with a 1:50.3 clocking. He followed that up by winning the NCAA 880 at Michigan.

As a junior, Sowell beat the seemingly unbeatable Mal Whitfield in winning the 800-meter event in the Pan American Games in the record time of 1:49.8.

In April, 1955, he led Pitt to a 72-59 victory over Navy at Annapolis. Sowell won the 440 and broad jump events, finished third in the 880 with teammates coming in ahead of him, and then ran a brilliant 46.7 anchor leg as the Panther mile relay team won that event in 3:16.6.

That same campaign, he tied the world's 1000-yard indoor record of 2:08.2 at the National AAU championships in Madison Square Garden. He also won the title in 1956.

Sowell won the half-mile three years in a row at the 1C4A meet. As a sophomore, he set an IC4A record of 1:50.3. As a junior, he lowered it to 1:49.1 — the fastest half-mile ever run until Sowell himself did 1:47.6 in the National AAU.

At the IC4A Indoor Championships at Madison Square Garden in 1956, Sowell won the 1,000-yard, anchored Pitt to a two-mile relay win and placed third in the long jump.

In a victory over Miami of Ohio at Pitt Stadium, he won the broad jump, the half mile, anchored the winning mile relay team and was third in the high jump.

In a triangular meet against Army and Ohio State at the Stadium, Sowell won the half-mile and quarter-mile, then anchored the winning mile relay team, making up a 15 yard-deficit on Ohio State's Meade Burnette, a top runner.

Ohio State's coach Larry Snyder cheered Sowell at the finish line. "We lost it to one of the greatest I ever looked at," said Snyder. "Sowell isn't only wonderful, he's impossible." Sowell had just run the fastest quarter mile ever clocked.

An Army cadet came up to Sowell as he was walking off the track into the dressing room. "Congratulations, Arnie, you're the best," said the cadet, as he vigorously shook Sowell's hand. "Thanks, that's nice of you," said Sowell.

He won the MVP awards for track and cross-country at Pitt in 1956, and was honored by a dinner held by the Varsity Letter Club at the Schenley Park Hotel.

Sport Magazine named Sowell the outstanding track & field athlete in 1956. "This kid," said Coach Olson, "has been publicized until he seems not human."

Sowell considers coming back to Pittsburgh to work. The place still holds a lot of appeal to him.

"I'm glad I went to Pitt, and I'm glad I was on the track team there, even though it never got the attention that I thought it should have," he said. "Under Olson, at the University of Pittsburgh, I was required to get an education. To me, that's the bottom line.

"Olson always told me that fame is fleeting, that they forget. He told me you can be a great athlete, and that was nice, but he asked, 'What are you going to do afterward?' That's what gives me the most pleasure about my Pitt experience."

"I had to admire him for what he did . . . he decided to go for it. He wanted to win. He made a valiant effort."

—Tom Courtney

Peery Family Made Panthers National Wrestling Power

By Bob Smizik

"Coach Peery was the greatest. He was tough, but he was fair."

—Jim Conklin

The year was 1949 and the sport of wrestling was nothing but a bad memory at Pitt. It had surfaced briefly twice, once even luring the legendary Jock Sutherland out for the team, and failed miserably both times.

To most Pittsburghers of that day, collegiate wrestling was unknown. To them, wrestling meant Don Eagle, Ruffy Silverstein, Gorgeous George, Gypsy Joe, Man Mountain Dan and Argentina Rocca on television.

But to Tom Hamilton, then Pitt's athletic director, it was a sport he thought belonged in the Panther athletic program. Past failures meant nothing to Hamilton. He wanted a wrestling team.

Towards that end he placed a call to Tulsa, Okla., to a man he had never met offering him to coach a team that did not exist.

The man was Rex Peery and though Hamilton did not know him, he had heard plenty about him.

When Hamilton felt wrestling's time had come at Pitt, he asked several people prominent in the field for recommendations. One name kept coming up. The name was Rex Peery, a high school coach in Oklahoma.

When the call came through, Rex Peery had recently finished his 14th year of high school coaching in his native state. A three-time NCAA champion at Oklahoma A&M, he was a Sooner to the bone.

"Until I was 21," remembered Peery, "I thought Stillwater was the center of the universe."

Hamilton wanted him to come to Pittsburgh. Cliff Keen, the Michigan coach and a legend in collegiate circles, had been one who recommended Peery. Keen had seen Peery's Tulsa Central team practice and had been impressed. His recommendation was enough for Hamilton.

It was not enough for Peery. Leaving Oklahoma would not be easy. "We were born and raised out here," remembered Rex Peery. "It was very hard to leave."

Circumstances made it somewhat easier. "We had two boys coming up and unless they got scholarships we couldn't send them to college on a teacher's salary," said Peery.

So Rex Peery came East with his wife, daughter and those two boys for whom he wanted scholarships. Along with Rex, those boys — Hugh and Ed — were to change the face of college wrestling and turn Pitt into an almost-immediate national power.

In one of the most incredible family stories in all of sports, first Hugh and then Ed duplicated their father's feat of winning three NCAA championships. The drama of Ed winning the ninth national championship for the Peery

REX PEERY — He put Pitt on map in mat sport.

family was heightened by the fact that the title was won at the Pitt Field House in a bout so close that not even overtime could decide a winner. Those who were there recall it as one of the most exciting sports events they have ever witnessed.

Along with Hugh and Ed, seven other Pitt wrestlers won national championships during the Peery years, 1949-1965. There were none before and none after. And it wasn't just a few scattered individuals that Peery coached to greatness. Twice the Panthers challenged the mighty Big Eight teams for the national championship, coming in second.

Some of the great ones were Joe Solomon, Ed DeWitt, Tom Alberts, Ron Schirf, Paul Powell, Larry Lauchle and Jim Harrison — NCAA champs all. But they all take a back seat in the Pitt wrestling story to the fabulous Peery family.

And though he was the one who never stepped on a mat for Pitt, it was Rex who made the program one of the finest in the nation.

He was a coach from the old school. No fooling around during wrestling time. When he expected from his wrestlers, he had done himself.

He was fond of telling a story about himself when he was at Oklahoma A&M, later Oklahoma State. The Aggies

PIONEERS — Pitt's first wrestling team in 1914-1915 season.

were on a long bus trip from Oklahoma to New York for a series of matches. Early on in the trip, Peery ate well. When the team stopped along the way to work out, Peery discovered he was significantly overweight and would not be able to wrestle when the team reached New York unless he did something about it quick.

"When ever the team stopped for a meal," related Peery, "I'd start running. They'd go in and eat their normal meal, and I think they took some extra time because they knew I was running. When they finished they got on the bus and started on their way. When the bus caught up to me I got back on."

Peery made weight for New York.

It was that kind of attitude that he brought into coaching. Asked to describe Peery, one of his wrestlers said, "He was very, very demanding. He was very strict and expected a lot from people and got it. He didn't tolerate any fooling around. He was very strict. Everyone had a lot of respect for him. They knew not to challenge him. If they did, he'd run you right out of the program. Not that anyone would ever try."

The wrestler assessing the coach was his son, Ed Peery.

But before Hugh and Ed matriculated to Pitt there were some hard times, which was not unexpected since the two previous tries to start the sports had been so enormously unsuccessful.

From 1914 until 1919, Pitt fielded a wrestling team and did not win a match while losing 13. Jock Sutherland was a

member of some of those teams. The sport came back from 1934 until 1937 and the Pitt wrestlers won two while losing 17.

The pioneer coaches were Leo Collins, Charles Reinecke, Joe Orsini — who doubled as the boxing coach for two seasons — Earl Oster and Ed Mozeski. None of them produced winning teams, and the overall wrestling record at Pitt prior to Peery's arrival was 2-30-1.

Rex Peery was to end all of that. By the time he had the Pitt wrestling program established, Tom Hamilton was to call him "The best coach I've ever seen in any sport."

The Panthers were 0-10 in the 1949-50 season and Peery, who retired to Oklahoma after leaving Pitt, remembered that season as well as he remembered the great ones.

"I came up there and we had quite a little schedule to face," said Peery. "We opened with Lock Haven and had Michigan, Michigan State, Penn State, Ohio State. The only matches we had a chance in were Franklin & Marshall and Gettysburg."

They won none of them despite the efforts of Jim Conklin, a four-time PIAA champion, who lost only once all year even though he was competing while in his second year of medical school.

Conklin's story was an unusual one, to say the least. After a brilliant high school career at Waynesburg and half a year at Waynesburg College, he joined the service. When he came out he matriculated to Indiana U., where he wrestled for two seasons and made rapid progress

ART DETZEL
Wrestling team captain and All-American guard in 1935.

JIM HARRISON
Pitt's last NCAA wrestling champ in 1963.

towards a degree by taking summer classes at Waynesburg.

He was admitted to the Pitt medical school still shy of an undergraduate diploma from Indiana. While Conklin was a freshman in medical school, Peery, on a campus visit, spotted him wrestling in intramurals. Though Conklin was some 50 pounds over his wrestling weight of 157, Peery liked what he saw.

"He came over and asked me if I would consider wrestling again because I still had two years of eligibility left," recalled Conklin. "I needed some help getting through medical school, I was married, so I went out for the team.

"Coach Peery was the greatest. He was tough, but he was fair."

Conklin went on to wrestle two years for Peery and lost only two matches.

The wrestling team was given old Trees Hall as its practice site. "There was a stage in the building and they put what mats they had up on that stage and that's where we practiced," said Peery. "The meets were held at the Pitt Pavilion, underneath Pitt Stadium."

The first team had been largely recruited by soccer Coach Leo Bemis, who had been put in charge of the program until Peery's arrival.

Help was on the way the next season. Peery had some new wrestlers and they helped produce seven victories in a 14-meet schedule.

Ray Cappelli, a 123-pounder, was 10-1-2, not losing until the final match of the season against Waynesburg. Gail Ellis was 6-1, Frank Skirpan 8-4, Harold Miller 12-2 and Conklin, now a plastic surgeon and on the faculty of the Pitt medical school, lost only once despite battling a knee injury most of the year and being heavily involved with his third year of medical school.

A program was starting to develop and it hit full stride the next season. Hugh Peery, who had finished his senior year of high school at Oklahoma during his dad's first season at Pitt and was a member of the freshman team in his second, gave the Panthers one ace and Joe Solomon

another to go along with some strong wrestlers from the previous season.

The Panthers opened the 1951-52 season with wins over Indiana State and Yale and then stunned Michigan, 15-14. The world of college wrestling had found out what Rex Peery was doing at Pitt. The Panthers had a 16-meet winning streak when they took on Penn State the next week and an astounding crowd of 1,937 came out to see the match. The Panthers lost, 16-12, and lost again later in the season to Michigan State, but those defeats did nothing to dim the accomplishments of this wrestling team, which finished with a 9-2 record.

The Panthers had truly arrived weeks later when Hugh Peery, a 115-pounder, won his first NCAA title. "I really don't remember it all that well," said Hugh, who later went to dental school and established a practice in the Pittsburgh area. "I beat the guy real bad."

Peery qualified for the Olympic team and traveled to Helsinki that summer. He lost to a Russian and finished sixth.

"The Olympics were never really a goal of mine," he said. "The style was so much different from what we wrestled in college. My goal in life was to win three NCAA titles. It was my life's ambition."

He took another step towards that ambition the following season, again winning the NCAA 115-pound championship as Pitt posted a 10-1 dual meet record.

The Panthers were 9-1 the next season, 1953-54, and Peery won his third national title. This time he was joined by Solomon as the Panthers finished second in the national championship to Oklahoma. Fittingly for the Peerys, the nationals were held in Norman, Okla. that year.

It was during the 53-54 season that the Panthers began competing in the Eastern Intercollegiate Wrestling Association (EIWA). Peery's team wasted little time in establishing dominance over their new rivals. Hugh, Charley Uram, a 147 pounder, and George Bereford, a 177 pounder, won EIWA individual titles and the Panthers the team title. In all, Rex Peery was to produce 23 EIWA champions.

Hugh finished his Pitt career with three NCAA titles, one Eastern title and only one dual-meet loss, suffered in his sophomore year to Bob Hohman of Penn State.

Thanks largely to his efforts on the mat, Pitt was near the top of the college wrestling world and Rex Peery intended to keep them there. And why not? Another son was coming along.

Ed picked up where his brother left off. The Panthers were 9-2 in 1954-55 and won their second straight EIWA title. Ed, Solomon and Bill Hulings won Eastern titles. Solomon did not repeat his national championship of the previous year, but Ed won the NCAA 123-pound title and Pitt finished third.

The following year was another great one for the Panthers. The team was 10-0 in dual meets and DeWitt, Don Huff and Dave Johnson won Eastern titles. It was the first of three for Johnson, the only Pitt wrestler to ever perform that feat. Ed Peery was upset in the Easterns that year by Joe Allissi of Springfield. It was the only loss of his collegiate career.

He redeemed himself later in the season by winning his second national title and DeWitt joined him as a champion.

It was to be the following year that was to be the Panthers greatest. They were undefeated in dual meets until losing the season finale to Penn State, 14-11. And though they were a bit of a disappointment in the Eastern championships, finishing second, — as Peery, Johnson and Schirf won titles — it was in the NCAA championships, the ultimate challenge, where they were to shine.

The event was held in Pittsburgh that year as Ed Peery went after his third national title.

It was a moment of high drama at the Pitt Field House. The entire family was there. "We lived with it night and day," said Hugh, who was finishing up a stint in the Navy as an assistant coach at the Naval Academy.

Ed Peery has films of the match, in which he wrestled Harmon Leslie of Oklahoma A&M.

"It would probably go down as one of the real tension bouts," he said. "There was tremendous pressure. The intensity of the wrestling was something. But by today's standards it isn't a very interesting match. At the time they permitted a great deal of stalling. By today's standards they probably would have thrown us both out of the match."

Leslie led by six points going into the second period as a packed crowd at Pitt groaned with the Peery family. Peery still trailed by four going into the final period. Leslie began the action on top.

"In order to get into a tie situation, I had to escape, take him down and get riding time," said Peery. "I did all of that."

The match went into overtime, two two-minute periods. Peery rode out Leslie in the first period to take a riding-time advantage. Leslie allowed Peery to escape in the second period and then scored a two-point takedown late in the match. The overtime ended 2-2.

The match would be decided by a referee's decision. "I felt sure I had won," said Peery. "I felt I was the aggressor. He scored points when he had to, but I was more aggressive."

Still, as Peery waited for the decision to come down, he remembered the last time he was in such a situation. He owned two PIAA championships and was going for his third in the finals of his senior year. "It came down to a referee's decision and I was sure I won," said Peery. "But they gave it to the other guy."

This time they gave it to Peery and there was jubilation at the Pitt Field House. But the Panthers were not done. Alberts won the 167-pound title and Schirf the 191-pound title. The Panthers finished a close second to Oklahoma State for the team championship.

"If one more guy would have placed we could have won the whole thing," said Ed Peery.

No one knew it at the time, but this was to be the high point of Pitt wrestling.

To be sure, there were more great years to come, but none to match 1957.

Powell won a national title in 1958, Lauchle in 1961 and Harrison in 1963. Four lightweights dubbed "The Mitey Mites" — Dick Martin, Lauchle, Daryl Kelvington and John Zolikoff — made the Panthers a great dual meet team in the early '60s.

Lauchle, Alberts, Zolikoff, Tom Hall, Martin, Kelvington, Harrison, Mike Johnson and Dino Boni won Eastern titles. But as a team Pitt never again challenged for national honors.

Two years after Harrison won Pitt's last national championship in 1963, Rex Peery stepped down. He was bringing in great wrestlers and they were not staying in school. Pitt's dramatically improved academic standards were taking a toll on the wrestling program.

DAVE JOHNSON — Pitt's only 3-time Eastern champ.

Dave Johnson, the three-time Eastern champion, took over for his old coach. But Johnson was practicing dentistry and trying to coach at the same time.

"I think he did a good job," said Hugh Peery, "but the support wasn't there."

Johnson had seasons of 2-7 and 2-8 and was replaced by Dave Adams, a promising young coach who had been an Eastern champ and national runnerup at Penn State.

Adams brought the program back to respectability, producing five Eastern champions — Ralph Cindrich, Kevin Love, Craig Tritch and George Bryant, who won two — but Pitt never reached the heights it had under Rex Peery. Winning seasons were more the norm than losing ones, but the Panthers no longer wrestled with the Oklahomas and the Oklahoma States.

After successive 13-4 seasons, but no Eastern title in the EIWA or the Eastern Wrestling League — which Pitt joined in 1976 — Adams, whose career record was 98-64-1, stepped down from coaching in 1979 to become an administrator at Pitt.

In addition to the EIWA champs he developed, Adams also produced five EWL titlists — Rande Stottlemyer, Bill Bailey, Skip Bolin, Mark Stepanovich and Glenn Maxwell. A year after resigning as coach, Adams was named athletic director at San Diego State.

His successor was one of the best wrestlers of recent times at Pitt, Stottlemyer. He was 68-16-2 in a career frequently hampered by injury. No other Pitt wrestler ever had more wins.

"My philosophy," said Stottlemyer upon taking the job, "will not be to make champions who win trophies, but to make strong men — inside and out — who will be champions as a result of their character."

It is a noble purpose. But it was only half of what was accomplished by Rex Peery. Peery produced men of character and wrestling champions.

Wrestling seems to be on the upswing at Pitt. At the Eastern meet in the winter of 1982, the Panthers captured their first two individual titles since 1977 with 150-pounder Jeff Jelic and 158-pounder Doug Haines.

"Winning at EWL gave us credibility," said Stottlemyer. "You can talk all you want, but we didn't have the credibility. But when we won, people started to take notice."

Stottlemyer landed five outstanding prospects who entered Pitt in the fall of 1982. They include Jack Uppling of Meadville — "the class of Pennsylvania as far as big guys are concerned" — who holds the state record for career wins (134), was a state finalist three years and won the gold medal at 185 as a senior.

Other newcomers include Kyle Nellis of Shaler, a state champ at 119 with 126 wins; Joe Bond of North Allegheny,

state runner-up at 155 with 100 wins; John Hnath of Mt. Lebanon — "one of those sleepers" — and Gary Bolin of Shaler, the WPIAL's 126-pound champ.

"In two years, we could really be awesome," said Stottlemyer. "We would be willing to take anybody on."

Perhaps the most fitting shrine to Pitt wrestling is located not in Pittsburgh but in Stillwater, Okla. at the College Wrestling Hall of Fame. Rex Peery is there, among the first inducted. Hugh Peery and Ed Peery are there, too, inducted in 1981.

The Peery family is the story of Pitt wrestling and that the whole family is in the Hall of Fame speaks so well for the history of Pitt wrestling.

CHAMPIONSHIP LINEUP

HUGH PEERY

ED PEERY

RON SCHIRF

JOHN ZOLIKOFF

TOM ALBERTS

LARRY LAUCHLE

WRESTLING

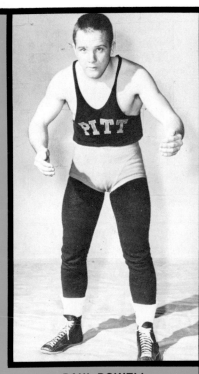

DARYL KELVINGTON

DICK MARTIN

PAUL POWELL

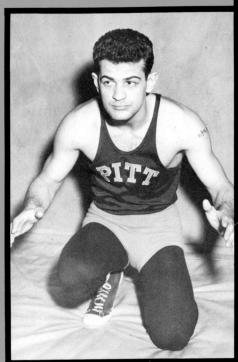

ED DeWITT

TOM HALL

JOE SOLOMON

Women's Sports Didn't Start With Chapter IX At Pitt

By Maria Sciullo

"It was a joy to be in varsity competition and travel. Everybody isn't a football player."
—Vee Toner

The women's sports program at Pitt has undergone extensive change since it fielded its first knickered basketball team in 1916. These changes — some good, some not-so-good — were mostly due to the fact that the administration and young women involved weren't quite sure which direction they wished to take.

For example, in 1927, after ten highly-successful seasons, the lone varsity program — basketball — was discontinued. "Maybe they thought it was too strenuous," offered Vee Toner, who played on the Pantherette team during its last few seasons.

Just as likely is this explanation from the 1930 OWL, the Pitt yearbook:

"Carrying out the idea that sports have come almost to mean the participation of the few to the deprivation of the many, and that we have emphasized our national community, and school heroes in all lines of sport to such an extent that we have lost sight of the true value of sports, Miss Margaret A. McClenahan, professor of women's physical education, was instrumental in doing away with the last trace of intercollegiate competition for Pitt girls when the basketball team played its last game in 1927."

It is rather odd that Margaret A. McClenahan, the chief "doer-away," in 1927, was also the team's coach and had played center on Pitt's first teams. Sounds a bit like Roy Chipman urging the athletic department to dump varsity basketball, but McClenahan apparently believed that varsity and intramurals could not co-exist harmoniously.

For the next 43 years, co-eds at the University of Pittsburgh were content to take advantage of an extensive intramural setup that offered everything from horseback riding to archery to clinics on fashion and posture.

Toner, who also was active in intramural swimming, field hockey and tennis, said that she enjoyed all the sports, but added, "It was a joy to be in varsity competition and travel."

Indeed, for their day, the Pantherettes were a much-travelled crew.

They played the locals from Slippery Rock and Geneva, of course, but by the mid-20's, their schedule included road trips to Washington, D.C., New York, Cincinnati and Philadelphia.

The 1924-25 squad completed its 10-game schedule undefeated; road victories were against Swarthmore College, Temple University, New York University and Thiel.

"I remember our trip to New York — we had a ball!" recalled Toner. "Those trips were just wonderful. After they cut it (the varsity program), I felt sorry for the outstanding players who didn't get to play as we had."

VEE TONER — "It was a joy"

Before she became Vee Toner, Venus Shakarian was an intracollegiate tennis champ and played "side-center" on the basketball team. Women played "three-court" basketball, which meant that each side assigned two players to three different zones on the court.

There were two forwards, two guards, a center and side-center. After each basket was scored, the center would handle the ensuing jump ball. She would tap the ball to Toner, who in turn passed it to a forward.

Scores usually resembled those of modern-day football: 33-13, 29-10, 17-14. But relatively speaking, said Toner, her teammates wouldn't have done poorly against players of the 1980's. Team captain Ruth Stultz, for example, scored 152 of her team's 190 points in 1927.

"Dottie Russell . . . Grace Austin, Ruth Stultz . . . wonderful players who could show up anyone," Toner added.

In the days before professional sports dominated local papers, the Pantherettes received their fair share of coverage. "The late Al Abrams and Chet Smith, they used to put our lineups in the paper all the time and they'd run our scores just as they do for basketball today," said Toner. "In those days, they paid a little more attention."

In 1919, the only organization governing women's sports at Pitt was the Women's Athletic Council. Created by McClenahan and former basketball player Ethel James, the council later joined the National Women's Athletic Association and from there was known as the W.A.A.

According to the 1934 OWL, "W.A.A. was organized in 1919 and has ever since retained its two-fold purpose, that of fostering clean sportsmanship and promoting higher physical efficiency among the women at Pitt."

Each week during the mid-30's, members of the W.A.A. could catch a ride out to the riding stables in Ingram, swim at the local pool, or brush up on golfing skills in the basement of the Oil and Gas Building.

The introduction of "games days," or "Play Days" as

they were known at Pitt, appeared to be a popular substitute for inter-collegiate competition. One school would invite others to participate in a day of contests, although women would be placed on teams irrespective to school.

The purpose was "to eliminate intercollegiate competition and foster a spirit of play," according to the 1927 OWL. Play days became a tradition that lasted until the 1950's.

The W.A.A. kept in touch with the times. Part of its 1942 calendar included "Hard Times" and "Farewell Afternoon" dances for Pitt men who were inducted into the services.

The W.A.A. became the Women's Recreation Association at the start of the next decade — with the small gym in the basement of the Cathedral of Learning as a center of such sports activity — and now it seemed that the OWL was no longer taking women's sports seriously.

Following the "I Love Lucy" mentality that permeated the 50's, the yearbook report of 1952 W.R.A. activities included this bit of fluff:

" 'I'm glad we went to W.R.A.'s Freshman Party,' said freshie Arlene Morrisey. 'The mixer square dances were such fun and the food . . . out of this world! Wasn't that sucker doll I won in the second contest a cute prize,' added Audrey Stewart. 'I'm going to insist that all my girl friends

VEE FOR VICTORY — That's Vee Toner, then Venus Shakarian, sitting at the right in the second row. Her teammates included, front row left to right, Sylvia Perovsky and Dorothy Russell. Second row, Jean Muter and Ib Zeigler. Third row, Peg Thompson, Helen Lloyd, Kathleen Burgun, Ruth Stultz, Dorothy Koch, Coach Margaret McClenahan.

HORSEBACK RIDING AND ARCHERY were among many athletic activities for women in earlier years.

go to the next fun and frolic nights and the swimming party.' "

By 1970, Pitt finally returned to intercollegiate sports. The physical education department sponsored five varsity teams in basketball, volleyball, field hockey, swimming and gymnastics.

The first three teams on this list were coached by Sandra Bullman, who is now Pitt's assistant athletic director in charge of women's sports. Although the athletic department didn't begin sponsoring the women's program until 1974, it did award varsity letters to the ladies four years prior to the switch.

"I think that we were probably the pioneers in the western part of the state to get women full-fledged scholarships and coaching staffs," said Alfreeda Goff. Goff was in charge of the Pantherette track and field program for five years and was an assistant for one through 1975-80. Now she is an assistant to the athletic director in charge of programming and scheduling.

Although the Pitt program now embraces eight varsity teams, said Goff, it has "sort of hit a standstill due to finances."

While four Pitt teams compete at the Division I level in four sports, the other four — track, tennis, field hockey and cross country — enter regional and national competition at the Division II level.

"These sports have not been de-emphasized, but we can't compete — money-wise — for scholarships with some of the other schools. We moved down to be more competitive," Goff explained.

During the regular season, however, these teams still may compete against Division I schools.

The implementation of Title IX in the mid-70's has done much toward equalizing men's and women's athletic programs on the high school level, but according to Goff, it has not had much impact on the college scene.

SANDRA BULLMAN — Women's Athletic Director

"I believe that Title IX is going to be a thing of the past," she said. "The NCAA is going to end up being the governing body (of Pitt's men's and women's programs), so when you have one body governing, there will be no discrimination per se on the national level.

"Now, the individual schools will have to decide, 'OK, where are we going to put our money. . .' "

"Pitt's Winnin' Women," was the sports information department's slogan for its ladies during the 1977-78 season. That year, Pitt's winningest woman was swimmer Kathy Stetler.

As a junior, Stetler became the first Pantherette to win an individual national championship when she won the Association of Intercollegiate Athletics for Women (AIAW) 50-meter butterfly title.

Several weeks before striking AIAW gold, the Riverview (Oakmont, Pa) High School graduate won seven events at the Eastern collegiate championships. Her performance was so overwhelming, the coaches created a special Most Outstanding Swimmer award just for Stetler.

Now a dental student at Pitt, Stetler joined former Panther running back Tony Dorsett as the University's only four-time All-Americans.

Another All-American Pantherette was gymnast Lisa Shirk. As a freshman, Shirk placed second in the 1981 AIAW all-around, by far the best showing in Pitt women's gymnastic history. She suffered from bone spurs in one foot during the 1982 season, but the spunky competitor from Connecticut bounced back and won a national championship in all-around competition.

Three Pantherette track and field performers have done exceptionally well in the national championships. In 1976, Elizabeth's Marie Ribik Kennedy finished fourth in the AIAW high jump, but All-America status was not awarded to track athletes until several years later.

Peri Jude Radecic and Gwen Murray, however, received such status in 1982. Radecic, a Brentwood native, finished third in the AIAW Division II discus, while Murray ran to fifth place in the 400 meters.

Two years earlier, Murray competed for the United States in an international meet in France. Like Kennedy and Radecic, Murray is also from the Pittsburgh area with Butler as her home base.

A number of Pitt teams always seem to do well. Each year, the swimming Pantherettes qualify some of their ranks for nationals, and All-Americans at Trees Pool have become almost commonplace.

Under Coach Mike Hebert, who later moved on to the University of New Mexico, the volleyball team asserted itself as the best in the East during the late 70's. Hebert's teams won two EAIAW titles and one year toured the West Coast and Hawaii.

Four different women have coached the basketball Pantherettes since Bullman's coaching days: Jean Condo, Pat Wallace, Jean Balthaser and now, Judy Saurer.

Although the women's basketball program has never made it past the opening round of regional competition, players such as Debbie Lewis, Debbie Jones and Wanda Randolph gained attention for Pitt.

Sixty-six years after the first Pitt Pantherettes hit the basketball court, there is still room — and opportunity — for change.

The AIAW, which has governed women's athletics since the national resurgence of women's athletics, has had its position severely threatened by the NCAA.

WINNING SMILES — Jan Ujevich, left, and Kathy Stetler smiled often as repeat All-American swimmers at Pitt.

"The way I see it, I don't think there is going to be an AIAW much longer," said Bullman. "Financially, they're weak . . . even if the AIAW is still in existence (after this year), the only smart thing to do is get involved with the NCAA."

The NCAA began sponsoring national championships for women in 1981, although the AIAW still maintains theirs. Schools are currently given the chance to divide their programs between the two.

Pitt's gymnastics and basketball programs are going the NCAA route; the other varsity programs will stay, for now, anyway, with the AIAW.

If and when the NCAA takeover occurs, said Bullman, Pitt will have to adapt to some rule changes. For example,

the AIAW allows an athlete to transfer to another school without losing a year of eligibility. The NCAA does not. Recruiting rules also differ.

Bullman said that she foresees the increase in recruiting trips and expenses, not to mention scholarship money, if Pitt wishes to compete in the big time. "We're going to have to change our budget," she noted.

Vee Toner has kept in touch with her alma mater, and she agreed with Bullman. The women's athletic program, she observed, "is moving, but I wish it would move a little faster. I'm very close to Pitt . . . but women should get a little more attention. There are not enough scholarships for women.

"Everybody isn't a football player."

ALL-AMERICA LINE-UP

| GWEN MURRAY | SUZANNE PULLEY | DEBBIE LEWIS | LISA SHIRK | PERI RADECIC |
| Track | Swimming | Basketball | Gymnastics | Track & Field |

1982 ALL-AMERICA SWIMMERS: Front row, left to right, Diana Firth, Jan Ujevich, Amy Jackson. Rear, left to right, Sue Heon, Julie Terrell, Nancy Henry. They boosted Lady Panthers to highest finish — eighth — in national competition in school history.

Other Sports

By Jim O'Brien

There are lots of sports activities at Pitt for just about everybody's tastes, even if they don't get as much publicity or attention as the football and basketball teams.

There are club teams, for instance, that have been organized by the students and receive no financial assistance from the athletic department.

They include, in alphabetical order, bicycling, bowling, chess, Chinese Kung Fu, fencing, frisbee, gaming, ice hockey, judo, martial arts, road racing, rifle, rugby, sailing, skiing, unicycling and water polo.

Up until a few years ago, water polo was played for a brief period as a varsity sport. The men's team even turned out some Eastern champions. It was eliminated in a budget cut about the same time that golf was abandoned. Pitt also used to field varsity rifle teams.

Ice hockey was played as a varsity sport way back in 1906, and lasted a few seasons, and was started up again at the onset of the 30's.

Boxing was also a varsity sport at that time, and lasted for a decade. The first sports competition between Pitt and Duquesne, for instance, was in boxing in 1930.

There was a varsity fencing team that was organized in 1914 — the same time wrestling debuted as a varsity sport — and Pitt competed in that foils game against several Ivy League opponents.

Volleyball is a varsity sport at the school. Pitt hosted a regional championship in men's and women's volleyball at the Field House in the spring of 1982. The men were upset early, but the host women's team won their end of the tournament. There is also field hockey for women.

In addition to its tennis teams, Pitt has also been represented in squash racquets competition. In addition to track & field there's been cross-country.

So there's something for everybody at Pitt, or almost anyhow.

Anyone for darts?

Dee Dee Kantner competed in field hockey as well as varsity basketball.

Varsity fencing team of 1914 strikes classic pose.

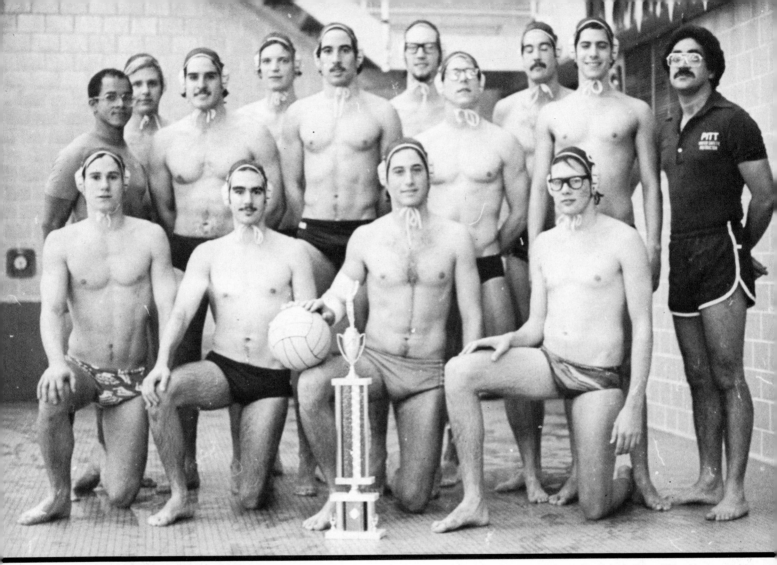

EASTERN CHAMPIONS IN 1978 — Pitt's water polo team consisted of (front row left to right) Barry Ford, Luis Toro, Mike Mere, Gary Hild, and (back row) Asst. Coach Juan Curet, Greg Taulbee, Butch Silva, Steve Feller, Papo Ruiz, Wynne Hunkler, Dave Plocki, Mike Schofield, Jorge Machicote, Head Coach Miguel Rivera.

Real Sports

Two organizations that merit the full support of the University community, and followers of Pitt sports are the Golden Panthers and the Pitt Varsity Letter Club.

The Golden Panthers is an organization interested in helping to finance Pitt's athletic programs. Bob Heddleston serves as the executive director of the fund-raising group. Their fund-raising efforts were influential in the dramatic turnaround in Pitt's sports fortunes.

When he announced his retirement as athletic director in the summer of 1982, Cas Myslinski said his greatest ac-complishment in nearly 14 years at the head of Pitt's sport department was founding the Golden Panthers.

Former Pitt football player Bob Rosborough looks after the affairs of the Varsity Letter Club in the school's alumni center. It's an alumni organization that encourages a closer and supportive relationship with all facets of the Pitt sports programs.

Those who wish to donate funds to other school departments can do so through the Annual Alumni Giving Fund.

PITT IS IT because of such organizations.

THE PANTHER FOUNDATION

This book was made possible through the private sponsorship of The Panther Foundation — formerly Bellefield Educational Trust.

CHAMPIONSHIP TEAM — Editor Jim O'Brien, front left, and Illustrator-Publisher Marty Wolfson proudly display their book, "HAIL TO PITT: A Sports History of the University of Pittsburgh." Behind them is the executive committee of the sponsoring Panther Foundation, left to right, Charles R. Wilson, president; Paul Martha, Dr. George Fetterman, and Charles L. Cost.

THE PANTHER FOUNDATION BOARD OF TRUSTEES

WILLIAM R. BAIERL   W.F. DONALDSON, JR.   HARRIS F. HAWKINS   IRA R. HILL

HARRY S. KALSON   FRANK W. KNISLEY   EDWARD W. MICHAELS   C. ROBERT MILLER   GEORGE S. STEWART